Anthropological Futures

EXPERIMENTAL FUTURES:
Technological Lives, Scientific Arts, Anthropological Voices
A series edited by Michael M. J. Fischer and Joseph Dumit

Anthropological Futures

MICHAEL M. J. FISCHER

Duke University Press
Durham and London
2009

*Duke University Press gratefully
acknowledges the Massachusetts
Institute of Technology, which provided
funds toward the production of this
book.*

IN HONOR OF

ha-Fischerim, Eric and Irene
husband (1898–1985) and wife (1907–)
participant-observers of the twentieth century changes described
herein, and authors, respectively, of

The Passing of the European Age;
A Question of Place;
Minorities and Minority Problems;

and

Geometry;
Geodesy, What's That?

and for

new generations of twenty-first century cousins: roboticists,
breakthrough thinking consultants, brain scientists, musicians,
political sociologists, and social workers

students, colleagues, friends,
and always Susann

CONTENTS

Rekeying Key Words for the Contemporary World

Culture, nature, body, personhood, science, and technology are among the key words of anthropology, the study of human beings in the world and in their worlds—including their social and cultural worlds and the environments, ecologies, and planetary forces with which they interact. Key words, of course, key different registers of meaning. Like strange attractors, they describe dynamic patterns through which, since at least the eighteenth century, anthropology has engaged, unfolded, and refolded itself. Or, to shift keys again, perhaps they are like proteins with multiple surface receptors to which alternative stem cells can attach. Anthropology, Immanuel Kant suggested in the eighteenth century, following David Hume, is foundational to any critical philosophy of use to human beings.[1]

Culture is both that which is distinctive, local, colorful, artistic, philosophical; and that which is universally human. Culture is that which is cultivated (*gebildet*, civilized, woven) and that "complex whole which includes knowledge, belief, art, morals, law, customs, and any other capabilities and habits acquired by man as a member of society" (Tylor 1871: 1). Culture speaks to our aspirations (*cultura*, a future participle) and to that which is tied to our nature. Culture is where meaning is woven and renewed, often beyond the conscious control of individuals, and yet the space where institutional social responsibility and individual ethical struggle take place. At issue are not just better methods but a return to some of the most fundamental moral and cultural issues that anthropology and cultural analysis have long addressed: issues of class differences, culture wars, social warrants, social reform and social justice; of mental health and subjectivation; of democratic checks and balances, institutions of ethical debate, regulation, and the slow negotiation of international law; of access to information and the formation of new kinds of public spheres. Cultural analysis has become increasingly relational, plural, and aware of its own historicity: its openness to the historical moments in which it is put to work makes it capable, like experimental systems, of creating new epistemic things (chapter 1). Return to fundamental moral and cultural issues, like the return to religion which Jacques Derrida points out in his commentary on Kant's notion of religion at the limits of reason, is never a return to the same, but more like respiration, a return after taking a break, a renewal of inquiry.

The cultural skeins of science and technology (chapter 2) make more realistic the demand for attention to the reconstruction of public spheres, civil society, and politics in our emergent technoscientific age. No longer can we rest on broad claims about the alienation of the market, the technicization of life, or globalization. Just as we have moved from Mertonian sociologies of science to analyses of what scientists actually do, so too we need to pay attention to civic epistemologies and cultures of politics as they are transduced across the cultural switches of the heterogeneous communities within which the sciences are cultured and technologies are peopled with the face of the other.

Nature (chapter 3) is our other, but also ourselves. Even as ourselves (my character, my body, my selfhood), our nature is often other, that which we attempt to control and separate ourselves from, but on which we are dependent and which always escapes our reach. Like language, like biology, like the unconscious, nature poses powerful ethical dilemmas of whom and what to help live and whom and what to let die. Nature is both a label for the reality effect and sites of moral testing. In chapter 3, nature is unpacked as environment; as contingency, accident, and risk; as biology repaired, enhanced, deformed, and reconfigured from inside out or nano-, molecular, cellular, and tissue level up; and as dealing with and accepting alterity.

Our *bodies* are our nature, and they are culturally inscribed. The more we tinker and experiment with the body, the more the nature of bestiality and divinity are redefined, the more bodily markings take on new connectivities, significations, intensities, and transductions (chapter 4). We have always been able to read the aging body for traces of experience, but increasingly we now enter the age of biological sensibility. The haptic and proprioceptive body is natural—the ground of perception—the body out of control is bestial, the transported body is divine. Like the old chain of being or the merit-reincarnation sequence of bestial, natural, and divine, the contemporary topology of natural, bestial, and divine is like a Möbius strip twisting back on its own implications. This biological sensibility informs the productivity of much contemporary thinking and poesis, weaving back and forth between contemporary biotechnology and ethical/anthropological stakes that are signified in the face, the communicating body, and the traumatic body. These must be understood in their social dynamics—class markings, gendering, sexuality, racial inscriptions, postcoloniality, asymmetrical powers, etc.—not just as individualized bodies or codes.

Aging is in our nature, our bodies, our (sense of) *personhood* (chapter 5). Aging, more often than we like, manifests in otherworldly topologies, surreal and psychodynamically twisting inside out (like Klein bottles and Möbius strips), with memory, language, and behavioral fragments oddly sutured and scarred; and revealing of natures we never imagined existed, certainly not in our sense of who we and our loved ones are. Even in aging, as in early and adolescent development, however, transitional objects like linguistic and other symbolic objects (remembered snatches of Virgil's *Aeneid* memorized in childhood, for instance) are vehicles of self-fashioning, temporary ego stabilization, recognition of self, self-esteem, personhood, as well as registers of historical agency and, however uncertainly, reality checks. The geoid drew me into multiple worlds—earth sciences, mathematical shapes, ancient Greek and early modern geodesy, new marine and satellite explorations, detective sleuthing across nationalist guarding of data, bureaucratic warfare, and gendered conflicts. Eratosthenes is where the geoid and the quest for the Figure of the Earth (size and shape of the earth) began. Or was it with John O'Keefe, with stories of the Vienna Circle, Norbert Wiener, and Vassily Leontiev? Or was it with a high school geometry textbook? These names evoke a community that my mother and I can share in her autumn years. They help to orient her world, reaffirm her personhood, allow her dignity amidst the indignities of old age. In this community, at this time, it is less important that sometimes fantasy and the dream world intervene, that logic gets confused, that reading cannot be managed, that what was once intellectual challenge is now "too technical." What is important is the self and its relations, the ability to feel oneself as sentient, as having accomplishments, as being recognized. The geoid is a transitional object. In the past it condensed the geodetic interfaces of surveying and gravimetry, of oceanography and astrogeodetics, and of gender in a man's world; it condensed the interfaces of bureaucracy and science. But now the geoid is a transitional object in another sense, a vehicle for negotiations of old age, a territory for which the geodesy is as complicated as those new geodesies whose technologies outpace their ability to securely tell noise from signal.

Anthropology is exploration of all this and more. The methods of exploration, of pragmatic knowledge, extend across technologies and sciences, as they grow and change, shift and reconfigure, across historicized cultural horizons. The *anthropology of science and technology* periodically requires a new generation of robust switches to translate (even transduce) legacy genealogies into new public futures. Hannah Arendt, Kant, Ibn Khaldun, al-Biruni, Fa-hsien, and Herodotus, among others, were prolegomena, building upon travels, comparison, and exploration of moral and political duties, constructing a cosmopolitan ethos. Their legacy categories, including culture, nature, body, science, technology, are still with us, changed, morphed, and refunctioned. With these tools—culture, nature, the body, aging, science and technology—we recalibrate, recompose, revise, and renew the anthropology to come.

Anthropologists among Humanists, Social Scientists, Natural Scientists, and Engineers

The anthropologist, as in the neurologist Oliver Sacks's essays *The Anthropologist from Mars* and in locutions like "What would an anthropologist make of what we are doing?" points to a figure of general inquiry—Greek *historie* in Herodotus's time meant "inquiry"—about what we can expect of human beings. Anthropology, in other words, has a philosophical status between the humanities and the social sciences and refers not just to an academic discipline. Indeed, it has four referents:

(i) Anthropology in its general philosophical, not academic disciplinary, sense is the study of *anthropos* ("mankind") and of, as Kant put it, what we can expect of our societies and their capacities. Just as we do not expect all who write histories of the present to be historians, or all who write about literatures of the present to be literary critics, so too not all who use the tools of ethnography and social theory or who write anthropologies of the present are professionally disciplined anthropologists.

(ii) And yet, there is something valuable and specific about how professionally disciplined anthropologists continually update their discipline in order to explore the emergent worlds forming around us. Among the most exciting of these updates are the ways in which anthropologists have had a powerful hand in creating, over the past two decades, new kinds of science studies, challenging and reshaping the canon of science, technology, and society (STS) that has been dominated by social studies of knowledge (SSK), social construction of technology (SCOT), philosophy of science, and history of science. This is both a historical or genealogical acknowledgment and a warrant for new interdisciplinary work, whether done by anthropologists or others. It has something important to do with the ethnographic perspectives of anthropology, without anthropologists being the only ones using variously tailored ethnographic methods these days.

(iii) Third, anthropology is a call for not being overly focused on Europe and America. It is a characteristic limitation of many science studies and much of the social sciences, including theories of development and modernization, that they continue to view the world fundamentally in terms of center and periphery. (The evasion "My study is limited to Western cases" is exactly that, evasion, in the service of continuing to do exactly what one has done before, as if the rest of the world did not exist both outside and inside the West.) One of anthropology's distinctive features, both in its Kantian philosophical sense and in the disciplinary social science sense, is its call for multidimensional, linguistically and culturally informed, comparative and cross-cultural perspectives—in the sense not only of acknowledging that cultural perspectives interreference one another but also of showing how and where they interfere with other ways of seeing, evaluating, valuing, and categorizing. A corollary feature of anthropology's ethnographic sensibility is its call for attention to the multileveled peopling of technologies and infrastructures that shows them not to be smooth-working machines, but in fact humanly fraught endeavors, full of what Kant called the unsociable sociabilities, antagonisms, value differentials, and competitions of humankind. Why should not someone or some group throw a wrench into (or hack) the machine if he can gain advantage? We have responsibilities for nudging social institutions to robustly deal with such unsociable sociabilities.

(iv) Fourth, there can be the possibility of multiple anthropologies analogous to the computer scientists' talk of multiple ontologies that they encode in their engineering. Assertions of a common human nature, psychic unity of humankind, universal capacity for language, basic affective needs for social bonds, and so on do not, in the end, tell us much, even if true at a minimalist level. Despite all efforts at socialization, we remain biologically, culturally, and linguistically lively, not precision tooled and identical. Both the ways societies are structured (descriptive or empirical anthropologies) and what their inhabitants think can be expected of them (philosophical anthropologies) have been and continue to be variable. An ethnographically powerful illustration in today's technoscientific worlds is to recognize that, for instance, computer scientists versus molecular biologists or biochemists versus structural biologists focused on the mysteries of the protein-folding properties beneath the wave lengths of the humanly visible have different anthropologies. The former insist that proteins, atoms, and all other building blocks are in the end machines at different scales, while the latter demur that biologies cannot be separated from context or milieu, have path-dependent histories and complexly emergent properties, slip their bonds with heat or change reaction with ph, and are in general lively rather than fixed—"Nature as wily coyote," in Donna Haraway's lovely metaphor, revitalizing an old Native American insight, characterization, and mytheme.

What Is the *Anthropos* in Anthropology?
And the Possibilities of Many Anthropologies

It is nicely symptomatic that in Persian there is a debate about what term to use to designate the field of modern anthropology: *adab* might be the appropriate translation for what G. W. F. Hegel called *Sitte* or *Sittlichkeit*, customs, norms, proprieties, but anthropology is a bit different even if taking account of customs; *tarbiat* might be the translation for socialization, being civilized; *bi-adab, bi-tarbiat,* "uncultured," "unsocialized," are frequently used disciplining negatives. But the debate about the translation of "anthropology" is whether it should be *ensan-shenasi, mardom-shenasi,* or a kind of *jome'-shenasi? Ensan* refers to the double meaning that is conveyed in German by the word *Mensch*: it is both the person and the moral character. To be a *Mensch,* in the English borrowing from Yiddish, stresses the moral quality of personhood. It is different from the mere number of *Menschen* (individuals) in a population. *Mardom* stresses the other meaning of *Mensch*: it is the collective noun meaning "people." Unlike the German *Volk* ("folk") and English "nation," *mardom* is not the carrier of an essentialized *Volkgeist* ("folk spirit" or "genius") or of an autochthony of birth. Indeed, the translation of "nation" in the early twentieth-century constitutional period in Iran was troublesome. The term *meillat* was adopted and is still used for formulations such as the national bank (*Bank-i Melli*), but that word derived from and was used by the Ottoman Empire to designate confessional communities.

For Kant's *Anthropology from a Pragmatic Point of View* both *ensan-shenasi* and *mardom-shenasi* might be appropriate in different places, but so might a third term, *jome'-shenasi:* the study of groups, societies, sociology. Culture involves another term, *farhang,* although, as in En-

glish, it often means high culture rather than culture in the anthropological sense. For Kant, Emile Durkheim, Sigmund Freud in his work
on group psychology, and Jacques Lacan grappling with the social
nature of language as a symbolic arena knotted together with the
imaginary and the real—for all these modern authors, individuation,
personhood, relative autonomy, character occur only in groups, in
increasingly differentiated social structures.

Kant speaks of these processes at the macro level of politics, both
republican politics within states, dramatized for modern Europe by
the French Revolution, and confederated structures of universal
peace. Kant's idea for such confederated structures is, like the European Union, not a world state but legal structures resulting from histories of unsocial sociabilities and antagonisms, trade relations, regulations, and negotiations. Kant's analogy for such a confederation is the
ancient Greek Amphictyonic League. Kant probed the limits of law
and reason, searching for positive constitutional orders that could
promote maximal human freedom and creativity within social formations (not as individual isolates), within distributed nexi of trade and
politics that (rather than power, force, or sovereignty) would demand
such constitutionalism. The early twenty-first century's obsession
with discussions of varieties of cosmopolitanisms and cosmopolitics
to resolve the inequalities and dangers of the world in the post bipolar
Cold War period repeatedly returns to these Kantian questions, to
anthropology from a pragmatic point of view. Interestingly, the sociologist Ulrich Beck recognizes ethnography, along with cultural studies
and geography, as a key tool for correcting what he calls zombie categories of sociology premised on social statistics' presupposing of
nation-state units (2004a: 26).

Similar shifting elements in what we mean by anthropologies in the
philosophical, empirical, and pragmatic senses are worth exploring in
many language formations and historical horizons. *Anthropologie*, in
German for instance, often still means primarily physical or biological
anthropology and needs a modifier to clarify when one means the
larger subject. What, then, did *anthropos* mean in the Greek from
which Indo-European languages get the modern term "anthropology"?

According to Cornelius Castoriadis, two opposed meanings were
held in tension for the Greeks of the fifth century BCE. For Aeschylus
in *Prometheus Bound* (c. 460 BCE) *anthropos* stands between animals
and gods (*therion e theos*), between the bestial and the divine. Aeschylus works with a structuralist anthropogony or genesis of *anthropos*.
Before Prometheus's gifts to humankind—of fire and the arts of culture, of memory and foresight of death, of discerning the potentials of

action and creation (*prattein, poiein*)—men and women were like zombies. They saw without seeing, heard without hearing, lived in sunless caves unable to distinguish the seasons, and were without discernment (*ater gnomes*). Men and women were, in other words, placeholders in the structural scheme between gods and beasts and were transmuted into human beings, alchemically or by mutation, as it were, by Prometheus's gifts.

By contrast, for Sophocles in *Antigone* (c. 443–42 BCE), *anthropos* is a drive, a compulsion of self-fashioning, that weaves together the laws of the polis and the equally strong passions of political life. *Anthropos* in this account is self-educating (*edidaxato*). *Edidaxato* is self-reflexive, an example of the grammatical middle voice in which agent and object of agency are indistinguishable—a grammatical form which no longer exists in modern Indo-European languages. Of anthropos, Sophocles says, "Numerous are the wonders and terrors [*deina*] but nothing is more wondrous and terrifying [*deinon*] than man" [*polla ta deina kouden anthropou deinoteron pelei*]. The gods, like comic book characters, are fixed in their qualities, but man is self-creating, self-modifying, and challenged to weave together (*pareiron*) the bonds of polities. *Antigone* is a play about the need to weave together loyalty to ancestral tradition—the Burkean republicanism of incremental conservatism—with loyalty to the self-legislating rule of law—the Jeffersonian republicanism of new constitutions every twenty years. The tragedy comes from the *hubris* of Antigone and Creon, each of whom is loyal to one principle and unable to weave the two together (*pareiron*) into the passionate embrace of the work and working of the polis (*astuonomous orgas*, whence also orgasm, explosive passion).

The fifth century BCE, Castoriadis stresses, was an extraordinary period for Athens: the Peloponnesian peace treaties were achieved in 446–45, the Parthenon was built in 447–38, Pericle's Odeon was built in 443, Phidias's colossal bronze statue of Athena was put on the Acropolis in 450, Herodotus came to Athens and perhaps read from his *Histories*, Protagoras was named legislator for the Panhellenic colony in Thourioi in Italy and proclaimed "*Anthropos* [man] is the measure of all things," Euripides won the prize for tragic drama in 441, Sophocles defeated Aeschylus in the Dionysian competition in 468. This, in other words, as Castoriadis puts it, was "the creative social-historical space from within which emerges the verse, *polla ta deina kouden anthropou deinoteron pelei* (numerous are the wonders and terrors, but nothing is more wonderous and terrifying than man)."

Castoriadis also claims the fifth century BCE was a hinge between myth and history, between Aeschylus and Sophocles/Herodotus, between *two different anthropologies.* He would like to see another break after Jean Jacques Rousseau. I am less convinced of a Rousseauian break, preferring a denser mesh, screen, or matrix of discriminations. Both Kant and Freud draw on Sophocles. But the delineation of contrasting anthropologies can be a valuable exercise, and Castoriadis is particularly helpful in identifying the violent misreadings of the Greek texts by Martin Heidegger in his attempt to impose on the Greeks his own antidemocratic, mystical antimodernism. As Miriam Leonard (2005) points out, the Greeks once again became important in post–World War II French thinking about democracy, ethics, and postwar reconstruction, often in contrast to earlier German readings of *die Griechen* (especially those of Hegel, Friedrich Nietzsche, and Heidegger).

In an effort to reopen the questions of anthropology from both a philosophical and a pragmatic point of view, I will return to Kant's *Anthropology from a Pragmatic Point of View* and his *Idea for a Universal History from a Cosmopolitan Point of View* in chapter 6, the conclusion, and the epilogue. I am interested as well in other predecessors, such as Herodotus's account of the Persian wars, in which the Persians are accorded ethical insights and blindnesses equal to those of the Greeks.[2]

Anthropologies and Emergent Forms of Life

For the moment and overall, however, I want to keep the accent on the challenges that today's emergent forms of life pose for anthropologies of the twenty-first century.

Chapter 1, on cultural analysis as experimental systems, plays off a rhetorical device Clifford Geertz used in "Religion as a Cultural System" but turns his definitional exercise into a reflexive historical analysis of how culture keyed different semantic registers at different moments of its formulation. The chapter was conceived in one of those flashes (*Augenblick*, blink of an eye) of dialectical illumination (in the ruins of terms whose aspirations need to be recovered from their decay) of which Walter Benjamin wrote, in response to a request by the editors of *Theory, Culture and Society* that I write an essay on culture for what was described as a kind of encyclopedia. The challenge, I thought, was to do something analogous to Raymond Williams's *Keywords*, but at greater depth. I wanted to stress the relational nature of the cultural and to revivify what gets lost if the cultural is homogenized into instrumental reason, rational choice, and simple rule-governed behaviorism—not that each of these cultural devices might not have its place, uses, and misuses. It turned out that *Theory, Culture and Society* wanted something much shorter and chose to take a short excerpt (*Problematizing Global Knowledge: Special Issue*, [2006]: 23:2–3). I was delighted when the full essay, with its rhetorical and intellectual integrity, found a home in *Cultural Anthropology* (vol. 22, no. 1, January 2007), the journal of the Society for Cultural Anthropology. It seemed an opportune moment, also within the discipline of anthropology, to reexplore the liveliness of cultural analysis and how this old key term might yet be further retooled for the contemporary world, thinking of culture and cultural analysis as analogous to contemporary biological experimental systems as described by Hans-Jörg Rheinberger (1997), expanded upon by Avital Ronell's *Test Drive* (2005), and in various ways also described by Donna Haraway's notions of material-semiotic objects (1997). The interface between science studies and anthropology not only was an area in which I had been working for the past decade and a half (Fischer 2004), but also was widely recognized as a crucible of developments in anthropology.

As I was finishing the revisions on the version of chapter 1 that appeared in *Cultural Anthropology*, the new editors, Kim and Mike Fortun, asked me to participate in a panel on the genealogies of anthropologies of science and technology at the Society of Cultural Anthropology meetings in Milwaukee in 2006. This allowed me to end the cultural analysis essay with a promise to complement it with one on the cultural genealogies of STS. I wrote what turned out to be an energetic manifesto, "Four Haplotype Genealogical Tests for Anthropologies of Science and Technology in the Twenty-First Century." The rhetorical conceit here was to draw on metaphors from biology, specifically the notion of haplotype clusters that was displacing the term "race" and that for me could displace the equally problematic term "genealogies," which, as we know from many detailed ethnographies, are structures, frequently manipulated to fit political realities while professing to be natural justifications for alliances, jural roles, and inheritances, biological as well as property. The juggling of four kinds of assays or tests for haplotype clusters worked well in a manifesto, but as it transformed into a longer essay several readers insisted on taking the metaphors literally, wanting something like definitive assays to establish each of the four haplotype clusters rather than understanding the clusters as overlapping families of resemblance with differing profiles.

Two influential readers whose work in this arena I respect urged me to keep the haplotype metaphor. I have compromised by revising the chapter title and by shifting some of this meditation from the text to an extended note (chapter 2, note 4). "Four cultural genealogies" works as shorthand for more complex relations (and more genealogies). The note reminds that the present formulation is itself an unstable experimental system whose utility and generativity may lie in its further transforms, metaphors, and developments.

In any case, chapters 1 and 2 operate for me as a pair. Chapter 1 narrates a history or trajectory of sociocultural anthropology as it interacts with shifting adjacent fields, an important one today being science studies. Chapter 2 inversely examines science studies and excavates four of its quite different cultural formations or genealogies and identifies key contemporary stakes for an anthropology of science and technology. Among these stakes is a more global anthropology of science and technology studies, something that should come naturally to anthropology and that is part of my current research efforts. I am grateful to the Carnegie Corporation of New York for funding fieldwork on which the global genealogies are partly based.

Chapter 3 was written for theologians at the Divinity School of the University of Chicago, who convened a workshop (fall 2005) and then a conference entitled "Without Nature: A New Condition for Theology" (October 2006). As foils they invited a biologist, an ecologist, an urban geographer, and an anthropologist to describe how each of these fields deals with nature in today's world. It was wonderful to be in the company of Stuart Newman, Peter Raven, and Ed Soja. In the grand traditions of the University of Chicago, the conveners David Albertson and Caleb King, the participants, and the keynoters Wendy Doniger and Loraine Daston could not have been more stimulating. I thought of this essay from the beginning again as a pair to chapter 1. The old polarity culture versus nature has long outlived its utility. No serious scientist, except one writing for the public, would take either of these terms at face value. Obviously "nature," just like "culture," needs to be retooled, rekeyed to the world of contemporary anthropologies. Although we could never get the theologians to quite spell out what the stakes were for them, I presumed it had to do somehow with the doctrines of natural law. And so in my anthropological perversion (*per-version*, as in a traveling through, detouring, a lovely pun from Lacan) I determined to focus on the four ways in which contemporary science and technology seem to be reworking traditional understandings of nature, including such ideas as accidents of nature, first and second natures, the reengineering of the body, and new questions raised by ecological relationships, cross-species coevolution and cohabitation. The very linguistic notion of nature is ambivalent and, if listened to, opens into a range of dilemmas and fascinations that are proving to be not just intellectual puzzles but also policy debates.

Ivan Crozier invited me to prepare a chapter for a volume he was editing on the twentieth-century history of the body (chapter 4). By now I was on a roll of key terms: culture, nature, body. Since, together with a number of colleagues, I had been watching developments in molecular biology, biomedical sciences, and bioengineering, it seemed natural to expand upon what in chapter 3 I called reengineering the body from inside out. These colleagues include Byron and Mary Jo Good, with whom for over a decade I have been teaching a course at the Harvard Medical School on the social studies of the biosciences and biotechnologies, and in whose Friday morning seminar I have participated over the years as well as in the "Anthropology of Subjectivities" seminar that I have twice cotaught with Byron. The body is a staple in all these venues, but the molecular biology imagination flourishes particularly in the environments of the medical school and MIT. The medical school course has been an opportunity to engage with an extraordinarily stellar list of bioscientists, physician-scientists, and bioengineers, including, to mention only a few, David Altshuler, Rox Anderson, Anthony Atalia, Fritz Bach, Stephen Bergman, Paul Farmer, David Fishman, Judah Folkman, Ferenc Jolezs, Jim Kaye, Jim Kim, David Kuter, Eric Lander, Robert Langer, John Parrish, Julie Richardson, Brian Seed, J. Vacanti, Michael West, Michael Zinner. One year, three of these colleagues—George Daley, Michael Myerson, and Irving London, the founder of the joint MIT–Harvard Health Science and Technology Program (HST)—merged their molecular biology class with ours. I hope to have more to say elsewhere about these explorations, but for the present chapter my imagination has also been stimulated over the years by ongoing discussions with the structural biologist Rob Meijers; the bioartists Oron Catts, Ionat Zurr, Adam Zaretski, and Joe Davis; and with STS colleagues and students in the Boston community: João Biehl, Joe Dumit, Mike Fortun, Nate Greenslit, Evelynn Hammonds, Sheila Jasanoff, Jonathan Kahn, Lily Kay, Evelyn Fox Keller, Hannah Landecker, Natasha Myers, Adriana Petryna, Kaushik Sunder Rajan, Sophia Roosth, Aslihan Sanal, Karen-Sue Taussig, Charles Weiner, and Sarah Wylie.

Chapter 5 was produced at the invitation of Sherry Turkle to write about an object. It was part of her larger initiative to get MIT to think about the affective relations people have with objects. MIT is an engineering school. People's passions are invested in the objects they engineer or otherwise model, discover, play with, or transform. Invoking

Freud, D. W. Winnicott, Melanie Klein, Lacan, Claude Lévi-Strauss, Jean Piaget, and Seymour Papert, among others, Sherry often alludes to object relations, transitional objects, evocative objects, and objects to think with. She has psychoanalytic training and wrote her first book on Lacan. So I began to think about what around me could help me explore affective relations. In another of those flashes of illumination, deriving from my daily care for my mathematician mother, I was led to another key term of anthropology with a long tradition of social theoretical writing from Marcel Mauss and Alfred Schutz to Clifford Geertz and others: personhood. It was a major topic that George Marcus and I reviewed in *Anthropology as Cultural Critique* (1986, 2d ed. 1999, "Conveying Other Cultural Experience: Person, Self and Emotions") and, as mentioned above, the subject of a graduate seminar on subjectivities that Byron Good and I cotaught with the psychiatrist-anthropologist Alisdair Donald in fall 2005 and again in spring 2008.

The geoid seemed to me to work beautifully as a transitional object when I was a teenager for learning about modeling and science as fields of competition and persistence, as well as in the present for helping my mother stay centered as a person in her late nineties. Even more, thanks to trying to be an advocate for my mother, I had realized how little interesting literature there was on aging (not to mention the astonishing dearth of gerontologists), especially in comparison to the literatures on infancy, childhood, and adolescence.

Figuring the size and shape of the earth became a metaphor for figuring old age. More generally, I had long used my relationship to my parents' scientific careers as resonators for skeptically evaluating much that was written about scientists, especially women scientists, by journalists and other laymen. The intensity of the drive, joy, and jouissance of science, of puzzle solving, and of making the world one inhabits is something only a few journalists and sociologists manage to capture in a realistic way amidst all the rivalries, bureaucratic blocks, deceits, and other impediments. My mother's is a survivor's story on multiple levels, and I recommend her scientific autobiography, finally published during the writing of chapter 5, to all those who claim there are not enough accounts of model women scientists (I. Fischer 2005). Chapter 5 represents the most personal of the present essays in rhetorical style, but I think there is a lesson in that as well: something about the relation between form and content that anthropologists and colleagues explored in the initiatives begun in *Writing Culture* (Clifford and Marcus 1986), *Late Editions* (Marcus 1993–2000), and *Critical Anthropology Now* (Marcus 1999) as well as *Anthropology as Cultural Critique* (1986, 2d ed. 1999). For more synthetic essays on subjectivity and personhood, I might direct readers to my pair of essays, as well as the others, in the volumes *Subjectivity: Ethnographic Investigations* (Biehl, Good, and Kleinman 2007) and *Postcolonial Disorders* (Good et al. 2008) and to the index entries on psyche, psychiatry, cultural psychology, and subjectivity (under STS concepts and vocabulary) in *Emergent Forms of Life and the Anthropological Voice* (2004). Chapter 5 has been excerpted in Sherry Turkle, *Evocative Objects: Things We Think With* (2007).

Chapter 6 began life as part of the prologue. Reflecting upon the remaking of anthropologies and the dilemma of how anthropology, on the one hand, has become central to a perspective on the mutability of life ("What would an anthropologist make of what we are doing?"; "We need an anthropologist to teach us about" how Iraqis, Iranians, etc. think, or how to make our organization more effective, or how to make our ads more culturally sensitive); and yet, on the other hand, has also become widely dismissed as not important among the scientific social sciences like economics and political science, I thought perhaps I should excavate what Kant (and those he was reacting to, Hume, Rousseau, and who reacted to him, Moses Mendelssohn, Salomon Maimon) meant by anthropology as fundamental both philosophically and to all of our practical endeavors. Once I started reading Kant again with contemporary reanalyses of his work, I couldn't stop. What was intended as a brief passing paragraph or two to push back the genealogies of chapter 1 another generation or two began to grow and to make claims of its own. I found it fascinating, for instance, that Michel Foucault should have begun by annotating Kant's *Anthropology from a Pragmatic Point of View*.

I first read Kant (and other European philosophers) with Maurice Mandelbaum, a philosopher of the social sciences at The Johns Hopkins University. He was delighted with a paper I wrote on Sir E. B. Tylor, invited me to join his graduate seminar, and sent me on to work with philosophers and anthropologists at the London School of Economics (J. N. W. Watkins in metaphysics; Karl Popper, Michael Oakeshott, and Ernest Gellner in moral philosophy; Gellner, Raymond Firth, Maurice Freedman, Lucy Mair, Isaac Schapera, Abner Cohen, and my tutors, Robin Fox and Anthony Forge, in social anthropology; with visits by E. R. Leach and Lévi-Strauss). I returned to Johns Hopkins just in time for the conference *The Structuralist Controversy* in 1966 (Macksey 1970, 1972), at which both structuralists and poststructuralists entered the U.S. academic stage. At the University of Chicago, I continued in anthropology during its golden age of symbolic and interpretive anthropology with David Schneider, Milton Singer, Raymond T. Smith, and Nur Yalman (Leonard Binder and Marvin Zonis nearby in political science) as my dissertation committee; Paul Friedrich, Eric Hamp, and Howard Aaronson in linguistics; Barney Cohen, Clifford Geertz, Lloyd Fallers, Ray Fogelson, McKim Marriott, Manning Nash, Ralph and Marta Nicholas, A. K. Ramanujan, Terry Turner, and Victor Turner, as active faculty; Sol Tax and Fred Eggan still in the wings; and Michael Silverstein, Judy Shapiro, Shep Forman, and Stanley Tambiah just arriving, Mel Spiro leaving, Marshall Sahlins not yet arrived. I also continued to dabble in philosophy (with Elizabeth Anscomb and Peter Geach, students of Ludwig Wittgenstein), discovering on my own Hans-Georg Gadamer's *Truth and Method*, Jürgen Habermas's *Legitimation Crisis*, and Benjamin's *Origin of German Tragic Drama*, sitting in occasionally on lectures and seminars by Arendt (originally also from Königsberg), Paul Ricoeur, and Mircea Eliade.

Ann Kaplan, by inviting me to participate in the twentieth-anniversary conference for the Humanities Center at Stony Brook, gave me the opportunity to turn the recovery of Kant's *Anthropology from a Pragmatic Point of View* (in its Foucauldian, Lyotardian, Derridian, and other contemporary inflections) toward the future (the epilogue). The cosmopolitan and cosmopolitical dilemmas that were anticipated in the eighteenth century have deepened and expanded as the world around us explodes in violence beyond the mere unsocial sociabilities of which Kant wrote. Learning from catastrophe in the tradition of Benjamin, Arendt, Habermas, Foucault, Emmanuel Levinas, Jean-François Lyotard, and Derrida, among others, has become a recurrent necessity, and it is hoped that the pebbles anthropology throws in the way of violence will bring some relief and help—the violence that Levinas defines as acts done as if one were alone in the world and the world existed only to receive them, and the relief that Kant suggests might come from the capacities of learning to think from other points of view (the anthropological translation of the categorical imperative).

Throughout I have tried to use images less as illustration than as themselves performing a visual thread and counter- or cross-stitching to the arguments, and in this endeavor I have deployed long exploratory captions paralleling the two text boxes in the early chapters. Many thanks for help to the photographer Richard Chase; to Patricia Seed for turning the NASA images into what Duke University Press wanted; to the Houghton Library and imaging services at Harvard for the famous Benjamin cover of *Einbahnstrasse* (*One-Way Street*); and to the artists and friends who allowed me to reuse their images: Germaine Arnaktauyok, Eric Avery, T. R. Chouhan, Johannes Fabian, Dennis McGilvray, Shirin Neshat, Entang Wiharso, and Parviz Yashar.

This book owes much to my students in sts and anthropology and to intellectual communities at Harvard, Rice, mit, and Irvine and particularly to the ongoing stimulation and colleagueship of Hal Abelson, Orkideh Behrouzan, João Biehl and Adriana Petryna, Ryan Bishop, Candis Calison, Melissa Cefkin and Mazyar Lotfalian, Joe Dumit and Sylvia Sensiper, Didier Fassin, Kim Fortun and Mike Fortun, Yaakov Garb, Byron Good and Mary Jo DelVecchio Good, Bruce Grant, Nate Greenslit, Stefan Helmreich and Heather Paxton, Jim Howe, Jean Jackson and Louis Kampf, Erika James and Malek Ghachem, Sheila and Jay Jasanof, Henry Jenkins, Chris Kelty and Hannah Landecker, Rafique Keshavjee, Shekhar Krishnan, Wen-Hua Kuo, George Marcus and Pat Seed, Esra Ozkan, Mariella Pandolfi, Kyriaki Papageorgiou, Kris Peterson, Kaushik Sunder Rajan, Aslihan Sanal and Rob Meijers, Susan and Bob Silbey, Susan Slyomovics, William Urrichio, Santiago Villavecces, Chris Walley and Chris Boebel, Danny Weitzner, Livia Wick, Sarah Wylie, and only alphabetically next to last, but otherwise first, Susann Wilkinson.

Culture and Cultural Analysis | 1
as Experimental Systems

Culture is (1) that relational (circa 1848), (2) complex whole . . . (1870s), (3) whose parts cannot be changed without affecting other parts (circa 1914), (4) mediated through powerful and power-laden symbolic forms (1930s), (5) whose multiplicities and performatively negotiated character (1960s), (6) are transformed by alternative positions, organizational forms, and leveraging of symbolic systems (1980s), (7) as well as by emergent new technosciences, media, and biotechnical relations (circa 2005).

Without a differentiated and relational notion of the cultural—the arts, media, styles, religions, value orientations, ideologies, imaginaries, worldviews, soul, and the like—the social sciences would be crippled, reducing social action to notions of pure instrumentality.[1] When singularized, frozen, or nominalized, culture can be a dangerous concept, subject to fallacies of pejorative and discriminatory hypostatizations (we have reason, they have culture) or immobilized variables (their culture is composed of x features).[2] The challenge of cultural analysis is to develop translation and mediation tools for helping make visible differences of interests, access, power, needs, desires, and philosophical perspective. To anticipate the conversation that anthropology has been having in the past decade with science studies, I draw upon the notion of experimental systems as developed in science studies, particularly Hans-Jörg Rheinberger's *Towards a History of Epistemic Things* (1997), as a way of thinking about how the anthropological and social science notion of culture has evolved as an analytic tool. This chapter's end is the starting point, in reciprocal manner, in chapter 2 to rethink the cultural genealogies of science studies.

The modern social science use of the term "culture" is rooted in the historical milieus that arose with the dismantling of the religious and aristocratic legitimations of feudal and patrimonial regimes, and the agons of third world particularistic cultures against first world claims of universal civilization. These agons began with the English Industrial Revolution, the American and French bourgeois revolutions, and the efforts of peripheral states in what would become Germany and Italy—and later in what would be called the second and third worlds—to catch up without losing their identity.[3] The collection of folklore, epics, oral genres, ritual forms, customs, kinship terminologies, jural norms and sanctions, dispute mediation techniques, material-semiotic objects, musics, and the like were important in nation-building ideologies, in nostalgia-based constructions of identity, and in hegemonic struggles between what was counted as future-oriented modernity and what was counted, reconstructed, or reinvented as past-oriented tradition.

Official histories of anthropology often credit Sir E. B. Tylor's "omnibus" definition—"culture or civilization is that complex whole which includes knowledge, belief, art, morals, law, customs, and any other capabilities and habits acquired by man as a member of society"—as providing the first canonic counterpoint to definitions of culture as the best productions in aesthetics, knowledge, and morals.[4] While such elitist high culture definitions of culture arose in dialectical relation to more demotic or foreign cultural forms, the anthropological understanding of culture that Tylor began to unpack asserts the importance of understanding the relations between all cultural forms at play, in contestation within social formations.[5] The nineteenth-century rise of Quakers such as Tylor and scholars and reformers from other Dissenting Sects in England opened a space of critique of state-established forms of religious legitimation and cultural presuppositions, in synergy with scientific and political Enlightenment ideals of the previous century; these were taken up also in reform movements in India, the Islamic world, China, the United States, and elsewhere, as is acknowledged by the fluorescence of recent work on "alternative modernities" (e.g., Gaonkar 2001).[6] Simultaneously, political economy reformers, including Chartists, abolitionists, Henri de Saint-Simon, Auguste Comte, Pierre-Joseph Proudhon, Karl Marx, and others, provided a space for critique and organizing political movements to reshape the material environments and infrastructures of cultural formations. These nineteenth-century articulations would develop into the methods of cultural accounting of classical sociology, British social anthropology, American cultural anthropology, French structuralism, and poststructuralisms as well as considerations of alternative modernities.

The "jeweler's-eye view" of ethnographers of the early and mid-twentieth century succeeded in putting on the comparative philosophical map the cultural logics—and their social implications and historical circumstances—of the Trobriands, Nuer, Azande, Yoruba, Ndembu, Navaho, Kwakiutl, Shavante, Arante, Walpiri, and others. These cultural logics were used to create structural understandings of the possible cultural variabilities and their social implications in diverse domains, including exchange theory and kinship, political organization and cosmology, jural roles and personhood, speech genres and interactive sociolinguistic styles, economic spheres and informal power, gender roles and psychodynamic complexes, and the structuring of knowledge and awareness by linguistic grammars and cultural frames. The jeweler's-eye view means not only the ability to bring out the different facets, but also a constant back-and-forth movement between (loup-assisted) close-up viewings and sitting back for a more global view of the settings. Classic ethnographies, constructed as synchronic snapshots of a moment in time—classically an annual cycle and a half, or eighteen months—need and are receiving historical recontextualization through restudy and archival work. They have become documents of a historical horizon for the cultures and societies under analysis as well as for those of the ethnographers.

Just as we increasingly recognize the cultures of classic ethnographies, both as they were and as they have become, as always already reworked parts of cultures of larger national, colonial, imperial, regional, and global formations, yielding often out-of-sync alternative modernities, so too the interactions of proliferating kinds of cultures, indigenous, ethnic, occupational, expert, linguistic, local-regional, are becoming more complex and differentiated. New forms of globalization and modernization are bringing all parts of the globe into greater, but uneven, polycentric interaction. New multicultural ethics are evolving out of demands that cultures attend to one another. Within transnational and global technoscientific networks proliferating specialized vocational and class cultures must pay attention to one another in information-rich and multiperspectival institutions lest high-hazard, mission-critical operations such as chemical, aeronautical, and medical industries, or even just ordinary trade, for example, global advertising, production, and sales operations, go awry.

Culture, defined as a methodological concept or tool of inquiry, might best be understood in terms of its historically layered growth of specifications and differentiations, refined into a series of experimental systems that, in a manner akin to the experimental systems of the natural sciences, allow new realities to be seen and engaged as its own parameters are changed. To think of the methodological concept of culture as experimental systems is to assert that there is something both experimental and systematic: that social science accounts of culture emerge from intermediate and interactional spaces, both intersubjective and institutional, that were awkwardly or poorly handled by prior accounts.[7] Objects, theories, and techniques change in focus, resolution, or fidelity (to draw upon visual and sonic descriptive modalities) as we vary our cultural concepts. Historically, concepts of culture have been rhetorical as well as analytical tools in struggles over class and religion; universalistic versus particularistic claims about reason, aesthetics, morality; legitimate versus illegitimate forms of power; science, politics, public spheres, civil societies, and rights and justice. Alternative genealogies can be constructed for the word (*cultura* as a Latin future participle of what comes into being rather than what is), as can humanistic usages (Giambattista Vico's eighteenth-century notion of culture as that which is knowable because created by man). But the modern social science and anthropological construction of the term arises initially in the intergenerational reformulation between the grand comparativists of the nineteenth century and the in-depth fieldworkers of the twentieth century.

While science, technology, literacy, poetics, religion, and capitalism have, since Marx and Tylor, been central to discussions of culture, the focus of debate, the drawing of metaphors and epistemic analogies from the leading sciences of the day, and the refinement of methodological concepts of culture have shifted over the past century and a half, layering themselves as a set of lenses and devices of increasing generativity.

(1) Culture is that relational (circa 1848) . . .

Premonitions and protoformulations of what later would develop into four components of *relational* cultural analysis or cultural accounting can be found already in various places in the mid-nineteenth century. The emergence of *working-class cultures* in relation to bourgeois and artistocratic class cultures can be found in Friedrich Engels's proto-ethnography of working-class Manchester in 1844 (Engels 1887; Marcus 1974); and in the organized complaints of industrially displaced Luddites (skilled workers protesting not all machines but deskilling machines and the introduction of prices not related to custom and skill that would destroy their control over their means of production and turn them into unskilled proletarians), Chartists (workers who felt excluded by the suffrage Reform Act of 1832 and the Poor Law of 1834 and demanded charters of universal male suffrage and other political reforms), as well as the demands for "right to labor" at one's craft, rather than as proletarianized unskilled labor, in the revolutions of 1830 and 1848 in France. These organized complaints and political demands would develop into an explicit working-class culture in the late nineteenth century (Thompson 1968; Sewell 1980; Nimtz 2000).[8] The emergence of a *bourgeois culture* can be seen in the discussions of *Bildung* (culture) in Germany, institutionalized by Johann Fichte's new university in Berlin (Ringer 1969; Readings 1996; Lepenies 2006).[9] The emergence of *national cultures* becomes crystallized in the standardized national languages, creation of university-taught canons of literature and history in these languages, and the print-mediated literacy required by industrialization (Anderson 1983; Gellner 1983; Habermas 1962).[10] The emergence of *culture* as a dialectical agonist to *civilization* can be seen in the nationalist and nation-state building discourses, in which locality, nation building, and universality contest. The emergence of notions of *culture as hegemonic* power relations becomes explicit in the sketches by G. W. F. Hegel, Heinrich Heine, and Marx of why different groups in society might see their interests in agonistic fashion as well as why, critically, they often misrecognize their interests in ways that benefit others (ideology, hegemony), as so memorably expressed in Marx's essay *The Eighteenth Brumaire of Louis Napoleon* (1852).

Four components of relational culture begin to become clarified in the mid-nineteenth century by the agonistic diffrentiation and reorganization of modern societies: (1.1) folklore and identity; (1.2) ideologies and political consciousness; (1.3) class and status cultures; (1.4) pluralized, relational cultures versus universalizing civilizational ideologies.

1.1. Folklore and National Cultural Identities

The nineteeth-century novels of Sir Walter Scott (d. 1832) began in English literature an exploration of looking back at fading regional cultural settings from an insider-outsider perspective. A member of the lowlander elite writing about highlander Scottish society, Scott wrote novels that became key to Scottish identity for unionist United Kingdom and English audiences, thereby helping to define an emergent British national and British imperial identity. The debates of the period over James Macpherson's *Fragments of Ancient Poetry, Collected in the Highlands of Scotland, and Translated from the Gaelic or Erse Language* (1760), judged to be fraudulent and imaginatively composed, were not unlike efforts to compose national epics in eastern Europe and elsewhere, which Ernest Gellner credits as the background to the suspicion of Bronislaw Malinowski toward explanation by historical roots and insistence instead on the ideological functionality in the present of the formulation or retelling of such cultural forms (Gellner 1988: 175). Among such functionalities were also projections or models used in colonial settings: it is often remarked that Scottish clan structures provided models for William Robertson-Smith and others for understanding and characterizing tribal organization in Arabia, in the Hindu-Kush, and elsewhere. (See further, under late nineteenth century, below.)

1.2. Cultural Ideologies and Political Consciousness

Marx's *Eighteenth Brumaire of Louis Napoleon*, written in the aftermath of the failures of the revolutions of 1848, not only became a touchstone for later writers trying to puzzle out underlying structural patterns of social organization and cultural forms (Claude Lévi-Strauss says he would always reread *The Eighteenth Brumaire* before sitting down to write a new project), but is an early locus classicus for thinking about class cultures and how they are aligned under hegemonic ideologies. His resonant phrase about the peasants being like potatoes in a sack was not contemptuous but a summary tag for the ways in which their economic, organizing, and strategizing possibilities were fragmented and controlled.[11] His dramatization of a revolution running backward (propelled by each higher class abandoning the interests of the next lower one when it thought it might gain momentary advantage, but thereby in the longer term isolating and weakening itself) was a vivid way of charting the different class fractions in the revolution (class fractions resonating with petrochemical fractioning of different grades of oil as well as with the arithmetic of voting, just as class strata and stratification resonated with slower but active geological processes of sedimentation, upheaval, intrusion, and temporary consolidation).

At issue in both examples were problems of political consciousness and ideology, not just economic interests. Crucial to the stabilization of ruling classes, fractions, or coalitions was the ability to make their control appear to be the natural order of things, legitimizing their society's cultural forms, hierarchies, and practices. Marx was a pragmatic organizer, trying to prevent precipitous armed labor rebellions that could only be crushed and rethinking the failures of earlier conceptions as with the defeats of 1848. It became clear on the barricades of Paris in 1848 that this would be the last of the artisanal revolts and that an industrial proletariat would not come into political strength for many more years, and even then, as in Germany, would compete with a rapidly growing white-collar class for political power. Consciousness, alienation, commodity fetishism—cultural armatures of political economy—would be central to these struggles. Indeed, in the preface to the second edition of *The Eighteenth Brumaire* (1869), Marx contrasts his explanatory narrative with great-man-in-history accounts (Victor Hugo's *Napoleon le Petit*) as well as with deterministic ones (Proudhon's *Coup d'état*), insisting on the theatrical, linguistic-translational, allusional nature of cultural and social forms, including a fortiori revolutions, which draw upon and are haunted by cultural forms of the past and yet sometimes can leverage novel breakthroughs and transformations.

As Bendix and Lipset (1951) would put it in one of many meditations on why the concept of class seemed so much less politically resonant in the United States than in Europe, class in Europe was always an interpretive cultural construct involving theories of social change in which class becomes salient at times of misalignment between power and interests, as when a new class begins to challenge the power of a weakening hegemonic one. In the United States, as Lloyd Warner demonstrated in his *Yankee City* studies (1949–51), people tended to view class without any such theories of social change. Class was conceived as either objective indices—income, job type, education, church, and voluntary association affiliations—or as relative subjective feeling states, in which those close to but not at the top, the lower upper class or upper middle class, had the most sharply developed sense of the pecking order or hierarchy, that in any case could be gotten around by individualistic hard work or moving westward.

Distinctive working-class cultures became politically salient, organized through unions, workingmen's circles, sports clubs, and political parties, sometimes fueling thinking about social change and national or international futures, but as often, as Paul Willis's (1977) ethnography *Learning to Labor* described for later twentieth-century working-class lads in England, locking people into class position. The elucidation of various working-class cultures around the world, though usually grounded in political economic analyses, takes on a variety of cultural armatures, from C. L. R. James's situating of Caribbean working-class formations of respectability in relation both to empire and to fears of sliding back into the desperations of the poor, to the subaltern historians' teasing out of working-class cultures in India in the context of caste and language differences.[12]

1.3. Class Cultures and Status Distinction

It is with Max Weber's *Verstehende Soziologie* ("interpretive sociology" or sociology of understanding or meaning) that analytic tools for unpacking the cultural formations of estates, status groups, and classes began to come into sharper focus. Using a comparative approach to questions of power and legitimacy, education and bureaucracy, this-worldly ethics and inner motivations, Weber compared the mandarin examination system used to recruit bureaucratic officials in China to the use of Greek, Latin, and vernacular classics as a mode of recruiting officials from the new educational institutions (*Gymnasium*, the new universities in Berlin and elsewhere) for the new German bureaucratic state. Greek was not of particularly instrumental use in a modern bureaucracy, but, as with recruitment to the imperial cadres of the British Empire, it was one of a set of markers of status distinction. In German, the term for such cultivation (*Bildung*) had everything to do with the creation of the bourgeoisie as well as the civil service. *Bildung* involved *Kultur,* which in turn was part of universal civilization, but German *Kultur* was also distinctive, constructed around a canon of literature and philosophy. *Bildung* involved dress, behavior, punctuality, discipline, and various knowledge sets.

Modern capitalist class and ideological cultures come into being historically, according to Weber, through a conjunction of material and cultural causes. While feudal estates or patrimonial status groups have other motivations, values, and cultural styles, the culture of industrial capitalism comes into being through the conjuncture of five causal factors: (i) the anxiety structure of theological beliefs in predestination and need for signs of whether one is among the saved, which provided a this-worldly economic ethic of demonstrating God's pleasure through worldly success (the Protestant ethic); (ii) an organizational structure which disciplined its members to adhere to this work ethic (the sect); (iii) a position in the stratification system where such an ethic could be especially effective in achieving upward mobility or stable income—the lower middle and upper lower classes, small businessmen (Marx's low road to capitalism); (iv) a historical cultural change of values and lifestyle among mercantile classes of the seventeenth century, who stopped using profits to buy land, positions of nobility, and luxurious lifestyles and began living Spartan lives and investing profits back into productive enterprises (Marx's high road to capitalism); and (v) world-historic changes in global markets and technologies.

None of these causes is sufficient alone, Weber cautions, nor exclusive to Protestant communities: other religions have their forms of anxiety structures, organizational discipline, and finely measured religiosities that may be equally productive of this-worldly economic drive (Jains, Jews, and Parsis are among his examples) and may become part of industrial capitalist modes of production, given the proper conditions. In *The Protestant Ethic and the Spirit of Capitalism*—two essays written from a vivid comparison of North Carolina and Germany, part of his larger comparative sociology of religions, in turn part of his larger comparative studies of economy and society, for which motivating and legitimating cultural forms are central—Weber tries to account for the elective affinity of causes.

The multicausal analysis, as well as Weber's attention to the varieties of Protestant forms and their changes in social locus over time, protects both against the chauvinism of attributing all progress to Christian or Protestant grounds and against scapegoating Jews or similar groups for the ills of capitalism.[13] The work sparked a parallel debate over the rise of the modern sciences in seventeenth-century England (Merton 1938), a debate taken up again in the 1980s with a Weberian attention to the material, literary, and social "technologies" of experimental sciences as well as the synergy or "coproduction" between a particular field of rationalization and other arenas of legitimation of authority (e.g. Shapin and Shafer 1985).

What is crucial here for the study of cultural forms is Weber's insistence on understanding the cultural frames of reference of the motivations and intentions of actors. Even a concept such as power for Weber is famously defined as the probability that an order given will be obeyed, and therefore the strongest form of power is neither force nor economic monopoly but culturally formulated legitimate domination, on the grounds of tradition or that the person giving an order is legitimately entitled to do so. Thus religion, as a central component of culture, is often analyzed by Weber not only as differentiated by social position—priestly classes and laity have different relations to the symbolic, ritual, and belief systems—but as legitimating ritual structures for state formations, especially for the ancient empires and their patrimonial successors.

Classic Weberian accounts utilizing the more detailed knowledge of twentieth-century fieldwork or utilizing the questions raised by such an ethnographic sensibility include Clifford Geertz's account, in *Religion of Java* (1960), of how class and status stratified religious and cultural formations in a decolonized, modernizing "new nation"; E. P. Thompson's *History of the English Working Class* (1968), which, albeit a more self-described Marxist account, analyzes the cultural formation of work discipline and the role of the religiosity of the dissenting sects; and Joseph Gusfield's *Symbolic Crusade* (1963), a study of the temperance movement in the United States that likewise illuminates the religious-class inflected antagonisms of small-town elites feeling themselves losing political ground to Catholic and urban immigrants, all formulated through the language of cultural legitimacy.

1.4. Culture(s) and Civilization(s)

Nineteenth-century England and France saw themselves as the vanguard of universal civilization, carriers of comparative knowledge from which education and reason could devise progressively more humane, efficient, just, and free societies (*liberté, fraternité, egalité,* in the French version; white man's burden in a tutelary vision of the task of colonialism). Germany and other nations on the periphery saw cultures in dialectical relationship to the French and English metropoles rather than only singular civilization. German social theories would thus emphasize the plurality of cultures, and even more importantly the dialectical relationship between first world cultures and second or third world ones, beginning with Marx's sensitivity to the contradictions of class positions and their cultural perspectives or dialectical (in)abilities to develop political consciousness and also with his notes on the relation between labor in the colonies (Ireland, the United States, and India) and conditions in England.

As the Moroccan historian Abdullah Laroui would put it in the 1970s, Marx was the model third world intellectual, to be followed by many others, moving to the metropole to study and strategize ways out of his homeland's subordinate position in a globalizing world, paying particular attention to what would come to be called dual societies, underdevelopment, deskilling, and proletarianization. For colonial political leaders and social theorists (M. K. Gandhi, B. R. Ambedkar, Frantz Fanon, Albert Memmi, O. Mannoni, Aimé Césaire, C. L. R. James, W. E. B. Du Bois) the dialectical relationship between self and other, between the conditions of the colonized and the colonizer, could never be forgotten in a simple universalistic account. Laroui would emphasize a quintessential cultural dilemma in *The Crisis of the Arab Intellectual* (1976) in the last quarter of the twentieth century: one could adopt a Marxian ideology and, as in South Yemen, seize control of the state but then have to impose a tutelary dictatorship until the population catches up to the cultural perspective of the vanguard (all the more oppressive the smaller the vanguard); or one could attempt to mobilize change by utilizing the cultural language of the masses, Islam, but then have to deal with a cultural language vulnerable to theocratic or fundamentalist capture.

The nineteenth-century terms "culture" and "civilization" became pluralized in the twentieth century, and at the core of this pluralization in both cases were notions of cultural symbols and meaning structures, usually with deep histories, as in "Islamic," "Persian," "Indian," or "Chinese" civilizations, each containing numbers of cultures within.

Culture is (1) that relational (circa 1848),
(2) complex whole (1870s) . . .

Sir E. B. Tylor's second key contribution, complementing the omnibus definition of culture, was his paper pointing out the arbitrariness of Victorian charts of progress, made nowhere more obvious than in the field of morality. Indeed, while British anthropology remained within a general self-congratulatory evolutionary paradigm through World War I, it is crucial to recognize that the fight waged by anthropology on behalf of rationalism and empiricism against the dogmatics of the established church was part of a larger series of social struggles having to do with the various reform acts of nineteenth-century England, including those which enfranchised more and more of the population, reformed penal law and social policies for dealing with the poor and reserve labor force, and reformed marriage and family law. Anthropologists were often associated with the Dissenting Sects of the rising shopkeeper, artisan, and independent professional classes, espousing individualism and self-reliance and hostility to older relations of hierarchy, status, and ascribed rather than achieved position. And some, such as Robertson-Smith, even on occasion lost their chairs for their outspokenness against the dogmas of the established church.

While in England utilitarianism became the new social theory, in Germany (and France after the Franco-Prussian War), the rapid industrial revolution and state formation under Otto von Bismarck would lead to a recognition that the second industrial revolution required a social theory more integrative or institutional than a merely utilitarian dependence on the decisions of atomized individuals.

The four components of the relational culture concept that began to emerge in the mid-nineteenth century now became engaged, in the last quarter of the nineteenth century, (2.1) in England with the elaboration of utilitarianism both as a tool for rationalized social reform and as an ideology of Victorian culture; and (2.2.) on the European continent with the reformulation of cultural nationalisms and universal civilization(s), including at least an intellectual engagement, through philology and comparative religion, with universal civilizations other than Christendom.

2.1. Utilitarianism as Native Social
Theory, a Class Culture, and a Professional Culture

Within the various emergent forms of utilitarianism in England and elsewhere, socialisms of both the Marxian and Fabian varieties were accommodated under the calculus of the "greatest good for the greatest number" and the social welfare of society. This calculus left little explicit room for notions of culture except in the form of values and preferences which might be factors in utility curves. Yet the educational curriculum in public schools in preparation for the colonial service and public administration at home was based more on classical humanities than on engineering or other practical skills. Culture was carefully constructed and enacted, while being misrecognized as merely the "best that civilization has to offer." England being one of the two most powerful global empires of the day, the temptation was to see English utilitarianism as a universal logic rather than itself a conceptual machine that could be used to erase or obscure the presuppositions, assumptions, and cultural logics that allowed the calculation to work. "Formally free labor markets" in which workers might bargain with employers by organizing were recognizable but less easily recognizable were the nonmonetary elements that went into the reproduction of the labor force. Utilitarianism tended to obscure why it might be in the interest of plantation laborers in Jamaica or British Guyana to work only until a certain amount was earned each week and then use the rest of the week for their own nonmarket subsistence agriculture, therefore being stigmatized as lazy, nonmaximizing, and noneconomic actors with low productivity; or why paying copper miners in Northern Rhodesia insufficient wages to support families back home for their lost labor in the tribal economy might cause agricultural collapse and famine (Allen 1964; Dumont 1957; Richards 1939; Rodney 1972). Culture in these colonial conditions often became a pejorative mode of dismissing the rationality and sophistication of subaltern populations: their culture, their values are different.

Utilitarianism of this reductionistic sort remains powerful in such professional cultures as classical and neoclassical economics (in competition with the more cultural-analytic fields of institutional, historical, political, family, or feminist economics), and it continues to bestow several important legacies. The first is the ability of rationalistic models to serve as probes against which reality can be measured and new questions generated. The second is the optimistic, prudential reformism, the insistence that because society and culture are made by human beings, they can be improved, a formulation that goes back to the Italian humanism of Vico but reformulated in terms of restructuring social institutions and moral education.[14] A third legacy, central to nineteenth-century utilitarian reformism, was Jeremy Bentham's insistence that the rules of government be published and made public, thereby tempering the arbitrary capriciousness of a monarch, tyrant, dictator, power elite, imperial president, or executive's will.

Culture begins to emerge in these very practical fields, first as a conceptual tool for making visible the often counterfactual assumptions on which rational choice models are constructed; second, as a professional or disciplinary formation with its own incentives and sanctions on thinking otherwise; and third, as embodied in material media and forms of communicative action and performance, as in Bentham's demands for public accountability

Two problematics develop in the twentieth century alongside these articulations of culture. The first has to do with democratic theory: what Carl Schmidt called the dilemmas of constitutional democracies (how to deal with political forces that want to destroy the constitutional form, but forces which nonetheless cannot simply be excluded [Kennedy 2004]), and what Jürgen Habermas called the decay of the public sphere (the manipulation of common sense and public opinion [1962, 1973]). The second has to do with the atomization of cultural accounting, whether in political economy (individualist "contract theory"), evolutionary theories that debated diffusion versus independent invention of cultural traits (the "shreds and patches" version of culture), at best recognizing culture complexes of traits that seemed bound together, or stories of how universal reason might triumph over local superstition.

2.2. The Reformulation of National Cultures

The demotic omnibus definition of culture as everything produced by human beings provided a productive foundation for including in social science accounts the cultures of peasants, religious groups, migrants, and a variety of others, contesting the dominance of high culture and figuring culture as a field of contestation and differential interpretation among social groups. Epics, poetry, and folklore collections were often important to nation building and their ideological legitimation. Canonic collectors of folklore were often influenced by modernist movements: the brothers Grimm in Germany, Charles Perrault in France, Itzhak Manger for Yiddish Poland, Yangit Kunio in Japan, Sadeq Hedayat in Iran. Contending nationalist mythologies continue to be used as mobilizers of irredentism and communal strife.

Sir James Frazer's collection of folklore in *The Golden Bough* remains one of the most influential works of this phase of the culture-civilization dialectic. On the one hand, it powerfully influenced a generation of early twentieth-century European writers in search of symbols and imaginative forms to expand their literary and cultural repertoires (Vickery 1973). As a work of comparative ethnology, it remains a descriptively rich collection that repays returning readers. It is particularly rewarding on ancient Middle Eastern and East African rituals, the notions of sacred kingship, and the assimilation of the Christian ritualization and sanctification of Jesus as one more of the Middle Eastern seasonal renewal rituals. And for the study of English culture of the late nineteenth century, *The Golden Bough* is itself a testimony to the ideological drive for modern reason against superstition and clerical authority.

On the other hand, for the development of anthropological methods, Frazer became the benchmark against which the next generation of methodological innovation defined itself, eschewing his "amongitis" (comparing items from different cultures out of context) and his reduction of meaning to the common sense of his own culture (not having methods of access for richly understanding the "native point of view" and thereby discounting the intelligence of the other).

The struggle between utilitarianism and culture (Durkheim 1912; Parsons 1939, 1951), culture and practical reason (Sahlins 1976), and idealism and utilitarianism (Kant 1781, 1788, 1790, 1798) is an enduring tension between the recognition of society as open to reform and directed change and the recognition that when one tries to change something, others things often change concomitantly, often in unexpected ways. Some of these concomitant changes may be anticipated if one has both a structural and a hermeneutical understanding of the interconnections of cultural understandings and institutions.

Culture is (1) that relational (circa 1848), (2) complex whole . . . (1870s), **(3) whose parts cannot be changed without affecting other parts (circa 1914)** . . .

At the turn of the twentieth century the notion of culture comes to partake of a vision of structure and function widespread across intellectual disciplines (geology, biology, linguistics, psychoanalysis, Durkheimian sociology, British social anthropology), a search for relations among parts and a sense that phenomena have structures and functions integral to their existence, adaptability, growth, and decay. Central to the emergent formulations of culture in this period are the methodological discussions of how to study the meanings or symbolic structures that make culture a level of analysis not reducible to mere biological, psychological, or sociological frames. These discussions about the *Geisteswissenschaften* and *Verstehendes Soziologie* (or interpretive, hermeneutic, or symbolic analysis of social communicative action) were central to philosophy (Wilhelm Dilthey), history (Max Weber), sociology (Emile Durkheim), linguistics (Fernand de Saussure, Leonard Bloomfield), and anthropology (Franz Boas, Bronislaw Malinowski, Alfred Kroeber, Edward Sapir, A. I. Hallowell).

The evolution of class structures (especially the growth of the white-collar classes faster than the industrial proletariat in Germany), changes in the bureaucratic requirements of the second industrial revolution and large-scale societies (no longer built upon small feudal and parish institutions), and new forms of urban life mediated by commodity fetishisms (crowds, boulevards, shop windows, walls decorated with advertisements) are key grounds upon which culture now became formulated in direct opposition to the cultural theories of utilitarianism and early industrial capitalism.

In a formulation that became canonic for mid-twentieth-century sociology, Talcott Parsons suggested that while utilitarian social theories were based on atomism (actors as individuals), means-ends models, and an unordered, ever-growing, and infinite number of possible wants, desires, and ends, Durkheimian sociology and other social theories of the second industrial revolution challenged all three of these axioms: Individuals are divided entities, only partially socialized by their families, communities, and nation-states. Values are organized through collective representations or systems of symbols and the *conscience collective*, punning on conscience and consciousness, a moral force as well as a system of representations. Short-term, means-ends rationalities very often do not account for the choices and actions of individuals and social groups. Weber similarly distinguished between short-term instrumental rationalities and long-term value rationalities that were organized into systems of "legitimate domination" which allowed the exercise of power through individuals' feeling that orders given should be obeyed because they were right and legitimate; Marx earlier had delineated this phenomenon as the ideological ability of ruling political factions to make their perspective on the world appear to be part of the natural order.

In the early twentieth century, four analytics of culture began to take on methodological rigor: (3.1) culture and linguistics; (3.2) culture and hermeneutics; (3.3) culture, social structure, and personhood; (3.4) culture and the comparative method.

3.1. Culture and Linguistics

The structural linguistics of Fernand de Saussure, Leonard Bloomfield, Nikolay Trubetzkoy, Roman Jakobson, Edward Sapir, and Benjamin Whorf and the semiotics of Charles Sanders Peirce were to become growing influences on anthropological theories of culture. From nineteenth-century efforts by Sir Henry Maine and Louis Henry Morgan to deal with systems of kinship terms and totemic systems as ordered linguistic and jural sets, the movement was toward the model that Saussure classically formulated: meaning is established by a system of differences. Just as each language selects but a few phonemes from the possible set of phonetic sounds, so too languages and cultures divide up grammatical and semantic spaces differently. (*Mouton* in French is not the same as *mutton* in English.) The Sapir-Whorf Hypothesis generalized the recognition that Native American languages expressed mood, place, aspect, and tense in radically different ways from Indo-European languages and that therefore common sense, presuppositions, and worldviews would be quite different. Pierce's notions of icons, signs, and symbols and of how both relations among referential systems and speakers and addressees operate would become one source of thinking both about the pragmatics of language use, sociolinguistics, and about the relations among communicative units not reducible to morphology, grammar, or semantics. In mid-century this thinking would be combined with work on cybernetics and information theory, with further work in sociolinguistics and pragmatics and, in the 1960s, with structuralism, ethnosemantics, the emic-etic distinction, the Kuhnian notion of paradigm, and symbolic anthropology.

Crucial to all of these elaborations is the probing of the interconnected systematicities of binary distinctions and complementary distribution (upon which the phonemic model of language and information theory more generally depend)[15] creating meaning or value, and the distinction between native knowledge and structural rules that can operate beneath the consciousness of the native speaker: e.g., a native speaker can correct grammatical mistakes and thereby teach a novice, child, or linguist without being able to articulate the grammatical rules being used (but which the linguist can elicit through systematic binary pairs). Lévi-Strauss made it a rule of thumb not to trust native models or explanations but to systematically analyze for the underlying structural rules. On the other hand, equally important for the study of knowing how actors understand their worlds is eliciting their native points of view, their hermeneutical modalities of interpretation, and their critical apparatuses of evaluation.

3.2. Culture and Hermeneutics: Vico, Dilthey, Weber, Freud

The late nineteenth-century debates about the methodology of the social sciences, in distinction to the natural sciences, turned upon the paradox that if actors become aware of the description of their actions by an observer they may well alter their actions to make those descriptions appear nonpredictive. Sentient actors do not behave like crystals or atoms. The *Geisteswissenschaften* (the German translation of the English "moral sciences") became defined as the study of meaning to the actors, something that could be "objective" because dependent on the public nature of language and communication. All social action by individuals is intersubjective and can be analyzed like any other linguistic phenomena in terms of message, sender and receiver, context, and pragmatics. While the roots of these formulations go back to Vico, were then elaborated by Friedrich von Schiller, Johann Gottfried von Herder, and other German Romantics, and were reformulated for the human sciences by Dilthey, it was the generation of classical German sociology, including Weber, Georg Simmel, and Ferdinand Tönnies, that laid the groundwork for the notion of culture used by symbolic and interpretive anthropology in the 1960s. Contributing to their formulations were the sharp contrastive contexts of Germany vis-à-vis England and France and of the accelerated pace of social change in Germany formulated as a transformation from feudal rural, agrarian, and customary *Gemeinschaft* (community) to industrial, urban, more impersonal, contractual, commoditized, and bureaucratic *Gesellschaft* (society).

Weber, the master sociologist of the period, worked out a methodology that paid attention both to causally adequate explanations such as economics, law, and politics, and explanations adequate at the level of meaning to the actors, such as culture and values. His study of the interaction between the Protestant ethic and the spirit of capitalism, for instance, as already described, insisted on a multicausal explanation of an anxiety structure induced by Calvinist notions of predestination and election to being among the saved by faith alone; an organizational disciplinary mechanism (small voluntary organizations where members helped discipline one another); a social structural analysis (effective at especially the lower middle class, upper lower class strata); a cultural or value-orientation shift (from using accumulated wealth to buy land or luxury goods to living spartanly and ploughing earnings back into production); and a world-historic accounting (that this-worldly economic ethic combined with an emergent moment of cap-italist organization helped a system transition to a new cultural-and-economic mode of production that subsequently would not need the legitimation to the same degree). The texts, journals, letters, and ac-counts of church methods of the early Protestants, as well as his own observations in Germany and North Carolina, afforded access to the cultural forms through which the actors felt themselves compelled to act and by which they justified their actions. In order to understand and to formulate predictive models good enough for governance, one needs to find cultural patterns systematic enough to be at least predic-tive "ideal types" or "as-if" accounts. Weber here is not as fully herme-neutic as later scholars armed with tape recorders and engaging in longer term participant observation might be, but he provides the beginnings of an intersubjective methodology that can lay claim to empirical objectivity and that can be iteratively tested and corrected.

Freud, the master hermeneuticist of the period, elaborated a set of elicitation and story-structuring techniques. There were, first of all, his theatrics of elicitation: the couch, the analyst outside the vision of the analysand, the fixed time, free association, and dream reporting. There were the dramatic markers of emotional truth: the way in which a suggestion would either be confirmed by vigorous further elabora-tion or by violent denials and changes of subject. There was the hunt for clues in slips of the tongue, rebus visualizations, word substitu-tions, and the like. There was the production of the case history as a literary form which weaves together different plots, story lines, and temporalities: those of the order of discovery, the order of presenta-tion of symptoms and development of illness, the reconstructed etiol-ogy or causal sequence (Brooks 1984). There were the cultural tem-plates for patient and physicians to use as analogues, often drawn from the Greek mythologies on which the educated middle class was raised, such as Oedipus. And there were the social issues of the day: the shell shock of World War I, which also preoccupied W. H. R. Rivers in England, bourgeois sexual repression, and status anxiety, as wonder-fully recontextualized in the case of Dr. Schreiber by Eric Santer (1996). Finally, there was the metaphysical topology of *das Ich* (ego), *das Es* (id), and *das Über-Ich* (superego), functioning somewhat dif-ferently in the colloquial German from the more Latinate English intended to bolster the authority of the discipline, but again function-ing as a cultural template to think about the way the unconscious works its uncanny and subterranean tricks (Bettleheim 1983; Ornston 1992; also Riceour 1970 for a hermeneutic reading of Freud).

In a brilliant commentary and transformation, Lévi-Strauss would juxtapose a Cuna healer's technique to that of Freudian talk therapy: in the one case an ostensive personal life history would be *elicited from* the patient and recoded into a collective myth (e.g., Oedipus); in the other case a collective myth would be *told to* an individual to get her to identify her pain with the characters and movement of a collective story. Lévi-Strauss's analysis would provide the basic form of many anthropological accounts of healing rituals. The ambiguity of whether Freud's techniques were cultural or universal would be explored in the 1930s by many anthropologists, who not only had themselves ana-lyzed but would take Rorschach and other tests to the field to test whether an analyst not familiar with the culture would come up with the same analysis as one familiar with the culture and whether the range of results would fall within universal patterns or needed to be standardized in each culture locally (Du Bois 1944; Kardiner, Du Bois, and Linton 1945). There was also an ambiguity about the degree to which patterns found among individuals could function also on the collective level, as in Freud's speculative late essay *Moses and Mono-theism* and, in a different, more functionalist fashion, the anthropolo-gist Mel Spiro's elaboration of cultural defense mechanisms (1967).

3.3. Culture, Social Structure, and Personhood

Methodological functionalism, the obligation of an investigator to ask how changes in one part of a social system affect other parts, became a fieldwork guide for a generation of British social anthropologists trained by Bronislaw Malinowski and A. R. Radcliffe-Brown and in intellectual dialogue with Emile Durkheim and Marcel Mauss's journal *L'anné sociologique*. Mauss's canonic *The Gift* (1925), which continues to generate commentaries, draws upon Malinowski's fieldwork on the kula ring in Melanesia, Elsdon Best's account of Maori exchange, Boas's fieldwork on potlatch exchange up and down the rivers of the northwest coast of North America, and examples of other exchange systems from ancient times to modern France. These exchange sys-tems demonstrate how ceremonial trade circuits not only carry along ordinary trade, but also stimulate production, require ritual both to regulate social relations and environmental ones, organize politics, elicit competitive agonism, and generate elaborate jural distinctions, typologies of gifts, and stages of gift-giving.

Mauss's essay provided an alternative account to Jean-Jacques Rousseau's and Thomas Hobbes's notion of fictive social contracts as necessary to social order, showing how hierarchies of power, regional economies, temporalities, and cosmologies could come into being through modalities of reciprocity. In Radcliffe-Brown's articulation of structural-functionalism, roles and statuses in a social structure were seen as tools for a comparative method that did not tear institutions out of their contexts. Such comparative work with societies ethnographically well studied were pursued in volumes on political systems and marriage systems (Radcliffe-Brown, and Forde 1958), as well as in Radcliffe-Brown's own efforts (1933, 1952) to show that emotions and joking relations were patterned by social structural relations (as Durkheim had argued in *The Elementary Forms of Religious Life*).

For Durkheimians and the British social anthropologists, the formation of personhood was likewise formed by the social structure. Persons were partially socialized and partially unsocialized. The process of socialization and formation of cultural personhood operated not only through parenting but also through rituals and larger cultural forms. Malinowski's essays in *Sex and Repression in Savage Society* (1937) were a cultural and anthropological challenge to those interpretations of Freud that assumed the Oedipus complex to be universal. If one were to take the Freudian argument seriously that adult personality is crucially formed in early childhood by family dynamics, then in a matrilineal society, where property and authority pass through the female line rather than the male line, dreams, crimes, and patterns of transgression should be different from those in bourgeois Vienna (Malinowski also sketched out a third pattern of Polish peasant family life that also contrasted with bourgeois Vienna). This line of Freudian attention to the cultural formation of personhood in different cultures and social structures was taken up by the culture and personality school of American anthropology in the 1930s and 1940s, which included Margaret Mead, Ruth Benedict, Cora Du Bois, A. I. "Pete" Hallowell, and Clyde Kluckohn, and by later Freudian psychological anthropologists like Mel Spiro, Anthony Wallace, Gananath Obeysekere, Robert LeVine, Robert Levy, and Waude Krache.

The culture and personality school experimented with statistical distributions of personality types selected by a culture. Margaret Mead's *Sex and Temperament in Three Primitive Societies* (1935) and *Coming of Age in Samoa* (1928) contributed popular understandings that norms of child rearing and gender roles were variable across cultures and could be reformed at home. The later generation of Freudian psychological anthropologists introduced a series of new concep-

1. *In Return I Give Water*, 2005, etching and aquatint print by Germaine
Arnaktauyok. A perfect illustration of Mauss's *The Gift* (1925) and the culture of
mindfulness of reciprocity between humankind and the environment, the return
gift of fresh water is to aid the seal in its journey into the next world. Arnaktauyok,
of Yellowknife, Northwest Territories, Canada, remembers as a girl coming upon
her father on the ice engaging in this rite. Born in Igloolik (now Nunavut) in 1946
to the carvers Therese Nattok and Isidore Iyotok, she is well known for her prints,
children's book illustrations, and the design of "The Drummer" on the two-dollar
Canadian coin (1999), celebrating the creation of the Territory of Nunavut (as well
as for her mother-and-child design for a two-hundred-dollar gold coin issued in
2000). Photo by Richard A. Chase; print owned by M. Fischer; reprinted with permission of Germaine Arnaktauyok.

tual tools: Anthony Wallace (1969) reworked the notion of distributions of personality type into a general recognition that individuals
participate in but do not necessarily share culture. His notions of
mazeways and revitalization cults argued that the Seneca, under pressure, might be seen as using ritual processes to rework their psychological orientations, using reports of their dreams as pieces of evidence. In
similar fashion, Obeysekere used Freudian analytic clues to interrogate
case histories of nine ecstatic priests who were part of the formation of
a new Buddhist-Hindu cult in Sri Lanka. He was able to use Freudian
suggestions to generate hypotheses and see if they were confirmed or
not in the lives of these priests (1981). He then also attempted a wider
cultural analysis of South Indian and Sri Lankan Hindu psychology
through the cult of the Goddess Pattini (1984). Krache (1978) uses
dreams and small-group dynamics to explore the psychology of a band
of South American Indians. And LeVine (1973), more generally, building on child-rearing studies, attempted to create a field of cultural
psychology.

There is now a third generation of psychoanalytic approaches in
anthropology utilizing Jacques Lacan's rereadings of Freud, proceeding via linguistics and topology, Michel Foucault's notions of subjectivation, and Slavoj Žižek's interpretations of contemporary politics,
particularly in the postcommunist Balkans and Eastern Europe, but
also in American popular culture. Two recent collections that reflect
some of this anthropological work are Biehl, Kleinman, and Good
(2008), and Good et al. (2008).

3.4. Culture and the Comparative Method

The understanding that cultures and societies need to be understood
structurally, hermeneutically, and in context presented challenges for
comparative research. Weber, even more than Marx before him, cast
his comparative net globally. Marx had been interested in the expansion of capitalism and imperialism into the colonial world, the resistances in semimonetized settings such as Asia and Russia but had
mainly confined his detailed work to western Europe. Weber's detailed
comparative investigations into the stability of states, political economies (*Economy and Society*, 1922), religious systems of legitimation
(*Sociology of Religion*, 1920), and status and cultural formations (mandarins, feudal estates versus capitalist classes, sociology of music, rationalization of cultural forms) extended from China and India to the
Middle East, North America, and Europe. While much of his work on
the ancient religions of India and China and on Judaism has been

superseded by more recent ethnographic and social historical work, his work on bureaucracies, taxation systems, empires, and modern nation-states remains part of the contemporary tool kit. The Durkheimian tradition in tandem with British social anthropology also ranged across the globe, albeit initially paying more empirical attention to small-scale societies in aboriginal Australia, Melanesia, Africa, and South Asia, but with equal concern for the implications for England and Europe. Durkheim's own major works included comparative work on suicide rates as indexes of more pathological or more healthy social structures, the effects of the division of labor, and the destruction of middle-level political organization by the French revolution on penal systems and the conscience collective.

Weber's concern with religious and cultural systems of legitimation would lead in the 1960s to such studies as Geertz's *Religion of Java* (1960) and Robert Bellah's *Tokugawa Religion* (1985), both placing cultural questions at the center of modernization theory and what later would be called alternative modernities. Durkheim's and Mauss's work would provide one source of French structuralism in the 1960s and in British and American anthropology would lead to work on the powerful effects of ritual and symbols in local contexts (Victor Turner) as well as (via Talcott Parsons) to a notion of cultural systems as principles which structure social action, and on ethnosociologies, such as David Schneider's accounts of American kinship as a peculiar mixing of ideologies of blood and code for conduct and McKim Marriot's accounts of the transactional logics of purity and auspiciousness that structure the caste system in India.

> Culture is (1) that relational (circa 1848), (2) complex whole . . . (1870s),
> (3) whose parts cannot be changed without affecting other parts
> (circa 1914), **(4) mediated through powerful and power-laden
> symbolic forms (1930s)** . . .

The crisis of the 1930s—reactions to the trauma of World War I, to the global economic depression, and to the growth of mass politics, advertising, and the culture industry—elicited a powerful set of revisions of the methodologies for the study of culture. Of these, enduring contributions were made by (4.1) Ernst Cassirer's *Kulturwissenschaften* (rather than *Geisteswissenschaften*), (4.2) the dialectic between documentary realism and surrealism, and (4.3) the Frankfurt School's reworking of Marx and Freud in its study of the culture industry and modern media.

4.1. The Logic of Symbolic Forms

Cassirer, an important influence on Geertz and 1960s symbolic and interpretive cultural anthropologies, addressed the crises of knowledge—the separation of knowledge into epistemologies of mathematical physics and those of the historical sciences—by examining the common logical structure of concepts at work in both and by undertaking a phenomenology of perception.[16] The notion of mediation via symbolic forms is key. As earlier argued by Vico, Herder, and Simmel, perception is constituted as objective through language and art, neither of which merely "copies" pregiven reality. The expression of the "I" is an act of discovery, not just one of alienation. By externalizing itself, the I or self establishes itself through the mirror of its work. In *The Myth of the State* (1946), Cassirer criticizes the philosophies of Spengler[17] and Heidegger[18] as having enfeebled the forces that could have resisted modern political myths. By constructing decline and *Geworfenheit* (literally, "thrown-downness," the accidents of existence) as the logic of our time, they abandon the active, continuous construction and reconstruction of cultural life. More helpful, but still requiring correction, are the later Edmund Husserl's *Lebensphilosophie* with its focus on "life-worlds" and production of the good life and Henri Bergson's phenomenology, which, while suspicious of symbolic forms as life-denying reifications, directs attention to embodied perception. For Cassirer, the self perceives the resistance (*Widerstand*) of the world, of the alterity of the object (*Gegenstand*) against which the I arises; so too language, art, and religion are tangible for us only in the monuments we create through these symbolic forms—the tokens, memorials, and reminders of the reciprocal processes of continuous reanimation of self, cultural object, and context and of physical existence, objective representation, and personal expression.

Cassirer, Alfred Schutz (1939), Kenneth Burke (1941, 1945, 1950), and Susanne Langer (1942, 1967, 1972, 1982) form an important set of precursors to 1960s cultural anthropology. Schutz extended the phenomenological method in a sociological direction, Burke stressed the performativity of rhetorical, symbolic, and cultural forms, and Langer was both a translator of Cassirer and a best-selling philosopher of symbolic forms in logic, art, and ethnopsychology in her own right.

4.2. Realism and Surrealism

Close documentary realism, especially through photography and the projects of the Works Projects Administration (wpa), but also by the tradition of community studies in anthropology and sociology, was one response to the crises of the 1930s. Particularly through the photographic documentation of the Great Depression, but also in newsreels, theater, painting, dance, and fiction we now have, post facto, a visual imagery not available to people at the time (Stott 1973, MacLeish 1937, Lange and Taylor 1939, Agee and Evans 1941, Stott 1973, Marcus and Fischer 1986). There was a hunger for reliable information at the time and suspicion that newspapers were manipulating the news and that government officials denied problems in hopes of boosting business confidence.

The Chicago School of community studies was imbued with the documentary spirit and established the groundwork for investigations of social mobility, neighborhood patterns of succession, local community organization, processes of immigration from Europe and from the South into the industrial cities, and symbolic arenas of competition for cultural hegemony and control. William Lloyd Warner's *Yankee City* studies (1949–51), W. F. Whyte's *Street Corner Society* (1943), and the various studies of Chicago by Louis Wirth, Robert E. Park, Ernest W. Burgess, Roderick D. McKenzie, and their associates were important ethnographic beginnings. Warner's studies of the tercentennial parade in Yankee City (Newburyport, Mass.), of the strikes and political campaigns, and of church and voluntary organization affiliations as cultural markers of class and status remain exemplary.

Mead's studies of child rearing, sex roles, and emotions in Samoa and New Guinea to critique American patterns and call for their modification was a mode of cultural critique that entailed juxtaposing a foreign perspective, gained from firsthand, long-term community studies. One can read British social anthropology and its development of the ethnographic monograph of communities as providing a similar kind of cultural critique. Malinowski engaged in social policy debates based on the comparative archive built up by in-depth fieldwork in the functional interconnections of institutions of society. The comparative volumes on political structure and kinship, while couched in more theoretical terms, were intended to establish new foundations for the understanding of moral authority (Fortes and Evans-Prichard 1958; Radcliffe-Brown and Forde 1958; Schneider and Gough 1961). Audrey Richards (1939), Godfrey and Monica Wilson, and the work of the Rhodes-Livingstone Institute were involved in probing the failures of the colonial system in agriculture and mining by showing their detailed workings via community studies documentation. Follow-up studies by this generation of anthropologists and their progeny would probe the dysfunctions of resettlement policies and underdevelopment.

While documentary realism and comparative juxtaposition constituted one set of responses to the crises of the 1930s, surrealism was another way of interrogating the present by exploring alternative potentials. In France, surrealism attracted both artists and some anthropologists as a way of breaking open and liberating the reified institutions of society (Clifford 1981), by connecting signs in a new urban world and reenchanting the worlds of science and technology, and by operating in contrast to Jean-Paul Sartre's anthropology based on humans as project-making animals (he was powerfully motivated by his experience in the Resistance to the Nazi occupation, making meaning out of a moral and cultural crisis), cultivating an anthropology based on a divided self of unease (Bürger 2002). If the condition of modernity is one of living in two worlds simultaneously, traditional and modern, rural and urban, craft and commodity (Hegel, Marx, W. Benjamin, Berman [1982]), the rise of fascism and Nazism elicited Antonin Artaud, André Breton, and Georges Bataille to focus on the double worlds of reason and madness as also the condition of modernity. Nazi race theory was recognized by cultural analysts as a delusional force: asserting that race is defining of an essence, yet knowing that it is constructed (Hermann Göring's "I define who is a Jew" and the training of Czech, French, and Polish young men in Napola paramilitary schools to strengthen "the race"; see Bürger 2002). Nazi followers indulged in harmony with the Führer and the power of the party, while recognizing themselves as insignificant and dependent upon an unreal world of signs (ibid.: 21). For Bataille the Nazis represented a Teutonic military order that was able to create a mythic spirit of strength. He wanted to create an equally powerful spirit based in premodern sacrifice and expenditure. The secret society *Acéphale* was an experiment to think (and possibly enact) a human sacrifice to build a community or church of sacral-like power. (It is said that although members were willing to be sacrificed, none could be found to play executioner.)

The legacies of surrealism continue to reverberate into the present, part of the stream of French attention to the body, sensuality, immediacy, and that which escapes language and reason, but which structures cultural fantasy, advertising appeal, dream worlds, and imaginaries; and in the work of such anthropologists as Michael T. Taussig (1987, 1992, 1993, 1997, 2003) (also heavily influenced by Walter Benjamin) on violence, fantasy, and the magic of the state.

4.3. The Culture Industry: The Politics and Poetics of Culture

For the generation of 1968 perhaps the most important predecessor in cultural analysis was the Frankfurt School's critical theory.[19] Combining Marxist and Freudian questions, Max Horkheimer and Theodor Adorno reanalyzed the dynamics of the Oedipal complex and family structure and, like Freud, found roots of the authoritarian personality in the replacement of the father by a political leader or movie star. Unlike the sons in agrarian families, who received both land and skills from the father, sons in modern society were more likely to learn skills of livelihood in school and then teach them to an increasingly out-of-date father. Rather than watching parents struggle to make pragmatic decisions, young people paid attention either to perfect role models disseminated through the media or to their peer group, forming thereby more rigid, brittle personalities that were less able to deal with ambiguity and adversity. Adorno was particularly concerned with the formation of a culture industry that increasingly shaped the superego through the lowest common denominator and the largest revenue-generating music and commodities, thereby reifying and deadening the critical faculties. Although some of Adorno's dismissals of jazz and other popular forms were elitist, Eurocentric, and uncomprehending, his concerns with the way media transform thought and with the possibilities for self-reflection, critique, and political subjugation remain intensely salient in our multimediated world.

More optimistic about the democratizing potentials of the new media, Benjamin after 1924 found his subject in the new industrial arts, architecture, photography, mass culture, and new avant-garde cultural forms in France and Russia. He became celebrated posthumously through the work of such commentators as Hannah Arendt and Gershom Scholem and, in the 1970s and 1980s, Martin Jay (1973) and Susan Buck-Morss (1991), who in turn stimulated what is now an increasing flood of work, including in the anthropology of Taussig and Michael Fischer. Benjamin's notion of dialectical images which flash up in charged moments was a way of reading advertising and commodity displays by juxtaposing the utopian hopes originally invested in them with their later commodity banalization as a way of reigniting the aspirations of making the world otherwise. It was a tactic not unlike Adorno's aesthetic theories for the avant-garde arts and the sociology of music, seeing art as a form of negative dialectics with which to see the world as it is and yet otherwise, abstracted and reconfigured.

Others of the Frankfurt School worked on the sociology of penal systems (Otto Kirchheimer, who inspired Foucault), the political

economy of money (Friedrich Pollack), the sociology of irrigation societies (Karl Wittfogel), the sociology of literature (Leo Lowenthal),
and psychoanalysis (Erich Fromm). The Frankfurt School was among
the first intellectual circles to be shut down when Adolf Hitler became
chancellor, and most members thereupon emigrated to the United
States. Adorno, for example, worked with Paul Lazarsfeld at Columbia
University on the study of propaganda and the authoritarian personality. After the war, Adorno, Horkheimer, and Pollack returned to
Germany to rebuild critical thought there. Herbert Marcuse stayed in
the United States, becoming a guru to the students of the generation
of 1968, as did, less flamboyantly, Lowenthal. Others associated with
the school or publishing in their journal (*Zeitschrift für Sozialwissen-
schaft*) included such figures as Arendt, Raymond Aron, Bruno Bettelheim, Bertolt Brecht, Siegfried Krackauer, Georg Lukács, Karl Mannheim, and Scholem. Intense concern with the psychology of cultural
forms, their instrumentalization by the culture industry of propaganda, advertising, movies, and popular culture, and their social force
in competition with other forms, were common concerns of these
theorists. Benjamin, an intense interlocutor with Scholem, Brecht, and
Adorno, was also part of another illustrious circle in Berlin that met in
the ateliers of László Moholy-Nagy, Ludwig Mies van der Rohe, and El
Lissitzky—the G. Group, who published a journal, *G. Zeitschrift für
elementare Gestaltung*—as well as with the surrealists in Paris.

The mix of immediate concerns about cultural power's ability to
influence socialization and individual psychology as well as mass politics, the destruction of the public sphere by mass advertising and
propaganda, the power of the market to direct what cultural and commodity objects would circulate, and the psychodyanamics of ideology
was a heady blend of ideas for the 1968 generation, which saw in the
Vietnam War, the resistance to the civil rights movement, the conservatism of the universities, and the restrictiveness of social codes a
parallel to the oppressions of the 1930s.

Culture is (1) that relational (circa 1848), (2) complex whole . . .
(1870s), (3) whose parts cannot be changed without affecting other
parts (circa 1914), (4) mediated through powerful and power-
laden symbolic forms (1930s), **(5) whose multiplicities and
performatively negotiated character (1960s)** . . .

Cultural studies, poststructuralism, and symbolic or interpretive anthropology, along with feminism, media and performance studies,

new historicism, and early studies of decolonization and new nations, transformed cultural analysis in the 1970s.

Symbolic anthropology drew upon the quasi-cybernetic paradigm of Harvard's Social Relations Department under Talcott Parsons, semiotics (C. S. Pierce, Ray Birdwhistle, Thomas Sebeok), structural linguistics (field linguistics classes became training grounds to learn systematic methods of elicitation and analysis of cultural units), and generative grammars (Noam Chomsky). The core course in the anthropology graduate program at the University of Chicago was organized into cultural systems, social systems, and psychological systems. David Schneider, founder of the Society for Cultural Anthropology and senior editor of the reader *Symbolic Anthropology* (Dolgin, Kemnitzer, and Schneider, 1977), argued that the cultural system provided the principles of organization for the social system; Geertz argued that the cultural system was logico-meaningfully integrated, the social system functionally integrated, and the psychological system psychodynamically integrated. Geertz thus wrote essays on religion, ideology, common sense, art, and moral thinking as "cultural systems."

Mel Spiro provided a foundation in Freudian psychoanalytic approaches, with a strong anti-Malinowskian insistence on the universality of psychoanalytic concepts (Spiro 1982); he smuggled culture back in, however, in the form of cultural defense mechanisms. (He then founded an anthropology department at the University of California, San Diego, with a strength in psychoanalytic approaches, recruiting Obeysekere and Levy). Schneider argued that the distinction between etic and emic could not be sustained, thereby making all systems of thought, native and scientific, merely variant modes of cultural accounting.[20] Victor Turner analyzed the Ndembu "forest of symbols" with a widely imitated combination of structural-functional (Durkheim, Arnold van Gennep) analysis of mythic charters and ritual process, with Freudian fusions of corporeal-emotive and cognitive-symbolic poles in symbol formation, and Burke's performative notions of motives and rhetorics.

The turn toward interpretive anthropology led by Geertz (1973) and Turner (1967, 1974) followed from the instability of the etic/emic and the cultural/social system distinctions and drew upon the hermeneutic and phenomenological traditions of Dilthey, Weber, Freud, Schutz, Paul Ricoeur (who also taught at Chicago), and Mircea Eliade (also at Chicago).

Meanwhile, in fall 1966, structuralism and poststructuralism arrived simultaneously in the United States via a conference entitled *The Structuralism Controversy: The Languages of Criticism and the Science of Man*, held at Johns Hopkins University (see Macksey and Donato 1970), with Lévi-Strauss, Jacques Derrida, Lacan, and others, an event that would lead to a dominant strand of cultural work of the next generation. In France, structuralism and poststructuralism were modalities of French response to the traumas of World War II, Americanization, and the influx of North Africans after the Algerian War of Independence. Lévi-Strauss brought together the enthusiasm of postwar thinking about set theory, linguistics, and cybernetics with an elegy and reconstructive method for aborignal cultures destroyed by colonialism in Australia and North and South America. He and his fellow structuralists, among them, Georges Dumezil, Jean-Paul Vernant, Michel Detienne, Pierre Vidal-Naquet, transformed the study of Greek mythology and myth studies in general. No longer could anyone identify deities with single virtues (god of wisdom) without considering that deity's structural position vis-à-vis others; no longer could one version of a myth be privileged without considering the entire set of transformations that a mythic structure makes possible. Lévi-Strauss seemed at the time to vanquish, in favor of deep, pervasive, regenerative mythic and social structures, Sartre's attempt to fuse voluntaristic, politically engagé existentialism with the inertial forces of history understood through Marxist lenses—albeit the charismatic force of Sartre's position arose from the moral crisis of sense making during the Resistance against the Nazi occupation. Lacan, the early Foucault, and Pierre Bourdieu were received in the United States as elaborations of this culturalist structuralism.

Structuralism and poststructuralism were influential moves away from behaviorist and symbolist models of communication.[21] Behaviorist models take words and symbols to be unproblematic tokens, combined and rearranged in meaningful chains of sentences or utterances, done in turn-taking, stimulus-response sequences. Analysts can thus build up models of culture based on sets of belief statements made by actors. Symbolist models recognize that symbols are not univocal simple tokens but have fans of meanings and that more is exchanged in any speech act than either speaker or receiver comprehends. Nonetheless, in symbolist models, symbols are still but more complex sign tokens—like overly full bouquets or pockets of fertile sediment—richly polysemic yet discrete. Indeed, the richest symbols are like black holes: the entire culture is said to be condensed there. Symbolist analysts organize their models of culture around key symbols, symbol clusters, and nodes of semantic networks, somewhat like a crystal structure. There is a reassuring sense of relative stasis or stability of the symbolic system. Structuralist, and particularly poststructuralist, models decompose symbols and metaphors into chains of metonyms or associations that play out into disseminating, ramifying, transmuting dynamics, attempting to model, in the structuralist case, the semantic-symbolic parameters of variation and transformation and, in the poststructuralist case, the transmuting ambivalences of meaning that keep texts and communication labile—unless forcibly controlled, in which case poststructrualist deconstructive sensibilities highlight the tensions and pressures of alternative meanings subversive to those intended and authorized by the controls.

Foucault's insights into disciplinary power and the birth of the clinic may have had something to do with a kind of Freudian *nachträglich* (post facto) recognition of his experiences as an adolescent: the reformatory to instill heterosexual codes and watching compliance to the Nazis in his native Poitiers ("we all have a fascism in our heads" [cited in Carton 2004: 25; see also Agamben 1995, 1997, 2003; Bernauer 2004; Raber 2004]). Derrida and Jean-François Lyotard were more explicit about the legacies of World War II. Lyotard's *Postmodern Condition* (1979), Carton points out, "turns—between chapter 9, 'Narratives of the Legitimation of Knowledge,' and chapter 10, 'Delegitimation'—on a paragraph devoted to Heidegger's notorious 1933 Rector's Address, . . . and the new chapter begins, 'In contemporary society . . . [where] the grand narrative has lost its credibility' " (Carton 2004: 24). The essay is about the coming of the computer and the information age, in which local language games and performativities will have more force than past universalist ideologies for mass mobilization (in the name of History, Reason, or Progress) and in which incommensurabilities among language games and value systems will challenge two centuries of standardized linguistic, religious, and educational nation building (as France copes with Muslim North African immigrants). Similarly, Derrida, from his first major work, *Of Grammatology* (1967a), takes on the "ethnocentrism which everywhere and always, had controlled the concept of writing . . . from the pre-Socratics to Heidegger" and introduces the image of ashes that would grow as a motif in his corpus, quoting Edmund Jabes, "Ou est le centre? Sous la cendre (Where is the center? Under ashes") (Carton: 24; see also Agamben 1995).

The question of Vichy France, the Nazi occupation, and the haunted, hidden collaborations of that period continue in the 1980s and 1990s slowly to be worked through as a challenge to cultural accounts that would treat culture as merely communicative, symbolic, and openly political, "what you see is what you get," uncompromised by hidden meanings, displacements, and self-deceptions. Indeed, here is one of

2. *Lumumba Makes His Famous Speech*, 1973–74, painting by Tshibumba Kanda Matulu. Both in artistic style and content, popular genre painting of the 1970s provides popular culture histories and cultural critiques of colonial rule and the period of decolonization and postcolonial struggles. Kanda Matulu's painting of Patrice Lumumba, on the day after Zaire's Declaration of Independence and his appointment as prime minister, shows him cursing King Baudo in of Belgium for the slavery of colonialism and demanding that all whites leave. The screws and chains of African subjugation are broken. The public plaza, microphone, and postal, telegraph, and telephone (PTT) communications media are in new hands. The painting is part of series of 102 paintings with commentary by Kanda Matulu executed in 1973–74, collected by Johannes Fabian (1996, 1998). The original painting is now at the Tropenmuseum, Amsterdam. Image courtesy J. Fabian. Photo by Richard A. Chase.

the roots or, at least, resonances of the continuing intense interest in psychoanalytic approaches to subjectivities and subjectivation (Foucault 1981–82), rhetoric (Derrida 1996b), feminism (Kristeva 1987, 1995; Cixous 2001), technology (Ronell 1989, 2005), and ideology (Rickels 1991, 2002; Žižek 1991). But France and Europe are not the only places to have experienced such histories of violence, cruelty, and oppression that are embedded in cultural topologies amenable to this sort of analysis, as anthropologists have explored in Japan (Ivy 1995), Indonesia (Siegel 1997, 1998; Good and Good 2008), and Thailand (Morris 2000), and some literary critics are exploring for China (B. Wang 2004; D. Wang 2004).

The stress in interpretive anthropology and poststructuralism on culture as contested meanings created, negotiated, and performed in locally polyvocal contexts dovetailed also with the rise of cultural studies. In Britain, cultural studies arose at Birmingham University from literary studies, branching out under the leadership of Raymond Williams and Stuart Hall into youth and popular culture, ethnicity, hybridity, race, and class cultures. In the United States, cultural studies grew out of American studies redirected by anthropologists and folklorists, initially at the University of Pennsylvania, and from labor and social history, as in the work of George Lipsitz (1990, 2001). For a period, centers for cultural studies sprang up to create interdisciplinary work between the humanities and social sciences, until the field was eventually reimperialized by English departments, losing not only its ethnographic and social science edge, but also its fledgling efforts to work in languages other than English (ironically the language of most writing about postcolonialism).[22]

> Culture is (1) that relational (circa 1848), (2) complex whole . . . (1870s), (3) whose parts cannot be changed without affecting other parts (circa 1914), (4) mediated through powerful and power-laden symbolic forms (1930s), (5) whose multiplicities and performatively negotiated character (1960s), **(6) are transformed by alternative positions, organizational forms, and leveraging of symbolic systems (1980s)** . . .

The 1980s produced revised modes of cultural analysis, followed in the 1990s by changing infrastructures such as media, environment, biotechnology, and violence that took on new cultural salience. The revisions of the eighties included new approaches to using ethnography to investigate and map the changing nature of cultural and social forms at the end of the twentieth century (*Anthropology as Cultural Critique: An Experimental Moment in the Human Sciences*, Marcus and Fischer 1986); inquiries into the multiple disciplinary tools that could be employed in making cultural analysis more trenchant and revealing (*Writing Culture*, Clifford and Marcus 1986); the incorporation of transdisciplinary approaches, including feminism, deconstruction, film and media studies, new historicism, science and technology studies, cyborg anthropology; the efforts to revive area and global studies with fresher ideas about how to do multisited ethnographies of mutually dependent activities in dispersed parts of larger systems or networks; and inquiries into second-order modernization and risk society (Beck 1986, Fortun 2001, Petryna 2002, 2005). Among the new journals that propelled these initiatives were *Cultural Anthropology* (1986), *Public Culture* (1988), *Positions* (1992), *Visual Anthropology* (1987), *Subaltern Studies* (1982), *Representations* (1983), and the eight-volume annual *Late Editions* (1993–2000).

In the 1990s, a new experimental, recombinant mode of cultural thought, writing, and visualization took material shape through the combination of commercial biotechnologies shaped by post-1980 legal, financial, and technological infrastructures and information technologies, particularly after the World Wide Web in 1994 and linked databases made the Internet an everyday medium. Lyotard's speculations in his *Postmodern Conditions of Knowledge* (1979) on the role of the computer in making information available suddenly seemed both quaint and prescient, quaint in failing to foresee the many-to-many communication uses, the way just-in-time accounting could reorganize the business world, and the way e-mail would speed up the pace of work and introduce new stratifications; yet prescient in the apperception of new local language games and formats, including increased communicative reach through flows, codes, and performativity rather than single propositions and arguments. (Viz. also: Gregory Ulmer's efforts to think Derrida through electronic media [1985, 1989, 1994]; Avital Ronell's rereadings of telephony in Alexander Graham Bell's America versus the place of technology in Heidegger's Germany [1989]; Friedrich Kittler's contrasting of the cultural formations carried by standardized German in 1800 and the grammaphone, film, and typewriter in 1900 [1985, 1986]; and Mark Poster's efforts to rethink the oral versus literate cultures debate [Ong 1982; Goody 1977] in terms of new electronic modes of communication [1990, 2001]).

As restratification processes proceeded in the aftermath of the implosion of the Soviet Union and the decline of the bipolar world, violence and religious legitimations repackaged themselves. Derrida suggested that globalatinization through the capital concentration and mergers of transnational media conglomerates would make Islamic and other putative fundamentalist resistance movements appropriate and be undone by the new media, like a kind of autoimmune disease, intense, virulent, and violent. Globalatinization is a taking on of a Christian or Western formatting of publicity: it is an argument about the nature of the current media which sets the theatrical format, enforcing a frenzy of position taking in order to maintain visibility. While the use of the latest media (Internet, Web, video) helps extend the propaganda reach, at the same time it reformats that propaganda into a new modality. The constant need for new positioning is exhausting and generates its own opposition among both traditionalist and modernist forces: hence autoimmune disease. Acquired immune deficiency syndrome (AIDS), one of the major plagues of these years, gave rise to new modes of cultural work, with activists pushing for changes in drug approval processes, using the Internet to challenge the hierarchical relations between doctors and patients, insurance companies and beneficiaries, and the entire health care system. Globalatinization, AIDS (and severe acute respiratory syndrome [SARS], multidrug-resistant tuberculosis, mad cow disease, and other viruses such as Ebola and the H5N1 avian flu), 1990s financial crises moving rapidly across the globe from East Asia to South America, and worries about climate warming, all made the eighties' cultural notions of alternative modernities seem, if not quaint, more relational than ever, differentially connected to the global patchwork of political and cultural economies. Ethnic and religious warfare intensified and led to renewed analyses of the limits and weaknesses of constitutional forms of governance and the lack of local rootedness of human rights and global humanitarian industries (Agamben 1995, 1997, 2003; Pandolfi 2002, 2006; Fassin 2002, 2003; Appadurai 2006).

> Culture is (1) that relational (circa 1848), (2) complex whole . . . (1870s), (3) whose parts cannot be changed without affecting other parts (circa 1914), (4) mediated through powerful and power-laden symbolic forms (1930s), (5) whose multiplicities and performatively negotiated character (1960s), (6) are transformed by alternative positions, organizational forms, and leveraging of symbolic systems (1980s), **(7) as well as by emergent new technosciences, media, and biotechnical relations (circa 2007)** . . .

Cultural vocabularies and social understandings increasingly draw analogies from the new technosciences of the 1990s and 2000s—especially the life and information sciences—instead of from the mechanical, physical, and physiological sciences, which provided much of the functionalist and structuralist imagery of the early twentieth century. Symbiogenesis and bacterial or viral abilities to shift genetic material among species offer enticing sources of new metaphors for reconceptualizing social interaction and cultural hybridization. As in work with immunological systems, which expose the conceptual inaccuracy of identifying diseases as fixed entities, so too it seems often fruitful to think of cultural and social patterns as emerging out of mutations, assemblages, viral transitivity, rhizomic growth, wetwares and softwares, and disciplinary discourses transmuting into even more pervasive and infrastructurally embedded codes and flows.[23] Cultural and social theorists have turned to the technologies and technosciences around which contemporary societies construct themselves for useful metaphors with which to describe, explore, compare, and contrast these societies with one another and with their predecessors. As Kim Fortun puts it in a review of the second edition of *Anthropology as Cultural Critique*, "Anthropology is at its best when understood to be operating *within* an open system, *as* an open system, and as the study and production *of* open systems" (2003: 172). Moreover, she notes, because scientists must learn to be open to interdisciplinary inputs with their cultural differences of language, assumptions, and protocols, the practices and experimental imaginary of scientists become a rich reference point for ethnographies of contemporary cultural worlds.

Circa 2007, then, three key areas of cultural change have become foregrounded: (7.1) morphing media environments and culturing connectivities; (7.2) cultural double-entry accounting amidst social traumatization and reconstruction after warfare and structural violence; (7.3) transformations in the life sciences, technosciences, and cultural life involving overwhelming flows of data, new modes of visualization, new forms of collaboration, and intense commercialization.

"Experimental systems, graphemic spaces."

Experimental systems are the working units a scientist or a group of scientists deal with. They are simultaneously local, social, institutional, technical, instrumental and, above all, epistemic units. [A]n experimental system [is] a unit of research designed to give answers to questions we are not yet able to ask clearly. In the typical case, it is, as Francois Jacob has put it, "a machine for making the future." It is a device that not only generates answers; at the same time, and as a prerequisite, it shapes the questions to be answered. An experimental system is a device to materialize questions. It cogenerates, so to speak, the phenomena or material entities and the concepts they come to embody. An experimental system can be compared to a labyrinth whose walls, in the course of being erected, simultaneously blind and guide the experimenter. The construction principle of a labyrinth consists in that the existing walls limit the space and the direction of the walls to be added. It cannot be planned. It forces one to move by means of checking out, of groping, of tatonnment. The development of such a system depends on eliciting differences without destroying its reproductive coherence. Together, this makes up its differential reproduction. The articulation, dislocation, and reorientation of an experimental system appears to be governed by a movement that has been described [by Jacob] as a play of possibilities (*jeu des possibles*). With Derrida, we might also speak of a "game" of difference. It is precisely the characteristic of "fall(ing) prey to its own work" that brings the scientific enterprise to what Derrida calls "the enterprise of deconstruction."—Hans-Jörg Rheinberger (1998: 287–88, 291)

7.1. Morphing Media, Culturing Connectivities, Soft Infrastructures

One might call new information technology and media environments culturing new connectivities, after the way biologists learn to culture tissue, to grow immortal cell lines, to use recombinant DNA techniques to grow knock-out mice for cancer research, and generally, as Rheinberger says, to "write with biology" rather than discover it, creating tools, molecules, and tissues that did not previously exist in "nature." The Internet, networked data banks, visual icons, video clips, film, animation, streams, and repetition of information flows are *repositioning* and enveloping older cultural media such as orality and literacy, *reshaping* the public sphere by changing power relations, as in doctor-patient-insurer relations, mobilizing money and attention in electoral campaigns, and drawing attention to alternative geopolitical narratives, as in al-Jazeera's transformation of the Arab public sphere, and *producing* new *lively languages* that, in interesting recursive loops, continually reference the morphing media and new infrastructures of life from which they emerge.

The move "from Web 1.0 to Web 2.0" collaborative tools is a metaphor for continuing efforts, beginning with the uncommercialized electronic frontier of the Web in the mid-1990s, to move from, as it were, Diderot's encyclopedia to Wikipedia: that is, from slowly produced, rigidly formatted, bureaucratically controlled, authoritative knowledge to platforms for quickly produced, flexibly formatted, and easily reassembled distributed intelligences and information cascades. These informatic tools, which harness many individuals working at "the edge of [their] competence on purpose" to expand creativity and knowledge frontiers, are but one small niche that promises "butterfly effects" of new cultural itches.[24]

China offers some of the most dramatic current examples if only because of the massive nature of Chinese demographics. Only thirty-seven million or so of China's billion plus people are Internet users, and only 6–8 percent of these are bloggers, but that is approximately two million bloggers. By June 2008, the number of Internet users in China reportedly surpassed that in the United States (Markoff 2008). Blogging exploded in China in 2005–6, driven by more than one hundred firms that are Internet providers, by venture capital, and by the money to be made through advertising. Delightfully, the characters for blogger mean "learned guest." Although the Chinese government has instituted filtering, censorship, and panoptic controls and although most blogs are about trivial matters and although the most linked-to blogs are those of celebrities, still the nature of the conversational, citational, and linking can have cascading effects.[25] Xiao Qiang, the editor of the China Digital Times Project at the University of California, Berkeley, has been collecting examples. He notes that the CEO of sina.com, China's largest and most prominent site hosting blogs, is married to the daughter of one of China's political leaders. It is thus the provider closest to China's power center and its efforts to control the media. Not only is the site connected to the communist party, it has the power to select what blogs to put on its front page and, via ads attracted to the most linked-to blogs, it is a node of economic power.

Yet one blog that appeared on the front page was by Fei Tei, who wrote innocuously about recipes for tomato soup, mentioning in passing that a particular Chinese herb makes the soup especially delicious. It is grown in western China, and it destroys the environment, but it is highly valued in Hong Kong, where its sales generate huge profits. As the shaggy dog story evolved, with its further links to information, it became a bit of investigative journalism on environmental degradation. As Fei Tei commented, he has an urge to bite society, but actually he only scratches it where it itches, and he wondered, "Am I making a difference?"

Another blog—by the celebrity artist Ai Wei Wei, who returned from the West and now owns bars and was a consultant to the architect for the new Olympic stadium—refunctioned a minor news story about a medical researcher who was victimized by the robbery of his laptop and who lashed out at the laxness of the police in repressing the criminality of homeless urban migrants. Ai Wei Wei chided the researcher for indulging in a shameless attack on human rights. The blog attracted eighty thousand hits with further commentaries, setting off a storm of discussion about discrimination and the treatment of rural migrants trying to make their way as urban workers.

What is happening via such examples, Xio Qiang says, is that the government is losing control of the narrative that only the communist party can lead and control economic growth. More obvious ways of undermining the government narrative include simple linking to official statements, such as "there are no bloggers in jail" and recirculating these with only the comment "Did you know?" or "Here's some news!" (Iranian blogs often use poetry in similar ways.)[26] The point, Xio Qiang suggests, is not that these blogs themselves are constitutive of a public sphere, but rather that they are creating the soft infrastructure for a future one by becoming rapidly circulating and widely disseminated information cascades that can set media agendas and provide space for emerging voices, so that when social movements do emerge, the most credible of these voices can emerge as leaders.

Soft infrastructures, here, are changing cultural norms and thereby contribute to emergent forms of life. In a useful heuristic, the constitutional and Internet lawyer Lawrence Lessig (1999) suggests that there are four main tools for building our cultural and information infrastructure through the Net: the law, the market, the code or architecture (or engineering), and cultural norms. The outcomes of battles over the future norms and forms of cultural life are by no means predetermined. It is crucial to continually debate and air in the public sphere precisely the cultural values being encoded through software code, market, and law to prevent unwanted shifts of ownership of information, barriers to access, and other infrastructural decisions and to track shifting cultural norms. Questions must be asked: Does information want to be free? Does commercialization stimulate innovation or channel innovation away from desirable lines of development? Is privacy impossible in an information society? Are speed bumps, which slow information flow, important protections against corrosive effects of commercialization? Can the balance between public domain and intellectual property rules be open to continual readjustment rather than becoming locked in? These and other questions are not just legal, economic, and software decisions but cultural switching points, values, and choices that make a difference in the directions cultural life will take (power-laden, performative, and negotiated, but constituitive, symbolic systems in the language of the anthropology of the seventies; shifting relations between forces and relations of production or consumption and of legitimation, in the earlier languages of Marx and Weber). Reciprocally, cultural critique needs an analytics that is sophisticated about the workings of

the infrastructural modalities through which culture is institutionalized and temporarily "hardened."

7.2. Double-Entry Cultural Accounting and Cultural Infrastructures in Zones of Violence and After Social Trauma

It has long been recognized that culture is not primordial but continually reconstructed and reworked after massive disruption, both
intended (nation-building projects, modernity ideologies as breaks
with the past both in Europe and elsewhere), and unintended (via
disease decimations of indigenous populations, wars of conquest, civil
wars, world wars, wars of independence, disorder after the collapse of
command economies and authoritarian regimes, massive migrations).
In the late twentieth century and early twenty-first, violence including
physical warfare, economic "structural violence," suffering and psychic
reorganization through new modes of subjectivation has again come to
the fore in the moral and political debates over cultural ideals. Cultural
analysis has a critical role to play as norms, justifications, and principles
are renegotiated over multiculturalism, sovereignty, prevention of ethnic cleansing, human rights, cultural survival, humanitarianism, environmental use, and physical and mental health. The very conceptual
categories are increasingly undergoing cultural morphing.

Warfare and armies, for instance, are morphing into dual capacity
fighting and policing forces that also (thirdly) even occasionally provide humanitarian and development aid. These functions are often
mutually incompatible, self-conflicted, or internally contradictory, although they are legitimated as being on the road to smart, flexible
organizational forms. Resistance organizations, whether political
movements or black market mafias, become equally, and in mirrored
self-contradictory ways, dual capacity guerilla and social welfare organizations building cultural legitimacy through their infrastructural as
well as their ideological cultural claims. As the eagle and the mole
again compete, the battlefield becomes ever more airborne with precision bombing that does not see the enemy up close and regrets collateral damage, continuing the process of displacing into media projections older cultural notions of heroism and tests of virtue;[27] while the
guerilla forces hide among and target civilians, hoping to leverage
terror and images of dying bodies with appeals to humanitarian and
human rights values to win through the media, public opinion, and
diplomacy what cannot be won on the battlefield.[28] Complicity inserts
itself everywhere, as do the media, as do dual capacity, double entry,
flexibility, adaptability, networking, mobility, interoperability, camou-

flage, gaming, mimesis, parasiting, infecting, symbiosis, delayed reaction, testing, and experimentation. These are our ever more insistent *cultural self-characterizations* of at least some of our emerging forms of life, contested, underdetermined, and turbulent.

We live in an age, for instance, in which the very institutions of humanitarian intervention are suspected of complicity, when the humanitarian industry all too often follows military intervention, like brigades of prostitutes and merchants in the wake of the armies of history, providing jobs and succor but destroying local initiative and creating new vortices of power and intrigue. Then they move on to the next urgent call, the next crisis, the next firestorm of emotion and outrage fanned by a restless telemedia machine that turns its theater lights and thundering and weeping program music from the elections in Poland to Tiananmen Square in Beijing, from Bosnia to Gaza, Rwanda to Chechnya, Colombia to Kashmir.[29]

Iraq joins Kosovo, Albania, Afghanistan, Sudan, and Palestine in becoming exemplars of the late-1990s shift from pre-1970s cultural paradigms of state-led modernization—Western, socialist, and third world varieties; and their dependency theory critiques—to emergence of less explicit and less culturally justified global regimes of North–South governance through networks of nongovernmental organizations (NGOs), donor governments, military establishments, private companies, and mercenaries. In various accounts of these shifts a contrast is drawn between the cultural terms of understanding of the North, with its increasing density of economic, technological, political, and military interactions between North–North networks among North America, Europe, and East Asia (with evolving transnational moral codes of conduct, such as refusing even democratically elected regimes with explicit or barely concealed racist ideologies, as in the case of Austria in 1999–2000) and the cultural terms of dealing with the South through international humanitarian aid and riot control in North–South networks in what are conceived of as failed or corrupted states or terrains of gated development and sacrifice zones of crisis (Castells 1996, 1998; Duffield 2001; Fassin 2002; Malkki 1995; Mbembe 2001; Pandolfi 2002).

Among the key features of these shifts, according to Duffield, are (i) a logic of consolidation and exclusion rather than expansion and inclusion; (ii) black holes of the excluded generating innovative and networked global criminal economies; (iii) increased competition for resources, including control of the state, utilizing older ethnic and tribal cleavages, banditry, and genocide; (iv) transformation of the nation-state from buffer between domestic and external economies to agency for adapting domestic economies for the global economy; (v) selective incorporation in the South of populations needing to show themselves fit for consideration by meeting accounting criteria for economic aid, tests of not harboring "terrorists" for NGO funding, compliance accounting for medical programs, and the like (Duffield 2001). There is a dovetailing between first world governments' insistence upon security being now more endangered by underdevelopment than by interstate conflict and humanitarian aid organizations' increasing focus on conflict resolution, social reconstruction, and transformation of societies into liberal political economies. "In studying the new wars," writes Mark Duffield (2001: 6) in his survey of the merging of development and security, based in part on his long experience with the Sudan, "one is largely reliant on the contribution of political economy *and anthropology*" (emphasis added).

Anthropology here is the ethnography of social context and of cultural webs of meaning in which subjectivities must be rethought—not just the individual or self versus the collectivity or conscience collective, but in terms of the conditions of possibility for forms of subjectivity. Attention must be given to the forms and forces—or knowledge and power, as Foucault and Gilles Deleuze put it—that turn back upon themselves in new folds of subjectivation, including new psychic complexes, hauntings, and posttraumatic stress syndromes which more and more are invoked as popular culture metaphors for the contemporary condition.[30]

7.3. Life Sciences, Technosciences, and Cultural Life

At issue here and in the sciences themselves are transformed terms for figuring out what is to be made to live, who is to be let to die, what is the good cultural life, and how it is to be lived. These are moral struggles over new medical technologies like stem cell research, global clinical trials, provision of drugs for AIDS and multidrug-resistant tuberculosis, and research for the world's largest killers such as malaria which no longer garner concern in first world nations; and moral struggles over migration, what Stuart Hall has called the "joker in the globalization pack, the subterranean circuit connecting the crisis of one part of the global system with the growth rates and living standards of the other" (cited in Tunstall 2006: 3). Articulating these moral struggles as a cultural analyst, Giorgio Agamben writes of "bare life," "states of exception," and changing forms of sovereignty and subjectivation, updating Foucault's notions of biopower,[31] Adorno's and Heidegger's pre–World War II discussions of hyperrationality and culture,[32] and Husserl's and Bergson's discussions of the life-world and of the closed and open worlds of tradition and science.

In 1935 Husserl gave a lecture (later expanded into his last book) to the Vienna Cultural Society entitled "Philosophy in the Crisis of European Mankind." A few years later, my father, fleeing Vienna on board a ship between the Old and New Worlds (a ship that was sunk on its return trip by a Nazi submarine), wrote his first English-language book, *The Passing of the European Age* (1943).[33] Husserl and his almost exact contemporary Bergson were concerned with how to reconnect the procedures of the natural sciences with the goals of the human sciences. Husserl's language was that of intentionality—anthropologists might call it a proto-sociolinguistic understanding that concepts are always *concepts for* someone—and the life-world. Bergson's language was that of the need for a dynamic interplay between closed (traditional) and open (scientific) worlds, the first providing emotions of security and well-being, the second feelings of joy (Smith 2006). Concern with the relationship between the natural and human sciences is again prominent today.

Changes in the life sciences, in particular, offer a heady mix of utopian promises and dystopian fears that call for cultural analysis and critique. New, often overwhelming flows of information, new modes of visualization, new forms of collaboration, and intense commercialization in the sciences deserve attention, as does the way patients, too, mobilize the Internet and other information technologies to force accountability on the institutions of science (Dumit 2004, forthcoming; Jasanoff 2005; Kuo 2005; Sunder Rajan 2006; Petryna, Lakoff, and Kleinman 2006). Life, it seems, for almost all disciplines and specialties, has outrun the pedagogies in which we were trained, and we must work anew to forge new concepts, forms of cultural understanding, and trackings of networks across scales and locations of cultural fabrics.

Genomics is one of several life sciences that has already begun to transform basic cultural constructs. Our understanding of illness, for example, as Ludwik Fleck might have predicted, has changed: whereas once we regarded it as a deviance or abnormality from health, we now recognize that we are all carriers of defective genes with variable predispositions for disease under the appropriate conditions. We are all "patients in waiting" and thus are compelled to examine the cultural logics of our condition both negatively and positively.[34] Positively, genomics and other information biosciences provide critical metaphors for cultural understanding, drawing out the creative possibilities of the virtual, symbiotic, morphing, and experimental.

Negatively, or with pragmatic precaution, we are all, as subjects, not just external analysts, probing the logics of life and death that the technoscientifically intense life sciences have produced. Medicine has, as Byron Good points out (1994), a soteriological dimension involving daily moral struggles of life and death in the clinic or hospital and also what can be called a procedural dimension, illustrated by cases in which there are regimes to test new therapies in places where standards of care do not match best practices and where participation in clinical trials is often the only means of access to any care. Medicine's "biotechnical embrace," that is, the pressure to do whatever is technically possible, as Mary-Jo Good argues, can be at the expense of the good death or other humane values in first world settings (1996, 1998) and deserves cultural analysis. The contradictions of high-tech medicine in countries where infectious disease and primary care are still the public health priority also deserve attention, exemplifying how the struggle between the positivist sciences and appropriate human sciences of people's life-worlds, highlighted by Husserl, remains in play today.

The cultural creativity that comes from these difficult social circumstances should not itself be pathologized. The lotus can arise from the mud, though the analytic demands are often high in the fast-paced, often contradictory or double-edged space that has emerged around the contemporary life sciences. As cultural analysts, we need to see (and construct) scientists as creative cultural producers and to account for the ways in which the tools and material infrastructures of science shape what we understand, perceive, and conceptualize and what is thereby occluded, repressed, and pushed backstage. Since most real-world problems in the life sciences involve multiple disciplines, with their different protocols, ways of seeing, and cultural formats, the spaces of interactions among these technosciences become particularly complex and interesting sites for cultural analysis, both for understanding emergent technologies themselves but more importantly for tracking implications carried over into culture at large (metaphor in the larger, not just rhetorical, sense of "carrying over"). These sites are increasingly "ethical plateaus," terrains where decisions about life and death, what matters and what is triaged as less important, are made not just for individuals but with ramifications downstream for later turns in decision making. Just as the new fields of synthetic and systems biologies and regenerative medicine are attempting to experimentally develop new understandings of biological interactions, so too emergent cultural models must handle similar complex relations, transcending simplistic oppositions such as hype versus truth—e.g., accommodating "promising" as a third term, a kind of feedback loop both for raising the necessary funds for experimental exploration and as legally protected and disciplined against injurious deployment.[35] Similarly, just as today's informatics-intensive life sciences are a key site for developing ways of understanding and establishing complex causalities (Fortun and Fortun 2007), so too cultural analysts need to continue the development of the rich tradition of dealing with causality begun by Marx (the feedback loops of commodity fetishism), Weber (multicausal factors at historical conjunctures), and Freud (layered and interacting narratives with different temporal connectivities). Herbert Spencer put it nicely in the nineteeth century: "Causation, should not be denied because it is hard to determine, but to put its isolation into the forefront of the endeavor, as if we were operating in old fashioned mechanics, is naïve." Even if mechanics continues to have its important place, we no longer live in a world wholly or primarily culturally conceived in mechanical terms.

Open Endings

Just as Lyotard might say, there is no Jew and we are all jews (female, queer, normalized, neurotic, vulnerable, struggling for recognition, autonomy, rights, community, place, citizenship), so there is no culture, and all we do is cultural. Culture is not a variable; culture is relational, it is elsewhere or in passage, it is where meaning is woven and renewed, often through gaps and silences, and forces beyond the conscious control of individuals, and yet the space where individual and institutional social responsibility and ethical struggle take place.

At issue are not just better methods, but a return to some of the most fundamental moral and cultural issues that anthropology and cultural analysis have addressed over the past century and a half: issues of class differences, culture wars, social warrants, social reform and social justice (viz. the special issue on American culture and social warrants, *Cultural Anthropology* August 2006); of individual rights, human rights, cultural tolerance, multicultural ethics (viz. the journal *Cultural Survival*; Allen 2003; Engle 2001; Povinelli 2002; Ramos 1995, 1998); of mental health and subjectivation (Biehl, Kleinman, and Good 2008; Good et al. 2008; Kleinman, Das, and Lock, 1997); of democratic checks and balances, institutions of ethical debate, regulation, and the slow negotiation of international law (Fassin 2006; Jasanoff 2005; Kuo 2005; Masco 2006; Pandolfi 2002, 2006); of access to information and the formation of new kinds of public spheres (Dumit forthcoming, Fortun 2001, Fortun 2008, Kelty 2008). As Ann-Belinda Preis says, "In the years to come, some of the most crucial intellectual, moral and ideological battles about human rights issues are likely to turn on their cross-cultural intelligibility and justifiability, a radically new and far more dynamic approach to culture is needed" (Preis 1996: 296).

It is to remind ourselves of the work that anthropologists have been doing over the past century to create such a layered and dynamic approach to cultural analysis that this chapter has been addressed. Cultural analysis has become increasingly relational, plural, and aware of its own historicity: its openness to the historical moments in which it is put to work makes it capable, like experimental systems, of creating new epistemic things. It is the jeweler's eye for ethnographic detailing and conceptual experimentation which often provides insight into (a) the excruciating, impassioned, and conflicted local crucibles of cultural conflict, and (b) the multisited detailing of networks and transduction from localities to transnational players, testing and contesting the efforts to assert canonic universal formulations by those players or by philosophers and literary critics (e.g., on multiculturalism and the politics of recognition, Okin 1999, Taylor 1992, but also such anthropological accounts as Povinelli 2002).

Karen Engel, in a review of formal statements by the American Anthropological Association since 1947, argues that one of the most troubling issues is the charge of cultural relativism, which is often said to lead to moral nihilism and inability to defend the principles of the Enlightenment and those of the UN Declaration of Human Rights and other ethics conventions from Nuremberg to Helsinki. But this is a fundamental misunderstanding of "methodological relativism," of the social conflicts involved in negotiating political and legal regimes, and of the cultural resources in any society for claiming and contesting legitimacy. Methodological relativism obligates an investigator to first explore the "native point of view" (Malinowski); motivations, intentions, and understandings of the actors (Weber); native models (Lévi-Strauss); modes of cultural accounting (Schneider); models of and models for social action (Geertz). Methodological relativism includes exploring cultural contestations within societies (M. Fischer 1980, 1982, 1986, 2004), struggles to form public spheres in different sociopolitical contexts and historical horizons (Habermas 1962; Anderson 1983; Fortun 2001; Lynch 2006; Appadurai 2006), and cross-cultural and cross-nation-state networks and alliances, including efforts to negotiate across "enunciatory communities" (Fortun 2001) and civic epistemologies (Jasanoff 2005). Increasingly, methodological relativism entails efforts to renegotiate what Donna Haraway (1997) has called "material-semiotic objects," such as genetically engineered or-

3. *About Finger*, 2002, painting in oil, sand, and acrylic on paper by Entang Wiharso. Wiharso's (2003) post-Suharto, Reformasi paintings express the fears and anxieties of running amuck, cultural suffering, and psychic reorganization in the aftermath of political repression. Here, rumors swirl amidst the yellow Golkar politics of the state, the red violence of transition, sliced sands of time, a detached, up-pointing finger with parallel down-pointing ice pick, and a detached ear inserted with a siphon-blade. The red neck, mouth, and ear of a businessman in coat and tie are running blood as a white screaming figure witnesses. A graduate of the prestigious Indonesia Art Institute of Yogyakarta, Wiharso hails from Tegal on Java's north coast and from lower-class migrant life in Jakarta, where his parents had a *warteg* (a cheap food stall open eighteen hours a day, seven days a week). His paintings emerge from and evoke flows of contending signs and objects from Japanese and U.S. media worlds, Islamic and secular worlds, and a split life between Indonesia and the United States. His work is described and analyzed, with further artwork, by Good and Good (2008). Image courtesy Entang Wiharso, with thanks to Mary-Jo and Byron Good. Photo by Richard A. Chase.

ganisms, both animals and plants, or the potential in synthetic biology to build organisms directly from biochemicals, which reorganizes conceptual relationships and expose, through copyright, trademark, and patent, new genders or marks of ownership and power.[36]

Methodological relativism and recognition of many cross-cutting complicities in social relations raise the bar on descriptive precision. Methodological relativism indeed can disrupt conventional moral claims, making inconvenient demands on understanding. But without such understanding, one cannot build the social legitimacy to propose or sustain change. It does not follow that understanding means agreement.[37]

Cultural analysis of the sort that is alive to the multiple discourses that compose cultural fabrics will find alternative possibilities for alliances and coalition where it might have been thought there was only dichotomy and opposition. Iranian dissident leaders in the fight for human rights and democratic freedoms, such as Akbar Ganji and Fatimeh Haghighatjoo, for example, have little sympathy left for immanent critique, using the cultural resources of Islam to reform Iran's political system.[38] Instead they appeal to Karl Popper's negative utilitarianism and to secular constitutionalism (separation of religion and state) and insist on the breaks of modernity: that the UN Declaration of Human Rights introduced a new concept, that women's rights are a modern concept, and that it is impossible today to derive such ideas with reference to the Qur'an.[39] One can understand, recognizing similar fights in nineteenth-century Britain and elsewhere, and yet wonder how a movement is to form if one rejects the language, the cultural resources—including the debate traditions of Islam, the histories of Sufi, and philosophical dissidents—of a large percentage of the population, not to mention the century-long tradition of democratic struggles. Whichever of the more than two sides one chooses or by circumstance happens to be on, it is ethnographically enlightening and politically crucial to understand how different parties analyze the state of play. Indeed, these confrontations and politics are front stage not only in Iran, but also increasingly, once again, in the United States.

Cultural analysis involves the work of interpretation. It requires charitable readings to get the "native point of view" in a form that natives recognize as right and to elicit the context for the work of analysts, native or otherwise. It also contributes to the poetics and politics of the living growth of cultural understandings. Anthropologists are among many who make such contributions, and it may be useful to compare their work to that of advertising creatives. Creatives often judge their own work as borrowing from popular culture and returning to it leveraged formulations, which, when successful, reso-nate, amplify, and ramify throughout the popular culture (hearing one's jingle being sung by a child on the train is a signal of success). Anthropologists hope to not just amplify and leverage popular culture, but to juxtapose different cultures—be they vocational cultures, cul-tures of different religions and secularism, scientific cultures, or na-tional cultures—in ways that bring a critical, comparative perspective and increasingly a perspective that helps make transparent, visible, or accountable the network of transductions and changes that cultural assumptions and recognitions undergo as they scale or travel up and down, across, around, over, and through networks. Lively languages animated by metaphors of local cultures and references and carried by cultural analysts to other contexts and frameworks may help make these transductions audible, visible, perceptible, and even, sometimes, democratically subject to accountability.[40]

Culture, then, is one of the names of the anthropological form of knowledge that grounds human beings' self-understandings (from Kant's *Anthropology* on, but empirically embodied, as in Alfred Kroe-ber's *Anthropology* [1948]). It is a form of knowledge inflected by warm engagement with people and oriented by a jeweler's eye for detail and precision. It is a form of knowledge characterized by the openness and joy that Bergson identified with science. It is a form of knowledge, ever evolving, urgently needed in today's world.

2 | Four Cultural Genealogies (or Haplotype

Genealogical Tests) for a Recombinant Anthropology

of Science and Technology

The call of and for an anthropology of science and technology requires a new generation of robust switches to translate legacy genealogies to public futures.[1] Just as we have moved from Mertonian sociologies of science (stressing the regulative ideals of organized skepticism, disinterested objectivity, universalism, and communal ownership of ideas) to analyses of what scientists actually do (the slogans of the "social studies of knowledge," or SSK, and "social construction" of technology, or SCOT, and of the anthropologically informed ethnographies of science and technology of the 1990s), so too we need now to formulate anthropologies of science and technology that attend to both the cultural switches of the heterogeneous communities within which sciences are cultured and technologies are peopled and to the reflexive social institutions within which medical, environmental, informational, and other technosciences must increasingly operate.

Public futures are playing out in culturally and socially contested sites around the world where knowledges are generated and infrastructures are assembled, empowering some and disempowering others, calling for effective engagement across cultural difference. These public futures can be seen emerging in today's sciences of climate change and biodiversity built upon knowledge of the Amazon, Central America, Indonesia, and the environment of circumpolar populations (Allen 2001; Barcott 2008; Callison 2007; Edelman 1999; Lahsen 2001, 2004, 2005; Leigh 1999; Lowe 2006; Ong and Collier 2005; Royte 2001; Vivanco 2006); in the way knowledge of the risks of toxic and radioactive waste is assembled from many different sciences and from the experiences at Minamata, Love Canal, Bhopal, Chernobyl, Woburn, and Yucca Mountain (Brown and Mikkelson 1990; Fortun 2001; George 2001; Harr 1995; MacFarlane and Ewing 2006; Petryna 2002; Reich 1991); in the differentiating implementation of the World Wide

Web through offices in eighteen countries; in harmonization conventions for clinical trials around the world contested by countries that wish to ensure their own local populations are part of those trials and not subject to standards set by other populations both for political economic and medical reasons (Kuo 2005; Petryna 2005; Petryna, Lakoff, and Kleinman 2006); and in molecular biomedicine and plant genetics laboratories in China peopled by postdoctoral fellows trained in the United States, or the tissue engineering of palms and fruit trees in Iran on an industrial scale.

Reflexive social institutions are responses to decision-making requirements when unprecedented ethical dilemmas arise.[2] Examples include: (i) in health care, the conflicts between patient demands for all possible care and doctors' sense that further intervention is futile, causing harm and wasting resources (requiring hospital level ethics boards), or the dilemmas iteratively reviewed in hospital ethics rounds with doctors, patient advocates, lawyers, nurses, and clergy; (ii) in biomedical research and policy, in scenarios anticipating social, legal, and ethical issues stemming from stem cell research, nuclear transfer cloning, and xenotransplantation; (iii) in critical technologies where multiple communities of expertise must be negotiated (e.g., engineers and managers in NASA technologies, visible in the space shuttle disasters); (iv) in environmental and ecological arenas, where toxic threats to groundwater and to plant and human health require Citizen Action Panels (CAPS) with limited ability to hire independent experts (as provided in U.S. Superfund legislation) to negotiate with less limited corporate, military, or government expertise and authority; (v) in computer infrastructure policy, as in legal conflicts over intellectual property and social access rights and struggles between copyright and "copy-left," or open source in economically and legally sustainable innovation. More generally, public futures are at stake where multiple technologies interact to create complex terrains or "ethical plateaus" for decision making. Reflexive social institutions integrate knowledge from multiple sources, often are self-organizing and learning organizations, and respond to new circumstances more easily than brittle bureaucratic forms of agrarian empires, industrial societies, and closed-system, input-output, command-and-control economies.

Reflexive social institutions are also responsive to the evolution of democratic decision making in perforce multicultural worlds. We need an anthropology of science and technology that pays detailed attention to civic epistemologies and cultures of politics, to epistemologies and presuppositions of policy formulation, making them more reflexive, inclusive, and open to airing and negotiating conflicting interests, situations, requirements, and demands in ways that build legitimacy, without thereby making them unwieldy or formalistic.

As we move into worlds that are increasingly dependent on linked data banks and informatics infrastructures that require new modes of reflexive social decision making and that are accountable not just to instrumental values but also to the differential cultural sensibilities of affected and invested people in different social and cultural niches, we will need enriched anthropologies of science and technology to inform, critique, and iteratively reconstruct the emergent forms of life already forming around us. No longer can we rest on broad claims about the alienation of the market, the technicization of life, and globalization. The programming "object-oriented languages" of ssk and scot and the cultural skeins and social analyses of anthropologically informed ethnographies of science and technology from the 1990s have made more realistic the demand for attention to the reconstruction of public spheres, civil society, and politics in our emergent technoscientific age.

Anthropologically informed ethnographies of science and technology, in distinction to ssk and scot style work, began, as a first approximation, with the work of Sharon Traweek (1988), Emily Martin (1987), and Donna Haraway (1989), and in slightly different sublineages Lucy Suchman (1987) and Sheila Jasanoff (1990).[3] The gendered differentiation from the almost exclusively male and rhetorically combative ssk and scot tradition is not incidental but a visible effect of anthropology's conversation in the 1980s with feminist studies, cultural studies, postcolonial studies, and media studies and of anthropology's call to turn the jeweler's eye of ethnography on the key technoscientific institutions of the first world and to reintegrate political economy with cultural analysis (Marcus and Fischer 1986). It is also not incidental that Traweek took on the "hard case" of high energy physics, a slogan of ssk and historians of science not to deal with soft medical sciences until the hard basic natural sciences had been shown to be socially constructed; or that Haraway created a reflexive project that focused on the interminglings of folk ideologies, anxieties, and practices with the scientific assertions of primatologists and sociobiologists. These scholars might be considered "moral pioneers" in the anthropology of science and technology, to borrow the term used by Rayna Rapp to describe women who faced critical decisions following amniocentesis tests. Like them, Traweek, Martin, and Haraway had to proceed without established guides, keenly aware of the high stakes involved, and affirming the power of multiple cultural, political, and ethical logics over and above the workings of scientific ones.

Since the 1980s, entry points into the anthropology of science and technology have further diversified. For simplicity of exposition, I will map four quasi-distinctive genealogies, (or haplotype clusters) of the anthropology of science and technology, that together channeled (as in séances, involving fantasies or hyperbolic claims; as well as serving as sober working reference canons or quasi-research programs) the 1990s into the early twenty-first century.

The metaphorical pun "haplotype genealogical tests" plays upon the fact that genealogies are retrospective tactics that are often inappropriately singularized narrations of plural elements for present political or other purposes, and simultaneously upon the ambiguous use of philologically related genetic tests for tracking ancestry even in the absence of more reliable reality checks. Genealogies almost always can be pluralized, as they are here.[4]

One of the reasons for beginning to think with the haplotype metaphor is its role in biomedical attempts to displace, but acknowledge, older racial genealogies that continue to bedevil epidemiological categories as well as having social legacies. My effort here is likewise to move beyond old grounds of debate in four research traditions, acknowledge their overlap of methods, and clarify their contemporary conditions. As a borrowing from contemporary science, the source or "vehicle" for the haplotype metaphor—haplotype maps, haplotype groups—is worth a quick review for its own tensions between fixed mapping and multiple recombinant configurations.[5]

Haplotype groups are statistically associated sets of genetic characteristics that can be used to define genetic populations, often situated geographically or ethnically. In modern biology, they displace old categories of race, emphasizing the statistical overlaps among such older labeling categories (Goodman, Heath, and Lindee 2003; Marks 1995, 2002). They thus do not deny the diversity in the biology of human populations but make the understanding of that diversity both molecularly traceable and more realistically complex. Disease processes may be similar in all humans, and yet we know that disease susceptibility and biochemical reactivity operate through microinteractions that vary from individual to individual, while still allowing for risk groups, hormonal gender differences, immunological defenses, and other category patterns.

Technically, haplotype, a contraction of "haploid genotype," is a set of single nucleotide polymorphisms (SNPS) on a single chromatid (one DNA strand of a chromosome) that are statistically associated. They are studied by genealogical DNA tests that examine the nucleotides at specific locations on a string of DNA. The reliability of tests for mixed ethnicity is of quite debatable validity, but such testing has become a small growth industry (Montoya 2007; Tailbear 2008). The International HapMap Project is one of a series of public and private research pairings that keep in dynamic competition and reconfiguration: the political economy of biotechnology, intellectual property issues, concerns by subjects of research about their benefits from the research, and cultural questions about the "ontology" of human beings. In this sense, as well, haplotype genealogical tests are not just metaphor but also prime social and cultural anthropological objects of study: that is, institutional sites, epistemic things, and technologies of experimental systems.[6]

The metaphor of tests or assays to characterize the four clusters or cultural genealogies or research traditions draws upon Avital Ronell's *Test Drive* (2005), and just as she explores many kinds of tests and experimental systems, citing Rheinberger as well, so too did I in the original manifesto (Fischer 2006b). Of the four kinds of assays, only one remains in this chapter to characterize the SSK, SCOT, and actor network theory (ANT) style ambivalences between philosophical or theoretical purity and pragmatic, experimental serendipity. I call these testing protocols or writing pro-grammed object languages.

For the 1930s debates about the cultural humanist engagements with modernity and the anthropological concerns with cultural sensibilities, I adapted beta testing and test drives. Alpha testing is done in-house by technology developers under controlled conditions. Beta-testings are the first test drives outside the lab by users in the real world. The inflection of test drives as having libidinal content (a drive) was also underscored and thematized in a section on the *libido scienza,* a term I take from Bruno Latour's provocative study of the contrast between the objectivity of the French administrative Conseil d'Etat and the passions of scientists. But it is Ronell, more than Latour, who extends the terrain of science studies toward psychoanalysis, affect, and *jouissance*, that is, excess or surplus enjoyment that can be mobilized for political and other ends somewhat like Marxian surplus value; or that can simply be expended in intensities of bliss or mastered and remastered in the abjections and thrills of the sublime, to borrow, respectively, from Lacan, Žižek, Freud, Deleuze, Julia Kristeva, and Kant.[7]

Anthropological and ethnographic work from the late 1970s to the 1990s was assayed as ethnographic "proving grounds," again playing off the wider contextual grounds for object-oriented programming languages, and the military fields for testing munitions with their toxic waste byproducts that have become so central to Superfund legislation and environmental debates. This characterization points to the forceful return of social implications and complexity to the discussion, much as in biology new holistic endeavors have begun to challenge older reductionistic protocols: viz. developmental and systems biologies, concern with epigenesis, cell milieux, proteonomics, and complex pathways, where the same gene switching on and off can have different outcomes.

The engagements with new comparative methods attuned to the anthropology of the current wave of globalization, in which the calls of the twenty-first century are routed through switches, transducers, translations, and satellites from Mumbai and Shanghai, Bandung and Tehran, Dubai and Singapore, and elsewhere, raise the question anew of whether these portals open into new epistemes, armatures, mythologies, and experimental regimes. And so I called these phenomenological alterities or alternative ethnographic proving grounds.

Each of the four genealogies, haplotype clusters, research or discursive traditions, although appearing in rough historical sequence, has a different temporality, trajectory, and methodology. They each voice a different future-anterior: a different sense of what will have become of us or of our work if we follow a particular trajectory or research design. Juxtaposed, they should generate a feeling of out of jointness— their futures are not the same. By combining them in different configurations or mosaics (in either the cellular or architectural sense), they should generate a feeling of richer future possibilities than currently exist in any of their literatures taken singly, as well as a richer sense of the ethical plateaus on which multiple technoscientific trajectories and choices crosscut and complicate one another. I am looking for generative futures in each of these research traditions. And I am interested in investing them in mutual funds or portfolios. Genetic elements in each tradition are often shared. However, they express themselves differently in their respective research environments, so it is the ethnography of their social contexts that is critical. Each research tradition situates itself in conversation or disagreement with a different set of others. The ethnography of how each community of researchers links itself to other fields and broader questions thus also is critical.

I: Cultural Skeins, Epistemologies, and Democracies to Come
(1930s and 1960s)

The 1930s, as shorthand for the feelings of crisis in politics, economics, and science and morals or ethics in the period between World War I and World War II and during the Great Depression, remain a major historical horizon against which debates about science and technology measure themselves. At least three of these interconnected debates continue to have ramifying legacies and consequences: debates over technology (Heidegger versus the Frankfurt School); debates over the demarcation, autonomy, and unity of science (Vienna Circle; J. D. Bernal versus Michael Polanyi); and debates over phenomenology (1920s–1950s) and its successors in the postwar period (1968): structuralism, hermeneutics, and poststructuralism as methods in the natural sciences as well as the social sciences.

From a twenty-first-century perspective, one can review the contending philosophers, sociologists, and anthropologists of science,

4. Original cover of Walter Benjamin's *Einbahnstrasse* (*One-Way Street*), 1928. Cover design, section titles, and typography draw upon the language of commercial signs and optical devices and effects: "Imperial Panorama," "Enlargements," "Technical Aid," "To the Planetarium," "Gas Station," "Fire Alarm." Repetition designed for movement, and the interruption of sight lines by signs, mimics the heterogeneity, clutter, and bustle of the modern cityscape lined with shop windows. Cover montage is by Sascha Stone and typography by Ernst Rowohlt. Benjamin was interested in exploring the uses of 1920s advertising and newspaper technologies, along with his experiments with radio broadcasts for children, such as his analysis in the "Flooding of the Mississippi, 1927" (see chap. 3). Image with permission of Houghton Library, reproduced by Harvard imaging services.

technology, ethics, and morals of the 1930s—with their similarities of language, sharp animosities, Eurocentric parochialisms, and sometimes fierce cultlike followers today—as working in a fertile milieu or medium of repetition and difference, reproduction and mutation, critique through mimesis with a difference, and metabolizing opponents, through which experimental, epistemic, and practical knowledge occurs.[8] Their debates, slogans, and misrepresentations of one another constitute a kind of prehistory of science, technology, and society (STS) studies, in the sense of temporally and conceptually marking a territory to be investigated, to be broken apart (analyzed), and tested (subjected to assay) by the in situ fieldwork of later generations. This era still structures deep but often misrecognized concerns for us today.[9] Key legacies of productive method as well as political and ethical stakes continue to resonate in today's equally, but differently (less Eurocentric, more globally), contentious world.

Science Wars: Autonomy and Demarcation of Science

Debates over the demarcation of science (William James, the Vienna Circle, the Pragmatists, and Operationalism),[10] the historicity and hermeneutics of the sciences (Ludwik Fleck), and the methods of the social sciences, especially with regard to the technicity of constitutions (Weber 1918), the culture industry (Walter Benjamin, Theodor Adorno, Paul Lazarsfeld),[11] and the autonomy of science versus demands to direct its development for social ends (the chemist Michael Polanyi versus the crystallographer J. D. Bernal), all remain fiery synapses of contention, even if some of their contexts of articulation have changed.

Hans-Jörg Rheinberger, the author of a historical ethnography of the Massachussetts General Hospital laboratory in which protein synthesis was elucidated by means of a rat liver experimental system (1997), in his most recent explorations of what I am calling the prehistory of the anthropology of science and technology studies, focuses on what he calls "the epistemology of the concrete," a nice allusion to Lévi-Strauss's "science of the concrete" (1962). In modern biology, he cites Gaston Bachelard's remark from 1928 that "the history of science teaches that every great step in the direction towards demonstrating a final reality shows that this reality turns out to lead in a quite unexpected direction."[12] This is, as Rheinberger points out, one of a range of similar comments by Edmund Husserl, Ludwik Fleck, and others who attempted to demonstrate that scientific progress is neither a process of perfection nor a movement toward teleological ends, but a continuous process of differential reproduction (Rheinberger 2006: 38).[13]

Such formulations in the 1920s and 1930s intervened in the debates over whether there was a difference in principle between the natural and human sciences, between the physical and biological sciences, or among the different life sciences, that is, evolutionary biology, developmental biology, physiology, bacteriology, immunology, genetics.[14] Husserl tried to show in his "Question about the Origin of Geometry as Intentional-Historical Problem" (1936) that one cannot maintain the sharp distinction between epistemological-theoretical *Aufklärung* in the sciences and historical-narrative-explanation *Erklärung* in the human sciences.

If it was Kant who set the agenda for thinking about democracies to come as scientific, moral, and pedagogic endeavors, it was Fleck, a German-Polish immunologist who in 1935 provided the first ethnographically grounded study of a biomedical science with his analysis of the development of the Wasserman test for syphilis and the evolving understandings of both test and disease as a case illustration and exemplar, both *Beispiel* and *Muster*, as Kant would say.[15] Fleck showed that there can be no epistemology without history, calling his approach a new realism of epistemology as process—scientific knowledge proceeds not through single experiments but through unending serial ones—in which all new understanding is always already cultural as well as technical implementations of precedents repeated with a difference (Fleck 1929, 1935). It is a synthetic process that is, in principle, if not always in fact, democratic and collective, if also built on trust and authority (Polanyi 1962; Shapin and Shafer 1985). In Bachelard's words again, "Since knowledge is absolutely inextricable from its method or conditions of discovery, one must also characterize knowledge through its mode of discovery."[16] This is not too distant from the slogan of the Vienna Circle that scientific meaning is in the method of verification or confirmation and that whatever is not in principle falsifiable or subject to empirical testing is metaphysical or scientifically meaningless, although it may be meaningful emotionally, poetically, theologically, or in other realms.[17] This is still what scientists today mean when they frequently call a question philosophical, that is, not resolvable scientifically, however otherwise open to discussion.

Fleck's self-described quasi-Durkheimian, quasi-logical-positivist account of the development of the Wasserman test centrally argues (i) that epistemology cannot dispense with history or culture in favor of logical reconstruction; (ii) that the ambiguity black-boxed by the shorthand approximation of saying that an infectious agent *causes* a disease is known by every medical practitioner and scientist to be technically wrong since such agents do not always cause disease in healthy carriers (and hence as Emily Martin was to repeat six decades later [1994], the metaphors of immunology as warfare against pathogens are inexact and even misleading); (iii) that principal actors in scientific discoveries cannot accurately tell us how the discoveries happened because their evolving knowledge is situated in what often turned out to be false assumptions and unreproducible initial experiments; (iv) that communication never occurs without transduction and transformation; and (v) that truth is determined within a conversational arena that, like any cultural form, is more like an orchestra's coordination than like a proposition or mathematical proof.

Looking forward to an emergent genealogy, Fleck's first argument above about cultural skeins has been interestingly elaborated in the history and sociology of mathematics by Loren Graham and Jean-Michel Kantor (2007), Sha Xin Wei (2005), and a few others. Fleck's sociological arguments were followed up and elaborated by Thomas Kuhn's (1955) essay *The Structure of Scientific Revolutions,* by the historical sociologist Steven Shapin's and the historian of science Simon Schaffer's study (1985) of the seventeenth-century English Royal Society experiments with the leaky air pump, and by Bruno Latour's account (1988) *The Pasteurization of France,* all treated in more detail later in this chapter.

In the 1930s there were struggles over "irrationalism," and rational use of science for development. Both of these struggles are perennial. While Bernal welcomed the Soviet example of the state direction of research so that funds and effort would not be wasted on useless speculations (an ideology adopted by many developing nations, in which scientific funding required justification in terms of its practical contributions to development),[18] Polanyi led the defense of free speculative science as a renewable source of often unexpected social returns but justifiable as an activity of the highest order in its own right.[19] The fight over irrationalism was a fight led in different ways by both the Vienna Circle and the Frankfurt School against the neo-ontologists such as Martin Heidegger (see under phenomenology below), who, they argued, mystified the fundamentals of reality in words that sounded profound, structured much like traditional mysticisms of illuminationism and partially hidden orders of being and reality.[20] And yet the appeal of a search for ultimate meaning or values, frequently grounded in philosophically tinged mystical language, if not in explicit existentialist theology, remains strong and no doubt is one of the reasons for the continuing reference to Heidegger in some philosophies of technology.

The regulatory ideal of the democratic, public, and open-ended status of science has again become important, particularly since the changes in the structure of funding and intellectual property rights in biology and biomedicine, dating from the Bayh-Dole Act of 1980 and the Chakrabarty Supreme Court decision[21]—renewing the need to develop new institutions for accountability and transparency for the scientifically educated community at large as well as for the expanding segments of the population whose lives are directly and indirectly affected by (i) the research being done or not being done for reasons of funding and proprietary control of information, and (ii) the powerful potentials for hidden controls through data bank mining, correlation, and analysis such as populations have already experienced in areas like credit ratings and insurance company decisions.

The 1930s provided potent cases of the misdirection of science through political control—Lysenkoism in Russia, for example, and racial science in Germany—whereas today concern is more focused on economic and regulatory controls such as funding and intellectual property rights inhibiting free flow of information and on an as yet underdeveloped interest in civic epistemologies and cultural presuppositions of those epistemologies (Jasanoff 2005). These are beginning to come to the fore in differences over regulations on biological research, such as genetically modified organisms and stem cell research, and harmonization debates like global versus national clinical trials, free trade treaty requirements, World Trade Organization negotiations. The arenas today of the most public concern are in biomedicine and environmental toxicities, from toxic wastes to climate warming, and it is in these arenas that the most social experimentation is developing for patient and citizen access to and control of their own information and of research information (Fischer 2003: chap. 9).

Technologiestreit

The interwar *Technologiestreit*, or debates about the implications of modern technology, involved a struggle over the need to have sociologically and historically detailed ethnographic approaches to technologies as opposed to merely instrumental evaluations (cost-benefits of particular instruments, machine assemblies, or engineering systems), essentialized "ontologies" or mythologies, or efforts to institute nostalgically misrecognized premodern social solidarities and relations with nature. This became inscribed as Malinowskian ethnographic anthropology versus transhistorical evolutionary anthropology; the Frankfurt School critical social theory versus Heideggerian phenomenology; American cultural anthropology versus symbol and

5. Otto Neurath, a leading figure of the Vienna Circle and of social democratic efforts at reform in Vienna, pioneered an international language for visual education, here applied to the Mississippi floods of 1927. Top: "The Flooded Area near the Estuary of the Mississippi and its Population." "Each blue square represents 2,500,000 acres inundated in 1927. Each man symbol represents 100,000 population of states [Arkansas, Louisiana, Mississippi]. On blue: population of flooded area." Bottom: "The Basin of the Mississippi and Its Tributaries: This is not the place to analyze the reasons why people did not build their shelters far from river banks that may be flooded" (from Neurath 1939: 104–05).

Neurath's "pictoral statistics," "isotypes," and "Basic" contributed to the development of international signs for roads, restrooms, and exits and other signs.[22] H. G. Wells predicted, "By 2020 almost everyone was able to make use of Basic for talking and writing" (epigram to Neurath's *Basic by Isotype* [1937], published in the *Psyche* miniature series). Neurath would be thrilled by twenty-first-century software such as Hans Rosling's Trendanlyzer, which converts statistics into moving and interactive graphics to show how trends develop over time (http://video.google.com). Rosling's goal, like Neurath's, is to promote "a fact based world view through increased use and understanding of freely accessible public statistics" (see www.gapminder.org).

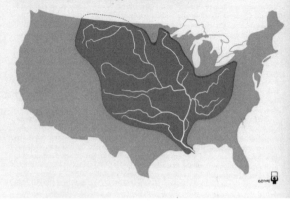

The Basin of the Mississippi and Its Tributaries

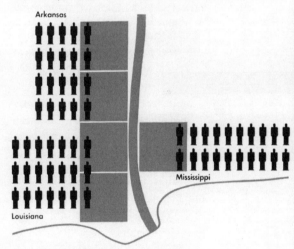

The Flooded Area near the Estuary of the Mississippi and Its Population

Arkansas

Louisiana

Mississippi

Each blue square represents 2,500,000 acres inundated in 1927
Each man symbol represents 100,000 population of states
on blue: population of flooded area

myth approaches to American studies[23] or generalized formulations by Lewis Mumford, Jacques Ellul, and E. F. Schumacher, popular in the 1960s, that technology needed to be balanced by local and religious or humanistic values.

To formulate these debates as being merely between materialists and idealists or between technological determinists and indeterminists fails to capture the richness of the historical horizon of the 1930s, when technology was, in fact, in concretely threatening ways, very much at issue.[24] The debates about the technological in the 1930s arose in the aftermath of two industrial revolutions: that of textiles mills advancing the division of labor, the separation of work and home, the increasing productivity of deskilled and disempowered labor, and the extraction of surplus value from this intensification; and that of steel, explosives, electricity, telegraph, and cinema, which required the coordination of large-scale engineering, bureaucratic, and statistical systems as the infrastructure of mass societies. The debates were also powered by a major world war in which, as Benjamin memorably put it, a new social technobody was being forged:

> Masses of people, gases, electrical forces were thrown into the open countryside, high-frequency sounds pierced the landscape, new constellations rose in the sky, air space and the depths of the ocean hummed with propellers. . . . During the last war's nights of destruction, the limbs of humankind were shaken by a feeling that looked like the thrill of the epileptic. And the revolts that followed it were the first attempt to bring the new body into their power. (1928, 147)

Within anthropology, nineteenth-century evolutionary anthropology's "long-wave," linear progessive accounts of technology development lost creditability to Malinowskian and Radcliffe-Brownian ethnographic insistence on not tearing tools and machines out of their social and cultural (meaningful) contexts, while Heidegger and many other so-called philosophers of technology continued the older tradition. In Heidegger's version, what passes for a criticism of modernity—mathematization, world-as-picture, and forcible extraction and storage of nature's energy as "standing reserves"—turns out to be a long-wave evolutionary sketch of transformations of worldview from fifth-century Athens to seventeenth-century scientific revolution to twentieth-century mass technologies of control of nature. Hannah Arendt pithily criticized Heidegger in her line, "Men, not Man, live on the earth and inhabit the world" (1958: 7).

Anthropologists addressed the social relations of technologies in agriculture; magic, science, and religion, or rational, pragmatic, symbolic, habitual, and transformative approaches to technology; magic and shamanism as pragmatic, if mystified, resistance to capitalism; religious legitimation of industrial relations; nonmonetized exchange systems within expanding capitalist ones; religious and media technologies as reworking the sensorium and as technologies of the self; and the interaction of traditional and modern biomedical systems. They did so within alternating currents and minor languages of multiple cultural and epistemic worlds.[25] In the 1920s and 1930s these cultural and epistemic worlds took the names of other cultures—Trobriands, Azande, Nuer, Bemba, Ndembu, Navaho, Kwakiutl, Shavante, Yanomami, Kayapo, Ilongot—or part societies—peasants, family firms and cooperatives, workers' cultures—and class or colonial relations. The epistemologies and representations of other cultures was a matter of debate among anthropologists and philosophers of mind (Gellner 1959; Winch 1958; Sahlins 1976, 1995; Obeysekere 1992), as were questions they raised about explanatory schemes, rationalities, and protection of belief systems against falsification (Malinowski 1935, 1948; Fleck 1935; Evans-Pritchard 1937; later Thomas Kuhn 1955; Mary Douglas 1966; Douglas and Wildavsky 1982).

The contrast between Heidegger's "The Question Concerning Technology" (1954) and Horkheimer and Adorno *Dialectic of Enlightenment* (1944) provides one access to the difference of their approaches to technology.[26] Both Heidegger and Horkheimer and Adorno directed attention to the difference between the multiple Aristotelian forms of causality, and how they had been reduced by the Enlightenment to the scientifically verifiable or technically efficient. However, while Horkheimer and Adorno analyzed this as a form of division of labor and differentiation of the sciences (from philosophy) and of professions among themselves, Heidegger directed us to turn back to the early Greeks, to *techne* as a form of *poesis* (not yet technology) that reveals "the primal: terror of existence, vulnerability to divine retribution, and to arbitrary fate"—precisely, McCormick notes (2002), the psychological terrain, according to Horkheimer and Adorno, from which the (unfinished) Enlightenment sought to free us, and out of which fascism emerged under the transformed conditions of modern mass society. The potency of the fascist ritualization and aestheticization of mass politics to use and counter such existential fears was analyzed by the Frankfurt School and others, such as George Mosse (1975). The Frankfurt School focused attention on the new media technologies used by liberal democracies and totalitarian or authoritarian regimes alike. This is thematized in the chapter "The Culture Industry" in *The Dialectic of Enlightenment* and in Benjamin's essay "The Work of Art in the

Mechanical Age of Reproduction" (1936) and its growing corpus of commentaries. It was a theme reiterated by Adorno in his unfinished, thousand-page *The Current of Music* (Adorno 2006; Hullot-Kentor 2006) and in the other studies he pursued in New York, the center of the broadcasting industry, and Los Angeles, the center of the movie industry (Jenneman 2007).

These are questions that remain vital: the political economy of the culture industry, the technological mediation of perception, and the consequences for subject and citizen formation. Although he got some technical details wrong, Adorno tried to analyze how, for instance, the technical medium of the radio made the production of music—live, not recorded music—transmission quite different from an audience hearing the same live music, an early instance of the idea of a reproduction without an original.

At issue in the technology debates of the 1930s were the balance between social direction or regulation on the one hand, and, on the other hand, individuation and moral responsibilities within organizational and infrastructural powers, as well as the appropriate deployment of the powers of symbol systems. This became focused in the immediate postwar period in the debates between phenomenology and existentialism on the one hand and structuralism on the other.

Phenomenology and Hermeneutics in the Natural and Social Sciences

Five transforms of phenomonology and hermeneutics complicate any simple reconstruction of the ferment of ideas, passion, and politics in the 1930s and their contemporary legacies for the anthropology of science and technology.

First in importance for science studies (but underexplored) are the relations between mathematics and phenomenology. Edmund Husserl began as a mathematician, and even after his conversion to philosophy under the influence of Franz Brentano—who influenced Freud and Heidegger as well—his first major work, *Logical Investigations* (1900–01), involved a theory of linguistic and nonlinguistic signs and was championed by the mathematician David Hilbert (Harmon 2007: 19).[27] One feels the parallel with the debates in mathematics between the realists (Hilbert) and intuitionists (L. E. J. Brouwer). Husserl, somewhat like Ernst Cassirer, viewed intentions as objectifying acts, including emotive intentions such as wishes, fears, confusion, anger. Intentional objects are never fully present; there is always more to them than is immediately visible or evident. Therefore, Husserl argued, one should attempt to "bracket" the world of appearances in order to get to the underlying reality. This is a realist endeavor rather than a search for a mystical religious insight, as it became for Heidegger.[28]

A second key transform of phenomenology involved the search in Protestant theology for a philosophical formulation of religious experience as a response to the Kantian threat of reducing God to merely a postulate or regulative ideal of ethical life (Moyn 2005: 123). While this might seem to be a lesser transform for science and technology studies, it is in fact a key genealogy for Heidegger's philosophy of technology and for the development of that line of philosophical thinking about intersubjectivity (the other, alterity) that seems to studiously avoid the parallel sociological development of intersubjectivity (Wilhelm Dilthey, G. H. Mead, Max Weber, Emile Durkheim, Alfred Schutz). Moyn seems quite correct to locate its power of attraction in a theological need to respond to Kant as well as to the anxieties and loss of meaning at the end of the nineteenth century and again in the wake of World War I in Germany (repeated to some extent in the immediate post–World War II period in France with the end of the Occupation and the collapse of Vichy France, as outlined by Leonard [2005]). This is the genealogy of Søren Kierkegaard and Friedrich Schleiermacher, Rudolf Otto, Karl Barth, Franz Rosenzweig, Martin Buber, and, after 1933, Emmanuel Levinas. Barth and Otto coined the terminology of "the Other" (viz. Otto's *mysterium tremendum*) and "alterity" or the "totally other" [Moyn 2005: ch. 4]). The study of religious subjectivity initiated by Wilhelm Wundt and William James seemed to give these theological formulations empirical and theoretical support (ibid.: 123). It is in this context that one might understand the otherwise strange claim that Heidegger secularized Christian theology as he moved from rejection of dogmatic Catholicism to radical Protestantism to a nationalistic religiosity rooted in Teutonic and forest myth and in *Volk* and *Heimat* —building upon Hegel's picture of the Greeks as explicable wholly in terms of their autochthonous development, of the *Geist der Heimatlichkeit*, in opposition to Schelling's exploration of Egyptian or Eastern cultural roots [Leonard 2005: 149]).[29]

A third key transform is the relationship between phenomenology, hermeneutics, intersubjectivity, and time. The tripartite relationship between present, past, and future and its relationship to intersubjectivity and social action, that is, intentional action as opposed to mere acts, was a core issue for thinking about the human sciences. Dilthey elaborated a compromise between the presumptive objectivity of describing objects (leaving quantum mechanics aside) in the natural sciences and the problem that descriptions of human action might affect the actions that the described humans take if they know about the description. The compromise was to recognize in public language and interaction a mode of negotiated intersubjectivity that can be objectively described. John Dewey would argue something similar in his schema of movement from viewing social action as merely self-awareness, to treating social objects as Newtonian interactions, to fully communicative transactions. George Herbert Mead is often seen as the pragmatist philosopher of the socially formed self.

The notion of intersubjectivity partially sidestepped the theological focus on prereflective, preconceptual knowledge, though this would return via bodily, emotional signaling and the play of the unconscious (transform four). This intersubjectivity could encompass the agnosticism of not actually knowing what is inside the heads of particular actors through models of patterned interactions (what Weber and Schutz called as if ideal types, and Karl Mannheim explored in his sociology of knowledge [1922, 1936]), the linguistics of describing the codes and pragmatics of communication, the sociolinguistics of recognizing that more is communicated than the actors themselves realize at the time, and the internal dialogues and heteroglossia of thought associated with Mikhail Bakhtin. Above all, perhaps, intersubjectivity could accommodate the notion of interpretive hermeneutics that all messages undergo and that in poststructuralist hands (Paul de Man, Jacques Derrida) would track alternative meanings carried in the ambiguities, tropes, and buried histories of modes of speaking and that were, in some sense, traces of absences, socially and culturally as well as logically, prior to the presence of speech acts and experiential moments. But from an anthropological and sociological point of view, as Arendt also argued, much of the philosophical literature on phenomenology had an unsatisfactory view of intersubjectivity, barely ever able to get out of a solipsistic transcendental ego (Dewey's stage of self-awareness).[30]

A fourth transform of phenomenology became the physiological, psychiatric, and perceptual phenomenology of Maurice Merleau-Ponty, particularly in his turn to Husserl's late work, *The Crisis of the European Sciences* (1936), and to the temporality of life-worlds. Merleau-Ponty's notions of "reversible flesh," of the ways in which we feel ourselves, and how we perceive through the body proved important for the anthropology of mental health, psychiatry, and culture (B. Good 1994; Desjarlais 1992), as did, to a lesser extent, the phenomenology of time explored by Henri Bergson. A cross-tie with the second transform above is the existentialist phenomenologists' focus on nausea and shame as moments when riveting to the body is inescapable, and one desperately seeks for evasions that are "otherwise than Being." It seems dubious that such "bondage" to the body conflicts in any way with the development of a responsible autonomous political self, said metaphorically to be phantasmically liberated from such bondage (the source of illusions of having a sovereign view from nowhere), and indeed Jean-Paul Sartre would insist that the ego is a complex structure of aporias that functions as a site or "moment of responsibility" (Rajan 2002: 58).

A fifth important transform is thus the relationship between phenomenology and freedom, of politics in public forums as the arena without which citizens and societies cannot achieve their potentials for freedom and justice. Arendt's notion of the "human condition in its plurality" is an important critique here of the solipsism of her teacher, Heidegger, and is today returning as a touchstone in thinking about how freedom is the result of agons of politics, of putting differences in play against one another, in order to generate a future in which all have some ownership.[31] Arendt died before the contemporary technoscientific and communication transformations, but the principles she invoked remain critical, especially in the face of seemingly overwhelming technological systems, analogous to the seemingly overwhelming political systems she analyzed. Even at the worst, individuals can band together in their differences "to people" technologies with the face and call of the other. Sartre attempted to fuse a Marxist notion of the structural forces of history with an existentialist and politically *engagé* voluntarism. It was against the excessive voluntarism and hopes to direct historical change, stemming perhaps from the relief of having survived World War II, that Lévi-Strauss and structuralism intervened.

Structuralism

There are two connected historical moments of structuralism important for subsequent anthropologies of science and technology: the structuralism that emerges from geology, Marxism, and linguistics and that was a general scientific language across disciplines in the early twentieth century; and second, the structuralism of Lévi-Strauss, Lacan, Althusser, the early Bourdieu, the early Foucault, and others in the 1960s. Like the functionalism of the 1930s and 1940s associated with Malinowski and Radcliffe-Brown, structuralism is often spoken of dismissively by those who, in a kind of figure-ground *Gestallt* switch, attempt to define new pathways against its background necessary to their own work (including the later Foucault and the later Bourdieu).

For the anthropology of science, the key double historical reference point in the structuralist moments has been, apart from the all-important understanding of structural linguistics as a defining method, the names of Thomas Kuhn and his predecessor in the 1930s, Fleck. Kuhn took the American academy by storm in the 1960s at the time of the reception also (in their different ways) of Noam Chomsky's generative grammar and Lévi-Strauss's structuralist studies of kinship and mythology. Kuhn was notationally important for science studies because he took on the "hard" sciences of physics and astronomy, a move that was important at a point before science studies felt confident enough to return to the "soft" sciences of biology and medicine that Fleck had pioneered and that Kuhn took as his inspiration. As the life sciences began to replace physics as the lead sciences of the day in the 1980s, Fleck's stock began to rise again.

Two things are important about structuralism as a set of methods for the anthropology of science. First, there is the important relationship of structuralism to mathematics: Lévi-Strauss and set theory, and Lacan and topology, first of surfaces, later of knots. This is not only metaphor: Lévi-Strauss and Lacan were in a reading group with the mathematician George Guilbaud and the linguist Emile Benveniste (Ragland and Milovanovic 2004: xx), and Lévi-Strauss's *The Elementary Forms of Kinship* was worked out in collaboration with the mathematician Andre Weyl (Rabaté 2003: 38).

Second is the much more general and now widely accepted notion, disseminated by structural linguistics (Ferdinand de Saussure, Leonard Bloomfield, Roman Jakobson) and semiology (C. S. Peirce, Thomas Sebeok), that significance is created by structured sets of relationships.[32] As Saussure (1916) famously put it, meaning resides in the system of differences. "Pill" and "bill" are phonemically different and meaningful thanks to a single binary distinction between a voiced and unvoiced labial puff of air. Linguistic meaning resides in such systematic binary differences. In a somewhat similar conceptual insight, equally powerful if practically more limited, Chomsky's famous *Syntactic Structures* (1957) popularized the idea that from a small set of grammatical rules one could generate the infinite number of grammatically correct utterances of a language—and perhaps of language in general.

This notion of generativity, the earlier notions of underlying phonemic patterns (Jakobson) and systems of difference (Saussure), and the later systematization of sociolinguistic rules of pragmatics and metapragmatics (ways that situational social relations are built into linguistic markers) provide the Lévi-Straussian distinction between deep and surface structures, the Chomskian distinction between competence and performance, as well as more general distinctions between models and reality, (as in finding best-fitting ellipsoids to model the geoid and calculate trajectories from the earth into space; see chapter 5). Speakers of a language invariably can correct the mistakes that a language learner makes—and this provides the systematic means of elicitation for field linguists in working out grammars and semantics—but they are themselves often unaware of and unable to specify the systematic rules of production. Similarly, class-linked linguistic styles (pragmatics and metapragmatics) often cause confusion or misrecognition across classes because what is intended as signaling trust, intimacy, or commonality in one system marks difference from another. Those who are able to operate across two or more systems (and we all do, to some extent) are thus said to engage in code switching. At the phonological level such code switching across languages frequently leaves traces of an accent.

Kuhn's notion of knowledge paradigms thus fell on fertile ground and was rapidly taken up both as a way to study the competition of different scientific research programs in terms of their internal conceptual coherence and resistance to falsification and also as a way to integrate the understanding "that political, social, and intellectual and scientific revolutions have to be discussed in a common context."[33] Over the course of the 1980s and 1990s, Peter Galison (1997) would break apart Kuhn's overly unified *Gestalt* or paradigm approach for physics by stressing (i) the differential changes among theory, instruments, and practice (they do not move in lockstep), (ii) the necessary pidgin or creolized languages of trading zones among paradigms of different disciplines involved in the interdisciplinary work of most contemporary sciences; and (iii) the inputs of perspectives, instrument traditions, and practices from outside a given scientific field proper, as in the relationship between Victorian interests in environmental turbulence and the development of cloud and bubble chambers, or the relationship between electronics and detectors in particle accelerators. Moreover, in this same period Fleck's arguments about the historical nature of epistemology would again come to the fore (see below). Both moves facilitated a rapprochement and new engagement between historians and anthropologists of science and technology.

Poststructuralism (1968)

For science and technology studies, poststructuralism has provided analytic strategies for dissecting and reevaluating the discursive and

6. The 1960s were profoundly marked by the visual icons of the space program. "Earthrise" and "Whole Earth" were widely disseminated NASA images that were said to have fostered an ecological appreciation of "space ship earth," i.e., that environmental problems on the earth, such as acid rain, were not local, but globally interconnected. Behind this popular interpretation were the emerging postwar fields of systems analysis: operations research, cybernetics, information theory, closed and open systems models, ecological models of energy, nutrient, and radioactive flows, as well as geodesy increasingly supported by satellites and new mainframe computers, with increasing accuracy required for parallax calculations of the distance to the moon. Homeostatic versus generative systems, structures and their transformations, models, and paradigms (as in the difference between oceanographers' versus geodesists models of the normalized ocean surface) were part of everyday scientific discourse.

In Figure 6, geodesist Irene Fischer, with her model of the geodetic depression in the Hudson Bay region (*right*), explaining geodetic deflections of the vertical (charts on *left*). The Fischer 1960 and 1968 Ellipsoids were important for the Mercury and Apollo space programs. The lunar parallax calculations were among her tasks (see also chap. 5).

7. Earthrise (NASA AS 8–14–2383). Apollo 8 photograph of Earth taken from lunar orbit, December 1968. Credit: NASA.

epistemic structures of various sciences and technologies as well as their ethical and political entanglements, including the magic pad-like historical complicities and displacements of subjectivities, desires, joys, and *jouissance*. Poststructuralism arrived in the United States along with structuralism in a conference on criticism and the sciences of man held at The Johns Hopkins University in 1966 (Macksey and Donato, 1970). The term "poststructuralism" is an Anglo-American invention: the French simply used "structuralism" (Rajan 2002: 34). In France poststructuralism, or the period around 1968, had to do with a broad reworking of structuralist, hermeneutical, and existentialist approaches of the immediate post–World War II period, meaning in part a reworking of the dialectical themes of machinic systematicity associated with language (metaphorized as the inhuman or antihumanism) and the indicativeness, referentiality, or metapragmatics of all that is beyond, marginalized, or on the other side of the signifier— what Derrida for a time called the margins of philosophy when referring to Algeria, Vietnam, or the student rebellion of 1968. These debates carried political inflections in which (post)structuralist rereadings of *die Griechen* (German interpretations of Antigone, Oedipus, and Socrates) provided palimpsests for rethinking the relations between politics, subjectivity, and ethics (Leonard 2005). The issues of the 1930s were revisited with an accent on emergent new technologies of the postwar period.

Derrida's work, in particular, pervasively evoked and drew attention to programming, telemedia, and molecular biology, some of his work being explicitly read in these terms (Ulmer 1985, 1989, 1994; Johnson 1993; Rheinberger 1997; Fischer 2001). Jean-Francois Lyotard similarly speculated on the effects of computers in *The Postmodern Condition of Knowledge* (1979) and on visual modes of communication. Gilles Deleuze created concepts and philosophies on time-images and moving-images in cinema, on alternatives to genealogical and typological reasoning in various fields, and on the makeshift assemblages of the technological and conceptual rather than their "totalizing" systematicities (1983, 1985, 1990, Deleuze and Guattari 1980).[34]

These and other works have provided productive intertexts for a number of science and technology scholars, particularly those in literary and cultural studies, but also those working directly in the history of technology, science, and the technosciences (Kittler 1985, 1986, 1997; Ronell 1989, 2005; Rheinberger 1997, 2006).

More generally, Derrida prepares the ground for genealogy 4 in helpful preanthropology of science fashion. He argued that "ethnology [Lévi-Strauss's structuralist challenge] could have been born as a science only at the moment when a decentering had come about: at the moment when European culture—and in consequence, the history of metaphysics and its concepts—had been dislocated . . . and forced to stop considering itself as the culture of reference." Moreover, he continued, "this moment is not first and foremost a moment of philosophical or scientific discourse. It is also a moment which is political, economic, technical, and so forth" (1967b: 283). At issue was a shift toward a world of informatic assemblages of codes and flows in which the globe is a space of differential generation.

In sum, the emergence of the second genealogy of science studies (SSK, SCOT, and ANT) in the 1980s was partly in reaction to these debates of the 1930s and 1960s. Polemically directed against a mischaracterization of the philosophy of science of the Vienna Circle and of Karl Popper as being insufficiently sociological, it also attempted a soft recovery of Bernal's sociology (after whom one of the prizes of the European Society for the Social Studies of Sciences is named), but of neither his activism nor his Marxism.

II: Programming Object-Oriented Languages:
SSK, SCOT, ANT (1980s)

In computer programming, object-oriented languages allow the pro-
grammer to drag-and-drop convenient objects that are already pre-
translated into machine language and thus ease the programming. It is
a kind of black-boxing but may be more productively thought of as a
creation of concepts or vocabulary that others can use without having
to fully rederive and reargue their utility, meaning, and justification.
The utility of the metaphor is to suggest that some of the arguments in
this style of STS take on a type of programming format, not unlike the
way in which scientific experimental systems, once stabilized, become
tools rather than discovery systems (see the Rheinberger passage in
the text box, and passim, in chapter 1).

Like technoscientific systems as theorized by Rheinberger, the
object-oriented languages in this style of STS are doubled entities,
simultaneously tool or protocol that reliably reproduces and generator
of excess, surprise, and the unprecedented. Defenders of scientific
reductionism and technical terminology—jargon, shorthand labels,
heuristics, black-boxing—correctly adduce their efficiency for cumulative building of experimental and theoretical scientific work and as
well-defined communication tools. This is the protocol and tool side:
take x, add y, modify by z; find a farmer's *field*, add a bacteriological
laboratory as an *obligatory point of passage*, produce a reversal of
power ratio between fieldworker and lab technician, add carefully
staged public demonstrations, produce a vanguard scientific *expertise*
over a (hygienics) *social movement.*[35] At the same time, the messy
surplus of surprises, unassimilable information, interesting but apparently irrelevant anomalies, and similar kinds of "noise" are not only set
aside, but over time become buried and forgotten. Yet these surpluses
generated by unstabilized testing often, when rediscovered in other
contexts or frames of thought, prove to be valuable new resources.
One needs both tool and surplus in dialectical tension or double-bind:
tools and protocols for reproducibility and reliability and surplus-
generating experimental systems for new effects and questions. While
the object-oriented languages of this genealogy of STS have indeed
been powerful tools, I will suggest that this puritan (disciplining, Apol-
lonian, pure reason) protocol side needs some loosening in favor of the
gay (Nietzschian, Diyonesian, excess producing) experimental side.

Contributions of the SSK, SCOT and ANT Genealogy.

The so-called new sociology of science, SSK (social study of knowledge), SCOT (social construction of technology), and ANT (actor network theory) style STS (science, technology, and society) constructively wielded a series of sound bites, slogans, and magical words.[36] For anthropologists, the slogan "social contructivism" may sound naïve and blunt, a belated rediscovery of long-practiced anthropological social and cultural analysis.[37] Granted, these often treated the natural sciences and technological systems marginally at best, but particularly medical anthropologists have expressed irritation that these styles of STS suddenly became prestigious while much of their investigative technologies were long practiced by medical anthropology.

Still, the contribution of these styles of STS to anthropologies of science and technology has been profound, particularly in forging the study of "epistemic objects" as experimentally produced through testing and turning unstable experimental systems in turn into at least temporarily stabilized tools. It is a shift from viewing scientific objects and cultural forms as things to be discovered to recognizing that the process of discovery is increasingly one of active production, of reconfiguring our worlds into new formations. This is never done by individuals alone, but as socially organized productions, where the articulation of the organization is more important than the word "social." The tools forged by science studies not only help explain central infrastructures and institutions of our contemporary societies, but they also help us in other arenas of changing cultural identities, categories, objects, or forms to find vocabularies and approaches that are less vague than "hybrids," "cosmopolitanisms," "multi-culturalisms," "glocals," or "hegemonies versus resistances." This is in part the challenge of the recombination of approaches for an anthropology of the technoscientific worlds of the twenty-first century.

Remetaphorizing this STS style or mode of focusing attention in terms of a genealogy of tools and methods foregrounds its generative capacities, its ability to produce healthy analysis as well as predispositions to certain illnesses (in Nietzsche's terms). Perhaps the most distinctive contributions of this style of STS to the anthropology of science and technology are (i) focused attention on the internal workings of science and technology from an ethnographic and sociological point of view, in contrast to reconstructive idealist and idealizing accounts of philosophy of science and intellectual history, (ii) a vocabulary of terms and methodological obligations, including (iii) the ethnographic study of laboratories and scientific controversies, and (iv) the production of scientific or epistemic objects such as model organisms and experimental systems.

SSK, SHOT, and ANT succeeded in doing what in Latour's terms might be called public recruitment or in Deleuze's terms the forging of an assemblage, relying on ideas that the basic utterances of language are "order-words" or slogans and that language is machinic and enunciative, coordinating relations among literal social bodies and thus constituting a kind of material politics; Fleck described "magic words" as performing similarly.[38] The publicity success of SSK, SHOT and ANT made the "science wars" of the 1990s possible, both for good (the Hollywood slogan "all publicity is good") and for bad (the inability to have productive conversations with some scientists who misunderstand the social analysis as a claim that there is no resistance from "the real"). In this light the primary contribution of this genealogy of science studies has been the production of vocabulary and methodological obligations, including the injunctions to always pay attention to the triad of social, material, and literary technologies (Shapin and Shafer 1985; "literary" here meaning, and restricted to, the actual writing of protocols so people not present can in principle reproduce the experiments or mentally become virtual witnesses); the difficulties of transferring laboratory skills and tacit knowledge of new experimental protocols (Collins 1974, Polanyi 1966); the micropractices and semantic discriminations that ethnomethodological observation shows as permeating scientific practice and thought (Lynch 1993, viz. Garfinkle 1967); the modes of drawing and representation (Lynch and Woolgar 1988); the points of obligatory passage, centers of calculation, asymmetric and reversible ratios of power/legitimacy (Latour 1987, 1988); the disjunctive histories or intercalations among the instruments, theories, and practices of a field (Galison 1997; Pickering 1995); the procedural and organizational differences among the experimental sciences (Galison and Stump 1996; Knorr-Cetina 1999); and the controversies that open and close black boxes, the networks of human and nonhuman actants that redefine agency, and the enrollments necessary for the success of projects over time (Latour 1993).

Other injunctions are of more limited value for particular purposes: so-called methodological symmetries of accounting for failures as well as success stories or for dealing with nonhuman actants in the same way as human actors. These injunctions can be defended: for example, the first as a reminder that the openness of a field of action not be recounted retrospectively as if the outcome were obvious or preordained; the second as a reminder that parasites, disease vectors, technological systems, and assemblages can be powerful causal factors in human affairs. But their generality is limited, and in the case of ANT and granting nonhuman actors their due, the locus of responsibility can easily be discounted. Institutional settings for ethical decision making are themselves increasingly important objects of study for anthropologies of science and technology, as they have long been for medical anthropology, development anthropology, human rights studies, and the anthropology of other institutions of public policy, regulation, and political cultures.

Allied vocabulary and methodological obligations from anthropologists and medical and social historians who interacted with SSK, ANT, and SHOT communities have also taught us the necessity of paying attention to differential pedagogies, mentoring styles, and patronage networks (Traweek 1988; Warwick 2003); gentlemanly science in the seventeenth-century Royal Society (Shapin and Shaffer 1985) obeyed protocols that were different from those of earlier courtier science practiced by Galileo (Biagioli 1993) or of later public demonstration science practiced by Louis Pasteur (Latour 1988; Geison 1995). Anthropologists have directed attention to circuits of knowledge dissemination and differential practical responses to technologies (Martin 1994; Traweek 1988; Dumit 2004), while some historians have adapted anthropological notions of pigeon languages and trading zones between disciplines and subdisciplines (Galison 1997).

An important project has been the delineation of different kinds of experimental systems (Kohler 1994; Rheinberger 1997; Cambrosio and Keating 1995), transitional objects and alternative styles of learning (Turkle 1995), and differences among field sciences, laboratory sciences, and simulation sciences. Cyborg anthropology (Haraway 1985; Downey and Dumit 1997) produced efforts to think through how mechanical-organic objects change cultural networks of meaning and social organizations and how assemblages of humans and nonhuman actants create new modes of agency. Anthropologists have directed attention to how scientific visualizations are manipulated and interpreted and how they circulate (Dumit 2004), how clinical trial data are manipulated through tactical "ethical variability" (Petryna 2005), how advocacy works in arenas of limited knowledge (Reich 1991; Brown and Mikkelson 1990; Fortun 2001), and how enunciatory communities thicken and contest the more instrumentalized or singularized notions of stakeholders and interests (Fortun 2001). The differentiation of different kinds of science has helped clarify presupposed social requirements or exclusions: the debate over statistically normal accidents and where in different social structures problems are likely to arise (Perrow 1999) has focused attention also on the differences between normal science, working within stabilized paradigms (Kuhn 1955), consultancy science, working with well-defined questions and given information, and regulatory or postnormal science, in which consequential health and environmental decisions must be made in the absence of good data or well-formed questions (Funtowicz and Ravetz 1992). These last vary considerably from country to country owing to differing cultural presuppositions and civic epistemologies (Jasanoff 2005), which in turn create different boundary objects and coproduce regimes of knowledge and power.

Limitations of the SSK, SCOT, and ANT Haplotype Group

While SSK, SCOT, and ANT have helped put science studies on the intellectual map of disciplines, provided essential object-oriented programming languages, and produced lab studies, studies of controversies, and studies of the development of particular technologies (from bicycles to high energy particle accelerators and intelligent transportation systems), the polemical edge of the field has been directed at correcting one particular strand of philosophies of science: a particularly flat, and even polemically mischaracterized, reading of the Vienna Circle "logical positivists" (excluding their pragmatist and operationalist side), and of British analytic philosophy. Except for Latour's claim to be an acolyte of the science and humanist polymath Michel Serres, the SSK-SCOT style of STS has displayed little interest in the so-called Continental traditions of philosophical accounts of science, particularly those of the phenomenological, psychoanalytic, and structuralist/poststructuralist traditions.[39]

There are several key problems in the SSK, SCOT, and ANT approaches. First, few practicing scientists take traditional analytic philosophies of science seriously, or do so only as idealized accounts in public explanations for laypeople, often to counter claims that ultimate meaning must reside in religion, opinion, or particular (unrepresentative) everyday experiences. The Nobel laureate and physicist Steven Weinberg is a case in point: although he writes periodic idealist accounts of science for the *New York Review of Books* (e.g., Weinberg 2001), when pressed in 1994 at the meeting of the right-wing National Association of Scholars to polemicize against science studies accounts, he noted that there is no single scientific method, that one needs to look at what scientists actually do, and that science studies was hardly an enemy—the real enemies of scientists were those with the money and votes in Congress to kill scientific funding for particle colliders and school boards that impose creationism or, nowadays, intelligent design in science classes as if they constituted falsifiable theories.[40]

Second, the seeming effort to tell scientists that science studies might teach them how to do or interpret their science better tends to create barriers rather than elicit the shared wonder and pleasure in the serendipity, competitions, passions, even irrationalities that are part of science and technological projects and about which scientists delightedly talk in private. These aspects have tended to be overlooked or devalued by this tradition in STS and instead have often been best, if partially and unsystematically, captured in novels (e.g., the novels of Richard Powers, the early John Banville, Carl Djerassi, Rebecca Goldstein, and Allegra Goodman, among others) and in drama (e.g., *Arcadia* by Tom Stoppard, *Copenhagen* by Michael Frayn, *Oxygen* by the chemists Djerassi and Roald Hoffmann, *Proof* by David Auburn, *Small Infinities* by Alan Brody, *On Ego* by Mick Gordon and the neuroscientist Paul Broks, and at least three plays about Ramanujan by Vijay Padaki, Ira Hauptman, and David Freeman).

This points to a third set of ills: the exclusions of interest in imaginaries and the literary dimensions of science (except in the restricted sense of the literary technologies of writing protocols so that experiments can be witnessed at a distance or virtually and be replicated or the conventions of writing scientific articles) and the devaluation of the psychological or affective dimensions of science. As a result, such approaches have often provoked an aggressive hyperdefensiveness in some scientists, expressed in insistences of objectivity and foundationalism beyond probable cause or plausible belief (e.g., Gross and Leavitt 1994). Such overdefensiveness may sometimes be associated with an always uncertain funding environment or with fear that airing the uncertainties, the constructiveness of experimentalism, the competitions between research groups and paradigms, and other social and psychological dynamics might put at risk the forward-looking statements, claims, and hype that are used to sell their projects. A more receptive anthropological attitude that establishes a venue and audience for scientists to assist in exploring the complex dynamics of the central scientific and technological structures of our society—which are otherwise increasingly exposed and contested only in the public media, with their short attention span and often distorting repetitiveness—may prove to be better than a predominantly corrective and oppositional science studies style.[41]

A fourth set of shortcomings of the SSK, SCOT, and ANT approaches is the attenuation of interest in larger sociopolitical institutions of the very sort that Robert Merton, Weber, and others in the 1930s genealogies explored and that these "new sociology" approaches wished temporarily to get away from (with the important exceptions of Shapin and Shafer 1985, and Latour 1988). This at a time when the very production of science, particularly in biology but also in the information sciences, is inextricably entangled with market and regulatory forces, patent law, and promissory investments, as big science and big technology have been since World War II and the Manhattan Project, the founding of the National Science Foundation, and the start of the space program, through the Superfund legislation of the 1970s and beyond. On the political side, the charges against the administration of George W. Bush for falsely manipulating scientific data for political ends is a public sphere issue that has mobilized scientists and others (Shulman 2006); and on the market side, the role of protection of forward-looking statements to investors, secrecy about proprietary rights, the role of media marketing to consumer groups for drugs and medical therapies, and enforcement of World Trade Organization rules have made the ideals of an autonomous republic of science ever more in need of vigorous probing and testing of validity claims. The so-called science wars of the 1990s, by contrast, had other, less momentous dynamics (Fischer 2003: 5–6). Many of these issues become even more obvious from within the context of postcolonial power relations.

The fifth set of problems with SSK-, SCOT-, and ANT-type approaches is laid out most clearly by Michel Callon and Latour, the authors of ANT, themselves. They had misleadingly called it actor network theory, insisting upon enrollment, nonhuman and human assemblages, agency for objects and things, and coproduction of scientific and political authority, as if they were revising sociological role theory to include technological objects. However, as Latour explained in "The Trouble with Actor Network Theory" (1996), the emphasis really should be on the nodes as metaphysical Leibnitzian monads (back to the seventeenth century), nodes that have "as many dimensions as they have connections." This is a notion of network derived from Dennis Diderot's *réseau* in the eighteenth century, in opposition to René Descartes' dualism of matter and spirit; in sum, it is a notion that really has much in common with Deleuze's and Guattari's rhizome and with chaos and complexity theory. It is, Latour suggests, really a bottom-up theory of "material resistance," perhaps like Foucault's microcapillaries of power: "Strength does not come from concentration, purity, and unity, but from dissemination, heterogeneity, and the careful plaiting of weak ties."[42] This reinterpretation of actor networks as cultural skeins opens up Latour's work into his more recent fascination with making things public, with matters of fact being really matters of concern, and (back to the 1930s) with John Dewey's (1927) notion of the public as "states of affairs," as the non-transparent, unintended, unwanted, invisible consequences of our collective actions and thus precisely not the superior knowledge of the authorities but their blindness (Latour 2001c, 2001d, 2004, 2005a).

In these moves, Latour reveals his anthropologist's instincts and provides a transition toward more anthropologically informed ethnographies of science and technology and toward the kinds of social theory analyses pioneered in the 1930s and 1960s. In this he rejoins Haraway's insistence that biology is civics; Ulrich Beck's notion of risk society and reflexive institutions of second-order modernization; Jasanoff's comparative studies of regulatory sciences, stressing different civic epistemologies and political cultures, which she analogizes to multilocal or multisited ethnographies (Jasanoff 2005; Marcus and Fischer 1986); Funtowicz's and Ravetz's (1992) policy-relevant, non-consultancy sciences; Gibbons et al.'s (1994) "mode two knowledges," Perrow's (1999) "normal accidents," Kim Fortun's (2001) "enunciatory communities," and Fischer's (2003) "emergent forms of life," "deep play," and "ethical plateaus."

Latour acknowledges Beck's notion of risk society and reflexive institutions of second-order modernization, saying that "Dewey invented reflexive modernization before the expression was coined" and that "risk" is "an understatement of the entanglements" that ensue as "we live with non human entities brought into our midst by laboratories at MIT and Monsanto" (2001c). Like Beck, Latour stresses that "nothing is left of this picture" of closed sites (laboratories) in which small groups of experts scale down or up phenomena which they could repeat at will through simulations and models, and then scale up, diffuse, or apply in the world and teach to the public in a trickle-down manner. Instead the "lab has extended to the whole planet, instruments are everywhere," and one needs a new definition of sovereignty in which there is "no innovation without representation." Despite his admiration for Dewey and American pragmatists, Latour suggests that the United States is still too powerful and too steeped in inherited modernity, and Asia, Africa, and Latin America still too full of dreams of being modernized; so that it falls to Europe to tackle the task of "adding technical democracy to venerable traditions of representative democracy" and that Europe's efforts to find a workable "precautionary principle" ought to be understood (using again an American referent) as "no innovation without representation," meaning informed consent (2001a).[43]

III: Anthropologically Informed Ethnographies of
Science and Technology (1980s–Present)

Anthropologists in the 1980s and 1990s tended not to start from science and technology studies but encountered the need for them. Two genealogical traditions and historical horizons come together in this encounter. First, anthropologists bring with them the ethnographic and social theoretic traditions described in the first section, finding the intellectual need for science and technology studies in the debates about the changing worlds of modernity (or modernities). They often traced their differences with SSK, SCOT, and ANT to those alternative ancestors of the 1930s and 1960s and their concerns sketched in the first section.

More important, the anthropologically informed tradition of ethnographies of the sciences and technologies began to form during the 1980s and 1990s, in puzzling out together with technoscientists in the field the nature of the rapid changes within which all were working. With the exception of Traweek and Haraway (and Latour), few came directly from science studies. Some came from medical and feminist anthropology (Emily Martin, Rayna Rapp) and were invited after their ethnographies appeared in science studies meetings, learning to enjoy an additional affiliation. Some came from French theories of modernity (Rabinow, prior to producing *Making PCR* [1996a], had written the Foucault-inspired *French Modern* [1989]). Some came with influences from feminist postcolonial theory (Kim Fortun claims her work [2001] has been more influenced by reading Gayatri Spivak and Drucilla Cornell than Haraway or Latour). Sciences studies took on the role that critical theory, feminism, media studies, cultural studies, and postcolonial studies had performed for an earlier generation of anthropologists in the 1960s.

Hence the ethnographies produced by these scholars look different from those of the SSK, SCOT, and ANT tradition. They have a wider range of actors, institutional accountabilities, political economy, and media focus, class-linked cultural analysis, and other interests. What makes them science studies as opposed to just general anthropological works is that they also exhibit an intense interest in the materials, tools, technological assemblages, and epistemic objects of the sciences and engineering technologies, and how these in turn structure the world in nonintuitive ways. This often required investigation in tandem with the scientists and engineers who often share parallel puzzlements and concerns, even as they add to the patchworks and work-arounds, new circuits, experimental systems, data mining correlations, conceptualizations, and heuristics of technoscientific worlds.[44]

New reflexive social institutions for decision making surrounding emotionally charged technoscientific issues provide another focus of attention. This focus leads beyond accounts of policy debates to ethnographically curious social and cultural analysis of the many actors, interests, perspectives, and cultural commitments that are often put into dramaturgically rich spaces of repeated and recursive tournaments of ethical decision making. Such institutions include new forms of ethical rounds in hospitals performing organ transplantation, heroic end-of-life interventions, and other contested medical procedures. They include the evolution of ethical guidelines for clinical trials around the world. They include differing civic epistemologies and assumptions about such research arenas as genetically modified foods, stem cell research, and xenotransplanation that get played out in commissions of inquiry, parliamentary debates, court decisions, and global trade conventions. And they include in the management of software innovation and networked worlds what Chris Kelty has called "recursive publics" (see below).

There is a second, more STS difference between the anthropologists and SSK-style ethnographies which also has to do with how the two sets of actors seem to have come to science studies. Physics continued to provide the key exemplary field for SSK as the hard science to show that it was cultural and socially constructed; the focus remained on a problematic of fact making inherited from an epistemology-centered philosophy of science. But it was the rise of molecular biology and biotechnologies in the 1980s, and then the computer network and web technologies in the 1990s that began to draw the attention of anthropologists as two technoscientific fields of innovation without which one could not understand the broader events, underlying rationalities, and ethical enrollments and disqualifications of emergent forms of life around us. These emergent forms of life entailed fundamental changes in the legal system (intellectual property rights), the market (the introduction of venture capital and new relations between government, university, and industry), the sense of physical body and social self (operating in virtual as well as real life-worlds), and the increasing comfort with the double worlds of ordinary (family, sensory, psychological, and other sociality located) versus scientific (instrument-mediated, systems integrated) epistemological common sense about the composition and attachments of the world.[45]

A third emergent arena beginning to take off in the twenty-first century is that of environmental and ecological knowledges seen as sites requiring not only interaction of multiple expertises or sciences and technical tools, but also requiring systems analyses beyond the localities and punctuated industrial accidents or environmental disasters of earlier work (see also note 53 below).

Older concerns with technological systems (electrification, irrigation, fish stocks, agricultural production, food processing and transport, energy production and transmission, infrastructural development for the third world), medical systems (traditional, alternative, and modern, experimental and regulated), physics (cosmology, accelerators, quantum mechanics, and relativity as epistemological challenges to everyday experiential worlds) took on an archaic feel but could be reinvigorated by refocusing anthropological questions through the lens (or new epistemic common sense) of the biotechnological, environmental, and informatics fields. Thus, for instance, the life sciences industry reframed studies of the history of medicine and epidemics. Bacteriology laboratories at the turn of the twentieth century were now reanalyzed as key cases in a historical series of laboratory science sites from the seventeenth-century Royal Society to contemporary molecular biology labs that provided new ways to analyze the conquering of epidemics (Latour 1988; Hammonds 1999). More important, the new life sciences made old distinctions between basic versus applied sciences harder to maintain and the hostility toward histories of biomedical fields exhibited by history of science enclaves, such as the Dibner Institute for the History of Science at MIT, perverse. At issue was also the requirement of new fields such as regenerative medicine to promote a tight collaboration between very different fields of expertise, a nexus analogous to anthropology's traditional interest in cross-cultural translations and practices. Similarly, technological systems again took on renewed salience, with the Internet, viral pandemics like HIV-AIDS, multidrug-resistant tuberculosis, and SARS, new media technologies, global financial systems semiopaque to financial traders and to the businesses financed and traded alike and to the countries' stock exchanges and currency markets. Physics, too, is being reimagined via anthropologies of mathematical modeling and analyses (Graham and Kantor 2007; Sha 2005), just as physicists themselves have migrated into the life sciences with their cultural presuppositions of how to analyze and model things and relations.

STS-styled finance studies, for example, is one of a set of new topic areas emerging from a need to understand the political economy of biotechnologies and other technoscientific arenas (Sunder Rajan 2006; Dumit forthcoming; Petryna 2005) and as a field for which the application of SSK-type analyses seems also well designed (Knorr-Cetina and

Bruegger 2002; Riles 2004; MacKenzie 2006; Lepinay 2005a, 2005b, 2005c, 2006).

While the anthropologically informed ethnographies of science and technology of the 1990s and early twenty-first century adopt many of the same tools or genetic elements, they often differ from SSK, SCOT, and ANT ethnographies in terms of the audiences they address, the arguments they oppose, and the degree to which they address the questions of the genealogy about cultural skeins and sensibilities, epistemological objects, and configurations of differently situated modernities.

Biology and the Life Sciences

One of the key arenas for the development of an anthropology of science and technology has been biology and the life sciences precisely because the science itself, as well as its institutional, conceptual, technical, legal, and ethical components, seemed to be rushing quickly beyond the pedagogies in which everyone in these fields had been trained. In addition, these rapid changes in the life sciences have more general implications for the common sense of personhood, politics, and ethics. The "molecular vision of life" (Kay 1993), understanding the transitional nature of the idea of the gene (Kay 2000; Keller 2000), and the way in which the language of information technologies colonized but did not satisfy the "cracking" of the biochemical code (Kay 2000) have led to a politics of health in which we experience ourselves biologically as patients-in-waiting (Dumit forthcoming), neither just healthy or ill but as carriers of risks and susceptibilities that make us, our organs, our tissues, our cells "bioavailable" (L. Cohen 2001) for economic exploitation, for reengineering the body and intimate connections to family and others, and for politics beyond illness and health and beyond old notions of good and evil (Nietzsche 1886). There are new, emergent forms of regulation, choice, and decision making, sometimes reinforcing and sometimes reworking older cultural ideals and inequalities (Biehl 2005, 2007; Cohen 1999, 2001; Fox and Swazey 1974, 1992; Petryna 2005; Rapp 1999; Sanal 2005).[46] Emergent forms of life are both biological forms and social ones. Nikolas Rose even suggests an elective affinity, in the manner of Weber, between a novel "somatic ethics" and the spirit of capitalism, which "accords a particular moral virtue to the search for profits through the management of life" and "opens those who are seen to damage health in the name of profit to the most moralistic of condemnations" (2006: 8). While this is perhaps a bit too "orthopedic" (after all, Weber found a series of five elective affinities that went into the spirit of capitalism), the intensities and *jouissance* of the ethical debates and dilemmas at the intersection of new technologies in the life sciences are indeed a moral terrain or set of ethical plateaus on which new reflexive social institutions are emerging and to which anthropologically informed ethnographies can contribute.

Anthropologically informed ethnographies, including historical ethnographies and multisited peregrinations through the distributed sites of biotechnological production (e.g., Sunder Rajan 2006 for the United States and India; Heath, Rapp, and Taussig 2004 for "genetic citizenship" groups, based on having, being a family member of one who has, or being carriers of susceptibility for such conditions as Marfan's syndrome or achondroplasic dwarfism) have been creating a mosaic of jeweler's-eye accounts of the recombinant, evolving forms of patient advocacy groups *and* health care providers, the market *and* government regulation, national competitions over potentially economically productive biotechnologies *and* transnational cooperation in such large-scale and high throughput technological projects as the Human Genome and HapMap projects, *along with* tense North–South relations of biocapitalism, threats of biopiracy, and differential clinical trial ethics and promises of benefit for different populations.

Scientific fields have been transformed dramatically by new machines (as in the case of the Applied Biosystems 3700, high throughput sequencers, which transformed the Human Genome Project from a public endeavor to a public versus private competition, raising moral as well as economic and legal intellectual property rights questions [Sunder Rajan 2006]) as well as by experimental systems (Rheinberger 1997) and by experimental systems that can be turned into biological tools (Rabinow 1996a; Cambrosio and Keating 1995; Landecker 2007). Ethical dilemmas have become no longer containable only through self-policing by scientists, as had been the case with the recombinant DNA technologies in the 1970s (the Asilomar Conference of 1975 leading to National Institutes of Health rules for containment facilities, which with experience were relaxed). This is partly because of the vast amounts of money in play in a field that in twenty years had transformed from one in which at least academic biologists steered clear of entanglements with corporate profit drives to one in which almost every successful academic biologist is involved in a company as a necessary means to protect patented discoveries and produce them in forms that are no longer merely experimental but can be used, licensed, traded, and put to therapeutic use. Biology has been transformed from a republic of science in which the flow of information, at least in academic settings, was largely free to one in which the biologist always tries to patent before publishing and much data is closely held and no longer freely available. At every level, there seem to be not just small changes, but changes that synergistially accumulate toward complexly interactive systemic change.

Ethnographic and historical ethnographic work continues on model systems (Kohler 1994 on the *Drosophila* fruit fly; Rheinberger 1997 on the rat liver experimental system; Creager 2002 on the Tobacco Mosaic Virus; Haraway 1997 and Rader 2004 on the production of standardized genetically modified mice for research), on reproductive technologies (E. Martin 1994; Rapp 1999; Hartouni 1997; Franklin and Ragoné 1998; Franklin and Roberts 2006; Thompson 2005), and on epistemic objects (A. Martin 2004 on chromosomes). Newer work on the use of living tissue as a tool in biology (Landecker 2007 on immortal cell lines), on robotics and systems biology (Fujimura n.d.), and on genetically modified foods and stem cell research (Jasanoff 2005) cannot be contained within the walls of the laboratory, but necessarily entails cultural and social entanglements.

The parallel with the phenomenology discussions in the 1940s on the inherent indexicality of language—referring to the world outside the linguistic signs and thereby destabilizing efforts to get to a stable underlying ontology, transcendental a priori, or invariant universal truth—is striking. Immortal cell lines, which had been regarded as neutral tools in the 1950s, became racialized in the 1960s and commodified in the 1990s (Landecker 2007). A-life experiments with "genetic algorithms" to explore complexity theory, however superficially for the science, were often talked about in terms of American folk theories of kinship (Helmreich 1998). Computer algorithms now were being experimented with to model biological processes and thus to overcome excessive reductionism in biology (systems biology), while biochemical elements were being algorithmically experimented with to make new biological systems and new biomimetic devices (synthetic biology). The translation of computer cultures into biological cultures is not easy and is the source of much synthetic and systems biology corridor talk about blindnesses and insights of the respective engineering versus life science styles of thought. This should provide a wonderful contested cognitive space for anthropological mapping, as were the earlier contestations between cryptographic efforts by physicists to crack the genetic code versus the biochemists, who eventually began to unravel the complex biochemical cascades and pathways (Kay 2000). Other such interdisciplinary spaces include the kinetic ways in which crystallographers, with 3-D simulation algorithms, figure out functionally significant complicated folding patterns that wet biologists must then prove out (Myers 2007).

These biomedical, bioscientific, and bioengineering terrains include ethnographic work on institutional innovations since the 1980s (Rabinow 1996a, 1999; Sunder Rajan's *Biocapitalism*, 2006 and *Lively Capital*, forthcoming);[47] and statistical strategies for clinical trials that ideally enroll everyone as patients-in-waiting and objects of "surplus health" extraction, pioneered by such cholesterol-lowering drugs as Lipitor (Dumit's *Drugs for Life*, forthcoming), or that capitalize on "ethical variability" across global populations in the search for populations that are drug naïve (Petryna 2005; Petryna, Lakoff, and Kleinman 2006). Such projects use statistical sets of single nucleotide polymorphisms that can signal a predisposition for the possible increased risks of various diseases and that can capitalize populations for biomedical research, as pioneered by the Icelandic company deCode genetics (Fortun 2008). The resulting databases can be used to manipulate physicians and consumers through "detailers" and statistical monitoring of pharmaceutical companies (Lakoff's *Pharmaceutical Reason*, 2005; more generally Rose 2006, and the new journal *BioSocieties*).

Institutional accounts of the creation of molecular biology as a discipline (Kay 1993), the shifting uses of metaphors and rhetorical forms in the conceptual structuring of the sciences and their imaginaries (Keller 1995; Doyle 1997, 2003), the creation of new material-semiotic objects such as oncomice and other engineered research animals (Haraway 1997, 2003, 2008) as well as a vision of how we are now beginning to write with biology, rather than merely discover it, creating biologicals that have never previously existed (Rheinbereger 1997), are transforming the ways in which we understand the relation between technoscientific production, society, and our biological and ecological conditions of existence.

Perhaps distinctive about these works is the degree to which they are based on working with, rather than objectifying, scientists and their work, adopting precisely the opposite stance that Woolgar and Latour took up *Laboratory Life* (1979), assuming a more anthropological insider-outsider tacking back and forth. Rabinow found a key insider patron to work with in Tom White, the scientist-manager of the research projects in Cetus Corporation that led to the transformation of the polymerase chain reaction (PCR) from idea to experimental system to marketable commodity; Angela Creager, Lily Kay, Hannah Landecker, and Kaushik Sunder Rajan come from backgrounds in biology, and Rheinberger continues as a working molecular biologist as well as a trained historian of science; Haraway comes as a trained

historian of biology but also with social democratic and feminist commitments, with an eye to seeing up close, ethnographically, technically, and conceptually, how things might be done otherwise.

A second possibly distinctive feature is the mosaic nature of the
work: no monograph or study stands alone, but contributes to a series
of studies analogous to old area studies projects, in which a number of
people would collaborate by working on different aspects or at different locations. No study is a microcosm; rather, each is a piece of the
larger puzzle (see again, for example, note 53).

But even more important are the conceptual tools and the institutions for decision making about unprecedented dilemmas and technological dangers. Material-semiotic objects is a particularly interesting idea: an object whose creation changes the way the semantic system
operates. Experimental systems, in contrast to testing devices which
reliably reproduce the same result over and over, generate the novel
through differential reproduction. Experimental systems differ from
ideas—the scandal of giving Nobel prizes to an idea but excluding the
people who created the experimental system that made it work. Standardized marketing kits or tools are yet something else having to do
with entanglements of standardization and market share.

Networked Worlds

Computers, software systems, the Internet, and local networked systems are key sites on which "the postmodern conditions of knowledge" (Lyotard 1979) have been puzzled out. Intimations, even seismic
rumbles, in the humanities began not only with structuralism and
linguistics, which in their Lévi-Straussian and Chomskian forms
claimed ambitions of integration with the neurosciences, mathematics, and computer or machine languages, but also with Derrida's *Of
Grammatology* (1967a), which argued that a reconfiguration of the
general economy of writing, codes, and programs was creating new
spaces for the human sciences and their engagements with the natural
sciences, on the one hand—especially molecular biology and the algorithmic or programming approaches of the computer sciences—
and, on the other, with philosophy, meaning the assumptions and
presuppositions that go under the names of metaphysics and ontology. Indeed, computer scientists, including computer game designers,
would soon call that which they write ontologies. Ontologies became a
language game.

Lyotard's (1979) report for the Quebec university commission, *The
Postmodern Condition: A Report on Knowledge*, insightfully identified

the multiplicity and performativity of local language games, which would be enabled by software programs. They would functionally replace or "bracket" the hegemonic master narratives of the march of Reason, History, Progress that had disciplined the Cold War period, dating back to the Enlightenment of the French revolutionary period, if not (as Derrida argued) the whole logocentric tradition of philosophy from Plato to Heidegger. Bill Readings's (1996) follow-up of thirty years later, *The University in Ruins,* argued that the university is being cut adrift from its nation-building functions, symbolically centered on humanities' canons in standardized national language literatures and histories, in favor of audits and accountings of performativity and productivity and "centers of excellence" for global competition. Henri Lefebvre (1967) was only one of many who feared the emergent world as one of the cyberanthrope, in which cybernetics and machinic Chomskian and structural linguistics would bring about even more surveilling and controlling, "totalitarizing" and "anti-humanist" cultures and societies.

But in the real world of ethnographic detail and anthropology from a pragmatic point of view, life and code are much more full of intrigue, puzzling, and gaming, involving plenitudes of passions and reasons, hacks and bugs, patches and work-arounds, values and interests, social imaginaries and institutional demands. It is a world, in Deleuze's and Guattari's (1980) vocabulary, of assemblages rather than unified machines, freed from the state apparatus, "available for a postmodern pragmatic anthropology" (Rajan 2002: 36; see also note 32 above).

A few recent ethnographic accounts provide strategic access to these worlds. Kelty's (2008) rich account of free and open software movements, the efforts to create open commons for education, biodiversity, medical data, scientific data and results, music, text, and video, digital archives and libraries, copy-left adjustments to intellectual property law, and open access publishing not only describes and analyzes how such efforts are incrementally evolved as experimental systems, but more generally poses them as a new form of reflexive social institutions that, as noted, he calls recursive publics. This is a mutation of the eighteenth-century public sphere created through newpapers and coffeehouse debates, with its regulative ideals of rational debate of public issues in spaces between civil society and the state (Habermas 1962), and of Dewey's notion (1927) of the public as the unintended consequence of policy making that the experts have failed to see or anticipate. A recursive public, Kelty writes, "is vitally concerned with the material and practical maintenance and modification of the very means of its own existence as a public, as a collective independent of other forms of constituted power" (2008: 2). It is constantly modifying, standardizing, remodifying, and experimenting with its technical standards and protocols, coordinating the various layers of volunteer-contributed software, debating the cultural significance of changes to code-enabled infrastructural options, monitoring the portability of academic and commercial code, and pressing for ways in which the law and the market can help maintain rather than inhibit openness through copyright and trade secrets. It is thus not only a reflexive social institution, but "raises questions about the invention and control of norms and the forms of life that may emerge from these practices." Recursive publics, he suggests, come to exist "where it is clear that such invention and control need to be widely shared, openly examined, and carefully monitored" (ibid.: 21).

To accumulate the details that compose his account, Kelty invokes contemporary anthropological fieldwork's "distinctive mode of epistemological encounter . . . suited to a problematic of emergence." Such encounters are multisided and in situ but also mine the vast online archives and discussion lists (2008: 22). In so doing, Kelty is able to access the normative and cultural dimension that the legal constitutional scholar Lawrence Lessig deals with less fully in his recognition of four key kinds of tools—law, market, code, norms—which can be used to configure the Internet and other networking tools (1999, 2001, 2004).

Gabriele Coleman (2005) engages with the Debian Project, an open source distributor of Linux, and Anita Chan (2008), doing fieldwork in Brazil, Mexico, and Peru, studies efforts to mandate government uses of open-source systems such as Linux. Microsoft and other corporations are responding to the competitive popularity of open source by making some of their code partially open as well. Linux has proved to be not only popular among hackers and geeks, but also widely used in mission-critical large-scale tasks. Interestingly, geeks have been less interested in making the front end of these programs more user-friendly to nongeeks. Perhaps this is another cultural index of open but meritocratic- or competence-based norms of admission and competition that goes along with the generally libertarian attitude toward the world.

At the frontiers of emergent forms of dependence on computer code and data banking are reliability studies and new forms of knowledge generation that use large data sets as experimental systems. The STS scholar Donald MacKenzie (2001) explores the ambiguities and problems in the internal validation of computer models; Fortun and Fortun (2007) explore the emergent informatics field of toxicogenomics, in which various data banks are experimentally cross-mined for possible correlations, patterns, and interactive effects. Schienke (2006) similarly explores simulations at three scales in efforts to model complex ecologies and environmental problems in China. Bowker's survey of memory systems (2005) as well as Bowker and Starr's work on classification systems (1999) sketches a terrain for this larger entry of informatics as the software of our emergent distributed knowledge systems, something that, in a philosophical register, Lyotard (1979) foresaw, if only partially, as one of the conditions of postmodern knowledge.

Finance is one of the most mission critical of the computer-mediated infrastructures of the contemporary world and has become one of the fastest growing topics in the anthropology of science and technology studies (Aboulafia 1996; Beunza and Stark 2003, 2004; Beunza and Garud 2005; Callon 1998, 2007; Ho 2005, 2009; Holmes 2006; Knorr-Cetina and Bruegger 2002; Lepinays 2005a, 2005b, 2005c, 2006; LiPuma and Lee 2004; MacKenzie 2006; Maurer 2005a, 2005b, 2006; Miyazaki 2003, 2005, 2006, forthcoming; Riles 2004; Zaloom 2004). The studies of finance are an explicit proving ground of transfer of science studies and ethnographic techniques. They follow the move that science studies made from Mertonian institutions to actual practices of scientists in the laboratory by moving to the actual calculative practices of actors at work (Beunza and Stark 2004). And while they begin with analyses of components of the "quantitative revolution" in finance (mathematical formulae [MacKenzie 2006] and virtual worlds [Knorr-Cetina and Bruegger 2002]), just as science studies began with laboratories, conflicts, instruments, and model systems, they now move to more anthropologically integrative accounts of entangled networks and cultural skeins integrating a heterarchical, distributed intelligence network of humans, machines, and formulae that is flexible and responsive to uncertain and fast-changing circumstances (Beunza and Stark 2003).

Karen Ho's "Situating Global Capitalisms: A View from Wall Street Investment Banks" (2005) initiates the semiotic study of the usage of "globalism" or "global presence" as a coinage that gets invested in some localities and not others and as a code that marks weaknesses and competitions among banks, an operational code that depends upon a duplicity or doubleness of hype (to clients) and decryption (to competitors). Here the close anthropological eye deconstructs and puts in its place the promiscuous use of such symbolic words as "globalism," showing, as Wittgenstein might say, how its use exposes conflicts and power relations, rather than the flat earth surface it seems to denote.

Bill Maurer pursues two epistemic objects in the world of finance:

the "form" of "due diligence" (Maurer 2005a) and, through juxtaposition with the Ithaca Hours, an alternative currency, several Islamic financial instruments that operate as epistemic "plays within the play" of capitalism to draw attention to unmet moral aspirations and memories (Maurer 2005b, 2006). In both due diligence forms and Islamic finance, these objects are moral tools, not reducible to, albeit constrained by, economic calculations. Islamic finance instruments are inherently ambiguous, caught in the debates among Islamic scholars betwixt and between efficiency and moral equity, and between *hiyal-e shar'i* (legalistic deceits of accommodation to capitalism) and claims to recover the original meaning of *riba'* as not "interest" but usury and even the requirement to detour all exchanges through the general equivalent of money so as not to exchange two kilos of lower quality dates directly for one kilo of higher quality ones (Fischer 1980a). Maurer perhaps underestimates the potential significance of Islamic banking by seeing it as expressive only of moral aspirations and as a minor alternative experiment, like Ithaca Hours. The recent Seventh and Eighth Harvard University Forums on Islamic Finance (April 2006, 2008), which I attended, brought together an impressive array of bankers and analysts from Wall Street, Paris, Geneva, Dubai, Bahrain, Malaysia, Pakistan, and Indonesia. A Paris- and Dubai-based analyst from McKenzie International put up comparative charts of the Islamic banking sector by country and dollar amounts, by profits relative to conventional banking, and by services offered. There is even a Dow Jones Islamic Market Index, initiated in 1999, and the London market is currently (2006) debating instituting an Islamic bond market to attract the more than $750-billion Islamic financial market. The McKenzie analyst stressed the ways in which particularistic interpretations in different Islamic countries have become open to negotiation.

These negotiations are a form of reflexive social institution due on the one hand to the social composition of national regulatory boards and their need to adjust to international regulatory conventions (Basel II), and on the other hand to the ways in which outreach to local communities of entrepreneurs and businessmen feed back into the negotiation of financial instruments as forms of political economy. As the demand for services increases, as Islamic banking moves from large funds to retail markets, these pressures will increase. As Robert Bianci stressed at the conference in 2006, in his comparative analysis of *shar'ia* boards in Malaysia and Pakistan, ensuring independence and technical competence will be a sharp political issue in these moral and efficiency negotiations. At issue is the continuing effort to reform and domesticate capitalism, a cultural matter, not just a financial one.

Maurer's study of Islamic mortgages in the United States (2006) similarly stresses the mainstreaming of Islamic mortgage forms that have the trappings of bureaucratic formality and legality over those that rely on particularistic charisma of a given Islamic authority and the social trust of a handshake.

Derivatives, one of the experimental technical instruments of the financial markets, opens another window onto unstable epistemic objects amenable to anthropology of science and technology analyses (LiPuma and Lee 2004; Lepinay 2005a, 2005b, 2005c). Having worked as a trader, Vincent-Antoine Lepinay wrote an ethnographic study of a Wall Street financial institution in which he tracks how financial trades are repackaged as they travel from trading floor to back office clearing to archives, a circuit in which the glamorous deal making of the trading floor must be converted by clearance and other modes of scrutiny into value, which, when fudged, becomes false coin and the criminal grounds for failure of due diligence. At the same time, Lepinay tracks the construction of objects (formulas of indexes) which are intended to concentrate and represent the world, or at least the world economy but tend to break apart over time. In Lepinay's case, these objects are capital guarantee derivatives, a financial instrument pioneered by a Swiss bank and constructed by combining the indexes of the New York, Tokyo, and London stock exchanges, guaranteeing the capital, and producing a surplus return based on the growth of the world economy. The Swiss bank miscalculated, nearly bankrupted itself, and canceled its offering of these instruments. New York banks picked them up and recalibrated the instruments, and it worked during the financial bubble of the 1990s but no longer.

This technical and sociocultural analysis begins to demystify a key abstractive and speculative commodity fetish, as does Analise Riles's (2004) account of Japanese bankers' efforts to use similar indicators abstracted from the flow of exchange rates. These financial instruments and indexes provide strategic access to points at which one can monitor the construction and breaking apart of tools that channel and redirect the flows of the world economy. These become anthropological small, intimate worlds, but ones that have nuclear power, with chain reactions, many near disasters, occasionally explosive implosions, and always-expansive cultural and social reverberations.

Indeed, the use of such epistemic objects which very insecurely provide illusions of information control but have practical consequences are further explored by Daniel Beunza and Raghu Garud (2005) using Goffman's notion of frames and Latour's notion of "trials of strength." They analyze how stock analysts produce persuasive analyses in situations of uncertainty. The frames consist of categorizations, analogies, and metrics. The example is Amazon.com and three trials of strength among different frames of analysis between December 1998 and June 2000. The leading frame in this period was Henry Blodget's categorization of Amazon as an Internet company that should be analogized to Dell Computer (rather than to a bookseller such as Barnes and Noble). They should thus be appraised in terms of revenue growth deferred for three years. This frame was able to overcome competitive frames for two years, but finally, as revenues failed to materialize and decisions to not yet pursue revenues continued to be made, Blodget's frame lost support. As with due diligence, the frames here are uncertainty-reducing procedures and are calculative and transparent but do not approach certainty or absolute truth; and as with Kuhn's paradigms, on which "trials of strength" are perhaps microversions, once anomalies build up and there are alternative frames, frames can shift. Above all, these frames are a way to explore how financial intermediaries function to allow actors to understand the operations of capital markets embedded in mass-market transactions. Analysts are neither straightforward forecasters in a probabilistic world, nor lemmings merely imitating one another in a world so uncertain as to make calculation impossible.

Many of the above components are brought together in a sociotechnical assemblage in Beunza's and David Stark's ethnography of an international securities arbitrage trading room in the former New York World Trade Center. The arbitrage trading room is a strategic access to the "silent technological [quantitative] revolution" that has swept over Wall Street in the "last two decades . . . ignited by the rise of derivatives such as futures and options, of mathematical formulae such as Black-Scholes, of network connectivity," and of exchanging the traders of the 1980s, characterized by riches, bravado, and suspenders, with engineers with "MBA degrees in finance and Ph.D.s in physics and statistics" (2003: 138). In arbitrage, value is generated through novel associations of securities in ways not previously recognized, depending upon access not to better or more timely information but to communities of interpretation using Bloomberg terminals that allow financial value to be represented in many alternative ways. Algorithms for computerized robotic trading are closely supervised by "statistical arbitrage traders" who stop their mechanical trading when the market situation changes.

With the destruction of the twin towers, elements of the sociotechnical network became starkly evident. Reconstruction of ID access to accounts held by deceased partners proved to be possible only through

intimate knowledge of these colleagues and guessing what their passwords might have been. But also as firms relocated, it was clear that as
virtuality of trading increases, the importance of physical proximity
among the traders becomes more important (Castell's paradox), while
that of the location of the computers and support can be elsewhere.
The development of new formulae exerts pressure to isolate one's
traders from competitors, and so rather than reassembling in Manhattan, some firms are choosing to move to Connecticut to minimize
inadvertent leaking of innovative tools. A new financial geography is
emerging, one that is calling for new anthropologies of technoscience
and its cultural and political-economic skeins.

As a proving ground, Beunza and Stark argue that traders recognize
opportunity "by making of their trading room a laboratory, by con-
ducting experiments, by deploying an array of instruments to test the
market" (2004: 371). Moreover, "calculation is not detached" but involves judgment, and "whereas the trader is emotionally distant from
any particular trade, to be able to take a position, the trader must be
strongly attached to an evaluative principle and its affiliated instruments" (ibid.; see also Zaloom 2004 on the bodily and psychological
discipline of the trader).

In sum, the third genealogy is composed of investments in the worlds
beyond the lab, a problematic of emergence, and an anthropologically
informed ethnographic method of epistemological encounter.[48] While
it has begun to reengage the worlds beyond western Europe and North
America, the reconstruction of the cross-cultural, geographically distributed, linguistically accented, and historically varied anthropological project is only just beginning to unfold.

IV: Emergent Cosmopolitical Technoscientific Worlds
of the Twenty-First Century

At the Institute of Technology of Bandung (ITB), an innovative generation of computer scientists has tackled the challenges of networking
the vast rural areas of the Indonesian archipelago with extreme low-
cost wireless technology, through guerilla education, and by moving
into the Ministry of Technology and Research.[49] At the Institute of
Physics and Mathematics (IPM) in Tehran, a remarkable group of
scientists helped keep the scientific culture of Iran alive through a
period of cultural revolution when the universities were closed and
Islamically purged.[50] It was the first site in Iran to be connected to the

Internet and is home to a world-class string theory group. Iran also has developed Bt rice, industrial-scale tissue-engineered propagation for date palms and other fruit trees; and it has experimented with new social models for paying donors for kidneys and providing free transplants and for WHO-designated best practices programs of HIV/AIDS triangular clinics.[51] In Egypt, Sekem, an experimental farm built with technosavvy combined with the ideas of Rudolph Steiner and Sufi ideology has not only proved it can grow and market organic crops, but has maneuvered the Egyptian government to ban cotton pesticide crop dusting and support healthier growing techniques.[52] In Taiwan, a cadre of biostatisticians has inserted itself as power brokers in the disputes over the International Conference on Harmonization for global clinical trials (Kuo 2005). In Brazil, tower experiments in the Amazon to determine whether the tropical forests are carbon sources or carbon sinks are interpreted differently by U.S., European, and Brazilian scientists. The six-hundred-plus scientist Large-Scale Biosphere Atmosphere Experiment Program is intended to chart the sustainability of the Amazon ecology, the role of the Amazon forests in the global carbon cycle and thus in regulating the global environment, and to train a new generation of Brazilian global environmental scientists who can work from contexts independent of the currently hegemonic American and European assumptions about how forests work, one of the contentious North–South divisions over the global political economy (Lahsen 2001, 2004, 2005; Lahsen and Pielke 2002). In Costa Rica, ecological research has become a model not only for pushing beyond equilibrium and human-free frames of thinking, but also for its deployment of ecotourism as funding source, as pedagogy (both domestically and for international tourists), as a contested site of local concerns and neoliberal pressures, and as part of emergent transnational technical networks responsive to the struggles against privatization of water in the 1990s and for new models of private–public goods that can guarantee water access as a human right, based on case studies of local experiments in integrated water management shared on the web.[53]

These and numerous other initiatives constitute the terrain of new genealogical and network structures for the anthropology of science and technology studies. The historical horizon is quite different from that of colonial, development, new nations, and even postcolonial studies (e.g., Grove 1995, 1997 on colonialism and environmental knowledge; Ihsanoglu 2004 on science in the Ottoman Empire; Mitchell 2002 on expertise in Egypt; Pyenson 1989 on colonial science in Indonesia; Stuchtey 2005 on science in European empires; Watts 1997

8. At the new GMP stem cell facility in Trabzon, eastern Turkey, two generations of Turkish science. Serdar Bedi Omay (*lower left*), M.D./Ph.D., trained in Japan and Turkey, hematologist at Trabzon's Karadeniz Technical University Medical School, and one of three founders of Advanced Technologies Industries (ATI). The acronym also mean "future" in Arabic (Persian *atiyeh*). ATI has built a good manufacturing practices (GMP) certified clean-room facility for stem cell therapies such as bone marrow transplants, cancer vaccines, and organ tissue engineering. Sociologically and economically, ATI is of interest for having raised money for its construction through local entrepreneurs, and then investors elsewhere, promising to produce autologous stell cells for patients across the country. (Interview with Omay and microbiologist Murat Ertürk, 21 July 2007; see

also the ATI website: www.atiteknoloji.com). The Turkish bone marrow transplantation registry was established in 1995, and has collected and analyzed data from fifteen tranplant centers on 437 adult lymphoma patients (185 Hodgkin's, 252 non-Hodgkin's) undergoing autologous hemopoietic stem cell transplantation from 1992 to 2002 (Journal of Clinical Oncology 2006:17517).

Omay stands in front of a photo of S. T. Aygun, veterinarian, virologist, and pioneer in stem cell culture and tissue engineering. He is credited with blocking the importation of Thalidomide to Turkey from 1958 to 1962, thereby averting the tragedy of deformed babies that affected thousands in Europe and Africa. A proponent of cell culture and tissue engineering, and opponent of experimentation on live animals, Aygun was concerned that the testing on animal models for safety and efficacy by Grünenthal Pharmaceuticals, the German developer of Thalidomide, were insufficient. Aygun is regarded not only as a national hero for averting tragedy in Turkey, but also by the ATI founders as a person who will eventually be recognized internationally as a pioneer of today's stem cell research field. Photo by M. Fischer.

(Thalidomide was also refused approval by U.S. Food and Drug Administration reviewer Frances Kathleen Oldham Kelsey until full safety testing had been done, for which she received a Distinguished Federal Civilian Service Award from President Kennedy. Once its structure and effects were further elucidated in the 1990s—including its antiangiogenic effects, as well as its teratogenic or birth defect-causing left-handed isomer—Thalidomide was approved for multiple myeloma, leprosy, and several cancers, under the condition that physicians and patients go through a special System for Thalidomide Education and Prescribing Safety, or STEPS, oversight program.)

9. On technology incubator at Sabanci Research Park, Istanbul, western Turkey, humans scaling and vault-ing over the walls of knowledge. Photo by M. Fischer.

and Jones 2004 on imperialism and disease; Edney 1997 on develop-ment of cartographic techniques through the Great Trigonometrical Survey of the British East India Company; Bayly 1996 on information networks in British India), though the lessons learned from those frames of study and of policy making remain important, as do their institutional legacies. So too nostalgic pride in prehistoric, ancient, and medieval rhizomes of long and polygenetic histories of local and civilizational knowledges remains symbolically important[54] and occa-sionally contains intriguing scientific and technological curiosities (the ecologically efficient desert irrigation systems of the Nabateans, the conversion error between Arabic and Roman miles as the explana-tion of why Columbus's estimate of the earth's size was 25 percent smaller than that of the correct one by Eratosthenes [I. Fischer 2005: 278–86]) but is most useful when such studies can identify local ecolo-gies, synergies, and networks of knowledge production.

The global initiatives of the search for cheap nuclear energy in the 1950s (Atoms for Peace), the International Geophysical Year (1957–58) and other such global foci of attention on scientific knowledge, and the space programs of the 1960s (in India and Indonesia) still have legacies around the world today, as do efforts by newly independent nations to build scientific research and educational infrastructures. These include, in India, the Tata Institute for Fundamental Research in Bombay, the Space Science Research Center in Ahmadabad, and the Indian Institutes of Technology.[55] In China they include the algae bio-technology marine research centers, rocket programs, and now-bur-geoning biotechnology efforts.[56] They include science cities and sci-ence and technology parks, such as the Korean Advanced Institute for Science and Technology (KAIST) and science city at Deojeung and Tsukuba in Japan, with its KEK physics accelerator (being a sister devel-opment to Irvine, California, as a planned science city, physically simi-lar but with different dynamics), and the new science city and technol-ogy park under construction in Dubai (circled on figure 23). In Iran they include the technical universities such as Sharif University, the Institute of Theoretical Physics and Mathematics, Amir Kabir Univer-sity, Modares Tabataba'I University, and the Institute of Advanced Studies for Basic Sciences. In Indonesia they include the ambitious effort to build airplanes, ships, high-speed trains, and automobiles as well as endeavors in molecular biology, agricultural biotechnology, astronomy, and ecology.[57] None of these were smoothly accomplished and require a cosmopolitical perspective to understand how they emerged and what the conditions of possibility for the future are.

Some of these aspirations and tensions can be seen architecturally in the modernism and ecological sensitivity of new technoscientific buildings, ranging from sculptural touches of humans scaling and vaulting over the walls of knowledge on the Sabanci Research Park incubator building in Istanbul (figure 9); to the elaborate atriums, attention to sustainable heating and water uses, and health facilities at the InfoSys campus outside Bangalore and at the new Institute for Advanced Studies in the Basic Sciences (IASBS) in Zanjan, Iran (figure 13); to the fusion of traditional and modern architecture at the In-stitute of Technology in Bandung, ITB, (figure 14). Old colonial build-ings, such as the Eijkman Institute for Biotechnology in Jakarta and the Bosscha Observatory in Lembang (figure 19) have been refurbished, and International Style campuses built such as the agricultural univer-sity at Bogor (Institut Pertanian Bogor, IPB) (figure 22). The aspira-tions and tensions can be seen as well in the variety of leaders, in their educational journeys and struggles to create new institutions, ranging from former aeronautics lead-designer for Airbus, B. J. Habibie (figure 17), who returned from Germany to Indonesia to develop the aeronautics, high-speed train, and shipbuilding industries (and was briefly President of Indonesia after Suharto), to physicist Yousef Sobuti, a student of Chandrasekar at the University of Chicago, who led the physics department at Shiraz University for many years, and recently has started the postgraduate IASBS away from the politics of the big cities. The variety includes such entrepreneurial non-profit gurus as internationally known Onno Purbo (figure 18) who resigned from ITB's computer science department to be able to show much larger numbers of young people how to network their schools and villages, and to create a bottom-up demand to reform telecommunications infrastructures and regulations; as well as such industry-connected scientists as current ITB rector and petroleum geophysicist, Djoko Santoso (figure 21), trained in Japan, Thailand, and Indonesia, justly proud of the hundreds of ITB petroleum engineering graduates who work in the oil industries of the region from Malaysia to Burma to Pakistan. Students (figures 12, 15, 22) and young faculty (figures 11, 20) mix old and new—in dress style, in work style, in equipment—providing a sense of both local and global possibilities. Amidst this mixture, Ganesh, the logo of ITB (figures 16, 21) reminds that modern learning is not only under Western aegis.

The new generation of ethnographies of scientific and technological developments, especially in the worlds outside western Europe and North America, is part of a cosmopolitical technoscientific world in which one needs an ethnographic eye to clearly see the political, cultural, technological, financial, institutional, and human capital building blocks and barriers. Generalized frames of postcolonial relations, for instance, while they serve well to highlight legacies of inegalitarian and dependency relations, cannot explain the successes and growth points of new developments.

With today's shifts in scale, changes in chronotope, spatial relations, and social organizational forms facilitiated by the Internet and other communication, transportation, and dissemination modalities, a more detailed, ethnographic eye is required. Anthropology perforce is becoming a third space, a space of comparative and entangled frames and of emergent forms of life (Fischer 2003). Differential and dialogic epistemic objects appear in agonistic, competitive, and transnational relationships; civics and ethical discourse shift from universal rights and matters of fact to matters of concern, ethics of care, living with alterity, and the face of the other (Fischer 2006b; M. Fortun 2008; Haraway 1991, 1997, 2003; Latour 2005a). While STS studies are gradually beginning in many places—at the Institute of Technology at Bandung, the national Tsinghua and National Min-Yang universities in Taiwan, Tsinghua in Beijing, the National University of Singapore, Sharif University and the Institute of Philosophy in Tehran, the Universidad Nacional de Colombia, and at various places in India[58]—these programs often have to struggle against older paradigms of study that emphasize catching up, or center–periphery relations. As the topics in the opening paragraph of this section indicate, these are not always the most illuminating or useful in the present context.

What makes these sites around the world not merely extensions of postcolonial debates but instead switching points within third spaces is that they have the potential for transforming science, policy, and cosmopolitics both in their targeted locales and beyond. For example, geographical information systems (GIS) and other data bank, mapping, and networking modalities provide material technologies for countermapping, epistemic object creation, and enunciatory community development (Callison 2002, 2007; CRIT 2006; Schienke 2006). The Critical Research Initiative Trust (CRIT)'s Mumbai Free Map, for instance, makes public the ownership deeds, rents, and pricing data which previously were available only to developers, thereby shifting some informational power into the hands of local communities so that they can participate in or contest municipal and developer plans and even raise their own funding for new forms of housing and services. Similarly, digital assemblage of information and perspectives by developers, miners, environmentalists, and tribal leaders can make public an evolving cultural debate over jobs, community, resource management, development, and heritage on the Tahltan lands of British Columbia; or for Inuit filing environmental and human rights suits over climate warming (Callison 2002, 2007; Landzelius 2005 more generally on indigenous communities' use of the Internet). In China, digital tools for environmentalism may help preserve ecosystems, provide visual means to foster public pressure to reduce air pollution, and provide linkages between spatial information at different scales (Schienke 2006). Similar tools were once mandated, in the aftermath of the Bhopal chemical disaster, as worst-case scenario mappings for communities near chemical factories in the United States as part of right to know legislation (Fortun 2001). They are made available by Syracuse University's Transactional Records Access Clearinghouse (TRAC) to provide monitoring access for journalists and others on biased enforcement patterns of the U.S. Internal Revenue Service, FBI, Department of Homeland Security, Bureau of Alcohol, Tobacco, Firearms, and Explosives, and Justice Department prosecutions. In Israel

10. The founder of the Institute for Advanced Studies in the Basic Sciences, Zanjan, Iran: Professor Yusef Sobuti (*left*). Photo by M. Fischer.

(*below*) 11. Institute for Advanced Studies in the Basic Sciences, Zanjan, Iran: Professor Babak Karimi, head of the chemistry department, (*facing camera*) in one of the Institute's chemistry labs. Photo by M. Fischer.

12. Institute for Advanced Studies in the Basic Sciences, Zanjan, Iran: Microbiology Ph.D. student Shahareh Tavaddod (BA nuclear engineering, MA superconductivity, research at Delft and Amsterdam) explains her work on the motion of E. coli. Photo by M. Fischer.

13. Atrium of the Institute for Advanced Studies in the Basic Sciences, Zanjan, Iran. With the geophysicist and earthquake researcher Farhad Sobuti (*right*) the anthropologist Mazyar Lotfalian (*left*), and author (*center*). Photo by M. Fischer.

and Palestine, they are used by watchdog groups (B'Tselem; Applied Research Institute Jerusalem [ARIJ], Palestine Environmental NGOS [PENGO]) to monitor and expose house demolitions, land expropriations, olive grove destruction, and road blocks (Fischer 2006a).

What makes these efforts more than just new technologies for local community organization is their global connectivity, highlighting the frictions (Tsing 2005), speed bumps (Sunder Rajan 2006), or time "out-of-jointness" (Negri 1970) that form the changing grounds of governance. Conservation biology in Indonesia (Tsing 2005; Lowe 2006) is a preliminary example of shifts in cultural chronotope, cultural scale, and epistemic objects of governance. At issue are mentoring lineages in science and technology across the globe, flows of scientific personnel, the roles of transnational corporations not merely serving their own interests but as sites of learning and experience for scientists and engineers who move in and out of various-sized companies, academia, and government service; the establishment of new technology institutions, including incubators, science and technology parks, and universities (e.g., on Japan, Low, Nakayam, and Yoshioka 1999; on Korea, see Kim and Leslie 1998 and more generally Low 1998). Among the most interesting of new knowledges being produced are both the customization of technologies as they move from one ethnographic context to another and the production of local knowledges that are important to global issues—e.g., biodiversity, climate change, mechanisms of cross-species infection, species ecologies, and food chains.

Technoscientific cosmopolitics, which views the development of science and technology in a global—political, economic, material, network—context rather than in simplified chains of histories of ideas within disciplines, is a terrain or ethical plateau that transforms traditional thinking about center–periphery and imperial power relations, about the role of domestic and transnational scientists mentoring lineages, about the circulation of scientists, and about the plurality of real-world instantiations of projects, competitions, collaborations, and assemblages.

Prehistories for anthropologies of technoscience may usefully focus upon key leaders in science and engineering: C. K. Tseng, Tsen Hsue-shen, Homi Bhabha, Vikram Sarabai, B. J. Habibie, Yusef Sobuti. But anthropologies of technoscience focus on the ways in which these lives and those of their institutional colleagues fit into larger patterns and networks of several kinds. As Marx remarked in the preface to *The Eighteenth Brumaire of Louis Napoleon*, historical, or here, technoscientific structures and structural change, can be explained neither by reduction to great man stories nor by deterministic stories of power

14. Institute of Technology, Bandung, Indonesia. Photo by M. Fischer

15. Study circle, Institute of Technology, Bandung, Indonesia.
Photo by M. Fischer.

16. Institute of Technology, Bandung, Indonesia. Ganesh logo on "smart campus" and Microsoft partnership banner (a Microsoft effort to stop the widespread use of pirated software). Photo by M. Fischer.

17. (*on left*): B. J. Habibie, aeronautics engineer and Airbus designer; in charge of developing Indonesia's aeronautics, high-speed train, and shipbuilding industries; and former president of Indonesia. (*right*): the author. Photo by M. Fischer and Sulfikar Amir.

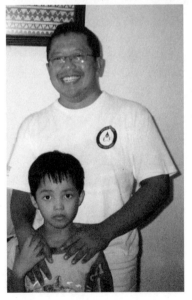

18. Onno Purbo, computer scientist, grassroots connectivity activist, with his son. Photo by M. Fischer.

19. Institute of Technology, Bandung. Astronomers at Bosscha Observatory, Lembang. Photo by M. Fischer.

20. Institute of Technology, Bandung. Astronomers: Tawfiq Hidayat (*back row second from right*), Mahasena Putra (*front row center*), Prenzana Premad (*back row far right*), and colleagues, with author. Photo by M. Fischer.

21. Institute of Technology, Bandung, rector and petroleum geophysicist Ir. Djoko Santoso and ITB Ganesh. Santoso has experience in the petroleum industry and has written software still used in the industry. He was educated in Japan and Thailand and received a PhD from ITB. Some two hundred ITB graduates work in the Malaysian state oil company, Petronas. Others work in the oil and gas industries of Myanmar, Pakistan, and other countries. Photo by M. Fischer

22. Indonesia's Bogor Agricultural University (Institut Pertanian Bogor, IPB). Photo by M. Fischer.

relations, whether class, colonial, imperial, or postcolonial. At issue is the creation of consciousness, in his case of political consciousness out of the inventive use of changing assemblages of political resources, here of technoscientific communities of understanding both among new generations of scientists, engineers, and physicians and among publics at large.

Prehistories for anthropologies of technoscience may usefully also chart the colonial and postcolonial building of institutions: e.g., Beijing's Tsinghua University, Taipei's Tsinghua University, Bandung's Institute of Technology (ITB) and its Bosscha Astronomy Observatory (Lembang), Bogor's Agricultural University (IPB), the Tata Institute for Fundamental Research (TIFR), the Indian Institutes of Technology, the Inter University Center for Astronomy and Astrophysics (Pune), the Pasteur Institutes (Tehran, Ho Chi Minh City, Tunis), the Abdus Salam International Centre for Theoretical Physics (Trieste), the Third World Academy of Sciences (Trieste). But anthropologies of technoscience will also explore the relations between these institutions and the building of communities of scientific understanding: e.g., the debate in Iran between those who argue that science textbooks should evolve Persian language vocabularies to stimulate fluid and culturally creative thinking and those who argue that English terminology is the language of science and should be learned from the outset; the debate in Pakistan over the destruction of educational standards under the Islamicization policies promoted under the Muhammad Zia-ul-Haq dictatorship (Hoodhboy 1991) and the somewhat parallel differences between the Ruzbeh schools in Zanjan and Tehran, the one producing secular scientists and intellectuals, the other producing religious ones; the role of the Sarabai Community Science Center in Ahmedabad; the role of the cosmologist Penzana Premadi in a religion and science forum that also coordinates local astronomy groups in Yogakarta and Bandung; the role of the cosmologist Reza Mansuri in pioneering a popular astronomy and science magazine in Iran that coordinates local astronomy groups.[59]

Again, prehistories for anthropologies of science and technology may usefully chart the ebb and flow of national science policy initiatives, the building of science cities (Cyberjaya in Malaysia, Biopolis in Singapore, Hyderabad's Genome Valley and Cyber Towers, Bangalore's Silicon Valley[60] and BioHelix, Dubai Internet, Healthcare, and Media Cities and Knowledge Village), science and technology parks, the laying of fiber optic cable, building of highways, manpower flows, brain drain figures, and recruitment strategies. But anthropologies of science and technology also explore communities of technological practice: Onno Purbo's strategy of bottom-up expansion of an Internet user base and demand in Indonesia, the efforts of Iran to find technology park models in postindustrial-divide Italy rather than in the massive top-down investment strategies of Tsukuba or Daejeong; the efforts of the national laboratories, new pharmaceutical company R&D efforts, and clinical trial hospitals in India to evolve hybrid organizational forms (Sunder Rajan 2006).

Prehistories for anthropologies of science and technology sometimes look to schools of traditional training as cultural roots for scientific breakthroughs, as in identifying Brahminic astrological calculations for a putative root of Ramanujan's thinking, or Persian cultural patterns for putative roots for Ali Asghar Lotfizadeh's "fuzzy logic" (aka soft computing). But anthropologies and cultural histories of science and technology look more closely at alternative derivations for similar or differential results and at actual networks of influence. Loren Graham and Jean-Michel Kantor (2007) argue that varieties of (mathematical expressions of) general relativity were developed differently by Albert Einstein (a more complicated gravitational equation to allow for different coordinate systems) and by V. A. Folk (a simpler equation that derived from his picking of a particular harmonic coordinate system and that made clear that the theory, in good Soviet Marxist fashion, was of absolute space-time or gravity and not "relativistic," as Einstein agreed he had misnamed it). Graham and Kantor argue in similar fashion that set theory was differently derived by mystical Name Worshippers in Russia (Dmitri Egorov, Nikolai Luzin) and by French rationalists (Emile Borel, René Baire, Henri Lebesgue). Fuzzy logic is perhaps a more interesting example. Introduced in the 1960s by Lotfizadeh, one of three prominent graduates of the first class of graduates of the School of Engineering at the University of Tehran, who pursued his career in the Electrical Engineering Department at Berkeley, fuzzy logic was initially a way of modeling natural language, relaxed the rules of Boolean logic, and became useful for control systems in a variety of arenas, initially for appliance manufacturing in Japan (Lotfalian 2004). What is interesting is how many Iranians have followed Lotfizadeh as experts into the field and how such soft computing upset the decade-long Japanese Fifth-Generation Computer Project (1982–95) to develop a revolutionary large-scale parallel processing computer system. Although Japan would still go on to develop the world's fastest supercomputer (installed in 2002 at the Earth Simulator Research and Development Center, Yokohama, and used for climate modeling), the fifth-generation computer was derailed by the processing speed, memory capacity of personal computers, and dis-

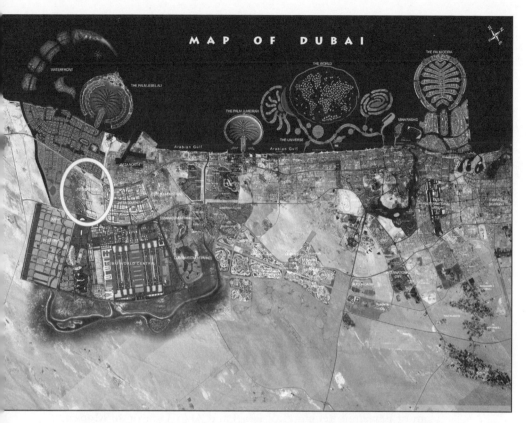

23. Science City and Technology Park (*circled*) in Dubai, seen near the Palm and World Islands, which have pioneered new engineering knowledge and solutions, now being proposed to address new barrier islands for the Netherlands (see National Geographic Channel's popular but informative video on the engineering of the Palm Islands). Aerial photo, courtesy of Dubai Technopark-Dubai Institute of Technology.

tributed computing through workstations as well as by soft computing techniques such as "fuzzy inference" and neural networks (Low 1998, Markoff 2002).

The weave of transnational connections, lineages of mentoring across countries, brain drain and return, and historical knowledge bases is shifting and expanding. A third of postdocs working in American biology labs are said to be Chinese nationals, many of whom are returning to China. Fellowships for Indonesian scholars are becoming more available in Japan and Australia, as they become less available in the United States and Europe, and Japan itself is beginning to export engineers to Asian countries as Japan moves its manufacturing abroad. Sharon Traweek (1996) has tracked some of the gender and cultural differences of physicists working at KEK in Tsukuba: the love of Americans for tinkering with equipment; the professionalized distance of Japanese from carefully machined equipment; the use of international postdoctoral fellowships for Japanese women scientists to evade the patriarchal hierarchies of labs in Japan and build intellectual capital and networks that can then be used to get ahead at home. Sarah Franklin (2007) engagingly shows that Ian Wilmut's team that developed somatic nuclear transfer "cloning" in Scotland (producing the sheep Megan, Morag, and Dolly) occurred in the context of a long historical tradition of breeding a diversity of sheep in Britain, but as interesting is that the second in the world to develop a human stem cell line was the team of Benjamin Reubinoff of Israel and Alan Trouson of Monash (Melbourne) and Singapore (who pioneered IVF technology in Australia and studied at Cambridge): the network is global and situates itself where opportunity arises.

At issue is not just a reconfiguration of political-economy competitions, but also a series of new ethical demands and configurations, highlighted by the stem cell debates. Franklin quotes Wilmut: "In the 21st century and beyond, human ambition will be bound only by the laws of physics, the rules of logic, and our descendants' own sense of right and wrong" (Franklin 2007: 32). Although he goes on to say, "Truly, Dolly has taken us into the age of biological control," what is more interesting is the notion of ethics being defined by the future-anterior, by "our descendants' own sense of right and wrong." This is indeed the challenge of designing reflexive social institutions that incrementally and recursively help us construct the publics forming around us. We do live in a new age of biological sensibility (not necessarily control), and one that through our expanding networked experiences is creating new kinds of recursive publics. The cosmopolitical worlds of technoscience are becoming ever more diverse, distributed, and dependent upon a heterogeneity that both requires and enlivens anthropologies to come.

Conclusions: Translating Legacy Genealogies to Public Futures

Four genealogies, like quadroscopic-lensed eyes, can provide complementary vision: cultural skeins and sensibilities; social worlds and institutions; technoscientific proving grounds; and spatially distributed, culturally heterogeneous configurations of technoscientific assemblages. Metaphorically, these are like camera lenses establishing long shots; close-up ethnomethodological lenses; motion picture lenses for emergences and motion-detecting midrange theory; and wide-angle, close-up lenses for situationally located experimental systems. The cultural skeins, programming "object-oriented languages," emergent forms of life, and cosmopolitical marshaling of ingenuity tracked by anthropologies of science and technology productively complicate and make more realistic the demand for attention to the reconstruction of public spheres, civil society, and politics in the technoscientific worlds we are constructing within and around ourselves. No longer can we rest on broad claims about the alienation of the market, the technicization of life, or globalization. Just as we have moved from Mertonian sociologies of science to analyses of what scientists actually do, so too we need to pay attention to civic epistemologies and cultures of politics as they are mediated by the paradox that the more networked, the more transparency, the more access, perhaps the less polis-like ability for localities to control local destiny (unless careful attention is paid to the infrastructural firewalls, speed bumps, accountability mechanisms, alternative valuations, sanctions, rewards, *jouissance*, intensities, sensibilities, and openness) and as they are transduced across the cultural switches of the heterogeneous communities within which the sciences are cultured and technologies are peopled with the face of the other.

3 | Emergent Forms

of Un/Natural Life

"Nature" is an ambivalent term, meaning both what is other to us and what is essentially ourselves. Even as ourselves (our characters, our bodies, our selfhoods), nature is often "other," that from which we attempt to separate ourselves and upon which we are dependent, which we attempt to control but which always escapes our reach.

Four kinds of nature as both other and self-defining—ecological, environmental, life science, and coevolutionary—seem to have risen to the top of political, philosophical, and moral agendas in the past quarter century: (1) so-called natural catastrophes and the problems traditionally associated with the control of nature; (2) industrial accidents and the unintended negative consequences of new technologies associated with first-order industrial processes and the military-industrial complex and with renewed calls for deliberative democracy, social accountability, environmental justice as well as the older environmental terms of remediation, preservation, and conservation; (3) contestations over agricultural and medical biotechnologies and the life sciences more generally and their potential for reorganizing conceptual categories of life, the viability of human beings and their habitats as well as more targeted concerns about genetic and pharmacological enhancements and inequalities; (4) shifting relations with companion species, both domesticated, including modified organisms for medical research, and wild, particularly viruses, such as Avian flu strains that map the changing relations among species and habitats.

We live (again) in an era in which new ethical and political spaces are thrown up that require action and have serious consequences, but for which the possibilities of giving adequate reasons ahead of the decision making quickly run out. Traditional ethical and moral guides seem not always helpful, particularly when some of the very categories of discussion (such as nature) seem to have morphed, disaggregated, and become distributed. We are often left to negotiate multiplicities of interests and trade-offs in legal or other tournaments of decision making over time. As an anthropologist, I am interested in the ways in which emergent forms of life embed institutional and ethical orientations, inventions, and productivities and in how these vary or contrast in different places and times. Are there pressures toward new reflexive or second-order modernization institutions? Or do we fail to learn from one crisis to the next, allowing involution of institutions, hierarchies, and sanctioned behaviors? What social, literary, and material technologies are used to frame and negotiate trade-offs, crises, and dilemmas? I take it as given that "one cannot change only one thing": interconnections are what are interesting, puzzling, and surprising and what spur to reframings and new institutions. This might be called the ecological rule.

Narrating First Nature: Catastrophe, Deep Play,
Repetition, and Social-Ecological Learning

As the devastation of Hurricane Katrina unfolded in 2005, I wondered if it was following a radio script of 1931 by Walter Benjamin, "Die Mississippi Uberswemmung 1927" ("The Flooding of the Mississippi 1927"). Benjamin did a series of radio "children's stories" on catastrophes, the Lisbon earthquake of 1753 being another celebrated topic. Both tales continue to have resonances today. In the Lisbon quake tale, Benjamin asked if new predictive technologies like seismology for earthquakes and satellite monitoring for hurricanes would make any difference. In the Mississippi River tale, Benjamin directly addressed social failures. The Lisbon earthquake was felt as far as Southeast Asia; the tsunami that devastated coastal Acheh and Sri Lanka in 2004 is rarely discussed as one in a long series that will continue as global warming continues and to that degree is not simply natural or an act of God; neither is it discussed enough as an event that has social implications for how, for instance, coastal communities are sited and protected.

At issue in the Mississippi Valley in 1927 was not only the struggle against the meandering of the great river to make it stay in its banks and flow more "efficiently" from north to south. More to the point for Benjamin was the dynamiting of the dikes protecting rural regions, forcing the rural poor to sacrifice for the capital city of New Orleans. Troops were called out to suppress the threat of civil war. As in 2005, St. Bernard Parish was flooded, but in 1927 the breaking of the dikes was neither a natural nor a necessary event, but a political decision to send a message to the New York and Chicago financial institutions that mea-

24. GOES-12 satellite image showing the status of Hurricane Katrina, August 28, 2005, at 1200Z, or 7 a.m., EST. Credit: NASA Goddard, Space Flight Center.

sures would be taken to protect their capital. New Orleans was not only the great port for agriculture, but also the banking center for the sugar and cotton interests of the Mississippi Valley. The banks were nonetheless wiped out, and agriculture, already in depression, was further devastated. Poor African-American sharecroppers in Greenville, Mississippi, and elsewhere, as John M. Barry details in *The Rising Tide* (1997), his book about the flood of 1927, were prevented from evacuating, lest they leave for good, and at gunpoint were pressed into rebuilding the levees, work that was paid at a dollar a day. Echoes might be heard in the Bush administration's lifting, in 2005, of the rules on paying workers the going rate and bringing in of fresh Mexican labor from Texas rather than employing either local labor or the many local illegal Mexican immigrants hiding from the authorities in the devasted city and surrounding areas. Benjamin commented on the destruction of the electronic communications system that ran along the levees. In 2005, again, one of the system failures was our much-vaunted communications networks, hampering first responders and rescue workers.

As a coda, Benjamin added the story of the three brothers stranded on a roof. Despairing that any rescue boats would stop for them, one

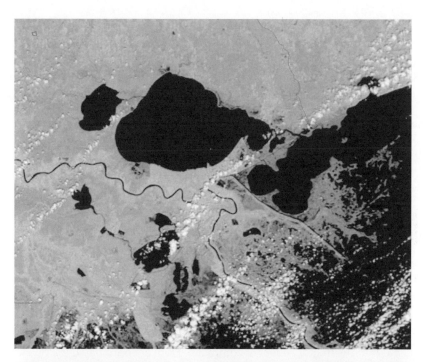

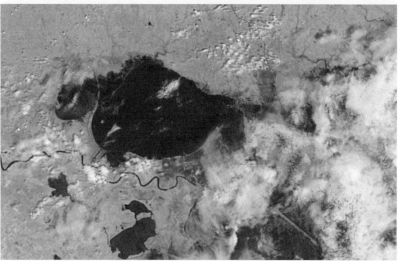

25.1 and 25.2. New Orleans before and after hurricane Katrina: August 27, 2005 and August 30, 2005, 11:45 a.m. Images taken by the Moderate Resolution Imaging Spectroradiometer (MODIS) on NASA's Terra satellite. After the hurricane struck, dark pools of water cover the eastern half of the city. Lake Pontchartrain balloons west of the city, and is separated only by a narrow strip of land from Lake Maurepas. Credit: MODIS Land Rapid Response Team at NASA GSFC. (http://earthobservat ory.nasa.gov/IOTD/view.php?id=5806.)

jumped to his death just before the other two were rescued. This figures as a miniature to the larger story and is part of Benjamin's polemic against techno-optimism. Catastrophes, Benjamin says, blast us out of the continuum of history and provide illuminations of different orderings of nature, history, limits to strategic planning, cost-benefit accounts, and other claims of rational prudence. They function analogously to traditional theological parables of human beings' best-laid plans going awry because of their inevitably partial knowledge.

The flood of 1927, caused by heavy rains from August 1926 through the spring of 1927, displaced over a million people from the lower Mississippi (Cairo, Illinois, to the Gulf Coast). Some 23,000 square miles flooded from Virginia to Oklahoma. People took refuge on the tops of levees, and 660,000 were fed by the Red Cross.

The flood was a transformative event in a number of regards. First, Barry argues, it dramatically changed the way Americans thought about the federal government's responsibility for its citizens. The federal government felt little obligation to provide food or shelter. President Calvin Coolidge refused to visit the disaster areas but did send Herbert Hoover, whom he empowered as a cabinet level officer and put into the military chain of command. Hoover coordinated the relief efforts of the Red Cross and other agencies. The newsreel imagery of the disaster and Hoover's coordination of relief propelled him into the presidency. Some of this footage can be seen in the documentary *Fatal Flood*, produced by Chana Gazit (2001).

Second, the flood changed race relations in the Delta and across the United States. Three times as many African-Americans migrated to Chicago, Detroit, Houston, and Los Angeles at this time than during the 1930s. Previously, because of a general labor shortage, the workers and sharecroppers may have been treated relatively well, but after the hampering of evacuation and forced labor, patrimonial relations with plantation owners was broken.

Third, the flood changed the way in which the Army Corps of Engineers attempted to control the river. From trying to work against the river's momentum, containing the river within narrow banks to increase speed of water flow and self-dredging for navigation—the so-called levees only strategy—the corps moved to a strategy of working with and leveraging the flow of the river, directing it via outlets and [James] Eads jetties. In 2005, a design flaw eerily similar to the levees only strategy operated: canals built in the 1960s to speed shipping funneled Katrina storm surges from the Gulf of Mexico into Lake Pontchartrain, Lake Borgne, and the city, adding to the destruction (Bohannan and Enserink 2005).

The Flood Control Act of 1928 initiated the largest civil engineering project, Project Flood, ever undertaken in the United States and shifted relations between the federal government and the states, constructing safety valves, controlled spillways, fuse-plug levees. In the 1940s the Mississippi Basin Model, a forty-acre physical model of the river, was built with German prisoner of war labor. It was used as an experimental system for testing large floods and control systems until 1973.

Whether Katrina in 2005 will have similar transformative effects remains to be seen, but a number of features articulate even broader concerns than those of 1927. There are suggestions of connections with anthropogenic climate warming, not just from civilian addiction to fossil fuels, but even possibly from Cold War military experiments' disrupting of the chemical and electromagnetic circuits of the planet.

I want to pose three kinds of analytic frames here: deep play, the balance between decentralized and centralized control systems, and monological-closed narratives versus dialogical-open ones.

Deep play: Catastrophic events and their associated political contestations often become deep play, sites where dynamically an increasing number of meaning structures implode or intersect and where society dramatizes to itself the meaning of its own representations about the moral order. It is said from various rational and cultural (e.g., Cajun backcountry) points of view that controlling the Mississippi in whole or in some of its parts and destroying wetlands along the way is hubristic and self-defeating. Yet, as with many death-defying sports—and some dangerous and death-challenging technologies —the struggle with the Mississippi has also been seen as the grandest of human agons: the Army Corps of Engineers against Nature.

The struggle with the Mississippi is a deep play in the Geertzian sense, giving meaning to endeavors to define human nature against its others. Over-investments of money, passion, and political resources constitute a nexus in which multiple registers of meanings are densely knotted. New Orleans, after all, is the great port of Midwestern agriculture, a great transshipment port of oil and petroleum, and the cultural entrepôt of French, Cajun, African-American, and southern cultural distinction. But in a Benjaminian flash of catastrophic illumination, the city reveals also the irrationalities of class and racial inequality, of the ethical or social justice unconcern on the part of political and financial elites, of bureaucratic fiefdoms, and of technological decay and miscalculation. The cost-benefit calculations of 1965, for instance, remain unchanged over forty years later. Cost-benefit itself might be challenged as a questionable methodology when lives are at stake. A measure of unconcern might be the token funding in 1998 of

the plans to save wetlands and rebuild the Louisiana coast, called
Coast 2050 or the Louisiana Coastal Area Project. This is a deep play
demonstration of meaning and values, dramatized, televised, and for a
time put out for public discussion. One might narrate these meanings,
as is usually done in the press, as a play of indictments and defenses, in
a mock litigious, American shadow play of skeptical civic epistemology in which truth, fact finding, and meaning are said to be established
through adversarial contestation, but in which testimony under oath
cannot be subpoenaed or compelled. The existential and ethical deep
play agons are refracted as well in plays, music, and the debates about
how much aid and succor should be provided by the government and
how much by civil society and faith-based organizations.[1]

Balance between decentralized and centralized control or governance systems: this second set of questions about alternative social
organizations has become "mission critical": what sorts of centralized
or decentralized governance might be most effective in dealing with
future hurricanes or similar events, including the building and maintaining of sea walls, levees, and wetland defenses, but also the preposi-
tioning of emergency supplies, the bolstering of local responders, shelters, and evacuation. Benjamin's question resonates: what use our
predictive abilities if the social institutions exacerbate the damage?

The comparative case of the sea wall in the Netherlands built after
the devastations of the floods of 1953 has been primarily discussed in
technological terms, but an anthropological science and technology
approach also should turn attention to the political and organizational
robustness required. The floods of 1953 killed almost two thousand
people and forced the evacuation of seventy thousand. It could have
been much worse. Half the country, including Amsterdam and Rotterdam, are below sea level. Dramatically, a Dutch sea captain sank his
boat in a widening breach to protect Rotterdam. The project to improve the sea defenses with a new design that allows water through to
maintain the wetlands in at least a portion of the coast caused a huge
domestic debate. The new design and debate also shifted the relations
between the central state and local water councils. Decentralized water councils have long been connected to Dutch democratic and self-
reliance organizations. Over the course of the twentieth century, the
state water control authorities created a symbiotic system of state
planning and outsourcing of construction and maintenance to private
sector companies. The new effort required new organizational forms,
both in negotiating the new plans and in the construction and maintenance (Bijker 2002). In the end, a compromise in the new design was
dictated by the politics of budgets. One leaves Bijker's account worried

with the Dutch about how secure the system is, albeit for the moment it seems to be functioning well. The Dutch debate whether one can hold the sea back as the land sinks continues. Perhaps, it is debated, one ought to invest in floating cities, and indeed in places new construction is required to be on pontoons. Other experiments for comparative attention are the floodgates on the Thames, on the Adriatic to protect Venice, the superlevees Japan is building, the concrete shelters on stilts in Bangladesh built in the aftermath of 130,000 deaths from the cyclone and storm surge of 1991, and California's "smart" levees that use "time-domain reflectometry" sensors to constantly monitor whether the dikes are weakening (Broad 2005: D1).

The loss of life and livelihood in these comparative cases should refocus attention on deep play meaning structures embedded in modalities of social organization. An estimated eight hundred to a thousand lives were lost immediately in the Katrina flooding (not considering excess mortality figures in the ensuing years), and almost immediately questions were raised about how many of these were from the poor, disabled, and minority communities and about what would happen to these communities and people as the city rebuilt and perhaps in the process gentrified. Kerry Emanuel, one of the scientists studying the connections with climate warming, pointed out that "tropical depression Jean the previous year—it was just a depression—killed almost 2,000 people in Haiti. Hurricane Mitch in 1999 killed 11,000 people in Central America. And a decade before that, a cyclone in Bangladesh killed 100,000 people" (Emanuel 2005).

Emanuel suggests that the United States is relatively lucky in the prevention of loss of life, that people should be encouraged to stop building along vulnerable coastlines, and that the differences between the vulnerability of the poor and rich are replicated in international comparative terms as in class terms within New Orleans. Charles Perrow, a sociologist of vulnerabilities in high-risk technologies, argues that New Orleans should be maintained at about one-third its pre-Katrina size, large enough to sustain the vital port functions but small enough to be defended against future storms and sinking coasts with technologies like those used by the Dutch (2007). New Orleans is already two-thirds its pre-Katrina size.

Even more went wrong in the New Orleans case with the breakdown of evacuation and relief preparedness. A previous evacuation effort in 2004 had resulted in gridlock on the highways. The repeated highway problems in 2005 indicate a certain failure in social learning. As Katrina approached, newsmen prepared forty-year-later reports on the disaster of Hurricane Betty in 1965, when eighty-one people died, a quarter of a million were evacuated, and the Ninth Ward was flooded, people had to be rescued from their rooftops, and rumors flew that water was pumped out of the mayor's Lake Vista subdivision into the Ninth Ward and even that the Industrial Canal was deliberately breached to flood out black people (Remnick 2005: 48, 53). Worst-case scenarios, with computer generated SLOSH models, were long in circulation (ibid.: 52). One wonders if any of the modelers or hurricane and other first responder agencies had thought much about Perrow's models of normal accidents (Perrow 1999). Apparently, in 2004 there was a $1-million hurricane simulation exercise in New Orleans that exposed many communication and logistical problems, which, however, remained unfixed (Klein 2005). Speculations began about what the long-term effects of the trauma will be on those who will remain separated from their social networks in the Ninth Ward and elsewhere: whether we will see, for instance, a run of suicides—two suicides were reported among the police during the storm.

Reflexive Social Institutions and Dialogic Narrative Capacities: Thus a third set of questions has to do with the creation of flexible and reflexive social institutions of second-order modernity that can make use of a rich interchange of communications and dialogue between decentralized capillary powers of decision making and central nodes of macrocoordinated support. Despite the multidimensionality of the deep play surrounding a catastrophe, reconstruction, restitution, and rehabilitation planning tend to elicit from government and major relief agencies a monological, rather than dialogical, form of mapping complexity within a semiclosed world of expertise that assumes everything can be viewed from a commanding height: the Mississippi Basin model that was used from the 1940s to 1973; a FEMA office in Washington; a simulation model in a university. One of the interests of comparisons with the Dutch case is to probe the possibilities of community, on-the-ground involvement, and investment in complex sociotechnical systems particularly under long-term anticipated changes such as climate warming and the anticipated rising of sea levels.

Among the intellectually most interesting and puzzling questions stirred by the Katrina hurricane are possible causal connections with climate warming, and the murky questions about military experiments with the atmosphere.[2] From a hydrological point of view, both the floods of 1927 and the hurricane flooding of 2005, despite their quite different causes and directionality, are part of a long series of Mississippi floods (1858, 1862, 1867, 1882, 1884, 1888, 1890 . . . 1927 . . . 1965 . . . 1993, 1995, 1997, 1998, 2001.) In 1965 Hurricane Betsy flooded New Orleans as Katrina did in 2005. And it was in 1965 that standards were last set for the strength of the levees on the dubious basis of cost-benefit analysis

The most significant of these floods in recent memory was that of 1993: the fourth "hundred-year flood" in eight years, a "five-hundred year" event, causing some $12 billion in damage. An unusual shift in the jet stream blocked a cold front and kept heavy rains over the Mississippi for six weeks. By August 1,083 levees had failed. This flood stimulated some changes in flood plain management, reinforced by the upper Mississippi floods in 2001. Instead of helping people rebuild in the flood plain, houses and even whole towns (e.g. Valmeyer, Illinois in 1993 and parts of Davenport, Illinois in 2001) were moved away from the flood plain. Some federal incentive programs for restoring wetlands began: an estimated half of all wetlands of the Mississippi basin are said to be gone, and in the Delta some of the farmland, now used for catfish farming, gets its water by pumping from the aquifers below. One study found that 40 percent of flood insurance payments goes to repeat victims, who represent 2 percent of policyholders; one house worth $114,000 received payments worth $806,000 for sixteen floods over eighteen years (Grunwald 2001; see also 2000, 2005a, 2005b, 2007).

Apart from these ecological, technical, and social management problems, there has been speculation about the role of climate change. While no direct correlation between individual events and climate change can be established, it is statistically the case that we are in a warming phase and that there is a correlation between the warming waters and the energy that goes into more intense hurricanes. The 1940s and 1950s were periods of intense, strong hurricanes, followed by a lull in the 1970s and 1980s, and we appear to be in another upswing. From the statistics of the Atlantic storms (11 percent of total storms) there is no way to associate the increasing intensity of hurricanes with anything but a natural cycle (Emmanuel 2005). On the other hand, Kerry Emmanuel also says that globally it appears that "the intensity of hurricanes is going up owing to global warming, and their duration is increasing, as well." He doesn't think we will see any direct evidence in the immediate future; it will take time for the connections to become evident. In half a century the connections will be more evident: insurance companies take note. But what has happened is that during the lull of the 1970s and 1980s there has been a great amount of construction and population increase along the coastlines, making these populations vulnerable.[3]

For New Orleans, climate change is experienced most directly by rising sea levels, which in time will put the city lower and lower below sea level. As Amsterdam, Galveston, and other places around the world testify, this is not necessarily an insurmountable engineering or social problem, but it is one that requires local knowledge and investment. For the greater New Orleans region, the rising sea levels are but one factor together with the loss of alluvium washed out to sea by the channeled Mississippi, material which otherwise might be deposited along the way, shoring up the coast and nurturing the wetlands protective zones. Deposits of nitrogen and other chemicals from fertilizer run off and perhaps other sources create hypoxia, or dead zones, in the Gulf. The slumping of land is also due to depressurization from offshore oil drilling, further contributing to loss of wetlands (Bourne 2004).

We come thus full circle in these first narratives of our nature. "Catastrophe" and "deep play" open windows onto our responses, passions, and meaning structures. They help us see ourselves as particularly puny microorganisms in the larger scales of the universe and our multiple worlds or frames of reference. Even very small organisms, we learn from ecological studies, have cascading effects that can change larger-scale systems (Wolhforth [citing Ed Lorenz] 2004: 149).

Second Natures: German Modes of Production, French Parliaments of Things, and American Regulatory Sciences.

Minimata, Love Canal, Bhopal, Chernobyl, and Woburn form a different series of engagements with the complexity of our environment and nature than do earthquakes, hurricanes, and tsunamis. They have to do with our chemical industries, our bodies, and our engagements with high-hazard, high-consequence missions, including medicine and public health, aeronautics and space flight, and nuclear industries. It was Friedrich Hegel and his generation that would conceptualize the transitions between the first and second industrial revolutions who elaborated the notion that men and women create around themselves a reworked nature, a second nature, a technological and cultural nature that is increasingly difficult to separate from nostalgias for a lost, primal, and mythic first nature. In literature and rhetoric, this lost pastoral was used to criticize and critique industrial, urban society (Marx 1964).[4]

But it is within the politically "green" lineage of concern—from Rachel Carson and Barry Commoner on in the United States of the 1960s and from the election in 1983 of the Greens in Germany—that a different register of work has emerged, probing for the voluntaristic,

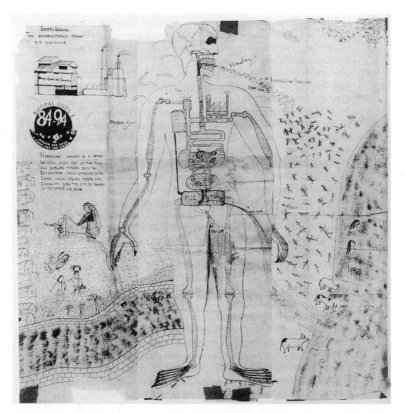

26. *Chouhan's Demon*, painting by T. R. Chouhan. "The Unforgettable Night" represents a demon that spews poison and people and crushes everything under its feet. The demon's body harbors Union Carbide's plant in Bhopal, India. The demon's bowels are the methyl isocyanate storage tank. Reprinted with permission of T. R. Chouhan. Photo by Richard A. Chase.

politically organized ways in which society could be reorganized to protect itself from the dark sides of its own production. While there are striking parallels across countries in the processual or dramaturgical responses to industrial disasters that affect the environment and public health across national boundaries (Reich 1991), there are also dramatic differences in cultural politics, in the presuppositions of how political decisions should be legitimately resolved: Sheila Jasanoff (2005) calls these "civic epistemologies"; and in the none routine and unstable coalitions of actors "called forth" by particular conjunctures of crises, social pressures, and double-bind commitments: Kim Fortun (2001) calls these "enunciatory communities."

The concept of "enunciatory communities" constituted in the vortex of contradictory demands helps make clear the importance of dialogical accounts (multiple play of arguments [logi] across [dia] interests, values, perspectives) that are often pushed into the background of monological expert summaries. In the Bhopal case, to take the double-binds of three of the key enunciatory communities, the Indian state attempted to represent the victims and at the same time publicly assert the hospitality of India to foreign capital; the women's association of gas-injured families asserted women's agency and yet had to recruit a male leader to talk to New Delhi, a leader who unfortunately fell into a typical male patriarchal mode of leadership antithetical to the women's organization; the lawyers for the gas-injured needed to appeal the dismissal of their suit in New York against Union Carbide on jurisdictional grounds (and that trying the case outside India implied the courts there were not competent) while at the same time asserting that their clients would be subject to a double standard and less compensation in courts in India.

Enunciatory communities and dialogical narrative formats are among the conceptual tools that can register and incorporate the multiple points of view that are required in *real time* lest complex social systems under crisis conditions break down. The best known of these formulations is, perhaps, Ulrich Beck's notion that we are entering a second-order modernization, coordinated and governed through new, reflexive social institutions. We increasingly live, he argues, in risk societies producing risks and dangers that are not calculable in the way the insurance industry constructed actuarial tables for factory accidents in the nineteenth century. Beck's narrative begins as a delightful, almost parodic, reprise of Marx's language on the transformation of feudal modes of production into industrial capitalist ones. It has the same doubleness of rhetoric, being simultaneously hortatory for a politics without which the transformation cannot occur, and descriptive of the internal institutional pressures to save old capitalist and bureaucratic forms from their brittleness and simplistic rationalities. Marx's notion of new modes of production arising from the accumulated pressures and contradictions of older modes of production is adapted by Beck to frame a structural account of shifts and changes.

Similar accounts arise out of green politics and regulatory sciences more generally in so-called Mode Two knowledge (Gibbons et al. 1994) or "post-normal" science (Funtowicz and Ravetz 1992), in the cosmopolitics of global harmonization conventions (Kuo 2005), and perhaps in the more philosophically eccentric tradition of French "political ecology" (Latour 2004; Serres 1990; Whiteside 2002).

Beck's elegant argument is that our chemical and nuclear industrial processes, among others, are producing risks we cannot see without scientific instruments, risks that respect no political or class boundaries and whose causality and thus liability is hard to trace. In preindustrial society, risks were largely not man-made. In industrial society insurance systems were based on understandings of systematic causation and statistical probabilities, so that rules of liability and compensation could be devised. But in risk society, risks accumulate slowly, are not limited in time and space, affect future generations, and are often testable only after the fact. The globe thus becomes used as a laboratory for toxic waste, the spread of illness vectors, and cascades of nonlinear causalities that make accountability diffuse and rules of polluter pays hard to enforce. In such circumstances corporate behavior becomes a shell game of defensive actions, as in publicizing the risks of another industry—the nuclear industry, for example, publicizing the ozone hole—or identifying sacrificial substances or products like the catalytic converter in automobiles as the answer to the destruction of the forests. The ad campaigns so generated contribute to wild swings in public moods between hysteria and cynicism. Politicians are urged to make dramatic policies based on such mood swings. There is growth of "parapublic" expert bodies to contain public anxiety and often to narrow and contain public debate. The logic of social divisions is reorganized, tourist industries, for instance, being opposed to chemical industries (the Po Valley is Beck's example).

These and many other systematic features of difference between industrial and risk society are elaborated by Beck for the 1980s (in *Risk Society*, 1986), in an updated transnational set of observations for the 1990s (in *What Is Globalization?*, 1997), and in three volumes for the early twenty-first century (*Power in the Global Age*, 2002a, *The Cosmopolitan Vision*, 2004a, and *Cosmopolitan Europe*, 2004b). Some of these features contribute to the decay and brittleness of legacy industrial society institutions. For instance, demands for ever-higher standards of scientific accuracy and causal linkage can be used to minimize risk and the need to take counteraction (Aaron Wildavsky's *But Is It True?*, 1995, is an example). But other features militate toward reparative and potentially transformative institutional forces such as pressures toward green production and the use of consumerism to drive ecological consciousness: rights of consumers to clean air and water, increasing market segments for organic food, citizen pressure toward mobilization of socially administered security.

One of the key features of these new institutional forms is reflexive social organizations which are able to integrate and use input from many different positions in society rather than relying on isolated top-down expertise of policy planners, factory designers, or laboratory scientists.

Minimata, Love Canal, Woburn, and Bhopal all are case examples of the agonistic battles to evolve reflexive social organizations. The dramatological pattern of citizens having to struggle against older corporate and bureaucratic structures is one of citizens noticing cancer clusters or what seems patterned illnesses, demanding from the state epidemiological surveys, being denied by the state and corporate authorities on the ground that the alleged causality is impossible, that the industrial processes in question were carefully constructed in the lab (for Italy, Japan, and the United States, see Reich 1991). That shop floor practices are frequently different from lab practices is often overlooked and denied, and in the case of the Union Carbide plant in Bhopal, of course, safety features were being dismantled as the entire plant was scheduled to be closed and moved. Citizens thus are forced to find scientists and epidemiologists who can collect sufficiently rigorous data to stand up in court, and once this barrier is passed, a long and arduous community organizing process must be launched to get remediation, restitution, compensation, and medical and other help. In the Minimata case, the effort was still ongoing after thirty years; in the Bhopal case, new charges were filed on the twentieth anniversary; and in Woburn, community activists are still fighting after twenty years.

Love Canal resulted in the formation of a toxic chemical clearinghouse alliance for communities across the country. Superfund legislation in the United States mandated Citizen Action Panels, providing the citizens some funding for hiring technical experts in their battles with corporations, military installations, and government facilities. Tactics of both citizen organizing and corporate defense have evolved over time. In the Louisiana chemical corridor, older civil rights organizing traditions helped with environmental organizing, only to be countered by petroleum companies' organizing of their own allegedly grassroots organizations (Allen 2003), a tactic which is the subject of at least one corporate how-to guide (Greife and Linsky 1995; see also Rampton and Stauber 2001). The Bhopal case involved litigation in the United States as well as India, and the parallels with struggles over Union Carbide's plant in Institute, West Virginia, illustrate that the Bhopal struggles were not merely "third world backwardness." In West Virginia, capital was less mobile, but labor was made mobile, Mexican labor being brought in to stop local union organizing. The post-9/11 concerns about terrorism reversed the drive toward right-to-know posting on the Internet for local residents of emission re-leases and worst-case scenarios (Fortun 2001; Perrow 2007).

Still, the argument for second-order modernization or reflexive so-cial institutions remains vital and more general than these particular cases of breakdown. Funtowicz and Ravetz note that "policy-relevant science," or what Jasanoff more felicitously calls "regulatory science," operates differently from normal science (in Thomas Kuhn's sense) or even consultancy science, in which there is thought to be an application of available knowledge to well-characterized problems: instead, highly uncertain, contested knowledge is generated in support of health, safety, and environmental decisions, and this requires a quite different sort of peer review, one that is extended to multiple stakeholders.

One of the most intractable (and hence interesting) of such re-negotiations of governance of environmentally damaged and hazard-ous areas is described in Joe Masco's study of the lands surrounding the Los Alamos National Laboratory (2006). Masco identifies quite different legal resources, perspectives, traditions, and data collection among the Los Alamos scientists, whose past hiding of facts has lost them credibility as objective stewards; Pueblos and Nuevomexicanos, both of whom are dependent upon Los Alamos for jobs; Anglos, often employing a romantic New Age environmentalism that is discon-nected from local political economies; and Washington bureaucrats. No longer is Los Alamos—or the University of California, as operator of Los Alamos—or Washington in control of all information and legal standing. This example should provide a comparative probe for other such sites around the world and connects the institutional reflections of this section with the shifts in environmental management and cli-mate warming debates in which the Inuit are engaged (see note 3).

The degree to which local knowledges, tacit skills, and intuition build up over long periods of practice and experience is critical to the flexibility and robustness of complex systems, whether they are tradi-tional knowledges, as with the Pueblo and Inuit, or situated on the shop floor of nuclear power and chemical plants (Perin 2004, Fortun 2001) or large engineering projects such as the space shuttle (Vaughan 1997) or in medical operating theaters and emergency disaster relief organizations. These are arenas that will repay detailed ethnographic attention in the coming years as the sites of some of the most conse-quential of ethical decision making. Philosophically (epistemologi-cally, methodologically), if not practically, the French tradition of po-litical ecology and what Bruno Latour calls the "parliament of things" can perhaps help keep thinking in this arena from falling into overly simple formulations. In sixteenth-century France, weevils and beetles were put on trial, accused by villagers of destroying their crops. Trials were held for insects, reptiles, rats, mice, leeches. Even dolphins were excommunicated for blocking navigation in a port (Ferry 1992: x).

The idea of natural contracts in French tradition has been picked up by Michel Serres (1990) but not so much as a matter of rights and standing in court, as in the famous law review article "Should Trees Have Standing?" (Stone 1972, also cited by Ferry 1992: xvii). Rather, Serres points out social contract theory in political philosophy was implicitly local, taking nature as given and as available for appropriation. As technological extensions make human reach global, this implicit relation to the environment encounters new forms of feedback and resistance. Human societies need to move from positions of parasitism to ones of symbiosis with natural cycles. Serres's notion of a natural contract, Kerry Whiteside explains, is not an ethical act in which people come to an agreement, nor is it grounded in a view of a pre-existing nature which is given judicial recognition (as in the sixteenth-century examples), but it is rather a literal *con-trahere* (gathering together), as in the image of tightening the ropes of the rigging of a sailboat, "a complex set of constraints and freedoms in which each element receives information through every adjustment" (Whiteside 2002: ch. 4).

Latour's "political ecology" focuses this French tradition of thought as one of shifting competences among "mélanges of things that transcend human control and of actions imputable to mankind" (Whiteside 2002: ch. 4; Latour 2004). Whereas premoderns sacrilized nature and feared nature's wrath, moderns attempted to create purified worlds they could control in science and politics. Today, however, Latour suggests, hybrids have broken through these efforts at purification: global warming, nuclear waste, and genetically engineered plants are among some of these unruly mélanges. In his provocative formulation, he suggests that what is needed is to give such hybrids or mélanges seats in our parliaments and representative assemblies, a parliament of things. The point seems to be that already all such things are matters of controversy and disputation among scientists, but also among human rights activists, ecologists, government agencies, and others. These backstage wars of position (to adopt a Gramscian formula) and negotiations need to be made visible, explicit, and part of our open representative assemblies. Latour insists that there is no nature independent of human interests and practices that might be used as a standard for preservation or restoration, that life is always in an experimental mode, and that what we need to pay attention to are the mediating instruments, inscriptions, and practices that form what we call objects.

There is an institutional move here, which perhaps can be seen if read together with Foucault's trajectories and assemblages of biopower. The modern creation of disciplines—labor/economics, language/linguistics, life/biology—for Foucault begins with the collection of social statistics, which then can be used by the state to discipline both bodies and populations. Other material devices such as the arrangements of prisons, schools, and clinics contribute to the construction of such disciplining. Latour pays attention to the material assemblages of things and people, the "mélanges of things that transcend human control and of actions imputable to mankind" in his studies of the rise of bacteriology (Pasteur's carefully staged public demonstrations; the creation of the laboratory as an obligatory point of passage; the reversal of ratios of power between farmers and scientists), of intelligent transportation systems (the shifting coalitions enrolled to make a futuristic technological system come into being or, in this case, fail to come into being), and of the constitutional court which adjudicates new laws in quite different fashion than science would.

Latour suggests that the parliament of things allows the contours of hybridization or mélange composition to be observed, and that the "moral effect" comes from not applying apriori ethical schemas but from a slowing down and modernization of the production of hybrids. This is not unlike the idea of "slow-motion" ethnography that Wen-Hua Kuo uses in his recent dissertation on the International Conference on Harmonization (ICH) of clinical trials among the United States, the European Union, and Japan (2005). At issue for Japan is the claim that because Japanese bodies are different in nature from European ones (drug dosages, for instance, are often adjusted), clinical trials must use Japanese bodies. In part this is an obvious political economy ploy to create a space for a Japanese clinical trial industry and to block pharmaceutical companies based in the United States and Europe from dominating the market. But by patiently examining the exchanges at ICH meetings step by step, the arguments about the state of the pharmaceutical market in Japan, and how clinical trials are done there, Kuo tries to show that more is at stake, that a hybridization of medical culture is at issue. Japan also is positioning itself to become an obligatory point of passage for larger regional and global markets with the idea of building a genomics database (that other Asian countries can ill afford).

In all these cases—chemical industry industrial accidents, nuclear accidents, and biological safety and efficacy—unitary expertise narratives seem increasingly less robust than dialogic (not two-person, but dia-logics, cross-arguments) ones involving persons who are differentially located, hold different stakeholder interests, and, in Fortun's terminology, are enmeshed in different "enunciatory communities."

Nature Inside Out: The Double Career of Bioethics in Cultures of Trust, Procedure, and Skepticism

Beyond second natures, we are now, via genomics and proteonomics, polymer engineering, material sciences, and other new molecular and nano-technologies, entering the promises of regenerative medicine, of rebuilding our natures inside out. The story of the remaking of our natures inside out—from cellular, genetic, or tissue level up, using technological manipulations too small to be seen by the naked eye, revealed thus only through the mediation of scientific instruments and graphical interfaces, and also heavily mediated and interpreted by advertising technologies on the part of companies on the one hand, and religious groups on the other—contains at least four moments. First, there is the evolution of institutions of regulation in their various public sphere settings. England, Jasanoff (2005) argues, relies heavily on trust in experts to test and establish regulatory rules, while Germany relies more on procedural correctness and the United States on litigation. These presuppositions about how decisions must be made are embedded in historically contrasting institutional developments.

Second, there are the contrasting policy outcomes, as in the application of the precautionary principle for genetically modified (GM) organisms in Europe versus "good science" calculations of probabilities and risk in the United States. The former is more cautious and more embedded in German procedural and bureaucratic traditions. American entrepreneurial traditions view the precautionary principle as inhibiting investment and market support for innovation and development of new technologies. In the case of stem cells, the House of Lords in England voted to permit cloning of human stem cells at the same time that President George W. Bush, on the advice of Senator Bill Frist, blocked federal spending on stem cells research except for the use of already existing stem cell lines (which proved to number fewer and fewer usable lines as time went on, and mostly unsuitable for research on human diseases because immortalized in mouse cells). In England a "pre-embryo" category (to fourteen days) was accepted by the House of Lords, whereas in the United States the term "embryo" or

27. The structural biologist Jinhua Wang demonstrates with his hand how his team solved a key component of the structure of Human CD4, the receptor on helper T cells for the human immunodeficiency virus (HIV) (published in *Nature* 348, no. 6300 [November 29, 1990]: 411–18). Structural biologists often use their bodies as well as their hands to demonstrate and viscerally imagine protein folds. See Natasha Myers 2007 for a discussion of how this works in pedagogy, in discussions among  colleagues, and most creatively in solving new protein structures by "reaching through" the computer screen and feeling how the folds must fall into place, a "feeling for the organism" as biologists at least since August Weismann have said. Folding the body in mimesis of the protein foldings associated with solving protein structures is a distinct skill from that of crystallizing proteins ("having green fingers"). Not everyone with one of these skills has the other. Various imaging models are used, including atom-by-atom balls, electron density maps, and cartoons like the one on the monitor behind Wang. The cartoons are particularly useful for describing the folds. Nowadays these are three-dimensional rotatable models. Wang is showing where a ridge on CD4 provides a hot spot binding site for HIV glycoprotein 120, the initial step in viral entry leading to a fusion of viral and T cell membranes. It involves the key binding residue Phe43 at the top right corner of the CD4 molecule (highlighted on the screen) forming a mini-beta ribbon. Gp120 competes with major histocompatibility complex (MHC), binding a thousand times more strongly than MHC, covering more surface area of CD4, and thus disabling the helper T cell's ability to fend off the virus: hence the name acquired immune deficiency syndrome (AIDS).

This image thus illustrates at least three features: the use of the flexibility of one's body to imagine and explore microscopic elements of the body; shifting and complementary modes of modeling nature; reimagining nature from inside out and health or illness from microinteractions to macro ones.

Jinhua Wang is known not only for the CD-4 work, but also for working out structures of many important cell surface receptors. In the 1970s he was part of the team of Chinese researchers who solved the first protein crystal structure of insulin in China. He is one of the Chinese national scientists to join the Harvard faculty and continues to maintain an interest in training Chinese postdoctoral fellows who return to work in China. With many thanks to Jinhua Wang of the Dana-Farber Cancer Institute. Photo by M. Fischer.

even "unborn child" was dominant because stem cells were often obtained from otherwise discarded invitro fertilization (IVF) procedures. Bush's Presidential Commission on Bioethics not so subtly reframed "reproductive cloning" into "cloning to produce children," shifting the connotations away from reproductive rights; and "therapeutic cloning" into "cloning for biomedical research," shifting connotations away from therapy toward experimental uncertainty and lack of control.

Third, deliberative democratic forms have evolved in such a way that they are not only different from country to country, but also now have considerable histories of international treaties, conventions, arbitrations, and adaptation of rules from one another. National Institutes of Health (NIH) rules on the handling of recombinant DNA after the Asilomar Conference in 1975 were widely adopted by other countries, and today clinical trial facilities in India and elsewhere follow NIH protocols closely so as to be able to provide services for companies dependent on the American market. On the other hand, good manufacturing practice (GMP) rules for therapeutic cell technologies (e.g. stem cells for bone marrow transplant) differ somewhat between the U.S. Food and Drug Administration (FDA) specifications and those of the European Union.

Fourth, the battles of marketing campaigns to control the semiotics of new drugs and other biotechnologies—as in the above example of "pre-embyros" versus "unborn children"—can sharply affect the understandings and the political room for maneuver of physicians, patients, politicians, and others. Indeed, all four moments involve the boundary work of what is natural or unnatural, of the relation between what can and what should be done, and between what is socially, not just ideally, possible and what is socially preventable and does not return by another route.

In the popular press and public discourse, many concerns surrounding molecular biology techniques—beginning in the mid-1970s with the breakthrough in recombinant DNA and proceeding subsequently to the biotechnology revolution of the 1980s, assisted reproduction technologies, genetic engineering, genomics, the promises of individualized therapies, and now the nuclear transfer technologies of therapeutic and potentially somatic stem cell cloning—focus on potential confusions and blurrings of categories: What is your kinship if your genetic material is cloned from so and so? Should organ transplant donors and recipients have any moral tie? What would be the status of living with xenotransplant organs: e.g., would one have to live with lifelong monitoring, and could that be ethically enforced? Will human-assisted gene transfer among plants, and potentially among mammals, change the course of evolution?

Anthropologically and sociologically more interesting, however, I think, are the coproductions of social venues for decision making as these technologies are shaped, because it is in these slow-motion, recursive, repetitive, and contested settings that new ethical stakes become visible, moral systems are developed, fears are distinguished from real danger, and utopian hopes are separated from real possibilities. Most popular accounts of the evolution of regulatory institutions for dealing with social, ethical, and legal concerns are chronological and have a sense that there is self-correcting, gradual social learning toward flexible, adaptable, second-order modernization or reflexive institutions. But the work of Jasanoff (2005) and Gottweis (1998) reminds that civic epistemologies, moral traditions, and cultural politics look different in different countries. Morevover, the work of Biehl (2005, 2007), Farmer (1990, 1999, 2003), Fortun (2001), Kuo (2005), Petryna (2002), Sunder Rajan (2006), and others reminds that global politics (variously called the New World Order, neoliberalism, empire, globalization) also have effects that reach far down into the fates of localities and individuals.

Ethical, legal, and social issues (ELSi) is the formula used by the Human Genome Project of the 1990s, which set aside a small percentage of money for discussions about these issues, but these concerns go back to efforts to regulate and provide oversight for the use of human subjects in experimentation (Nuremburg 1945, Helsinki 1964, Beecher Report 1966, Tuskegee syphilis experiment belatedly exposed by the *New York Times* in 1972), which produced institutional review board (IRB) oversight for U.S. federally funded research. More broadly these concerns led to the introduction of "bioethics," a term coined in 1970 by Van Rensselaer Potter and fostered by the founding of the Hastings Center (1969), the Kennedy Institute of Ethics at Georgetown University (1971), the issuing of the Belmont Report in 1983, which established the three ethical standards of respect for persons, beneficence, and social justice, and the Presidential Commission for the Study of Ethical Problems in Medicine and Biomedical and Behavioral Research (1980–83). Potter meant "bioethics" to refer to biology and values, encompassing medicine, environment, public health, and spirituality (Moreno 2005). But the term was instead rapidly professionalized into a focus on informed consent and the rights of individual patients. This was a period when the frontiers of medical knowledge were shifting from how to cure or prevent infectious diseases to chronic diseases as the key problem of first world medicine. In medical ethics, it was the time of a shift to an emphasis on patient autonomy (ibid.).

Professionalized bioethics has been severely criticized for being captured by medical schools and more recently by pharmaceutical and biotech companies to provide the ethical veneer to practices they wish to pursue; it has also been criticized by social medicine proponents for stressing individualist ethics over concerns with access, inequality, and social justice.

Yet, as Jasanoff suggests, a funny thing happened on the way to the forum. As biotechnology in the 1980s moved from laboratory research and the early containment fears of escape of new recombinant DNA organisms to the marketplace, civil society also appropriated bioethics as a vehicle for gaining a voice in policy and ethical oversight. Hence the "double career" of bioethics: a formal, professionalized form and a more open, public sphere one. Jasanoff suggests, moreover, that these public sphere forms work through different civic epistemologies in England, Germany, and the United States, which she tags with the shorthand labels, respectively, trust, procedure, and skepticism.

In the 1970s public concerns over escape of genetically engineered organisms from the laboratory and over the ecological and evolutionary implications of transferring DNA from one species to another were handled by calling for a self-imposed moratorium. Then, at the Asilomar Conference in 1975, regulatory controls were proposed that were made into NIH guidelines. By 1979 the debate over the safety of recombinant DNA research had been contained (to resurface later, however, in Germany and Switzerland regarding bovine growth hormone). As experience accumulated, the NIH guidelines were gradually relaxed. Jasanoff suggests that the experts at the time were not able to conceive that in the future this technology might destabilize kinship or farmers' rights to replant seeds. An important feature of such parapolitical modes of control (presidential commissions, National Academy of Science studies, etc.) is the way in which they narrow what is to be considered public discord and thereby contain it. As technologies move into the marketplace, Jasanoff suggests, these techniques of containment become subject to public scrutiny and contestation, and at the same time broad ideological positions become more nuanced.

Nineteen eighty seems a key year in the United States in the dramatically changing institutional and patronage environments for the biosciences and for the creation of a new power-knowledge nexus emerging around the new biotechnology institutions. Four arenas were changing: modes of funding, parapolitical modes of expert regulation and containment of disputes, market forces and the relation of scientists to the market (no longer distancing themselves), and legal changes. Nineteen eighty was the year of the Bayh-Dole Act, which fostered rapid development of new biotechnologies by encouraging NIH-funded research at universities to be patented and licensed to the private sector. The Supreme Court case of *Diamond v. Chakrabarty* in 1980 opened the floodgates to patenting of life forms as manufactured products, processes, and new composition of matter. Another Supreme Court case, *Foundation on Economic Trends (Jeremy Rifkin) v. Heckler*, found that the public interest was not satisfied by expert review but required more open deliberative processes. The Superfund legislation of 1980—the Comprehensive Environmental Response, Compensation, and Liability Act, or CERCLA—provided for Citizen Action Panels and Remediation Review Boards and appropriated some funding to empower citizens to hire their own experts independent of government agencies.

This is a period in which advertising becomes more and more sophisticated as well. Copyright, patent, trademark, and brand names, Donna Haraway (1997) suggests, are the "genders" (generic marks, "directional signals on maps of power and knowledge") of "asymmetrical, congealed processes which must be constantly revivified in law and commerce," especially in our new world of creating transuranic elements and transgenetic organisms. In 1991 the FDA streamlined approvals for biotech food by introducing the criterion of "substantial equivalence." Review would be triggered only if there was an indication that substitutes or changes in nutritional content of a product could cause toxic or allergic reactions. What is important, the FDA reasoned, is the product, not how it is made.

This rationale required revision in the struggles of the 1990s over organic food labeling. As Jasanoff points out, in 1993 recombinant bovine growth hormone (rBGH), or bovine somatotropin (rBST), was approved despite its questionable need in a dairy industry that already produced surpluses, its likely contribution to aid only large producers (and drive out small ones), and its possible effects of mastitis in the animals. Monsanto opposed labeling of rBST. Labeling what is (un)-natural is a powerful tactic in building a market. Lack of labeling means it is harder for consumers to opt out. Labeling, Monsanto argued, could negatively affect markets by suggesting that something was wrong. The civic epistemological form that opposition in the United States was forced to take was of developing counterscientific arguments: rBST is not obviously substantially equivalent because it has additional amino acid subunits (linker proteins).

Similar struggles over the labeling of organic foods in the 1990s eventually conceded to the growing organics lobbies that irradiation and use of sewage sludge as fertilizer could not be labeled organic. Not only the product was important, but also how it was made. By the time this point was conceded by the U.S. Department of Agriculture (USDA), organic farming had become a six-billion-dollar industry that provided 2 percent of the nation's food and was growing 20 percent a year (Jasanoff 2005).

Opposition to GM foods, Jasanoff points out, was always part of wider issues such as agricultural practices, nature preservation, and integrity of food and national styles of civic epistemology or cultural politics. In England, the bovine spongiform encephalopathy (BSE), or mad cow, crisis in 1996 created a breakdown in confidence in the Ministry of Agriculture, Fisheries, and Food and contributed to the defeat of the Conservative Party. New deliberative democratic forums were created to rebuild confidence under the new Labour Party. A public debate, "GM Nation?," was organized through a web site and over six hundred meetings, publicized via the Genewatch web site. A parallel citizens' jury was organized by Greenpeace with the University of Newcastle and the Consumers' Association, with the sponsorship of Unilever and the Co-op Group. The Prime Minister's Strategy Unit did a cost-benefit analysis with seminars on "Shocks and Surprises." The government chief science advisor organized an expert advisory process with open meetings and expanded panel membership. Jasanoff notes that in view of these displays of scientific and social unknowns, the government announcement of March 2004 to go ahead with commercial growing of GM crops came as surprise and betrayal.

At issue in civic epistemological terms in England was the culture of trust in experts, whereas in the United States, as illustrated in the FlavrSavr, rBST, and organic foods examples, the market (and litigation) became the arbiter, as it did again in the furor over insect-resistant StarLink corn animal feed (developed by Aventis Crop Sciences) which found its way into food products. The civic furor forced the recall of three hundred food products. In Germany, experiments with public hearings introduced after the Greens entered Parliament were gradually withdrawn, as the political tactics of environmentalists became obstructionary—e.g., demanding all documents to be translated into German and other delaying tactics. Not only was it argued that public hearings only make sense if they actually function as a Habermasian public sphere, requiring an informed public. Questions of "Whose rationality?" increasingly were foreclosed—e.g., the inadmissibility in the rBST debate of whether it would hurt small businesses. Issues of process in Germany are tied, Jasanoff argues, to constitutional requirements that the state protect human dignity. In Germany's stem cell debates, the Christian Democratic Union and Christian Social Union parties invoked this doctrine to forbid even the import of embryonic stem cells created abroad. The Social Democratic Party voted to allow the importing of stem cells for research on the grounds that they were not embryos proper and so do not require the same level of protection. The reprehensible act had already taken place, and the cells were not capable of becoming fully human. The Free Democratic Party voted to allow imports because they could benefit humanity and would not harm human beings or potential human beings. The law that passed in 2002 allowed import under supervision by an expert committee established by the Robert Koch Institute. This moved the discussion back into a contained deliberative environment, away from public debate.

Jasanoff summarizes part of her three-nation comparative study by saying that the rise of bioethics illustrates Foucault's account of how the growth of biopower ropes ethical debates into larger national narratives. In the United States the narrative is one of medical and agricultural innovation, in Germany it is one of building a principled *Rechtsstaat*, or state rule of law, and in the United Kingdom it is for maintaining a well-ordered space for research (Jasanoff 2005: ch. 7). The European Union becomes not so much a source of higher level rulings as a political resource in federal and *Länder* (local state) negotiations. Wen-Hua Kuo's analysis of the International Conference on Harmonization of clinical trials reveals a similar pattern, with Taiwan forging a nonofficial mediating role based on a cadre of returned diasporic experts in biostatistics (2005).

I will end my effort in this section to write a "double helix" account of new challenges to our sense of the (un)natural coming from the new biotechnologies as well as of the institutions through which we recursively and repeatedly revisit and renegotiate our cognitive understandings and visceral feelings by thinking about xenotransplanation as deep play. It is a deep play of the fantasies of abolishing disease and immortalizing life, sometimes at the expense of human rights, informed consent, equity, and access.[5] The American physicists went ahead with the bomb for Nagasaki, as Robert Oppenheimer memorably put it, because it was "technically sweet." So too today physicians and patients often go ahead with heroic experimental trials because they are caught up in what Mary-Jo Good (1996, 1998, 2001) calls the "biotechical embrace," doing what technically can be done under the Hippocratic formulation of preserving and extending life because it can be done, sometimes at the expense of the good death. The Austrian cartoonist Manfred Dix captures some of the fantasies in the picture of a genetically engineered pig, altered to be already a huge sausage, and in his mutant monsters (think post-Chernobyl) who have voting rights.

Xenotransplanation is one site among the biotechnologies where, because the science is so hard, there is some time to experiment with some creative thinking about new institutions and new ways of bringing into being an informed citizenry on a global scale that can provide civil society oversight, accountability, and decision making. Fritz Bach's call for a moratorium on clinical trials provides an overview of some of the changing venues for ethical and policy deliberation. Old institutions of medical ethics seem insufficient. The promise of a supply of organs from pigs, primates, or other mammals for increasing numbers of patients on waiting lists for organs is the public justification for xenotransplantation research. The other promise is that such research expands basic immunological knowledge that will be helpful whether or not xenotransplanation emerges as better therapy than, say, regenerative medicine. On the other hand, the threat of xenosis— and specifically of known and possibly unknown retroviruses from pig populations—that could unleash a pandemic like HIV/AIDS, however small the risk, is not something that can be dealt with in medical ethics models of doctor–patient relations or hospital ethics committees, which negotiate patients' demands for heroic care versus doctors' judgments that such care is fruitless and will cause needless suffering, or even national-level regulatory institutions.

Older methods of self-regulation by scientists in the Asilomar style of dealing with the fears about recombinant DNA in the 1970s seem no longer possible or adequate, and the recent experience of Monsanto with the "terminator seed" in the controversies over genetically engineered crops shows that the refusal to engage in public consultation can lead at minimum to public relations fiascoes. Bach has been experimenting not only with education modules at the high school, church, and grassroots levels and with national committee structures at the political level in several countries in both the first and third worlds, but also with new modes of global, web-based public consultation seeded with a network of opinion leaders in various countries. It will be interesting to watch this and other experiments in new institution and public critical knowledge building, especially in an environment in which calls for even limited moratoriums draw the ire of those who find it harder to raise research money and venture capital to push the science further.

Bach's interventions have come a long way from the model of Asilomar in 1975 and the handling of concerns over recombinant DNA research in the 1970s. That trajectory is one of the changing possibilities for parapolitical modes of expert self-regulation and containment of disruptive disputes and public politics. At issue in many of the debates over biotechnologies are questions of public safety. But equally emotional is what people feel is natural. How fast can what is natural change within what Durkheim would have called the conscience collective or moral sensibility, what Jasanoff more recently calls civic epistemologies, and what is often called by moral conservatives the slippery slope (to which scientists often respond that we are always already on various slippery slopes). To deal with the slipperiness, we need to characterize it and understand it better, not try to black box it.

Companion Species: Animal Models, Sentinels, and Alterities

J. M. Coetzee's Tanner Lectures of 1997–98, published as *The Lives of Animals* in 1999, foregrounds the debates over "animal rights" but evokes in the wings four series of questions about just what the natures of animals are in relation to: (i) human genetics, evolutionary development, and transitional medical artifacts, such as oncomice, that promise regenerative medicine to replace the slash, poison, and burn of today's brute medicine; (ii) "the morality of the table," or human ecologies of food and illnesses such as obesity and diabetes (Schuessler 2003); (iii) sentinels of climate warming and habitat change; and (iv) coevolving species who repeatedly mirror our sense of being in the world in uncanny and refractory ways. Coetzee's Elizabeth Costello, mother of people like most of us, English professor, and animal rights moralizer stands in for Wendell Berry, Troy Duster, Jim Hightower, Winona LaDuke, Michael Pollan, Peter Singer, Vandava Shiva, and many others who both rightly and irritatingly remind us of the sins of the social systems in which we participate and are complicit (all contributors to *The Nation*'s special "Food Issue," 2006, 283:7). Costello argues that in tasting the flesh of living things we violate animal rights and may be tasting sin, a trope that interprets the biblical story of the tree of knowledge/life in a particularly masochistic way.

Sin and rights may not be the most appropriate terms for thinking about our animal relations. Animal models, animal sentinels, companion species, and phenomenologies of emotion may be much more appropriate. Literature and philosophy all too often use animals as symbolic tokens but betray a disabling lack of interest in actual animals, their socialities, their sensoria, or how to interact with them.

Thinking of lab animals and work animals, Haraway asks what would happen to our conceptual and ethical stances if we thought of responsibility in terms of the category of labor rather than rights. She complains about Deleuze's and Guattari's appropriations of wolf packs and particularly about their dismissal of pet and other animal training relations as being merely regressive narcissism, rather than as critical epistemological and ethical sites.

Similarly, Jacques Derrida points out that while philosophers attribute muteness and therefore often also melancholy to animals (e.g., Alice Kuzniar's 2006 *Melancholia's Dog*), it is the human philosophers whose language, calculus of responsibility, and responsiveness fail. At best, Derrida demonstrates, invoking his cat, it is the return gaze of the animal that provides philosophers with an optical space in which to contemplate key zero points of phenomenology—nausea, shame, suffering—for recovering bodily, nonoptical modes of being.

Haraway gently criticizes her younger self, the author of *Primate Visions*, for not having gone into the field with the primatologists as an anthropologist would have and thus for perhaps having slighted the noncognitive, but critical ways, in which people (primatologists in this case) have learned to interact with, respond to, and become included in the communication styles of animals. And so, I turn to animal models, animal sentinels, companion species, and phenomenologies of affective communication.

Animal Models, Experimental Systems, and (Un)Natural Kinds

In arguing quite rightly against genetic determinism, the biologist Stuart Newman (2006) argues quite dubiously in favor of a classical notion of "natural kinds." The notion of natural kinds seems hard to reconcile with contemporary ecological understandings or with the unfolding of knowledge within molecular biology itself. At issue are at least two troubling dilemmas: animal models in medical research and life forms as technological instruments. I will deal with the first dilemma together with Haraway's interventions on companion species, both lab animals and work animals. I will deal with the second dilemma together with animal sentinels, including viruses as cross-species delivery systems. But why would a biologist draw on natural kinds?[6]

Newman, a cell and development biologist with a Ph.D. in chemistry, makes two crucial claims: that "species are 'natural kinds' . . . because they exhibit causal homeostatic mechanisms" (2006: 35); and that an epigenic, or "plasticity-based 'phenotype first, genetic programs later' scenario, rather than the gradualist, gene-driven processes of neo-Darwinism, makes the whole enterprise of improving phenotype of plants and animals by genetic tinkering all but irrational" (2006: 41). The claims for evolutionary developmental biology against genetic fundamentalism are an important corrective to much hype in contemporary science and biotechnology. Still, this is only one area of transformative ideas about nature that are being both discovered and rewritten, in the sense of creating objects, materials, and biologicals that have not previously existed. Newman's caution about experiments that seem to jump across the slow testing of natural selection seems well taken. On the other hand, his formulation seems insufficiently open to the slow, incremental nature of the experimental discovery procedures he seems to argue against. The sciences involved are not easy, and the time they take should allow us to understand the self-organizing properties and constraints, including homeostatic ones.

Newman is correct that in arenas such as agriculture and ecology we desperately need to find alternatives to the self-destructive industrial organizations and financial drivers that destroy us body and soul, though, scientifically speaking, I do not have the vaguest clue as to what Newman means by "soul," perhaps another metaphorical legacy, like "natural kinds," of philosophies that no longer quite work in our contemporary world. Were we to call the metaphorical "soul" in the expression "body and soul" something like cultural options, it might be more open to further productive analysis of how we pursue our bio-technical socialities. To do this, it may be helpful to turn to animal sentinels and animal companions.

Animal Sentinels: Ecologies of Food, Illness, Biodiversity, and Climate Change.

The likelihood of an H5N1 avian flu pandemic has emerged in recent years as one of the most feared (or perhaps most hyped) of threats to human populations. It is a more dangerous virus than SARS, experience with which has already put public health authorities on alert about the critical need to report outbreaks and the self-defeating dangers of denial or hiding of cases. The H5N1 avian flu threat is belatedly recalling from repressed memory the precursor influenza of 1918 that killed millions around the globe. And it is one of a series of recent viruses and retroviruses, including HIV/AIDS, Ebola, and dengue, that cross species and reinscribe into our consciousness our symbiotic repertoires.

Viruses operate as double figures in both the popular and scientific imaginaries of nature: (i) as a figure of thought for a variety of biological processes that disturb the understanding of natural kinds, species, and evolutionary trees; (ii) as means of drug delivery and new materials fabrication, which reconfigure the sense of the boundaries of natural kinds into more permeable and new ecologies of interaction. As figures that disturb the understanding of natural kinds, viruses are one of a series that includes infectious agents (bacteria, viruses), symbiogenetic forms and parasites (e.g., the wasp-polydnavirus-caterpillar), jumping genes, and lateral transfer.[7] Understanding the molecular mechanisms of host-parasite interactions could lead to a variety of new, hopefully more biologically gentle therapies.

As biological tools, viruses are used as drug delivery vehicles, are part of the experimental and still-dangerous technology of genetic engineering, but they are also now being used in nanofabrication technologies. Viruses subvert their hosts to reproduce themselves, but we are now learning to repay the favor and turn them into new optics and electronic material assemblers. Angela Belcher's lab at MIT has produced the first virus-assembled nanoelectrode and virus-assembled battery and is working on a virus-based transistor. She bombards a semiconductor wafer with nontoxic viruses to see which react, looking for ones with the chemical functionality matching the target material. Once found, the genes of the virus are manipulated so that they make protein coats that collect molecules of cobalt oxide and gold. Once altered, the viruses are inserted in a bacterial host, which replicates or clones millions of copies. They align on a polymer surface to form ultrathin wires circa six nanometers, or six-billionths, of a meter. Because viruses are negatively charged, they can be layered between oppositely charged polymers to form thin, flexible sheets that serve as an anode. (Batteries are anodes and cathodes separated by electrolytes.) Nanowire structures are used to assemble thin lithium ion batteries (from the size of a grain of rice to that of a hearing aid battery). The reactions needed can all be done at room temperature and pressure. The energy density of these batteries is two to three times that of other batteries. By harnessing the electrostatic nature of the self-assembly process with the functional properties of the virus, highly ordered composite thin films combine the function of the virus and polymer systems.

Viruses, bacteria, parasites, and the like provide experimental systems for exploring the permeability and symbiotic repertoires of natural kinds. Comparative genomics tracks some of the commonalities across living forms. But it is really ecological studies that provide some of the most worrisome questions about our futures, both tracking cross-species transfers that simultaneously map ecologies of human practices and transfer of organisms (food habits, transporting rats unintentionally in ships, introducing rabbits and cane toads into new environments, where they take over) and cataloguing, regulating, and redirecting the destruction of biodiversity and climate change.

Mobilization around the term "biodiversity" dates from the National Forum on Biodiversity in 1986, sponsored by the National Academy of Sciences and the Smithsonian Institution, led by Walter Rosen and including such key figures as Paul Ehrlich, Ernst Meyer, Peter Raven, and E. O. Wilson. They announced, "The species extinction crisis is a threat to civilization second only to the threat of nuclear war" (Takacs 1996: 38). These already senior figures could afford to join the newly growing field of conservation biology that understood itself to be scholarly advocacy and was viewed for that reason with some apprehension by the National Academy.

At issue are a series of wonderful (for the anthropologist and science studies scholar) ambiguities about how to guesstimate the decline of biodiversity and what such concepts as ecological system, keystone species, or even species and habitat should mean. On the one hand, it is crucial to the enterprise to emphasize how little we know and how much research needs to be done on the functional role of species in ecosystems. Takacs quotes Raven: "We know so little about biodiversity, the interchangeability of biodiversity in communities and all the rest, that we don't know what the limits are" (1996: 88). At the extreme is Wilson's observation that "the little things that run the world" (bacteria and insects) are hardly evident on the endangered species lists, which involve either primarily large animals that humans relate to or small creatures that are useful to block environmentally destructive development that should be opposed on other grounds, but the Endangered Species Act of 1973 is the most available tool to hand.

On the other hand, the notion of biodiversity nevertheless gets around both the charge that proponents wildly inflate the estimated rates of extinction and the endless task of making a species-by-species case for ecological integrity when we do not really know what makes for such integrity: whether one should be protecting maximum genetic diversity, genetically distinct populations, communities of tightly integrated organisms or larger ecosystems. The use of protection for larger animals requiring larger home ranges can serve as an umbrella for other organisms.

Even so, there are ambiguities in managing populations through the use of such tools as minimal viable populations (MVP) size that could survive genetic drift or catastrophic events. Debates over culling and over defining ecosystems are inevitably political and draw in economic interests. Among the most interesting efforts to leverage political and economic interests and to make the market incentives work in a green direction is the Costa Rican experiment of commodifying biodiversity around pharmaceutical, ecotourist, and scholarly renewable indus-tries. Especially interesting is the idea of retraining rural local people to treat their environment as an intellectual resource, thereby reenchant-ing the environment in new ways, capturing traditional knowledges, and building computerized databases with their help.

Conceptually this expansive view of biodiversity and ecology leads to what Takacs calls metaphysical holism. Again, he quotes Raven: "Peace, social justice, human order, the protection of biodiversity, the production of or promotion of a stable biosphere are all inextricably interwoven" (1996: 96). Warwick Fox is quoted as saying the process is a "this-worldly realization of as expansive a sense of self as possible." This is on the surface unexceptionable but, as the case of Wilson increasingly makes clear, can be a kind of priestly calling on the part of sociobiologists convinced that encoded in our genes is a biophilia evolved in hunter-and-gatherer pasts that has undergone remarkably little evolution, culturally, institutionally, or otherwise.

While the trope of the "disappearance of nature," often attributed to Bill McKibben, turns out to be a nostalgic one—nature doesn't disap-pear, it changes, becomes impoverished, etc.—somewhat like the im-age of the pastoral used in the nineteenth century to critique industri-alization and its destruction of the wild, perhaps the most trenchant structural argument for the loss of biodiversity and thus the loss of sustainable complex "wild" ecosystems is that by Stephen Meyer (2006). He argues that while the earth will continue to teem with life, it will be an increasingly homogenized assemblage selected for com-patibility with human beings. He claims that the extinction rate is now over three thousand a year, while less than one new species appears a year; and thus within the next one hundred years half the earth's species and a quarter of the genetic stock will disappear.

The argument is a structural one. There is a hierarchy of three kinds of species: Weedy species are adaptive, flourish in a variety of ecological settings, switch easily between food types, breed prolifically, and often have their needs met more efficiently by humans: raccoon populations are five times more dense in suburbs than in the wild, aquatic plants like hydrilla thrive in waterways enriched with runoff from farms, suburbs, and sewage treatment facilities; rats and white-tailed deer reach pest proportions. Relic species do not thrive in human-dominated environments and survive either in isolated areas or as managed "boutique populations": African elephant, giant panda, Sumatran rhinoceros, most of Hawaii's indigenous plants. Ghost species continue to exist but are past the tipping point of population collapse: African lion, gray wolf, prairie dog. Meyer claims that 90 percent of the stocks of tuna and swordfish are gone—sturgeon, which used to populate the East Coast of the United States, have been gone for many years—and that more lions live as pets and in zoos in the United States (ten thousand) than worldwide in the wild (seven thousand).

Meyer argues that while various factors in this "dumbing down" seem manageable, once one understands their cumulative interactions they become unmanageable. While some ameliorative efforts seem to work—numbers of whooping crane are increasing, tigers in India's Sunderban forest seem stable—most prohibitory, or protection, regimes are focused on relics and ghosts; most refuges and reserves are too small and thus illusory; the slogan of sustainable communities is usually an anthropomorphic use policy based on calculations of how much can be harvested, not on ecological models, with the result that much is driven by global markets.

"The race," Meyer says, "to save the composition, structure and origin of biodiversity is over: we've lost." What we can and should do, he argues, is "to purge ourselves of the humanistic love affair with the wild, landscape, and aesthetics" and do research on the functions of what is here and how it lives.

However apocalyptic or not one judges the ecological and species extinction crisis to be, the sentinel feedback that is given to us by our animal and plant environment is not to be disregarded: obesity and diabetes (the foods we eat), endocrine hormone disrupters (the chemicals we ingest and inhale [Krimsky 2000; Wylie 2006; Norris and Carr 2006]), multiple chemical sensitivity syndromes (involving the conceptual conundra of deciphering and measuring incremental and interactively cumulative injuries), the emergence of new infectious cross-species diseases (Davis 2006), the succession of invasive species (such as imperator grasses in former tropical forests of Southeast Asia and the epidemic of rabbits in Australia), the devastation of tropical forests and possible disruption of the earth's carbon cycle, the softening of the tundra and the disturbance of whale and caribou migration in the Arctic (Wolhforth 2004), the use of freshwater dolphin censuses to measure the water quality of the Orinoco River (Lakhsmanan 2006).

Indeed, as the columnist Ellen Goodman trenchantly remarks, with rising consumer interest in free-range poultry and grass-fed meat as well as in restocking such animals as wild turkeys, "there is a growing premium on domestic animals that live more naturally . . . [and] an explosion of wild animals living more tamely" (2007).[8]

Companion Species: Research, Domesticated
and Wild Animals.

I return to Haraway's and Derrida's complaints that most of the literary and philosophical literatures that use animals to think with do not actually deal much with the actual lives of these animals.[9] They do not even deal with the anthropological literature on how cultures categorize, name, and use different classes of animals; how animals carry mythic armatures of ecological knowledge; or how affect gets attached to animal figures through structural positioning in classifications from the domestic to the wild.[10] Deleuze and Guattari create new philosophemes with animal categories—wolf pack as a figure for multiplicity, orchid-wasp figures for symbiosis—but at the expense of the "points of view" of animals, most grievously, as Haraway complains, the dismissal of pet and other training relations as merely regressive narcissism, rather than as overlapping arenas of differential phenomenologies.

In this context, Haraway is perhaps one of the most useful of thinkers at the moment, coming from the broad world of the history of biology and science studies, both in the trajectory of her career from *Primate Visions* (1989) to *When Species Meet* (2008) and in the unresolved struggles that research animals especially pose, struggles that will grow in public awareness as the importance of biotechnologies continue to expand. With Haraway, perhaps we can prepare the ground for how to intelligently think about the dilemmas of the real world of illness and death, killing and making live, and *responsiveness* to companion species of all sorts, a responsiveness that parallels but is not exactly the same as earlier ecological notions of feedback in systems that will collapse or deteriorate if the component flora and fauna are misused or destroyed.

In *Primate Visions,* Haraway took on the newly developing profession of primatology, as it began to use anthropological style fieldwork to study baboons, chimpanzees, lemurs, and then other animals in their natural habitats and societies, rather than in laboratories or artificial colonies. *Primate Visions* turned the tables on the researchers, exploring their intellectual genealogies, hierarchies, and, above all, the ways in which they projected human cultural concerns onto their nonhuman subjects of study. This was elegantly done by charting decade by decade how changing theories of primate sociality correlated with changing popular human cultural anxieties. Second, it focused attention on female primatologists, helping raise their profile in a male-dominated field but criticizing them, in a friendly, puzzled way, for buying into the then-faddish sociobiology. Thus, third, it contributed to the wider anthropological critique of sociobiology's importation of American folk theories of reproduction, competition, aggression, sexuality, and status and of sociobiology's crude genetic reductionism (long before one could even map the genome or begin to unravel the mediations of protein, cellular, and other functionalities). Fourth, it was an exemplary exercise, a tour de force, in using and keeping carefully distinguished popular culture materials about animals such as hunting and photo shooting in the wild; interview and archival materials on a science in formation; and the gradually growing positive knowledge gained about animals and their socialities.

It is quite in character that Haraway should, in her most recent work, reflect back on *Primate Visions* and gently criticize her younger self for not having gone into the field with the primatologists as an anthropologist would have and thus for perhaps having slighted the noncognitive but critical ways in which people—primatologists in this case—have learned to interact with, respond to, and become included in the communication styles of animals. In her "Manifesto for Cyborgs" (1985) and her volume *Simians, Cyborgs, and Women* (1991), Haraway began to speculate on mixed technical and biological systems that would lead to the creation of animals with human genes and illnesses for medical research such as the OncoMouse. In *Modest_Witness@Second_Millennium.FemaleMan©_Meets_OncoMouse™* (1997), her concerns with the relations between technologies, animals, and humans had evolved into a set of reflections on the grammar of these relations in material reality as well as conceptually. These grammatical relations were signaled in the focus on cyborg creatures such as the OncoMouse, a humanly modified genetic organism (unlike the original NASA mouse fitted with an osmotic pump) designed to aid in research on human diseases. The grammatical relations were signaled in the title of the book and in section titles, adapting the usages of the computerized information environment with which biology has become infiltrated, embedded, and facilitated.[11] And they were conceptually signaled by Haraway's neologism "material semiotic objects," that is, real-world objects whose coming into being configure the way our semiotic and symbolic worlds work. OncoMouse is not only a biological organism, but a legal one that generated court cases and new understandings of the intellectual property rights regime that in the 1980s transformed the doing of biology and biotechnologies.

At issue throughout is the challenge that biology is civics. The several strands of grammatical relations alluded to above are also markers of our civic politics. Copyright, trademark, and brand have become, she wrote in a brilliant *bon mot,* our genders, generic marks on maps of power and influence. One of the essays in that volume is on the material and biological crossings (and material-semiotic changes they help produce) of the DuPont Corporation in polymer chemistry (nylon, rayon, synthetics), transurenics (nuclear power), and the new world of transgenics—a cross-section of our changing first and second natures.

But it is with *The Companion Species Manifesto* (2003) that Haraway begins to signal three important new themes: that to mistake pets for children is to endanger both the human and the animal: alterity is real and needs to be worked with in any useful animal-human ethics; that species contain rich histories of coevolution with humans, in their biology, labor regimes, and pedigree (consumption-branded) regimes; and that living with and loving animals can be a way of learning to live and work with diversity. I am particularly struck in a chapter on laboratory animals in *When Species Meet* (2008) by the honesty of struggle with commitments that resist simultaneous and seamless closure. These commitments are to medicine, to science, and to the principle that animals should not suffer. Haraway commits herself to thinking about how the humans in the lab might work, think, and interact with their animals otherwise. (See figure 8 in chapter 2 and the discussion of S. T. Aygun.)

Animal models for medical research attract the ire of animal rights activists, but they are still thought by most biomedical researchers to be necessary, not yet replaceable by computer models, regenerative tissue engineering, or other techniques. Of particular interest for the discussions of the nature of animals is that many, if not most, laboratory animals are genetically modified artifacts. This is particularly true of research mice and rats, which, according to the journalist Jennifer Schuessler, make up 95 percent of research animals, although the range of animals as experimental systems extends from nematodes and Drosophila (fruit flies) to dogs, cats, and nonhuman primates, mainly monkeys imported from abroad (2003).

Of particular interest in the current context of arguments about the (un)natural is Haraway's observations that rights language seems philosophically inappropriate, even if occasionally legal initiatives on such grounds may have tactical value.[12] Some utilitarian rights arguments (Singer's, for example) invoke pain and suffering as phenomenological grounds on which rights might be attributed. But while Haraway also invokes animal suffering and affect, she recognizes their alterity, a point she makes through a series of anecdotes about dog training and collaboration in agility competitions as well as through contrasts between dog breeds.[13]

"Intersubjectivity," Haraway points out, "does not mean 'equality'... it does mean paying attention to the conjoined dance of face-to-face significant otherness." Again: "To regard a dog as a furry child" demeans both, setting up children to be bitten and dogs to be killed (2003: 37). Morevoer, dogs have been bred for different subjectivities: metaretrievers, bred for herding, are not interested in chasing balls on the beach but can be totally obsessed with chasing retrievers as they chase balls, attempting to block and herd them away from the balls. Border collies bred through generations of competitive sheep-herding trials, when shown on British television, became popular pets, but then also were frequently abandoned when the owners could not satisfy the dogs' needs. How to live ethically in such heterogeneous relationships, Haraway suggests, is a training ground in alterity.

Acknowledging the emotional dynamics or responsiveness of animals, she asks how the humans in the lab might work, think, and interact with their animals otherwise. One thinks here of Karin Knorr-Cetina's *Epistemic Cultures* (1999), which shows not only how laboratories modify the organisms they form into experimental systems, but also how the human investigators are also remade into socialities whose dynamics are quite different in a high-energy physics lab from those of a molecular biology lab. At issue is that for the time being, in the laboratory as in nature, killing and illness are required.[14] As a first step, Haraway wonders about involving more hemophiliacs in the laboratory work of hemophiliac dogs used to study hemophilia.

Phenomenologies of Affective Communication

The philosophemes of Wittgenstein's lion, Levinas's dog Bobby, and Derrida's cat indicate something similar. The philosopher Stanley Cavell interprets the encounter with Wittgenstein's "mute lion" ("If a lion could talk, we would not understand him") as generating self-reflexivity: "Sooner or later it makes us wonder what we conceive knowledge to be" (quoted in Wolfe 2003: 3). But the dog and horse trainer Vicki Hearne objects: the lion is reticent, not mute, and it has presence; indeed, "if the chimpanzee Washoe learns human language and still remains dangerous," Cavell's epistemological mirror becomes confusing (ibid., 4).[15] For Hearne and Haraway, "the shared language of animal training makes possible a common world between beings with vastly different phenomenologies" (ibid: 5).

Levinas's dog Bobby, the "last Kantian in Germany,"[16] recognized and restored the humanity of the prisoners in Nazi camp 1492 (uncannily the date of Columbus's discovery and of the expulsion of Muslims and Jews from Granada) through a responsiveness that the Nazis denied in their stripping of the prisoners down to their presumptive species biological animality (a zero point undone by Goebels, "I decide who is Jewish"). As Haraway echoes in relatively more civilized circumstances, Levinas does not fail to acknowledge that humans, too, eat meat. But against Heidegger's callous leveling in 1949 of the difference between genocide and industrial agriculture, Levinas uses the juxtaposition of the two to raise questions about the various and different claims upon consciousness. As Derrida would more explicitly thematize, Heidegger's obtuseness is an object lesson in the ideology of difference. Levinas uses the fact of our consuming flesh as a zero point that exposes how the "I" is dependent on others, prior to distinctions between ego and nonego. Derrida radicalizes this: "There is no such thing as animality, but only a regime of differences without opposition" ("On Reading Heidegger," quoted in Clark 1997: 175).

Nausea and shame rivet us to our bodies and have served as phenomenological touchstones from Kierkegaard to Derrida for thinking about how the physiological body provides a substrate for consciousness. What philosophers fail to do is to expand this insight toward comparative ethology or even historical change. Derrida at least elaborates on Levinas using the story of his cat, whose gaze, when Derrida is naked, brings on a kind of shame, of revealed intimacy. As with Wittgenstein's lion, this could be taken to merely mean that there is a beastiary at the origins of philosophy, that the cat's gaze instills self-consciousness.

But Derrida speaks of the animal's point of view, something occluded by Cavell's reading and by philosophical discourse generally. "Believing that human conceptions of the animal are stuck in a language which generally does animals few favors, Derrida puns *animaux* into '*animots*,' presenting these language-laden composite creatures as something close to . . . botched taxidermy" (Baker 2000: 74). "Animots" puns on *mot* (Fr. "word"). Haraway's more material-semiotic version is to speak of dogs as *metaplasms* (Greek *metaplasmos*, remodeling or remolding), having separated from wolves, according to mitochondrial studies, some fifty thousand to one hundred fifty thousand years ago ("at the dawn of homo sapiens"), feeding off human-discarded food and thus coevolving with us.

Derrida's cat and his shame also index something like Wittgenstein's forms of life, language games, and metalinguistic meanings carried by the kinesthetics and pragmatics of communication. ("If you want to know what the bark of a dog 'means' you look at his lips, the hair on the back of his neck, his tail and so on"; and "If you say to a girl, 'I love you,' she is likely to pay more attention to the accompanying kinesics and paralinguistics than to the words themselves" [Bateson 1972: 370, 374, cited in Wolfe 2003: 40]). For the anthropologist, this indexing between the physiological and phenomenological carries also historically differentiated and socially formed anxieties.

Kathryn Milun (2006), using a century and a half of clinical reports on agoraphobia as an index of changing pressures on the collective technobody—empty squares at the heart of rebuilt European cities, urban freeways, and shopping malls—and the closely associated descriptions of nausea and shame in the phenomenological existentialisms of the late nineteenth century and early twentieth—Kierkegaard's objectless anxiety, Edvard Munch's agoraphobic painting *The Scream*, Dostoyevsky's agoraphobic *Underground Man*, Heidegger's abyss of death as the ground of authenticity, Levinas's analysis of nausea and shame, Sartre's nausea and nothingness—points out that these function as zero signs. Zero signs refer only to themselves. They occlude an organizing dimension, like the vanishing point in one-point linear perspective drawings, an invisible point that establishes the grid around which all other signs in its field are organized. Such zero points and their occluded organizing functions, as Levinas and Derrida delight in exposing, open up spaces for dissension, recover social contexts occluded by the zero sign (Milun 2006: 36).

Such is the function of companionate species, who, through comparative ethology, comparative genomics, animal experimental models, and sentinels of ecological deterioration and health, open up for us frozen categories, relationships, knowledges, and bases for ethical reconsideration.

Conclusions: The Four Trials of Anthropologies to Come

Durkheim, at the end of *The Elementary Forms of Religious Life*, argued that religion and science do not stand in a relationship of replacement, but rather that at the boundaries of what each society takes to be empirically knowable (science) are questions that demand answers supplied by religion, itself seen as a product of deeply socially structured relationships. E. E. Evans-Pritchard called this the two-spear theory of causality. Both science and religion are thus always changing with respect to one another. Return to religion, Derrida points out in his commentary on Kant's similar notion of religion at the limits of reason, is never a return to the same but more like respiration, a return after taking a break, a renewal of inquiry. (*Re-ligere*, to relink, to tie back, is one etymology of religion, a reknotting perhaps in the Lacanian sense.) As with Derrida's *animots*, Levinas worries that anthropomorphism, allegory, and other figural aspects of language can collapse crucial differences.[17] And yet, of course, some of the art of differences and *différances* in Levinas and Derrida comes from the multiplying of meaningful figurations. I am intrigued by the seeping-through of religious traces in the ambiguous denials/acknowledgments of E. O. Wilson's Baptist fundamentalisms (genetic, biophilia), Haraway's Catholicism (material-semiotic incarnational symbols, the "Christian realism" which she claims to decipher in much American science), Levinas's and Derrida's Judaism (expulsion, errancy of signification), or indeed in the title of the collection *Without Nature* (King and Albertson forthcoming), which I take to be (albeit on the surface McKibbon's notion of "end of nature") worrying the notions of natural law ("without nature").

My inquiry into the empirical places where ethical, political, and policy-making decisions are reformulated, adjudicated, and negotiated is an anthropologist's experimental effort to locate where contemporary moral thought could come into play with our emerging technosciences. This chapter has grouped these into four trials or places of moral testing: from nature as a place of context or environment; to nature as contingency, accident, and risk; nature as nano- and molecular culturing, cultivation, *Bildung*, from the inside out and bottom up; and nature as dealing with and accepting alterity.

Old metaphysical words such as "soul" or "presence" have meaning in today's world only by taking on a weak metaphorical or translational cast. They gesture toward helping people work through and clarify the conflicts in their lives and among the social forces in which they participate. Parables and stories have always been part of this tradition. They help point us to interconnections in society, to the ecological complexity of changing things, rather than to allowing the market, competition, and accumulation to define the nature of things. In this sense the old stories of Moses and Khizr still apply: We humans are always in possession only of partial knowledge (that is what we have to work with), with which we fashion our moral robustness (a social thing) as well as our ethics (a personal thing). We are tested with these tools in repetitive, recursive, ever slightly changing tournaments and ways.

So too the internal debates of religious traditions more generally provide narrative forms for ethnographic analysis of the social interests at stake. Like justice as an aspiration in contrast to actual decisions of the law, the terms "value," "ethics," and "morals" operate as aspirations, as regulatory ideas, as odd-job terms, generally left unspecified, and specified only in the context of particular cases. When dogmatized and claimed to be instantiated or perfectly embodied, they often undermine their own credibility. Just as minority opinions in legal decisions sometimes become majority ones in the future, so too with the formulations of religious thought. In the scholastic traditions of the three monotheistic civilizations, in the logical debate traditions of Buddhism, Hinduism, and Jainism, and in the parable traditions of Native American traditions, there is always dialectical room for alternative interpretation, particularly at the limits of reason and tradition. The old Aristotelian modes—visceral emotion, cognitive reason, and character—are institutionalized today as advertising, science and technology, and civic epistemologies.

To explore and define these positions, I have deployed in this chapter the notions of (1) narratives (Benjamin's catastrophes, Geertz's "deep play"); (2) second natures (modes of production, parliaments of things, litigations and contestatory, emergent "enunciatory communities"); (3) nature inside out (new biologies and biotechnologies, new forums for social definition of what is (un)natural); and (4) expansion of symbiotic repertoires with our animal familiars, analogues, and coevolutionary species.

I have used the dia-logues (cross-arguments) between comparative ethology, animal training, comparative genomics, and other emerging scientific fields, on the one hand, and phenomenological, philosophical, and psychiatric notions of agoraphobia, nausea and shame, and pleasure to come back to the question of the collective technobody with which I began in the first section.

My interest is in the changing "coevolution" of sites of dilemmas and ethical-political decision making, and charting emergent reflexive social institutions of second-order modernities such as regulatory forums differently handled by different civic epistemologies; tournaments of ethics rounds in medical settings, including changing definitions of mental and social health as agoraphobia (once defined in relation to space, now defined by pharmaceuticals as panic attacks without reference to space); to sites of interspecies and intercultural negotiation of radically different phenomenologies and social consciousnesses.

What might all this mean for an *anthropos* and an anthropology to come. Let me sum up with five hypotheses or queries:

1. Historically speaking, "nature" is an odd-job word, unlike "culture," which has an analytic history in anthropology as a quasi-technical frame of analysis (chapter 1). "Nature" no doubt has a history (e.g. Coates 1998) from classical times through the natural law tradition but in more recent times increasingly has lost its foundational referents and instead is a covering label for the paradoxical ambiguity with which I began (nature is that which is both our other and our "essential" self); and as our knowledge expands and reconfigures itself (biochemistry, neuroscience, comparative genomics, etc.) this ambiguity also expands.

2. Cross-culturally speaking, only in a heavily Christianized or "globalatinized"[18] world can one speak of the "death of God" or the dissolution of a foundational "natural law" (without nature). One need not be a holy fool, Sufi saint, Hindu guru, Jain monk, zen or dialectical Buddhist, Talmudist, or Spinozan to recognize that "God" diffuses into nature, leaving traces of divinity everywhere and that the decisions of the world are in the hands of the creatures and forces of the world. Thus to speak of God's death or absence seems not to make any sense, nor does the nineteenth-century fear (intensified by World War I) that without rules, metaphorized in traditional moral language as God, nihilism and chaos would ensue. "Death of God" and "without nature" are European philosophemes dating from before the mid-twentieth century.

3. In the *anthropos* and anthropology to come, nature can be no more than the output of humble, partial, experimental systems, meaning this less as a Darwinian idea than as a contemporary interoperable, kludgy, work-around, molecular, nano, and genetic, algorithmic, but also tissue and polymer conglomerate view, in which our epistemology is always already entwined, mediated, mutated, or transduced into (dis)-harmonic registers of Lévi-Strauss-like symphonies of meaning.

4. At issue here is a structure of feeling that as the world changes, as the scientific and pragmatic knowledges expand, our very vocabulary also shifts, increasingly inflected by the sciences and technologies of our time and the epistemologies and instrumentations through which they are elaborated. We need to embrace these languages and interrogate them for their "zero points" and other naturalizing and occluding features, in order to keep them, as well as our ethical stances in the world, lively and informative.[19]

5. An anthropology to come will need to be collaborative and intercultural, not only across traditional cultures, but across cultures of specialization, and it will need not only to incorporate the lively lan-

28. *Roadrunner in Tennis Shoes*, a woodcarving by Matt Yellowman Diné. While coyote is the trickster icon of choice by which Donna Haraway represents the wiliness of nature, roadrunner is equally a figure that moves between the pragmatic and the inspired. In Disney–Warner Brothers' Wile Coyote–Roadrunner tales by the animator Chuck Jones, Roadrunner trips up Coyote by stepping aside and observing "chaos engulfing his pursuer and nemesis, Wile Coyote" (Boje 1998). Boje uses the Wile Coyote–Roadrunner pair as a metaphor for the "cat and mouse" game between Nike Corporation and entrepreneurial activists who contest Nike's labor and environmental practices. A clan totem, the fast-running (up to fifteen miles an hour), occasionally low-flying roadrunner feeds off insects, scorpions, and even rattlesnakes, in which activity he parallels, in a down-to-earth way, the high-flying eagle. (Eagle is often pictured flying high with a snake in its talons. Roadrunner uses its strong beak to peck snakes.) Coyote nowadays, often pictured in kitsch greeting cards and cartoons nonchalantly wearing shades, is moving into suburban Los Angeles and other cities, a sentinel of the disappearing border between urban and wilderness (see Mike Davis's entertaining account [1998]). Roadrunner is everywhere from California to Kansas. But it is the tennis shoes and comic determination that moved me to buy this carving in (appropriately) the Tucson airport. (On Native American humor, see Fischer 1986, Ryan 1999; on the logic of animals as metaphorical operators, see Lévi-Strauss 1962, 1964: "Bird Chorus," 1967). Photo by M. Fischer.

guages of the new technosciences, but also reread, redecipher, and redeploy the palimpsests of traditional knowledges. Such collaboration is not easy: as with animal training, it involves translation, exchange, and responsiveness to different phenomenologies, epistemolologies, ways of doing, and ways of knowing.

Body Marks (Bestial/Natural/Divine) | **4**

An Essay on the Social and Biotechnological Imaginaries,

1920–2008, and Bodies to Come

Bestial, Natural, Divine Body Marks

The soul . . . is produced permanently around, on, within the body.
—**MICHEL FOUCAULT** *Discipline and Punish*

From the spectacular semiosis of the Renaissance body—albeit a body in pain—modernity fashions a new body for its own labor-intensive and empirical epoch. Modernity creates the status of two new bodies. . . . Concealed within the first body, [the second] is the diagrammatic, fibrous, structured, organized object of investigation . . . the object of the disciplinary interventions which will thenceforth sanitize it, train it, and prepare it for labor. . . . Throughout the culture of the modern period, the figure of the individual has been haunted by the figure of the artificial man . . . ghosted by the interference which that possibility offers to the task of sustaining the original sense of human authenticity itself.—**FRANCIS BARKER**, *The Tremulous Private Body*

. . . as was made terribly clear by the last war, which was an attempt at new and unprecedented commingling with the cosmic powers. Human multitudes, gases, electrical forces were hurled into the open country, high-frequency currents coursed through the landscape, new constellations rose in the sky, aerial space and ocean depths thundered with propellers, and everywhere sacrificial shafts were dug in Mother Earth. This immense wooing of the cosmos was enacted for the first time on a planetary scale—that is, in the spirit of technology. . . . In the nights of the annihilation of the last war, the frame of mankind was shaken by a feeling that resembled the bliss of the epileptic. And the revolts that followed it were the first attempt of mankind to bring the new [techno-cosmic] body under its control.—**WALTER BENJAMIN**, "To the Planetarium," *One Way Street*

The more we tinker and experiment with the body, the more the nature of bestiality and divinity are redefined, the more bodily mark-

ings take on new connectivities, significations, intensities, and transductions. We have always been able to read the aging body for traces
of experience, but increasingly we now enter the age of biological
sensibility.

Four score and a few years (1920–2008) from the concussions and
crutches of World War I through cancers produced by Cold War
radioactive tests, to endocrine disruptors, leukemias, and kidney diseases produced by pesticides, industrial and military toxic runoffs;
from *Wretched of the Earth* conditions producing *Black Face, White
Masks* and torture in North Africa, Latin America, Middle Eastern
and Asian "dirty" wars to post-traumatic stress syndromes of the Vietnam War, Tamil Tiger and Islamic jihad refunctioning of the body for
suicide bombings, and twenty-first century First Gulf War syndromes
and Second Gulf War enhanced prosthetic developments—these biologically traumatizing eighty-plus years have left new signifying marks
reverberating within, on, and projected through the bestial, divine,
natural body. Experimental sciences and engineering technologies attempt cosmic-cosmetic repair with lipstick and makeup, new organs,
prostheses, xenotransplants, autologous and regenerative techniques,
pharmakons, filmic and networked gymnasia of the senses. The demi-
urgical filmic eye is one of a series of prosthetic or cyborgian eyes that
allows passage between *Leib* (body) and *Körper* (corpus), "the first
oriented to humanity, the second to divinity."[1] The filmic and other
prosthetic eyes attempt to repair the inaccessibility of the body to
ourselves, the inability to see our face, our back, our whole head. The
filmic eye, like our senses, is productive of phantasms as well as illu-
sionary realisms by way of its artifactual editing, cutting, and suturing.

If time ("since 1920") suggests questions of the new, the sequence
bestial, natural, divine suggests questions of evolution, emergence,
and illness and healing, if not older languages of the great chain of
being and merit cycles of reincarnation. The bestial does boundary
work on one side of the natural body's ambi-valence, signaling internal
disease processes (the wolf of lupus, the crab of cancer), viral/retro-
viral species crossings (the fevers of mosquito-transmitted malaria,
HIV/AIDS from hybrid monkey SIVs,[2] Influenza A [H5N1] from birds
[avian flu], fears of porcine retroviruses should we pursue xenotransplanation), and parasite-host and prion relations out of control (mad
cow disease, or bovine spongiform encephalopathy, BSE). The divine
does boundary work on the other side: the miracles of healing, the
touch of ecstasy, empowerment, feelings of transcendence (illustrated
in Michelangelo's divine hand of God touching Adam's outstretched
finger and Eric Avery's photograph of the "space of healing" in reat-

taching a hand), the transports and transformations of drugs (oscillating between the demonic and the divine), and the extensions of electromechanical media (cochlear implants, lenses, the body electric, the cyborgian body). The natural body is an ambivalent term, meaning both our other and ourselves. Even as ourselves (my character, my body, my selfhood), our nature is often other, that which we attempt to separate ourselves from and which we are dependent upon, which we attempt to control but which always escapes our reach.

In matters of cultural imaginaries the dance between science and the arts can provide a dialectical cultural critique: science and engineering interrogating the current conditions of possibility; art exploring techniques, tools, and concepts in contexts unjustified beyond the aesthetic. In this dance, the arts are often early adopters of technique, yet often lag behind the frontiers of what can be done and of what scientists themselves plan and dream. They can serve as advance publicity to ready the public imagination as not only a fort-da mechanism of anxiety reduction, nor as just a carnival of the technoscientific, but also reminding the scientists of the real-world constraints and difficulties of implementation by exploring embedded demonic fears and anxieties of technologies going wrong, being misused ("in the wrong hands," exacerbating inequalities, discrimination), and unintended social consequences.

How new either the marks or their modes of inscription are is a minor key harmonic of this chapter along with its twin, the much-contested philosophical question of what "emergent forms of life" might mean.[3] Body marks since 1920 might involve at least three forms of the new. First, body marks inscribe cultural historicities, as in Michel Foucault's and Francis Barker's contrast of Renaissance and modern French epistemes. Second, body marks may be psychologically, ritually, and physically tropic, as in the writing of Flannery O'Connor (drawing upon Catholic corporeal theology, while suffering the wolf/lupus within) and the discourses of "reclaiming the body" by body modification artists in the 1990s, as described by the ethnographer Victoria Pitts (2003), or in any number of historically inflected anthropological accounts of ritual process, whether Catholic or Ndembu (Turner 1967, 1968, 1969, 1974), Jewish or Islamic (Crapanzano 1980; Derrida 1991a; Cixous 1975, 2001), Hindu or Buddhist (Obeysekere 1981).[4] Less historically inflected baseline measures for such historical inscriptions of the corporeal are provided by (i) Victor Turner's survey in "Bodily Marks" (1987) of growth and aging, clothing and headgear, masks and ornaments, permanent tattoo scarification and cicatrization, circumcision and clitorectomy, face and body painting, and the stigmata and

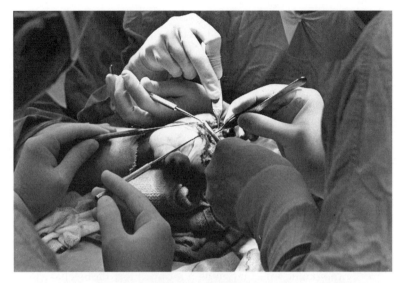

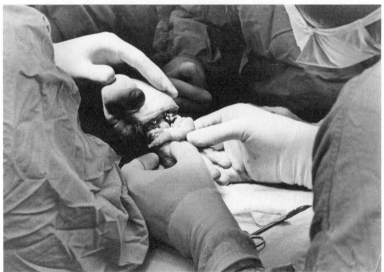

29.1 and 29.2. "Space of Healing," 1977. Photographs by Eric Avery.

signs of religious elevation; (ii) the *History of Tattooing* (1925) by Wilfred Hamby; and (iii) semiotic, hermeneutical, and cultural explications of the meanings of bodily marks in particular societies (e.g., Andrew and Marilyn Strathern on Mount Hagen in New Guinea; Terence Turner on the Chikris of Brazil; and Victor Turner's account in *Drums of Affliction* of cicatrization in Ndembu girls' puberty rituals, including erotic Braille around the navel "'to catch a man,' by giving him enhanced sexual pleasure when he runs his hands over them" and parallel cuts above the breast line "to deny the lover," one representing her premarital lover, the other her husband-to-be, the former never to be revealed to the latter so that they not fight (1968: 249).

A third measure of the new or of historically marking is contained in Walter Benjamin's suggestion that while the ancients' discourse with the cosmos was through the bodily experiences of ecstatic trance, twentieth-century technologies are transforming the sensorium, the collective technobody, biological exchanges (viruses, retroviruses, transfusions, organ transplants, grafts, genetic engineering, pharmakons, and biologicals), affect, and emotion. The new here is marked and inscribed not only by the technologies of war, but also by contemporary biotechnologies.

Traditional body markings—bestial, natural, and divine—remain potent in many contemporary worlds, as anyone dealing with the spirits that possess in Indonesia, the Persian Gulf, or Amazonia may attest, as they are potent also in snakebites as signs among snake handlers in the American Bible Belt, glossalalia among new Christians in Kenya, and snakelike dreadlocks among the ecstatic Buddhist-Hindu priests of Sri Lanka's new urban cults (whose psychoanalytic case histories are charted by Gananath Obeysekere in his cross-cultural, contrastively and comparatively titled and argued *Medusa's Hair*). Yet all these have their historically inflected new markings as well. Vincent Crapanzano dismisses the label "masochism," suggested by a psychoanalyst, for the ecstatic mortification of the flesh during Hamadsha trance dancing, not only because the conceptual category is misapplied from one culture to another, but also phenomenologically because it is too crude and undifferentiated for the different dance steps and breathing rhythms that make the body feel different, invoking different spirits (and, I would add, different historical indexicals).

"Divine eye," "natural skin," and "bestial body" are notational names for the parts of this chapter. These are crossed by the three forms of the new as well as by recombinatorial modes of emergence and boundary work. Markings on and by the body torque and twist together like

Möbius strips, Klein bottles, or knot theory creating the imaginaries of subjectivations and subjectivities.

The Divine Eye: Eye(I)ing the Bestial, Natural, Divine

The *eye*, acquiring cyclopean proportions when seen reversely through the magnifying glass before it, is not still . . . it might be said that the eye quivers . . . the gray-blue *iris* . . . also moves, though with a more calculated exactitude than the greater ocular structure. It moves economically and without caprice, as does the geometer. The circle at the center of the iris, the dark void known as the *pupil*, appears to be moving, but, in fact, the inside edges of the iris's striated membrane are contracting and relaxing, varying the magnitude of light information allowed to stream through the eye's lens and into the posterior chamber, to disperse through and illumine the thick jelly of the vitreous body, to bombard the retina's millions of photoreceptors.—MICHAEL MEJIA, *Forgetfulness*

Never still, marking and being marked, the eye is an organ both of transfer (Greek: metaphor) and interaction (affect, emotion, recognition, eye contact or avoidance, eye play, winks, and other signals). From the ancient mythic third eye of wisdom, the blind seer's insight, and cyclopean monstrosity to contemporary "posthuman" and cyborgian prostheses (colored contacts, shades, jewelers' loupes, newscasters' teleprompters, dentists' binocular microscopes, biologists' autonomic tunneling microscopes [ATM], scanning tunneling microscopes [STM], medical positron emission tomography [PET], computed tomography [CT], and magnetic resonance imaging [MRI], soldiers' night-vision gun sights and goggles, surgeons' and game players' virtual reality [VR] headsets), both the evil eye and the "postnatural" technoeye are never still, marking, noting, inscribing, glancing, hidden, opaque, glassy, jealous, envious, lecherous, inquisitive, probing, shifty, reconstructing rather than directly seeing, transferring, projecting, hallucinating, vehicle of psychic transference, missing the mark.[5]

The postmodern Islamic eye has come to the fore—posting back and forth between the modernist drive for women's equality and the modernist-fundamentalist reaction of reveiling—peeking out from its *hejab* seductively, marking gendered spaces, and in artful protest. Shirin Neshat has put her mark on the Islamic eye, filling it with calligraphic verses of martyrdom and eroticism, divine and physical love, witnessing (*shahid*: witness, martyr) to women's agency, resistance, oppression, female power under and out of control, marking contested moralities. The Islamic eye literalizes gendered spaces and interactions that elsewhere are more veiled: a woman makes eye contact with passing males but does not hold it lest it be taken as an invitation—a natural cue, say apologists, bestial assertion of power, say some feminists. Black-veiled female traffic becomes calligraphic form, ambiguously (un)surveillable, (un)readable by male eyes. In Elia Suleiman's satirical film *Divine Intervention* (2003), shot at the Qalandiya checkpoint between Jerusalem and Ramallah, a young Palestinian woman stylishly and sexily dressed, perhaps Muslim or maybe Christian, with determined eyes set straight ahead becomes a femme fatale upsetting the conventions of Israeli border guards, who, open-jawed at her boldness and beauty, allow her to pass unchallenged, as two visual puns underscore the point: their guard tower collapses, and she morphs into a Hong Kong aerobatic or ninja woman warrior as balloons with Yasser Arafat's face on them float across the border. Traces of divine intervention, undoing the best-laid plans and boundary work of men, linger in the drifting balloons, distracting beauty, and the filmic eye panning from close-up and intimate to long shots above the fray. *Memoirs of a Geisha* (2005) produces the same results when the novice practices until a male eye is so distracted by her beauty that he crashes his vegetable cart.

The eye is already marked in the 1920s by shock, the shock of the transgressive, the war, the psychosexually disturbed, the modern, the urban, and the cinematic. The shock of the eye is nowhere more sharply inscribed as a cultural icon than in Luis Buñuel's and Salvador Dali's film from 1928 *Un Chien Andalou*, portraying the terrifying slicing of an eyeball with a razor. George Bataille's *Story of the Eye* (1928), published the same year, further explored the disturbed/disturbing specular zones of indistinction of eros/pornography/sexual disorder, life/death, morality/amorality, sacred/profane, and emotions "beyond good and evil" in registers both of illness/dementia and "postdeath of God" sociality. Produced as part of his analysis with Adrien Borel, drawing upon childhood obsessions with his syphilitic (blind, paralytic) father and the amorality of dementia as well as debauchery, the book's authorship remained pseudonymic during his lifetime, functioning amphibiously across the divides of what is secret and public, noir and exposed, surrealist and antisurrealist modalities (Surya 1992: 93–103 *passim*). In his entry for "eye" in the journal *Documents* (1929), Bataille links the eye to horror, cutting, seduction, cannibalism, appropriation, and the uncanny. Bataille's Nietzschean eye, in the 1930s, eventually recognizes and agitates to counter the

30. "Offered Eyes" (1993). RC print and ink, 40 X 60 in. ©1993 Shirin Neshat. Photo by Plauto. Courtesy Barbara Gladstone.

rising choreographies of fascist mass cults that claimed heightened superman (*Übermensch*) experience through battle-hardening the body and submitting to a single will.[6] He anticipates the biology of excess and multiplicity, reacting against economistic scarcity as the dominant model for life.

In efforts to probe forms of seeing and interaction that can repair or extend this traumatized, diseased, and limited human (natural) eye, the terrain of existential, philosophical, and anthropological challenge moves ever more toward prosthetic cyborgian eyes and biological research on different kinds of eyes in the evolutionary palate. Snakes, for instance, see visually and with infrared sensors that create images of heat emitted from objects. The receptor cells on the sides of a rattlesnake's head can detect wavelengths of ten micrometers—ten times the power of the best current human-made sensors—and are self-repairing. Might such "eyes" help detect the temperature difference between cancerous hot tumors and healthy tissue?[7] Or might the vibrations of tumor cells provide such heat signatures sonically to a "listening eye," transducing vibrations into sound into images?[8]

The mammalian vertebrate eye has a cameralike structure with a spherical vitreous humor (a transparent gel that Buñuel's cut-eye image seems to spill) as focusing lens and an iris for regulating the intensity of light, and it detects light via a panel of retinal cells that convert light into electrical signals. Cats can focus the lens into slits and reflect light from the back of the retina, allowing better night vision as well as the reflective glow of their eyes in the dark. The brain of a newborn ferret can be rewired to lead electrical connections from the back of the eyes to auditory centers in the brain, which then begin to resemble visual centers in the cortex and allow the animal to see.[9]

An experimental VOICE technology developed by Peter Meijer at Philips Laboratories mounts a small webcam on the bridge of sunglasses that can scan the field of vision from right to left and convert height to pitch and brightness to loudness, producing a soundscape (through stereo ear buds) that allows several blind users to gain a rudimentary sense of sight that improves with habituation.[10] This "rerouting of the senses," Meijer claims, works better than retinal implants, also currently under development.[11] Steve Mann's earlier cyborg WearCom (eye tap camera and reality mediator), one of a series of experiments in WearCom (wearable computers), was a sunglasses-like device that records people's faces and matches them to biographical information from previous interactions so as to function as a memory device for those of us who forget or want faster recall. (It, and more recent eye taps, are linked also to the web to allow others to share in the wearer's vision.) Steve Furness's virtual retinal display (VRD) is a somewhat similar device that casts images onto the retina so that they float over normal vision, providing neurosurgeons, for instance, with brain scans over the surgical area on which they are working, or pilots with additional virtual flight scenes over their cockpit view (Geary 2002: ch. 2). In a sense, Meijer draws upon the body's resources, while Mann and Furness place the body within a distributed, neural-like, electronic network, paralleling in more medical or practical modalities the more bestial body arts of Orlan and Stelarc (see below).

Multiple functionality, rewiring, and different modes of seeing promise both prosthetic repair, supplementation, and extension of the eye and also potential directed mutation. Drosophila genetics allows eyes to be multiplied or placed in novel positions; Mann's composite "bug eyes" assemble multiple fragmented views.

The focusing lens of the mammalian eye functions like a camera, the modernist technology par excellence of the early twentieth century and of the 1920s' technology of the *Kino-eye* (1924) and *Kino-Pravda* (a series of shorts in the 1920s that collaged fragments of reality to make visible truths not normally visible to the natural eye) of Dziga Vertov (neé Denis Abramovich Kaufman). Filmic technologies—mi-

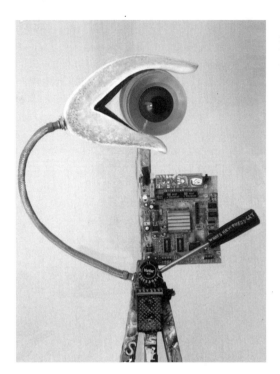

31. *The Journalist.* Sculpture by Parviz Yashar. Photo by Parviz Yashar.

crocinematography of cell movement,[12] telescope and microscope lenses, later ATM, MRI, PET, and other visual technologies—allowed the human eye and brain to experience what could never have been seen before: beyond, below, slower, faster, farther than the naked capacities of the human eye; cells, atoms, interiors of bodies and organs, distant planets and galaxies, daily traffic for crime control in urban spaces through networked video cameras, but also the night vision of guns, helicopter gunships, goggles, and remote control targeting.

This eye, the filmic eye, opens new aesthetic possibilities (montage, speed, derangement), including the simulation of science fiction bestial fears from Dr. Moreau's experiments with organ transplantation[13] and urban noir films (the detective eye) to the varied latter-day expressions of Friedrich Nietzsche's vision of the hypergrowth of eyes and brain perched on spindly remnant limbs and torso, an image of cognition gone wild, bestial and even, in a latter-day version, downloadable to a silicon chip,[14] which through a fantasy of escape from the body is a peculiarly perverse vision of the divine, a soulless variant of Neoplatonic, Illuminationist, and Enlightenment emanations, digitally purified.

The natural eye marked by and marking evil is revealed and embodied in John Howard Griffin's midcentury observation, "[A] 'hate stare' drew my attention like a magnet. . . . You see a kind of insanity, something so obscene the very obscenity of it (rather than its threat) terrifies you.... I felt like saying: 'What in God's name are you doing to yourself?'" (1961: 51–52). In God's name: the divine eye, of course, is a shifter and a metaphor for insight transcending and immanent in the everyday. When it becomes hypostasized in "god-tricks," as Haraway puts it (the view from nowhere, or from Heaven), in the fantasies of omniscient surveillance and control, it goes awry (see also Edwards 1996 on closed worlds). The eye as a biological nexus, a complex of signal transducers, a space of inquiry, a door of perception can be divinely open and can see such things as "a kind of insanity, something so obscene the very obscenity of it (rather than its threat) terrifies you."

The Natural Skin: Epidermal Scars, Tattoos, Pigmenting the Body

I have carried this number all my life, that I and others should never forget. Now before I die, I wish to expunge it. Not through any technique that would eliminate it, but through a superabundance in which it will be lost. It will become just one grain of sand upon a beach. I wish to be covered, from head to toe, in one mighty number. *This* number [indicating the number on his arm], in becoming just six consecutive digits within the greater number will be relieved of the weight of evil it has borne until now. Yet [simultaneously] the greater number will be what it is through the presence of that part within its whole. That is inescapable.—MICHAEL WESTLAKE, *Imaginary Women*

In body modification, you can take control of what you otherwise could not. —ANDREW, East Coast body modifier, quoted in Victoria Pitts, *In the Flesh*

The skin is one of the first successes of tissue engineering, of getting cells to grow on artificial scaffolds, of helping the body repair itself, the hope for regenerative medicine, an aid for burn victims. The skin, of course, is also a writing surface of scars, tattoos, pigmentation, legacies of encounters with the world. The surface of the body is the register in which the marks of biological crossings between species and technologies make their presence visible: from neurodermatological signs, retroviral, viral, and bacterial host-parasite relations to the fashioning of new organs for both the interior and the surface of the body: skin grafts for burn victims and tissue-engineered ears for infants born without as well as various forms of prostheses. Bioart follows along behind the advances of science as well as projecting ahead.

In 1959 John Howard Griffin—a photographer, novelist, physician, musician, sufferer of a twelve-year temporary blindness, rescuer of

Austrian Jews—chemically altered his skin color and visited racially segregated states for his book *Black Like Me* (1961). Hung in effigy in his home state of Texas, he moved to Mexico for nine months before returning to Fort Worth.[15] In 2006 Ice Cube, the rapper, actor, and filmmaker, with Hollywood makeup artist Keith Vanderlaan, and R. J. Cutler, produced a six-week documentary television series, *Black, White*, in which a black family is transformed with wigs and makeup into a white family, and a white family is transformed into black (Ryan 2006). First time as tragedy, second time not as farce but as "reality television" entertainment.[16]

The skin, its tattoos (marks of community and initiation) and brandings (of slaves and prisoners), its circumcisions and scars (marks of initiation, dueling scars, *qipu*-like [the Inca color-coded knotted strings] marks of diseases and injuries), pigments (racializing categories), and painting (eye kohl and mascara, evil eye prophylaxis, and sexual "war paint" makeup) have continued to mutate and proliferate since World War I as cosmic-cosmetic, as entertainment, fashion, political statement,[17] and self-marking, on the surface of the body and within.

The camp survivor's request (in *Imaginary Women*) to Molly, whose profession is "supplementing tattoos rather than trying to remove them" (Sullivan 2001:179), echoes, if in a different key, O'Connor's meditation on the agon of iconic versus aniconic hermeneutics in her story "Parker's Back."[18] Parker's wife, Sarah Ruth, disapproves of his tattoos. When Parker crashes his tractor, in reaction to his near death and in hopes of harmonizing his jumble of secular tattoos and finding an emblem his wife cannot resist, he has the Byzantine icon of Christ Pantocrator (Greek, "ruler of all," holding the Book) tattooed on his back. Sarah Ruth beats him with a broom, raising more welts and bleeding on his raw tattoo, reinforcing, as does his being put out under a tree in the yard, the connection with the suffering Christ. For O'Connor, Sarah Ruth is the heretic because of her "notion that you can worship in pure spirit."[19] "Thin and drawn" (without flesh), seeing sin everywhere, she is a puritan whose loss of sensuality in worship loses both the world and the divine, making the consubstantial insubstantial.[20] For Parker and O'Connor, on the other hand, there is a signifying chain from the Book held by Jesus in the icon and from the book of images of God in which Parker found the icon to his body as a book on which are inscribed the mysteries of incarnation, and which is a rite of initiation and passage attempting to configure or assemble meaning in his life among the tattoos of earlier experiences. Parker, Dennis Slattery notes (2000), doesn't use Parker's Old Testament names (Obadiah, "servant of the Lord," Elihue), preferring a New Testament image. Sarah Ruth, by contrast, goes by her (inapt) Old Testament names. Her preference for aniconic worship is treated by O'Connor as abstraction that destroys, disenchants, and disincarnates the word, in opposition to the Jewish reliance on the plenitude of the word, the signifying chain, leaving endless traces and loose ends everywhere for further lively embodied engagements. (Turner [1987] insists that the Old Testament forbids tattoos and bodily marks [Lv 19.28, Dt 14:1] but fails to notice in this context that circumcision becomes a defining rite for Jews [and for Muslims], something that Derrida turned into a philosopheme.[21] In the contemporary world tattooing among Muslims and Jews has become a site of negotiation.)[22]

The agon between body marks, the bestial, and the divine plays out in several registers. For Molly and the concentration camp survivor, the message is like that of Justice Louis Brandeis: the remedy for bad speech is not censorship but more speech. For O'Connor, suffering from an autoimmune disease, the lupus/wolf within, but also a gifted wielder of what Slattery calls a Catholic "theological poetics of corporality," bodily wounds and illnesses are terrains in which one experiences the deeper mysteries of the divine.

Circumcision (male in Islamic worlds and also female in East and West African ones), the anthropologist Vincent Crapanzano points out, is not just a purification and affiliation-initiation ritual, as the "native model" explanations often assert, or a simple change of status rite, as Arnold van Gennep would have it; rather, it is a paradoxical structure of contradictory messages that set up tensions to which the initiate returns again and again in efforts at resolution: at first sexual experiences, at hazing in the army, at marriage, in curing trance dances, and in colonial or authoritarian relations. The period of liminality of the ritual process does not end with the ritual itself but continues through life, as a constant "rite of return."[23] The circumcision in Morocco should not be done until the boy is "old enough to remember" both the pain and the paradoxical messages of "being a man" (e.g., not crying) and yet of submission (like Isaac or Ismail), of becoming a man by being unmanned. Muslim circumcisions are often explicitly referred to as weddings, the blood shed being like that of the wedding night, the boy's hands being hennaed like a bride's, and he wears an anklet. He is called a groom and is led on a horse but obviously is still too immature to be one, is handed to the mother to hold during the circumcision, and is swaddled like a baby and put on the mother's back afterward for a dance, which brings more pain. It is a rite of vulnerability as much as of making a man.[24] So, too, for women who undergo various forms of female "circumcision" (clitorectomy, infibulation) in order, it is said, to become excised of ambiguous male features, conform to the beauty of an adult woman, be desirable, even in some places to increase rather than decrease sexual desire; and, on the other hand, also said to decrease desire, thereby pacifying, controlling, and repressing young women.

In Toni Morrison's *Beloved* the relation between bestiality, divinity, and human body marks plays out on yet a different harmonic. Like the tattooed number from the concentration camp, a tree design has been whipped onto the back of Sethe, and freedom is achieved through transformative narrating, remembering, imagining. Like the icon on Parker's back, Sethe can feel but not see the marks on her back, which are described to her by Amy Denver as a tree design. Amy's words and her laying on of hands, easing Sethe's pain with spider webs (stringing the body like a Christmas tree, making of her body a narrative of the life of Christ) are like O'Connor's theological poetics of corporality. But there is another thematic as well, as Slattery notes: in the novel, bodies and words carry price tags and can be marketed to the highest bidder. Sethe must pay the tombstone engraver for "beloved" with her body and wonders if for another ten minutes she could have also gotten "dearly." All these themes reemerge in the stories of body modifiers in the 1990s, and Slattery observes that Morrison marks many of her female characters' bodies: "In *Song of Solomon*, Pilate has no navel, in *Sula*, Sula has a birthmark over her eye, in *Beloved*, Sethe's mother is branded with the cross in the circle and Sethe is marked by the whipping." Each mark is a shorthand narrative inscribed in a fleshy book of maturing, aging, and regenerative biological life.[25]

Peter Greenaway's film *The Pillow Book of Nagiko* (1996) brings many of these themes together with a foray into Japanese traditions of tattooing (*irezumi*), Japanese-Chinese ideograms, the dialectic between temporary and permanent bodily marks, and the more structural question of Oedipal scripting, private/familial scripts, and publishing/marketing, life/immortality versus death/impermanence, and the exchange rates among the currencies of sexuality, desire, money, writing, and relations of power as well (in Hélène Cixous's reading a call to a feminine writing from the body).[26] The establishing ritual occurs annually on the birthday of Nagiko Kiohara until she is seventeen: her father paints a greeting on several parts of her head, her aunt reads to her from Sei Shonagon's *Pillow Book*, the gramophone plays music from when her parents married, and her grandmother, mother, and aunt witness. The father whispers a spell about God calligraphing on his clay model of a human being, and when God was satisfied with his creation, he breathed life into it and signed his name. It is a creation rite, the father miming the original creation. The child smiles when she sees her painted self in the mirror. It is a mirror scene, with even the characters across her mouth cracking open in her smile. There is mirroring throughout the film between the tenth-century Sei Shonagon and Nagiko.

Greenaway describes the ritual as affectionate yet disturbing, setting up a ritualized tension, an emotional force that will enroll Nagiko in an economy of desire and productivity which she will pass on to her own child at the end of the film. The Oedipal dynamics are, as in Crapanzano's sensibility about the colonial and other hierarchical contexts of Moroccan circumcision, not merely patriarchal but also capitalist: the father's publisher is present at the ritual, and afterward the father is ritually sodomized by the publisher, linking his source of income and power in the external market to the family economy. Nagiko becomes a fashion model in Hong Kong ("for this fashion model this matter of surface is key" [Bruno 2002: 327]). She seeks out a series of lover-calligraphers, all of whom write on her body in nonpermanent ink, until she meets Jerome, a Western translator ("he knows about transfers" [Bruno 2002: 327]). She then herself takes up the pen, and in the end she has a permanent tattoo inscribed on her chest. Each of the experimental calligrapher-lovers has a different relationship to inscription, one even writing in invisible ink, invoking the Islamic prohibition on images and pointing to a television showing a documentary on Islamic calligraphy, which, unlike Chinese and Japanese ideographic calligraphy, is alphabetic, without obvious pictographic legacies. In the end, she is fully scripted into the Oedipal frame, with a permanent tattoo and a child to whom to pass on the script.

There is unexplored ambiguity, however, both in the substitution of milk for semen as the bodily symbol of cultural transmission (as Turner might have pointed out), at least raising a possibility of countering patriarchal tropes, and in the publisher's being killed by a sumo wrestler inscribed with the slogan, "I am old said the book; I am older said the body," suggesting the ongoing dialectic between "life-itself," and the "code of life." Greenaway, moreover, as Bruno points out, uses three screen ratios to mirror the diegetic play with writing the geometry of passion impermanently on the skin and more permanently in the haptic memory traces from her earliest imprinting that Nagiko seeks to reexperience with her lovers.[27]

The ritual process is often central to contemporary queer, lesbian, gay, and modern primitive body modification "body art" subcultures. As Turner writes and Greenaway screens, body modifiers deploy the bodily markers of the ritual process: shock, adrenalin, endorphins, percussion, heightened breathing, pain, blood, cutting, cicatrization, skin stretching, implants, hook hanging. And these visceral groundings are fused to cognitive-moral imperatives (self formation, community bonding, identity marking, productive tension of conflicting messages). Although claiming countercultural status as tribal, personal, political, or erotic, it is remarkable how often "reclaiming the body" by women seeking tattoos, piercing intimate body parts, branding, keloid-raising scarification (or cicatrization) constructs these acquisitions as powerful and communal rites of affliction in response to childhood or marital abuse, feelings of unattractiveness, and reactions to religious and other disciplinary regimes (Pitts 2003).

It takes but a small grammatical shift to change the point of view of agency without changing the psychosocial ritual process: "Instead of an object of social control by patriarchy, medicine, or religion, the body should be seen as a space for exploring identity, experiencing pleasure, and establishing bonds to others" (Pitts 2003: 11). "Karen," raised in a working-class Italian family, subject to childhood sexual abuse, a single welfare mother in her twenties, night school and law school graduate, lesbian, and breast cancer survivor has, among other tattoos and scarifications, a dragon tattooed on her breast as a talisman of overcoming fear, separating from her family, reclaiming her body, and being a person in her own right. The tattoo image came from a girlfriend's suggestion that she visualize a dragon guarding a cave.

"The purpose of that visualization was to give one an awareness of what they do with fear . . . and where their courage comes from. . . . Some people actually pick up swords and swipe the dragon mightily. . . . My way of dealing with it was to make myself one with the dragon and make the dragon become me" [Pitts 2003: 58]. She also had a scarification in the shape of an orchid, done by a professional body modification artist in a ritualized spiritual process among her SM group modeled on a Maui form of tattooing: sharpened shell to cut, then ash rubbed in. She compares this to Buddhist visualization practices: "I think it is the same or similar state that Buddhists, when they spend hours in a state of prayer—that place of acceptance, floating" (ibid.: 59).

As in other ritual processes, paradox and tension are maintained between what is allowable in the ritual versus secular space, intimate surfaces of the skin versus public visibility, as one negotiates employment and other social arenas. For some in queer culture, bodily marks are so visible as to enforce separation from employment outside tattoo, body-piercing shops. Matthew, who runs a profitable body-piercing studio, has stretched earlobes, scarring, and piercings and had himself branded onstage in an SM club by a well-known lesbian professional body modifier. The crowd, he says, was "awed by the power coming off the stage," and he himself felt lighter with each strike of the hot iron, until he got so high he had to separate himself from people and "really go into myself" in what he calls a spiritual experience. For "modern primitives," the romantic appropriation of Native American and other indigenous rituals is explicit, even if authenticity is devalued in favor of experimentalism (Vale 1989).

Body modification is semiotic, somatic, fetishized, commoditized, and flippable as pop culture (as investments are flippable from desired holdings to quick marketable gains). The ambiguity of what is customized choice, truly individualistic, or conventionalized, limited palettes for selection is always at play. As Girl Punk Melissa Klein notes, "Punk female fashion trends have paired 1950s dresses with combat boots, shaved hair with lipstick, studded belts with platform heels. . . . We are interested in creating . . . modes of contradiction" (Pitts 2003: 44). Cyberpunk style, drawing on such science fiction as William Gibson's *Neuromancer*, says Pitts, "is distinct in its futuristic, high-tech body projects use of biomedical, information, and virtual reality technologies" and views the body as a "limitless frontier" (ibid.: 153). This "iconic futurology," usually imbued with an individualistic ideology, is also physically experimental: Shanon Larratt, the founder of Body Modification E-zine (BME), experimented with small magnetic implants under the skin of his fingers to create an ability to feel the electromagnetic fields around him.

While the ethnic body may be marked in discriminatory ways, it can also, in the satirist performance artist Guillermo Gómez-Peña's hands, cross wires, borders, and categories into techno-ethnographic "undiscovered Amerindians," Mexterminators, Gringostroika warriors, geisha apocalipticas, and other forms of ethnocyborgs.

The surface of the body, likewise (or otherwise), is also the register in which the marks of biological crossings between species and technologies make their presence visible, and bioart, like literature and film, follows along behind the advances of science, exploring sociocultural embedded relations and projecting ahead.

Bestial Deep Body Marks: Biosurgical Arts, Bestial Dis-Orders
(Wolves, Crabs), and the Deranged Nervous System

Kantorowicz had two bodies, with Hawking we have three: the fleshly body, the distributed body, and the sacred body.—HÉLÈNE MIALET

What would happen if, instead of eyes, scientists had microscopes in their eye-sockets? . . . they would . . . become angels for then they would " . . . be in a quite different world from other people . . . : the visible ideas of everything would be different."—JOHN LOCKE, quoted by Hélène Mialet

To restore the human being to a free condition, we must put the body on the autopsy table for a complete anatomical reconstruction.—ANTONIN ARTAUD

La grande pellicule [film, skin] *éphémère.* Opening the Libidinal Surface. Open the so-called body, and spread out all its surfaces: not only the *pellicule* [skin/film] with each of its folds, wrinkles, scars . . . the immense membrane of the libidinal "body" . . . made from the most heterogeneous textures, bone, epithelium . . . [nerves, vocal apparatus] . . . All these zones are joined end to end in a band which has no back to it, a Möbius band. . . . Terror in the labyrinth is such that it precludes the observation and notation of identities; this is why the labyrinth is not a permanent architectural construction, but is immediately formed in the place and at the moment. . . . Each encounter gives rise to a frantic voyage towards an outside of suffering . . . there is no intensity without a cry and without a labyrinth.—JEAN-FRANÇOIS LYOTARD, *Libidinal Economy*

Not only the outer skin or hide, nor only the face and eyes, are bodily media for marks and signifiers. So too the material interiority. The more we tinker and experiment within the body, the more the nature of the bestial/divine and libidinal/fantasmic body are redefined, the more these bodies take on new connectivities, significations, intensities, and transductions.[28] Acoustic signatures, neural cell signals, genetic markers, and chemical signatures increasingly are new signifiers of the bestial/divine, ill/well, disconnected/connected body, available for performance and bioartists, physicians and bioengineers, retuned philosophical-anthropological understandings of our place in the world, and bioavailability[29] in biopolitics. Lyotard once claimed that we might lay out the body as surfaces, film, or membranes all the way through, following the lead of the surgeon, but with an eye to all the libidinal surfaces, sensors, and intensities.

   Gunther von Hagens's *Body Worlds*, displays of plastinated cadavers, has literalized this flaying of the body in a revival of public anatomical demonstrations, making available to the general public the muscles, sinews, nerves, vascular system down to the fine capillaries, and organs in a rare immediacy, showing prominently also the black marks on the lungs of smokers and occasionally the cancerous tumor. Surgeries also are being broadcast on television as public education. Dermatology, moreover, is gradually being transformed into photomedicine, exploring the ways in which our epidermal membranes can be penetrated by noninvasive, minimally invasive, and less and less invasive technologies, including lasers, endoscopes, and swallowable and probe-tipped cameras. Neural signals are experimentally being used to help the disabled control a prosthetic hand. Cells are listened to by nanotechnologists like Jim Gimzewski (see note 8) and by bioartists such as Joe Davis, who claims to be able to identify different bacteria and cells by their acoustic signatures, and Adam Zaretski, who plays music to E. coli bacteria to see if they can be stimulated to produce more antibiotics or otherwise change their modes of being. And, of course, forensics finds ever more ways of reading signs and marks in the ruins of the body.

Explorations with surgery by the performance artist Orlan, nerve and muscle connectivity by Stelarc, and tissue engineering by Ionat Zurr and Oron Catts juxtapose themselves to more direct expansions of the fragile body, such as the machines that keep the celebrated Cambridge University physicist Stephen Hawking functioning, the development of prostheses for war injuries, face transplants for accident and burn victims,[30] laser and regenerative medical techniques for life-threatening hemangiomas (vascular anomaly birthmarks), and construction of a congenitally missing ear by tissue engineering. Bioartistic experimentation beyond the current state of the craft of biology is in dialogue both with the (secularized) medical imaginary and with the religious and familial imaginary of people suddenly on dialysis machines, living with organs from others, with prostheses, immunosuppressants, and other interventions and pharmakons.

Quite apart from the wheelchair, oxygen, voice synthesizer, and other devices that allow Hawking to write, teach, travel, and appear in public, he has, Hélène Mialet suggests, three bodies (Mialet, 1999, 2006). There is the frail body, disabled by a form of Lou Gehrig (amyotrophic lateral sclerosis [ALS]) or motor neuron disease, which destroys the nerve cells in the brain and spinal chord that link to muscles, causing the muscles to twitch and atrophy, but does not impair the mind, personality, memory, or senses of taste, smell, touch, hearing, or sight, or the eye muscles, or bladder and bowel muscles. This frail body has become cyborg in the sense of being now accessorized with computerized facilitation. (On frontiers in the field of biocybernetics, see below.) There is, further, a soft "distributed body" (and intelligence) composed of all the personnel that not only attend to his cyborg and biological body but also include students of his who do the calculations and research he can no longer do. And there is what Mialet calls the "sacred body," the scientific corpus of the cosmologist and physicist. This divine body she compares to Ernst Kantorowicz's famous study from 1957 of the two bodies of the French king ("the king is dead, long live the king"), the physical body that is buried at death and the mystical corpus that embodies the sovereignty of the monarchical state and that is passed on to his successor.

In Hawking's case, Mialet glimpsed the making of a small piece of the sacred body by interviewing him. It is a long, very laborious process for him to type out on the computer answers to questions, yet he is an expert user of the Equalizer and Easy Keys systems and in saving what he wants and deleting the incidentals. No point, he indicated, for her to tape record or take notes during her interview with him: he would just give her a printout when the interview was over. However, to her surprise, the printout was sanitized of the questions he had asked in passing (of "why" she had been selected to write an article about him) and of requests ("legs") he had made to his nurse to adjust his position. So, too, of course, is the relation between scientific articles and the practices that go into their production. How important is his now-canonic anecdote about how his illness, in slowing him down getting ready for bed at an early stage of the disease, provided the time for him to think about "event horizons" and have his insights about black holes? Or how important is his topological or geometric intuition as a shortcut to arduous mathematical equations? In what ways do the three bodies "mark" one another? Certainly the distributed body (now made natural?) takes care to highlight the sacred body and veil the (raging, eliminating) bestial (and yet still natural) body. Hawking's three bodies are material-semiotic shifters redistributing the categories and their references.[31]

If Hawking's three bodies do mark one another, what of people on dialysis machines or undergoing organ transplantation with their required lifelong regime of immunosuppression? In interviews with end-stage renal failure patients in Turkey, Aslihan Sanal (2005) elicits a series of exchanges between old familial and newly religious bodies. The psychology of intimate familial relations is put under stress, and in one case, an Alawi young woman, upset by a number of hallucinatory dreams and psychological states, found herself questioning her paternity and identity as an Alawi and identifying rather with significant others in her dialysis cohort. This is more than the "tyranny of the gift" described by Rene Fox and Judith Swazey in their pathbreaking studies (1974, 1992) of early heart transplant patients who had to negotiate feelings about being unable to reciprocate the "gift of life" or being oppressed by unwelcome claims on intimacy by relatives who wanted to visit the heart of a loved one now in the transplanted person's chest (hence donations in such experimental procedures now are anonymous). At issue in routine organ donations (as with the construction of subcultural communities by body modifiers) are larger social solidarities negotiated through publicly regulated as well as gray or black market transplantations, through egalitarian public hospital social ideologies versus privatized market hospital systems, and through social boundaries and norms shifted by altruism or refused by transgressive acts (Sanal 2005).[32] Bodies of the poor, who donate for the money, are often weakened and stigmatized, marked by gender and class inequalities, and actively recruited into bioavailable commodification markets for body parts (Cohen 1999, 2004).

As with the discovery of "phantom limbs" during the American Civil War, the relations between the imaginary body and the physical body can be complex, not only a matter of maps in the brain (researched in the neurosciences) but also a matter of psychodynamic-interpretive and symbolic registers (traditionally explored in ritual and art). It is here that some of the experiments of performance artists and bioartists are of value in exploring the shifting boundaries that surgery, neural and muscle connectivity, and tissue engineering make possible. This is, Stelarc claims, more interesting when concrete consequences are at issue, not just science fiction or conceptual speculation, and when "images are cyber skins that transduce the physical body into the phantom entity" no longer just in the mind, but in photo and sonic physicality that feeds back into the material body and its nervous system (quoted in Goodall 2005: 12).

Indeed, the idea of reverse phantom limbs—the marking in the brain or writing "software" and "wetware" by the brain of new bodily functionalities—are technologies already in development for ALS and spinal chord injury patients, tetraplegics, stroke victims, surgeons, and pilots.[33] These are so-called biocybernetic technologies in which users train themselves to produce specific brain wave patterns on demand. These are read by electrodes that can move a cursor up and down, right and left on a computer screen or move a prosthetic limb, becoming after awhile part of the brain's body map. Niels Birbaumer of Tubingen University has designed a thought translation device that allows an ALS patient to select and type letters of the alphabet on a computer, which then, with a common word- and phrase-prediction software, can produce e-mail messages, somewhat analogous to the software used by Hawking but here by using brain waves. The "cognitive cockpit" is being developed at Britain's Defense Evaluation and Research Agency (DERA) to allow pilots with electrodes in their helmets and biosensors in their clothes to fly by directing attention (brain waves) to icon controls. The biosensors monitor vital signs, so if a pilot blacks out, an artificial intelligence (AI) copilot can take over. Somewhat more simply, bionic neurons (BIONS™) are being developed by Gerald Loeb at the University of Southern California for therapeutic electrical stimulation to prevent or reverse muscle atrophy in stroke and arthritis patients. These are sealed stimulators the size of a grain of rice injected into the muscles which send regular pulses of electricity, powered by a transmission coil and controlled by a hand-held computer (called a Personal Trainer™) with different programs to vary strength, timing, and duration of pulses. Cyberkinetics Neurotechnology Systems of Massachussets is testing a BrainGate™ two-millimeter-square silicon chip with an array of one hundred electrodes implanted into the motor cortex that samples patterns of neuron firings, and feeds them through a wire to a platform on the patient's head and thence into a computer. The BrainGate™ allows Matthew Nagle, who was stabbed in the neck and suffered a severing of his spine that left him paralyzed, to open e-mail, turn on lights or a television, play video games, and move a robotic arm. Jonathan Wolpaw, with help from the Altran Foundation's engineers, is testing a cap with sixty-four electrodes that does not require implantation into the brain to help an ALS sufferer use his eyes to send e-mail (Heuser 2006: A16).[34]

Stelarc's art performances only gesture in the direction of these technologies and seem crude in comparison, yet provide a kind of advance publicity in a realm protected from the ethical frontiers of medicine. One of the most interesting elements in these new technologies is the exploration of the idea that all sensing modalities are *transductions*, mediated transformations between one kind of signal and sensory system and another (see also Helmreich 2009). Abe Caplan, the technician helping Nagle learn to use the BrainGate™ by encouraging and adjusting the computer's settings for averaging the motion prediction algorithm, asks, " 'Want to hear it?' He flicks a switch, and a loud burst of static fills the room—the music of Nagle's cranial sphere. This is raw analog signal, Nagle's neurons chattering. We are listening to a human being's thoughts" (Martin 2005: 1).

In this sense the brain also "writes" software for mind-body disorders that are marked as disabling pain, such as, John Sarno argues (2006), tension myositis syndrome (muscle-nerve-tendon syndrome,

TMS), carpal tunnel syndrome, chronic pain syndromes, back pains, spinal disc problems, allergies, asthma, eczema, bulimia, anorexia nervosa, and neurasthenia/chronic fatigue. Many of these have physical marks that can be seen on X-rays or MRIs or can be documented by electrical tests (carpal tunnel syndrome) but are not caused by physical disorders and mostly are not resolved by surgery or other such physical interventions. The pain of TMS, he argues, is caused by the reduction of blood flow to the part of the body feeling pain, depriving it of oxygen and thus causing pain. Similarly, carpal tunnel syndrome, he argues, is not as often thought to be caused by nerve compression as by local ischemia. The root cause or source code of these problems is to be found in unspeakable rage and emotional pain that are displaced via the autonomic, immune, and endocrine peptide systems.

Thus, Sarno argues, Freud's notions of the unconscious and displacement were correct, if as yet underspecified. A similar argument is made by those studying the "second brain," the enteric nervous system of the gut, the neurons, transmitters, and proteins that line the esophagus, stomach, small intestine, and colon, which produces benzodiazepines, the antianxiety and antipain chemicals now made into Valium, Prozac, and other popular antidepressants which can thus also affect bowel movements (Gershon 1998, Wilson 2004).

If Freud is a founding figure from the early twentieth century for the explanatory tacking back and forth between the neurological and psychological as marvelously complex and worthy of exploration—bodily marks, signals, and transductions leading to new vistas and understandings both of the psychophysical body and of the relative autonomy of the ethical self and limitations thereof—the notion of Antonin Artaud (1896–1948) of the obsolete body, whose parts react involuntarily and which "needs to be put on the autopsy table for anatomical reconstruction," thereby freeing the human into a "body without organs" (BwO) provides a quite different but equally strong sur-realist set of frames of reference for the scientific, artistic, and philosophical imaginaries of the second half of the twentieth century. Artaud's suffering body—he was afflicted by meningitis, neuralgia, stammering, depression, opium and heroin addiction, peyote experimentation, electroshocks, colon cancer—provides material settings out of which the human emerges: Artaud's theatrical and poetic articulations, including in nonverbal sounds.

Like Freud, Artaud can lead in multiple directions. The performance artists Orlan and Stelarc both invoke Artaud's notion of the obsolete body. Gilles Deleuze invokes the notion of the BwO in a somewhat different way. In both cases a biological sensibility is emergent and perhaps comes together in the work of the bioartists Oron Catts and Ionat Zurr. Although Catts and Zurr have begun collaborations with their generational seniors, Orlan and Stelarc, they work more directly with tissue engineering to grow and cultivate the biological rather than to replace or reconstruct it. Tissue engineering is used to grow steaks ("victimless meat") from cells taken from frogs who happily continue to live on, pig wings (a more conceptual play upon how the impossible is no longer such), and a third ear for Stelarc and to colonize someone else's skin for Orlan. The idea of meat that can be grown rather than killed draws upon regenerative medicine, using techniques developed in some of the world's leading tissue-engineering laboratories, such as J. Vacanti's at the Massachusetts General Hospital, where Catts and Zurr were artists in residence for a year.

One might read the curious careers of Orlan and Stelarc as mid-twentieth-century probings of surgical and cyborgian imaginaries, part of the preparatory but brute technologies for the contemporary biotechnological revolutions (analogous to the "slash, poison and burn" technologies of surgical, pharmacological, and radiation oncology being slowly superseded by noninvasive and regenerative technologies). Born a year apart just after World War II, Orlan and Stelarc each now has a career corpus produced partly in conjunction with developing surgical and robotics technologies. The corpus of each is generationally marked also by highly literate vernaculars. For Orlan a key reference, in addition to Artaud, is the Lacanian psychoanalyst Eugenie Lemoine Luccioni. In her conferences, a performance format in which she is seated at a desk, or occasionally standing, reading from her texts, while slides and videos of her work are projected, she creates a distance between herself and her body in the images, and "despite her black lipstick and half black, half yellow hair, [she] comes across as a middle aged, French academic with self-depreciating humor" (Ayers 1999: 183).

For Stelarc it is Marshall McLuhan: "Well, I certainly have read Deleuze and Guattari, Baudrillard, Virilio, Lyotard . . . [but still McLuhan's] notion of externalizing our nervous central system is for me a central tenet." Born Stelios Arcadiou in Australia in 1946, Stelarc was named Honorary Professor of Art and Robotics at Carnegie Mellon University in 1997 and artist in residence for the city of Hamburg in 1999 and has worked with roboticists at Waseda and Tokyo universities. He has moved from prostheses (a third hand moved with leg and abdomen muscles, a left arm attached to electrodes which act as muscle stimulators), to "suspended animation" performances to make the body move and fly within electromechanical exoskeletons, to hybrid-human machines (including a brief interaction with NASA's project on cyborgs), to more recent explorations of parasitism (both the body within a networked and remotely controlled system and the body as host to agentive objects within).

Orlan, born in 1947 and now professor of fine arts in Dijon, has had a long career in painting, sculpture, dance, and public or street theater. She began as a youngster by causing small disruptions to rush hour traffic. In 1977 she lost her teaching job over the scandalous performance the *Kiss of the Artist,* in which she sat and sold kisses for five francs in front of a life-sized photograph of her nude body and one of her as the Madonna. By the 1990s she was exploring surgery and computerization first with a "carnal art" series of nine facial surgical *Interventions* (the seventh broadcast live by satellite to galleries and museums in Paris, New York, Toronto, and Banff) and then with her computerized *Hybridizations* of her own face with images of very different ideas of beauty, from pre-Columbian Olmecs with "flattened skulls, cross-eyed vision, and false noses" across many other cultures. She invokes as well the Mayan priest of the god Xipe Totec, who dons the flayed skin of his human sacrificial victims, an image that von Hagens also evokes in one of his dramatic plastinations with a real male body holding its own skin. Like Stelarc's, Orlan's carnal art requires collaboration with surgeons and information technologists.

Much of what counts as production of experimental knowledge emerges in these careers like much biological knowledge, as well as biological evolution, incrementally out of play and feedback, the exhausting of sets of structural possibilities. Successive projects unfold as sets of variations more than a precise working out of a long-term intentional plan. As art performances, such knowledge production requires careful planning, design, and coordination (engineering), but it partakes centrally as well in the inventive spirit of hacking and experimentation (science), often like the latter in small steps. This incrementalism—and ambiguity between knowledge and play, the trivial and the profound, the monstrous or bestial and the redemptive or divine—is what provides the time for ethical reflection. The slowness and space for ethical reflection of the hard work of the biomedical sciences and biomedical engineering contrasts sharply with the urgent temporality of the fundraising hype that is one of the necessary but disorienting conditions of constant production of technoscientific tools and platforms.

Pain and redemption are not signifiers in the performances of either Orlan or Stelarc. This is not ritual that uses pain to inscribe the body with significance, neither truth through torture, nor identity and healing, as among modern body art practitioners or traditional religion. Orlan says she wants to put the "naked body in the spaces opened up through scientific discovery," "realized through the technology of its time," and that her art, "lying between disfiguration and figuration . . . is an inscription in flesh, as our age now makes possible. No longer seen as the ideal it once represented, the body has become a 'modified ready-made'." Commenting on the surgeries and on the inability of some audience members to look, she advises, "When watching these images, I suggest that you do what you probably do when you watch the news on television. It is a question of not letting yourself be taken in by the images, and of continuing to reflect about what is behind these images" ("Autobiography"). In her operating theater "I can observe my own body cut open, without suffering. . . . I see myself all the way down to my entrails; a new mirror stage" (in Ayers 1999: 183; also in "Carnal Art Manifesto").

A new mirror stage, of course, is a reference to Lacan and psychoanalytic ideas about the misrecognition of the self. A text by Luccioni inspired her: "The skin is deceptive . . . there is an error in human relations because one never is what one has. . . . I have the skin of an angel but I am a jackal . . . the skin of a crocodile but I am a poodle, skin of a black person, but I am white, the skin of a woman but I am a man; I never have the skin of what I am. There is no exception to the rule, because I am never what I have." Orlan revels in the idea of being able to carry on a discussion with an audience by video feed while her body is open to the surgeon: "I read the texts as long as possible during the operation, even when they are operating on my face, which gave during the last operations the impression of an autopsied corpse that continues to speak." Her web page tells us that "famous designers, such as Paco Rabanne and Issey Miyake, have designed costumes for Orlan to wear during the surgeries. Poetry is read and music is played while she lies on the operating table fully conscious of the events taking place (only local anesthetic is used)." "In my work, the first deal with my surgeon is 'no pain.' I want to remain serene and happy and distant," and she wants to send "images of my body opened up with me at the same time having a completely relaxed and serene expression able to answer any questions" (in Ayers 1999: 183).

Orlan's trajectory from blaspheming to "technologies of our time" and the "naked body in the spaces opened up through scientific discovery," is recapitulated within her surgical series.[35] By 1993 her seventh surgical performance is called *Omnipresence*, punning on the telepresence technology and on the attribute of the Christian God. Her "carnal art," she says, works through augmentation, not self-mutilation. She has silicon implants put into her temples and broadcasts the surgeries to four interactive sites in Europe and North America. She draws on Greek (pagan) mythology: the implants in her temples as Dionysian horns, her bloodied lips as Bacchus's grapes in Dionysian rites of *sparagmos*, or tearing the body apart. She draws on the anarchism of her father, who was anticlerical, a Resistance fighter, and an Esperanto enthusiast, and Artaud: "I also use a lot of Artaud, because I am interested in the concept that the body is obsolete" (quoted in Clarke 1999: 193). Her show in 1997, *Ceci est mon corp ... ceci est mon logiciel* (this is my body ... this is my software)—using images from *Omnipresence* as well as *Hybridization* (done collaboratively and transatlantically with programmers in Canada)—points to an increasing concern with connectivity, telepresence, and the public sphere as well as to the BWO, releasing the human from its obsolete primate body. She also, along the way, gestures to writing, marking, with the blood that is part of the surgical release.[36]

A psychoanalytic reading of Orlan's work that is more conflicted than Orlan's own accounts is given by Parveen Adams. Adams points to a performative contradiction, the "work of anamorphosis."[37] Orlan, Adams writes, "directs under local anesthetic . . . [and] while Orlan experiences little pain, she makes sure that we experience a more substantial pain . . . of *jouissance*," of the gap between signifier and signified (Adams 1996: 142, 154, 156). Adams suggests we pay attention to three splits in the speech act, first, that between the performative effects experienced by spectators (like Freud's horror in looking down Irma's throat in his famous dream) and those experienced by Orlan ("while lying on the surgical table, what she experiences is the overwhelming desire to communicate"). Second, there is a split between the body and the pure subjectivity of speech. Orlan's "subjective account is that with each operation she becomes more distant from her body, it is as though she sloughs off her body to enter the pure subjectivity of speech" (ibid.: 154). And third, while Orlan claims to morph her face with art-historic images of women's faces ("flesh become image"), Adams thinks that instead she is showing that the image is empty, that the mask has nothing behind it, unhinging the grounds (even "all relations") of representation.

While Orlan "sets off on the highway of information," the spectator "is forced to tarry in this circus to witness something else, something which insists" (ibid.: 154).[38] Like Freud, Adams experiences horror as she watches the surgeon separate the ear from the face, shocked by the realization and recognition that the face is detachable. The "gap" or "space" that is opened as the skin is lifted "unhinges" the stabilities of inside/outside, mask/face, and any notion that the face represents something deep or interior.[39] Adams quotes Lacan's description of Freud's dream of Irma: "There is a horrendous discovery here, that of the flesh one never sees, the foundation of things, the other side of the head, of the face, the secretory glands par excellence, the flesh from which everything exudes, at the very heart of the mystery, the flesh in as much as it is suffering, is formless, in as much as its form in itself is something which provokes anxiety" (Lacan 1954–55: 154). In contrast to normal cosmetic surgery or that of transsexuals, where the goal is completion ("until my surgery I am unfinished"), Adams concludes, Orlan undoes any sense of such completion: "As the face becomes detached, it no longer projects the illusion of depth, it becomes a mask without any relation to representation" (1996: 145).

Of course, one might reply, somewhat pragmatically, first, that this dissociation is something medical students pass through in their training (Orlan's "technologies of our time . . . spaces opened up through scientific discovery"),[40] and, second, that facial transplants can be life restoring, even if they require lifelong immunosuppression (see note 32). Still, Adams crucially draws attention to the differences between the surface marks of the illustrated body and the deep marks of the traumatic body. The traumatic body is increasingly visible—as epidemiological demographics and as individual bodies—both through the cancers and other diseases that may be environmentally caused by our own productive activities and through the spreading pervasive effects of torture, war, and rape as a tactic of war; and visible no longer only in the men and women on crutches (World War I, the film *Kandahar*), but also in the silent ones (the world wars, rape victims), the symptomatic ones (Vietnam, the Gulf wars), and their stressed families.[41]

If Orlan has set out on the information highway, Stelarc has long been centrally concerned with these connectivities, with placing the "obsolete body" within the wider nervous and muscle systems in which the human body is being enveloped, intensifying Benjamin's observations of the immediate aftershocks of World War I, concretizing McLuhan's anticipations of telepresence and "externalizing our nervous central system." William Gibson gives an account of Stelarc not unlike Ayer's description of Orlan: "an utterly conventional looking man" who radiates "calm and amiability," and he adds, "but what I recall experiencing" from having watched Stelarc in performance with his third robotic arm "was a vision of some absolute chimera. . . . I sensed that the important thing wasn't the entity that Stelarc evoked but the labyrinth that the creature's manifestation suggested" (in M.

Smith 2005: vii–viii). Stelarc had swallowed a camera with great diffi-culty and medical help, and while it had unfurled properly it did not refurl; Stelarc, says Gibson, took the likelihood of needing surgery in stride.

Today there are swallowable cameras in pill-sized capsules for gas-trointestinal exploration.[42] Stelarc's *Third Hand* (Maki Galleries, To-kyo, 1982) was triggered by electromyography (EMG) signals from abdominal and leg muscles, and he was able to write in a coordinated way the word "evolution" with all three hands, while the interior sounds of his body were transduced and amplified through a speaker system. He describes this connectivity not as a simple insertion but as an implosive effect of technological miniaturization: "With the desire to measure time more and more accurately and minutely, the neces-sity to process vast amounts of information, and the impulse to cata-pult creatures off the planet, technology becomes more and more complex and compact. This increasing miniaturization creates an im-plosive force that hurtles technology back to the body, where it is attached and even implanted" (Goodall 2005: 8). Today, inversely, the noisy signals of Matthew Nagle's brain are parsed for functional feed-back so he can do things without his limbs.

As in Orlan's performances, in Stelarc's pain is separated from the performance. In *Fractal Flesh* (1995), Stelarc, in Luxembourg, was wired to a muscle stimulator that controlled the left side of his body, thereby splitting the nervous system. Parts of his body were under the control of external triggers; other parts were under control of his brain and central nervous system. Participating viewers in Paris and Amster-dam could enter signals via touch screen that would affect the left side of the body. In the *Extended Arm* (2000), one hand on a keypad controls long aluminum fingers, while the other hand is controlled by muscle stimulators that force it through a choreographed set of motions (Goodall 2005). Pain, Goodall remarks, "can be seen to pass in waves through the face, but is not part of the overall aesthetic" (ibid.: 17).

These waves of pain, she suggests, "are a reminder of how much is going on." Even more generously, Timothy Murray suggests that "the trauma of the body in regimes of high-technology is at the basis of Stelarc's practice" (Smith 2005: 98). But Amelia Jones (2005) demurs, insisting Stelarc's claims are ideological masculine denials and desires to escape the body.[43] Brian Massumi draws attention to the transduc-tion and extension of the body, arguing that even the early body suspen-sions on hooks were carefully calibrated to minimize pain and tearing of the skin (with eighteen hooks to distribute the body's weight), the skin stretched to the limit, the body in "suspended animation," and the body sounds transduced and propagated to fill the surrounding space. The "amplified body processes include brainwaves (EEG), muscles (EMG), pulse (plethysmogram), bloodflow (Doppler flow meter). Other transducers and sensors monitored limb motion and indicate body posture. The body performs in a structured and interactive lighting installation which flickers and flares in response to the electrical discharges of the body" (2005: 160).

Over time, Massumi notes, Stelarc has moved from exploring prostheses (*Exoskeleton, Goggled Eyes, Third Hand, Virtual Arm, Extra Ear*), all of which are extensions rather than substitutions for the body, to cybernetic networks rewiring the body's motion (*Split Body, Fractal Flesh, Stimbod, Ping Body, Virtual Arm, Virtual Body, Parasite, Movatar*). Always, Massumi suggests, Stelarc has recognized the idea of a single body evolving to be an absurdity, and conceptually all the experiments were stand-ins for extension into a collectivity, which "truly begins to unfold when the audience is let back in" (2005: 167), but also pragmatically as a function of the fact that most of his performances require medical and technical collaborators (Stelarc and Smith 2005: 216). Indeed, it is often most interesting when these collaborations and transductions fail, thereby showing the otherwise hidden work and fragility of the connections. In 1995, for the *Fractal Flesh* performance with participants in Paris and Amsterdam and Stelarc in Luxembourg, the early web was too slow, and a dedicated network of modem-linked computers had to be set up. But soon, with faster and broader band Internet connectivity, for *Ping Body* (1996), *Parasite: Event for Invaded and Involuntary Body* (1997), and *Parasite by Movatar* (2000), Stelarc could allow pinging over forty or more sites to feed back into the performance, varying the modalities of four kinds of body movement: voluntary, involuntary, controlled, programed (Massumi 2005: 180).

In using brain waves and EMG signals, Stelarc operates on the margins of neurological and biocybernetics research to reenable sufferers of Lou Gehrig's disease (ALS) and similar conditions of paralysis to move prostheses and screen cursors via brain implants or via merely reading electrical waves on the skull, like an EEG.

With *Third Ear*, Stelarc is beginning to move toward tissue engineering, and with *Prosthetic Head* toward "a conversational system." *Prosthetic Head* is an extension of old computer science experiments with expert systems technologies, beginning with the wildly successful first AI psychotherapy program, Eliza (1966), whose creator, Joseph Weizenbaum, left the field for fear such technology would be misused. The *Prosthetic Head* uses phrase recognition and prediction, selecting phrases from its human interrogator and mirroring conversational fragments, so that, as Stelarc quips, the AI is only as smart as its interrogator. But "Baldi," a conversational agent designed at the University of California, Santa Cruz, that, in conjunction with a cochlear implant, teaches deaf children at the Tucker Maxon Oral School in Portland, Oregon, is already much more productive. "Baldi" listens to a student, runs what it hears against a speech-recognition system, notes mispronunciations, and shows the student how to pronounce the "sh" sound by puckering its lips, the "th" by sticking its tongue between its teeth, and so on (Geary 2002: 39–41).

Suppose, Stelarc says, you add biorhythms so that the *Prosthetic Head* is grumpy in the morning and tired in the afternoon and has information about you through a vision system (à la Steve Mann) and can comment on your clothes or expression (Stelarc and Smith 2005: 321). Suppose you build in affective computing devices to read emotion, such as IBM's *Blue Eyes* software to detect excitement in the eyes of consumers, Rosalind Picard's affective computing devices at the MIT Media Lab, or the Salk Institute's and Paul Eckman's (UCSF) software for detecting deception signaled by facial muscle cues (Geary 2002: ch. 2).

Mimicking and interactive interfaces to read body marks move in one direction. But alternatively, suppose, Stelarc continues, one developed *e-motion* (not emotion) through sensors, such that an avatar could move your facial muscles, turning you into a surrogate body for its *e-motions*, causing your facial expressions (Stelarc and Smith 2005: 222). While this is a bit bizarre as a goal, it is an inversion not unlike his ideas about synthetic skin, which again extends what medically exists today to help burn victims. Suppose, he says, such a synthetic membrane were not only permeable to oxygen but possessed some photosynthetic capabilities, could produce nutrients, and dispense with the need for the gastrointestinal tract, circulatory system, and lungs, allowing the body to be hollowed out and making space to host technological components: a BWO (ibid.: 229); this is something perhaps he already gestured toward by having a camera introduced into his stomach to not only see but also "play" the music of the body—the opening and closing of heart valves, the slosh of blood—through Doppler ultrasonic transducers. Perhaps this is a retrogesture toward Manfred Clynes's and Nathan Kline's original ideas about cyborgs as preparation for space flight, and the idea that long-distance space flight would require the human body to undergo changes and machine-body hybridization.[44]

In an interview with Ross Farell, Stelarc says he is not trying to live as a posthuman body, but "it's important that it is not purely a fanciful idea or science fiction speculation, but rather . . . you try to cope with the precision and the complexity and the speed of this technological terrain, and you . . . live with the consequences. [mutual laughter]. . . . what constantly pleases me is that in creating these unstable situations with the body you generate unexpected outcomes with new interactive possibilities" (Stelarc and Farell 1999: 130, 133). In this interview, he suggests not the idea of a hardened skin with a hollowed-out body, but that with nanotechnology, we will "have the possibility that the body becomes the host for colonies of micro-miniaturized machines," an idea that some medical scientists also hold, particularly (or initially) nanobots that circulate in the blood sensing problems, doing repair, delivering adjustable dosages of medication.

The *Third Ear* is iconic for the way in which art lags behind reality while being suggestive of future possibilities. Ignoring current functional technologies such as the cochlear implant, the *Third Ear* is nonfunctional or reverse directional: it could come with a chip that emits rather than receives sound. The *Third Ear*, however, is visually and materially a reference to the famous tissue-engineered ear successfully implanted on the back of a mouse, a proof of concept that one can chemically engineer polymers as matrices for three-dimensional tissue growth, an interdisciplinary collaboration between the chemical engineers Robert Langer and Linda Griffiths, both of MIT, and the surgeons Joseph and Charles Vacanti, of Boston's Children's Hospital and the Massachusetts General Hospital. The tissue-engineered ear, designed for infants born without an ear, is connected to efforts by Anthony Atala's tissue-engineering lab to grow bowels and to his and a half dozen other such labs, including Vacanti's, to grow a variety of organs or help them to self-repair. In complex organs like kidneys and livers, the layering of tissues with polymer matrixes and lithographic-like techniques to guide capillary growth are among the key challenges.

The possibilities of repair and regeneration are at the heart of projects by the bioartists Oran Catts and Ionatt Zurr, who spent a year in J. Vacanti's lab expanding their tissue-engineering skills and working on their victimless meat project. Pictures of their bioart hang on the walls of the lab. Catts and Zurr, who are based in Perth, Australia, intend their projects as public education, not just about new biotechnologies, but more importantly about ways in which we can learn to live with, rather than consume and destroy, the ecological and reproductive forces of biology. In their early work growing tissue around small dolls as a "green" form of Guatemalan "worry dolls," to which one tells and thus offloads one's anxieties, they began an effort to install a biology lab bench at art shows to demonstrate how tissue engineering is done, to demystify and counter the anxieties publics have about this technology. In their more recent work growing meat from harvested cells, the effort is to think about how we can harness biological processes in symbiotic ways.

GATTACA: Back to the Future Body

Imagine the universe in expansion: does it flee from terror or explode with joy? Undecidable. So it is for the emotions, these polyvalent labyrinths to which only after the event, the semiologists and psychologists will try to attribute some sense. . . . We have nothing to do any more with the heraldry of the tragic. . . . It is not the tragedy of a destiny, nor the comedy of a character (it can be presented in this way, of course) . . . rather the strangeness of fictive spaces, Escher's waterfalls whose point of impact is higher than their source.
—JEAN-FRANÇOIS LYOTARD, *Libidinal Economy*

Maybe the problem is not biogenetics as such but, rather, the social context of power relations within which it functions. . . . Enlightenment remains an unfinished project that has to be brought to its end, and this end is not the total scientific self-objectivization but—this wager has to be taken—a new figure of freedom that will emerge when we follow the logic of science to the end.—SLAVOJ ŽIŽEK, *Organs Without Bodies*

Why not walk on your head, sing with your sinuses, see through your skin? . . . Find your body without organs. Find out how to make it.
—GILLES DELEUZE AND FÉLIX GUATTARI, *A Thousand Plateaus*

The haptic and proprioceptive body is natural—indeed, it is the ground of perception—the body out of control is bestial, the transported body is divine. Like the old chain of being or the merit-reincarnation sequence of bestial, natural, and divine, the contemporary topology of natural, bestial, and divine is like a Möbius strip twisting back on its own implications. It is of anthropological-philosophical interest that while analytic philosophy and Habermasian civic responsibility have remained modernist and suspicious of this regenerative twisting topology, so-called Continental philosophy (Nietzsche, Freud, Merleau-Ponty, Bergson, Lacan, Lyotard, Deleuze) has become enlivened with a biological sensibility. It is this biological sensibility (more than the irrationalist tonality of Heidegger and Nazi racism against which Habermas is still correctly vigilant)[45] that informs the productivity of much contemporary thinking and poesis (*Dichtung*). And it is that

productivity, the weaving back and forth between contemporary biotechnology and ethical/anthropological stakes, that I have aimed to
capture in the eye, surface marks, and deep marks, which are also the
face, the communicating body, and the traumatic body. It is anthropologically and ethnographically (historically and socially) critical that
they be understood in their social dynamics—class, gender, postcoloniality, asymmetrical power, etc.—not just as individualized bodies
or codes.[46]

Just as tattoos lose much of their meaning in the absence of personal
histories, so too do the new genomic, proteonomic, stem cell, and
nuclear transfer technologies and efforts at synthetic and systems biologies, which have stirred up ethical debate and geographic redistribution of scientists as they move to less restrictive environments in such
high-growth centers as Singapore and operate via cross-national networks of cooperating laboratories in Israel, Singapore, Australia, and
England and in the United States, Japan, and China. The bestial-
human-divine metaphoric theater shifts and morphs along with the
science and technologies. In Germany, the experience of World War II
has enshrined into the Basic Law a salutary defense of the inviolability
of human dignity. But this has meant a morally compromised position
on stem cell research, forbidding the creation of blastocysts for research but allowing the import of such blastocysts. The United Kingdom and the Netherlands, by contrast, operate with an understanding
that blastocysts are preembryos, life, but not yet human life: blastocysts are cells that, up to the fourteenth day of fertilization, have not
yet differentiated. In the United States the mass media, in collusion
with religious conservatives, have so far successfully inserted blastocysts into the term "embryo," insisting that their destruction is the
killing of human life, though the same conservatives say little or
nothing about the many embryos produced for possible in vitro fertilization that are thrown away or the many blastocysts that never make
it to term.

I am always reminded of the story of Mark Edelman, the last living
survivor of the Warsaw ghetto uprising. Edelman, a physician, was
collaborating with a professor of cardiac surgery who attempted a new
procedure in cases in which the patient was certain to die if there was
no intervention. The professor was afraid for all the normal reasons,
but also that, should he fail, his colleagues would say he was experimenting on human beings. Edelman urged him on. He lights up when
the game of death is on and one can outwit God: "God is trying to blow
out the candle and I'm quickly trying to shield the flame. . . . God is not
terribly just. It can be very satisfying because whenever something

does work out, it means you have, after all, fooled Him" (Krall 1977: 85). Our ethical institutions and moral imperatives have evolved over the past fifty years (Fischer 2003: ch. 10), and all interventions are not good. The lesson is that it is not abstractly but in recursive, incremental frameworks that ethical decision making occurs.

On May 9, 2007, MIT's Media Lab put on one of its periodic spectacular demonstrations of current research. Called "h2o" or "the Human 2.0," it was dedicated to unleashing a new era of human adaptability. It began with Oliver Sachs and his remarkable stories of awakening Parkinson's patients, the phenomena of phantom limbs and sensory substitutions, on which we are trying to build a new generation of prostheses using robotics, neuroscience, and bioengineering tools. It ended with three conversations, the first between the journalist John Hockenberry and the architect and designer Michael Graves, both in their wheelchairs. The second was among Michael Chorost, with his cochlear implant, the model Aimee Mullins, with her many sets of prosthetic legs, on which she has set long jump and sprinting world records, and the rock climber Hugh Herr, with his robotic legs and ankles. The third was between John Donoghue and John Hockenberry. Donoghue developed the BrainGate technologies to help people with spinal chord injuries and other severe problems use their brain's electrical signaling to move cursors to point and click and manipulate computer screens and machines. His statistics are amazing: thirty thousand Parkinson's patients have deep-brain stimulators that help them walk and reduce tremor, a hundred thousand people have cochlear implants, six now have retinal implants, and some three hundred people have his Brain-Gate with implanted wires in arm or leg muscles.

Hockenberry asked Donoghue about enhancements, not just replacements. Donoghue thought about this for a moment (or pretended to) and then said, Of course, this too could come, and he supposed his graduate students speculated about having ten fingers or such, but this is clearly secondary to helping people with severe problems. Hockenberry himself continually repeated throughout the show —he was the master of ceremonies—that it is the disabled who have the data that technologists, such as those at the Media Lab, need and that he, for one, has spent his year at MIT asking people how he could upgrade himself to a Human 2.0. The balance between hype (or fear) of the technological and the challenges of finding new solutions and upgrading our capabilities as networked human beings (socially, aided by technology) is where the excitement really lies. It lies perhaps in the skeins of five or more ways of reading body marks:

Reading body marks: My hair stands on end, I blush or maybe only redden (in embarrassment, love, anger), I wink or maybe only blink (voluntarily, involuntarily), I blink more rapidly (am I lying?), my pupils widen, nostrils flare, my cells scream, the cancer tumor heats up, the two genomes in my chimeric cells fight[47]—do you read me? When you feel me, do you also feel for me? When you catch my scent, can you tell if I'm afraid? To whom do my body marks speak: to you, to me (in my fantasies and misrecognitions of self-knowledge), to the instrumentation that listens through my skin to deep rhythms, vibes, heat, and other codes? Kismet, the robotic cartoon with camera eyes that follow my motion, head and eyebrows that move, and a voice synthesizer that responds to my comments (but no nose or other facial features), responds to my body's voice and motion, but where in this "sociality" does projection start and communication end, is it part of *my* libidinal body?[48] The space suit, pacemaker, and nanotech uniform that reads and adjusts my vital functions, even repairing some of my wounds, and the hospital tubes and electrodes that keep me alive are clearly exoskeletons. But what of the fingerprints, exfoliating skin cells, hair, and other marks that my body leaves behind so that DNA typing can ensure GATTACA-style surveillance?[49] Do you read me, will you still need me when I'm sixty-four?[50]

Ethical spacing of emergent bodily marks: bestial, natural, divine: What will the near and far future body be? How much of the past is projected forward to make sense of the new, like catacoustis?[51] Or like the artist's glimpses of past source images in current confusions and emergences?[52] How much of the future is reconfigured from the past like genetics reaching back into evolutionary history to track alternative branching points, alternative biological solutions? Is this the Nietzschean eternal return out of which liberation can emerge (experimentally) or be reconstructed (reverse engineering)? And is this the temporal spacing of ethics, the interactive "face of the other,"[53] the "given time"[54] to think about what we are doing, the feedback, and warning signals, signs of wisdom?

In Ray Bradbury's *Illustrated Man* (1951) the narrator meets a man with tattoos all over his body, each with a story that predicts the future. One bare spot fills in with the future of anyone who spends time talking to him. When the stories stop, the bare spot fills in with an image of the Illustrated Man choking the narrator to death, and he runs toward a town he knows he can reach before morning. Bradbury's cautionary tales about our technoscientific world do not contain inevitable predictions: we can escape the nightmare possibilities. Bradbury says that to survive we must build "empathy machines" or "compensating machines" and that the artist has a key role to play (Eller and Touponce 2004: 383). Such machines are perhaps like the robot grandmother in "I Sing the Body Electric" (1960) who gives the impression of imperfection but anticipates human desires, or Isaac Asimov's famed ethical programing commands for robots to ensure that they not hurt human beings.

Marked bodies of biopolitics: Tortured bodies, the wounded walking, and the living dead (zombies) are significant social and epidemiological categories today, the way the poor, the serf, the untouchable were in the unfinished past. So too are statistical groupings of the ill, often now networked or organized by disease for political leverage to get research done, drugs to market, insurance companies to pay. So too are the marketing categories of the "patients in waiting," the bodies whose genetic markings register probabilities of predispositions for future illness and who thus in the projected world of "individualized medicine" or pharmacogenomics could be prophylactically on "drugs for life" (Lipitor being a current example).[55] All these are marked bodies.

Markings of, and markings by, the body: Maurice Merleau-Ponty reminded us that the body is always a third term in the figure-background Gestalt of perception (1945: 13), Henri Bergson that perception comes with memories that the active body accumulates. The anthropologist Michael Taussig notes that synestheia is "the medley of the senses bleeding into each other's zone of operation" (1993: 57), the musicologist Steven Feld that sound can overwrite sight in cultural cosmologies (1982, 2005: 180–81), the anthropologist Constance Classen that cultural cosmologies focus bodily attention on different senses (Classen 2005), and the neurologist Oliver Sacks that case materials show the senses operate in different ways in different people (Sacks 2005). The body as filter, as switching receptors, as writing machine.

Marks of our time: We live with the transcribed body (in various codes like GATTACA), the psychotropic body (like Sacks's testimony to his own enhanced and precise control of visual imagery and memory under the influence of large doses of amphetamine),[56] the testimonial body (of aging, scars, torture, etc.), the libidinal body (of transferable intensities), the automatic body (nervous, wired, raging with hormones), the topological body (of misrecognition), the collective technobody, the signing, signaling, enigmatic, communicating body. These duplicitous, multiplicitous bodies bring us back recursively to the ethics of our puzzlements.

Against Habermas's warnings, deploying modernist common sense, that to manipulate the human body is to threaten the "ethical self understanding and can disturb the necessary conditions for an autonomous way of life" (quoted in Žižek 2004: 125; compare again the above epigraph from Barker), both contemporary bioscientists and philosophers who attempt to think through these biotechnologies posit the need to follow further the Enlightenment demands of inquiry: "There is no return to the preceding naïve immediacy" (ibid.: 126). Following the American chronicler of twentieth-century popular culture speculations Ray Bradbury, the artist, anthropologist, and philosopher can all play a role in making sure that the consequences of the speculations are not mere abstract nightmares or utopian fantasies but are lived in their micromultiplicities, feedback, reroutings, and reincorporations, in a density of experience and trial. The world into which we enter is emergent precisely in this mundane/profound sense that we run quickly out of reasons but still must act, and those actions have serious consequences which create forms of sociality that incorporate the face of the other, the call to be responsive to the other. This remains true even as we create new sensing biotechnologies, even as the overloads of sensations cause us to inscribe ourselves ever deeper into the ruins of the past, out of which we are emergent, different, and lively.

The geoid—moiré-like, simultaneously material earth and mathematical shape—has drawn me since my school days into worlds just beyond my current knowledge base, into realms inhabited by voices from the ancient past, the revolutionary modern, the geographically distributed, and the fabled worlds of terrestrial, marine, and satellite surveying, and, above all, into social worlds where the intellectual chase intersects with storied characters, competitions, and gendered conflicts.

"It's *my* article!" Irene complains about her 124th publication, the first of a nine-part abridgment of her scientific autobiography, appearing as she nears her ninety-seventh birthday: "Why can't they use the title the way I wrote it?" She's already worked out a compromise: "Let's divide the article into two articles, one having to do with its technical and military dimensions, and one having to do with the personal. That's the one people asked me to write, that's the important one. Write something personal they asked. These aren't my illustrations, why are they here, I didn't choose them."

The struggle for control has not stopped. She is confined to chair and wheelchair. Her eyes tire too quickly to read very much. "The doctors say there is nothing wrong with my eyes—that's a relief—so why can't I read? There must be something wrong with my brain, my *Gehirn*. I feel I have lost a piece of my *Gehirn*. Maybe I don't need an ophthalmologist, but a neurologist." She is all too aware both that the brain becomes confused and that her loss of ability to speak loudly enough, to hear distinctly enough, to parse quickly enough, threatens the social feedback that ensures her sense of personhood ("I used to be a public speaker, why can't I make myself heard? This place/condition is going to turn me into an idiot").

Wondrous epistemological conundrums ensue: "Don't tell me that's not so, it is *my* experience. If I can't trust my experience, how can I know what is real? Should I believe my experience or you?" And yet:

"You have to be my reality check." (I can't trust the doctors, the aides, the assisted living management: they all have their own agendas, mainly making money and keeping control. So I have to trust you to watch out for me.) And, of course: "How do I know what is real and what is a dream?" And even more importantly: "How do I keep the dream worlds from invading my real world?" Occasionally she can laugh at herself and at these conundrums, non sequiturs, and absurdities. Those are golden moments. More to the point: the aides, coresidents, and the assisted living management have no idea who she is or was, and so interaction with them, while often pleasant (when not a struggle over control), is merely banal. They also do not speak German, into which increasingly she slips without realizing it, even when repeatedly reminded by her daughter-in-law to speak English, English, speak English.

These are old-age issues of (loss of) control. They entangle themselves, however, with older issues of control: the researcher fighting the bureaucracy, a gifted mathematician and scientist staking out a place in a man's world, complicated in turn by the immigrant's struggles in a New World where, although a European education is highly valued, women's roles are retrograde relative to her generation's expectations in Europe. And yet, on the other hand, this New World career as an internationally renowned scientist would not have been possible in the socioreligiously divided Vienna of the 1930s.

She is right, of course. She usually is, even if the words don't always come out right. The title of her autobiography is *"Geodesy? What's That? My Personal Involvement in the Age-Old Quest for the Size and Shape of the Earth, With a Running Commentary on Life in a Government Research Office."* The words "with a running commentary . . ." run clockwise in open circle or spiral. She is fond of both the spiral and the signaling of the personal, the humor, and three entwined threads of the memoir: the ancient quest for the size and shape of the earth; the life of an immigrant scientist, wife, and mother; and the golden age of modern geodesy that was, and could only have been, pioneered in a government research unit with all its struggles between scientific, bureaucratic, and military cultures. She's right: the reduced title, "Geodesy? What's That?" is hardly the same: it sounds like a primer (she wrote a very popular one called *Basic Geodesy*), a technical introduction ("they already have that in many forms and places"), not a lively, sometimes sarcastic, ironic, humorous, and above all joyous account of a career she loved. "Joyous" is a word that often comes up in autobiographies of immigrant scientists of her generation. Indeed, the autobiography has a second title that appears on the table of contents and the preface: "Joys and Woes of a Government Researcher: My Personal Involvement in a Glorious Chapter of Cosmopolitan Geodesy."

She's not being entirely fair, of course. A number of people have put in a fair amount of work to get the abridgment serialized in nine bimonthly installments in the ACSM *Bulletin* (American Congress on Surveying and Mapping: January 2004 to June 2005), including her former colleague and fellow retiree Bernard Chovitz, who undertook to do the abridgment; Ed McKay, another retired geodesist, who re-typed her manuscript into digital form or corrected and proofed the scanned version I sent them; and the editor Ilse Genovese, who did a lovely color layout. Irene probably cannot see the light, pastel-colored hand flicking the earth like a marble. It's only a random fifty-fifty chance whether she would be amused or irritated by the image.

Among the many things I've learned from Irene is to keep focused on the task and goals at hand and not to get too distracted by the irritations along the way. *Geodesy? What's That?*, you can already see, is quite a ball of triangulated themes, entangled personal threads, and global concerns.

I

Eratosthenes is where the geoid and the quest for the Figure of the Earth (size and shape of the earth) begins—or is it with John O'Keefe? Or, in a way, with the Vienna Circle, Norbert Wiener, and Vassily Leontiev? For me, the geoid also begins with the high school geometry textbook Irene wrote in her spare time while I was struggling in high school to not besmirch the whiz-kid reputation my sister had estab-lished with the math teachers who taught her a decade before I came along. My mother was hired in 1952 when I was in first grade to work in the four-person Long Line Section, headed by Chovitz, of the Geoid Branch, headed by O'Keefe, of the Army Map Service (AMS). By the time I was learning geometry, she was also instilling in me the basics of geodesy. As she was being introduced to her future colleagues in 1952, O'Keefe casually asked her if she thought the Mercator projection was a purely geometrical projection onto a tangent cylinder. She had scanned Charles Henry Deetz's and Oscar Sherman Adams's *Elements of Map Projections* in anticipation of working at a mapping agency: "I was amused by the rather emotional remonstration against the error in many textbooks, which describe the Mercator projection as a cylin-drical projection rather than a mathematical arrangement of the paral-lels to make the rhumb line intersect the meridians under a constant angle. So that question . . . struck me right away as a shibboleth. And I watched with amusement the exchange of glances after my answer: I knew I was accepted." She had a similar attitude toward teaching high school geometry, which she had done in Vienna and again, before I was born, at Sidwell Friends School in Washington, D.C. The textbook she designed was color coded for three levels of students, with lots of little asides for the most advanced or most interested. I was called in as an "expert witness" to defend her against tendencies of textbook editors to cut to the lowest common denominator and eliminate anything that might actually interest a nonmath genius in middle or high school. (These were the years after Sputnik and the flurry of "new math" anxieties for American schoolchildren to catch up in math, engineering, and science.)

Teenage years are philosophical ones, or at least they were for me: how to get around the conundrums of solipsism, how to explore the world, how to know what is meaningful. I read Jean-Paul Sartre and Albert Camus and Jean Giraudoux. If today I am supposed to help keep Irene's thoughts grounded in something called the real, that was her role in those days, and she invoked her teacher Moritz Schlick, the founder of the Vienna Circle, and the pragmatism of the logical positivists, with their demarcation rules of what is scientific and what not and hence of what is worth arguing about and what is better to be simply acknowledged to be belief, emotion, tradition, or metaphysics. The math she learned with Hans Hahn, the calculus for which she studied with her fellow student and future MIT physicist Vicky Weisskopf, the logic she got from Rudolf Carnap and Carl Gustav Hempel—all at the University of Vienna—but above all the descriptive and projective geometry she learned at the Vienna Institute of Technology (Hochschule) would stand her in good stead when, as an immigrant in Boston, she got part-time jobs at Harvard grading blue books for Vasily Leontiev (until the Harvard men found out that, horrors, a woman was grading their exercises and exams) and at MIT grading for Norbert Wiener (if you don't grade those blue books, no one will), and on 3-D trajectories for John Rule. (When she tried to show Wiener the 3-D slides, she was disappointed to learn that he had only one good eye and so no depth perception.) It was the projective geometry again that began to make her name within the Geoid Branch under O'Keefe, when she insisted on a three-dimensional solution to the problem of conversions between the European and Tokyo datums or the Manchurian (Shinkyo) and Tokyo ones. Because of poor data and the need to have workable conversions during the war, two-dimensional survey grids were rotated until they fit into neighboring surveys when stretched to scale; and then they were "developed" onto a computational reference ellipsoid. But while this was a stopgap, Irene insisted that the future world datums would require three-dimensional approaches—which were deemed unnecessary and too complicated for local geodetic needs —and she began building the geoidal profiles that eventually she would turn into the world datums that would carry her name (Fischer Ellipsoid 1960, updated 1968; or Mercury Datum 1960 and Modified Mercury Datum 1968).

As Irene rose in the ranks, eventually becoming chief of the Geoid Branch and a GS-15, she began to explore a series of historical problems such as the one just alluded to: Why would conventional geodesy insist on sticking to obviously wrong two-dimensional shortcuts? Sometimes she pursued these puzzles in order to break conventionalized procedures that had become blockages to further conceptual development, as in the above example. Sometimes she pursued them just to solve the historical puzzles, as in determining why Eratosthenes' determination of the earth's circumference (250,000 stadia) had been reduced to 180,000 stadia by Posidonius (according to the 1973 *Encyclopedia Britannica*) or by Ptolemy (in the newer editions of the *Encyclopedia Britannica*), a fateful underestimation of the size of the earth that allowed Columbus to persuade his patrons that the distance westward by sea to India and Cathay would be shorter than eastward overland. Posidonius was quoted in the ancient literature with two results: 240,000 stadia by Cleomedes and 180,000 stadia by Strabo. The account in Strabo is confused: he admits not understanding the mathematics but is quite good on the need for repeated cadastral surveys in the Nile Valley, and hence why this should be where Eratosthenes' earth determination produced results so superior to others in antiquity, namely, the accuracy of the distance measurement between Aswan and Alexandria. Strabo seems unaware of the other half of Eratosthenes' procedure, the calculation of the astronomical distance by means of the shadows on a sundial at Alexandria and at a well at Syene marking the summer tropic (there is no shadow at noon at the summer solstice), but he admits that Eratosthenes' figure is good enough for all practical purposes. Further confusion was added in the literature by the claim that Hipparchus had added a little less than 26,000 stadia to Eratosthenes' figure. Since Hipparchus lived after Posidonius and before Ptolemy, his account refutes the claim that there was any generally accepted large reduction in Eratosthenes' number. Recalculating Hipparchus, using his more precise latitude for the summer tropic than assumed in Eratosthenes' time and using the alternatives of the upper and lower limit of Eratosthenes' uncertainty range, Irene arrived at a potential correction of 15,900 stadia. This was clearly on the right track, but 15,900 is not 26,000. "What could I have overlooked? Staring at Pliny's Latin quote: 'Hipparchus . . . adicit stadiorum Paulo minus XXVI M' it suddenly hit me: my 15,900 would be 'stadiorum Paulo minus XVI M,' a little less than 16,000. It would not have been the first time that a copier doubled an X by mistake!" (I. Fischer 2005: 285). But neither this nor other puzzles straightened out along the way explained the 25 percent reduction by Columbus of Eratosthenes' figure. "All clues had led to a dead end. But the corpse was still there: Columbus' underestimate . . . and America was still discovered through that mistake. As in all good mystery stories the solution came from an unexpected side that was there all the time," an unnoticed switch between the medieval Arabic mile, more than two kilometers, and the Roman or Italian mile, about one and a half kilometers. "So here was the 25% reduction through switching miles. It had nothing to do with the dimensions of the Earth" (ibid.: 286).

Irene's solving of historical puzzles of this sort was constant confirmation to me of the value of learning languages and of how much better my parents' European gymnasium education had been than mine. I took four years of Latin and some French and German, but my father had eight years of Latin and four of Greek, and my mother did Latin in school, Greek after school, English and Hebrew, and later taught herself Russian to read technical literature and Yiddish to translate a book about the Ukrainian village of her father's origin.

But perhaps more important in my teenage years of philosophical clarification was the example of the geoid as a model, the idea of manipulable geometric constructions against which a complicated reality can be compared, and of best-fitting ellipsoids, different ones of which might fit a portion of the earth better in different places, and thus the challenge of finding a single world datum or world geodetic system (wGS), as well as the empirical challenges of slowly over time building up the databases to make the modeling and comparison increasingly practical and useful as a launching and research platform. This historical work involved not only famous expeditionary explorations (such as the two geodetic expeditions sent out by the Académie Royale de Paris in 1735–36 to measure arcs in Peru and Lappland), systematic surveys (such as the 1870s Survey of India's extraordinary training of pandits and lamas to secretly measure the distance from Darjeeling to Lhasa hiding strips of paper in Tibetan prayer wheels to record the paces marched), as well as sextant and compass observations; but also the delicate negotiations by Irene and others to get the

South Africans, the Argentineans, the Brazilians, and others to contribute their national survey data to her geodetic world datums.

II

The geoid is defined as that equipotential surface of the earth's gravity
field that most closely approximates mean sea level. It is an uneven
surface with flattening at the poles and bulging at the equator, more
flattening at one pole than the other, and with depressions here and
there, like that around the Hudson Bay caused by the ice age (like a
thumb pressing in on a rubber ball), and differences between the sea
and land and between mountains and other geomorphological features. The Pacific and Atlantic sea levels are also not the same. The
irregularities of the geoid are measured against reference ellipsoids,
known by the numbers defining their flattenings. At every point the
geoid is perpendicular to the plumb line; the difference between this
perpendicular and that of the perpendicular to the best-fitting ellipsoid
is called the deflection of the vertical. Deflections of the vertical are
important indicators of how variations in the gravity force of the earth
from place to place might affect a missile's trajectory.

Sputnik signaled the coming of satellite geodesy, and in 1958 the
Vanguard satellite provided the AMS with a significant new figure for
the oblateness of the earth: 1/298.38+/-0.07. It was only slightly different from the previously accepted figure, but it had far-reaching
implications. "Some thought it not right that the satellite had again
taken sides in the east-west conflict in favor of the wrong side. The
Russians with their Karsoviskiy ellipsoid (flattening 1/298.3) had said
all along that the International flattening 1/297.0 used in the West was
wrong, and that they were right. But we had all the proofs in our
pocket; did the satellite not read the literature?" (I. Fischer 2005: 68).
O'Keefe, after making the public announcement of the new flattening
figure, began immediately to explore the geophysical implications,
pointing out that it contradicted the previous hypothesis that the
earth was essentially in hydrostatic equilibrium. Reanalysis of the
proofs for the old values eventually yielded a new hydrostatic value as
the one for geophysicists to use when studying the forces that shape
the earth.

O'Keefe's analysis of the observations collected by the satellite "also
led to (among other things) the now famous pear-shape of the earth
(O'Keefe, Eckels, and Squires 1959). With his flare for dramatics and

his great talent to drive the significance of a difficult concept home for the grasp of the uninitiated, he managed to transform a drab mathematical coefficient in an abstract theory into a colorful household picture that even made the comics in the newspaper. A "Peanuts" cartoon in 1959 shows Charlie Brown happy with a new globe, something he had always wanted to have. Then Linus tells him that according to the latest scientific discovery, the world is not round, it is pear-shaped; upon which Charlie Brown is so disgusted that he throws the new globe away" (I. Fischer 2005: 69). Twelve years later, when Irene wrote her booklet *Basic Geodesy, An Initiation into the Mysteries of Geodetic Concepts*, published by the U.S. Army Engineer School, Fort Belvoir, Virginia, and widely distributed, she "had wanted to include this cartoon, but quite unexpectedly and contrary to customary experience, I was refused copyright permission. . . . The Army editors, though personally sympathetic, did not dare to allow me to include even a paraphrased version of the cartoon nor the real life story of the elementary school teacher [who wanted to know what to tell her tykes who had objected when she taught that the world was round, that it was not, the earth was pear-shaped]. Even the subtitle of the pamphlet was too much for the Army and was at first dropped but then cautiously" made its way back into the preface (ibid.: 69).

My youth was spent in the aura of these satellite events, competitions with the Soviets, completing the surface triangulation of the long arc from Lappland to Capetown, across the Eurasian mass, extending terrestrial coverage across the Mediterranean and then across other marine expanses.

Part of this geographical extension was the diplomatic game among scientists for genuine international cooperation: one needed survey data from everywhere in order to piece together a global system for everyone's use. These ideals had to be fought for against nationalist control of data and Cold War competitive secrecy. I was privileged to be taken along to some of the international conferences and to meet the players, many of whom became sources for my growing stamp collection: J. J. Levallois and Suzanne Coron (the other female geodesist, "Mme Milligal," Irene suddenly recalls during one of our recent memory forays, a nickname for her command of gravimetric numbers) from France; Brig. Guy Bomford, the father (who referred to his equatorial bulge as an analogy for that of the earth's), from England; and Anthony Bombford, the son, from Australia; Weikko A. Heiskannen from Finland (and Ohio State); Erik Tengström from Sweden; Carlo Morelli from Italy, and many others. It was fascinating to hear stories of and occasionally myself watch Russian scientists being shadowed by their minders, only occasionally able to break away for a real conversation. In one dramatic game of sleuthing, Irene gave a paper in which she spoke of two calculations the Russians might have used and their implications; she then watched closely for the written reports of the conference in their journals. They reported her use of the correct figure, not even mentioning the false decoy, and so she could proceed. On a different, equally fraught historical horizon was the geodetic symposium in Vienna in 1967, her first return to the beloved city of her birth, a doubled town—"the lively town of the symposium, a beautiful town strangely suggesting that we may have visited here before; and another personal town that was crying with silence, a ghost town" (I. Fischer 2005: 157)—when she was greeted in a mixed Viennese rustic and courtly idiom by the host Austrian geodesist, Karl Ledersteger, "Gnädiger Frau, ich habe ein Hünchen mit Ihnen zu rupfen" [Madame, I have a bone to pick with you], wanting to know why she had forced him for years to speak English, not realizing that her mother tongue had been Viennese German.

But the greatest coup of these negotiations was enticing the Brazilians and particularly the Argentineans to give her their survey data so that she could construct a unified South American datum, given explicitly to her individually and not to her agency or government. It was not just a giving of data but an entirely new conceptual framework. Brazil and Argentina had good survey nets in their populated areas but practically none in the upstream river basins. The Andean states did not have very precise surveys, and, despite its name, the High Precision Navigation (MIRAN), and 'high precision' version of the Short Range Navigation System (SHORAN), connection of Venezuela and Brazil did not yield good accuracy. The Provisional South American Datum of 1956, which took as its origin point La Canoa, Venezuela, was affected by the proximity of the Puerto Rican Trench as well as by incomplete computation, and so its projection southward as a continental datum produced increasing distortions. Through the coaxing of the Argentineans and Brazilians to contribute their good survey net data and the selection of a new pair of origins points in both Argentina and Brazil with a dense, reliable geoid profile between them (and through a request for an extra hundred astro stations to strengthen the profile), two of the three necessary conditions for positioning a reference ellipsoid were met, the third point being in the Andes with a condition of less than fifty-meter geoidal height. The new tools of satellite geodesy—Sequential Collation of Range (SECOR), BC-4, and Doppler—were not yet perfected and gave divergent answers, but they were good enough within a range of values to correct the HIRAN procedures. As a further enticement for contributing their data, Irene arranged for the Argentineans to be trained on and be able to use AMS's computers to run their data. The result was an entirely new and useable South American Datum. Jealous bureaucrats in her agency prevented her from attending one of the conventions at which her results were presented, but the South American geodesists gave her a quite unusual and official "Vote of Applause."

The harmonics of these diplomatic games across national boundaries reverberate back into history and ahead into my own career. In 1963, as I was going off to college, Irene received a letter from Erik Norin, a professor at the University of Uppsala, asking for help in retrieving materials from AMS that belonged to the Sven Hedin Foundation of the Swedish Academy of Sciences. In 1946 AMS had agreed to compile a Central Asian Atlas from the field maps and notes of the Sino-Swedish Expedition to Central Asia from 1927 to 1935, led by Sven Hedin, accompanied by Norin and his brother-in-law, Niles Ambolt. Norin had spent some months at AMS on the atlas project in 1946 and 1947 and was still working on the book to accompany the atlas, which he hoped to have ready by 1965, the centenary of Hedin's birth. He had not received back all the materials from AMS, including his personal copy of a rare pamphlet of the Geological Survey of China. The pamphlet turned up. The book did not come out on time, but when Irene visited Norin at the time of a geodetic conference in Uppsala in 1965, she found a file number on a computation sheet in his possession that turned out to be an AMS file number and led to the discovery of a whole shelf of materials and microfilms which were then copied and restored to legibility (the materials had deteriorated over time) for Norin. Norin's *Memoir of Maps* was finally published in 1967, and the following year Irene was able to host him in Washington. He was now interested in using NASA photos of northwest Tibet taken during the Mercury and Gemini missions to improve his maps of that region. Irene understatedly remarks, "The episode of the Sven Hedin project at AMS shows clearly the difference between individual and organizational involvement in a long-term effort. The organizational facilities and manpower resources were needed for such a huge undertaking, but the personal continuity and involvement of Professor Norin prevented the scattering of the material and loss to oblivion" (I. Fischer 2005: 114).

In the following years my own career would repeatedly cross outposts of my mother's work. In 1982, when I taught at the University of Brasilia, I visited the elderly Col. Lelio Graça, who had, with the surveyor Pericles, shown my parents around the then-seven-year-old capital when Irene had come to a conference in Rio de Janeiro in 1967. He was full of fascinating stories of the era of President Juscelino Kubitschek in Brazil and its aftermath. In the 1990s, visiting Cape Town, the surveyor Ernst Fitchens of the Trigonometric Survey, who had shown my mother around in the 1960s, was excited to meet her son and show him around. In Houston, my meetings with and interviewing of the astronaut Storey Musgrave and the aeronautics engineer and lunar lander designer Jack Funk resonated for me through Irene's role in providing NASA with the Mercury Datum. In 1984, my wife and I spent half a year in Ahmedabad, Gujarat. I was studying changing social patterns in the Jain community and would later return to India to study scientists and filmmakers. We lived near the Physical Research Laboratories (PRL), a center of India's space research, established by Vikram Sarabai, and where the geodesist Narendra Saxsena, one of my mother's colleague's research groups had been. Some years later when I returned to India to interview scientists and engineers, I had some wonderful interviews with E. V. Chitnis, Sarabai's right-hand man, himself a physicist, who had become interested in communications. The PRL had pioneered uses of satellites for monsoon monitoring, agricultural crop estimation, radio and television broadcasting of information for farmers, and educational programing and movies for villagers. Filmmakers such as Ketan Mehta had their start in these ventures, and anthropologists had done village studies to track the impact. At the time India had won a bid for time sharing on NASA satellites, winning out over Brazil, but had also begun designing its own multipurpose satellites.

Everywhere I went, there were points of attachment, people and memories that allowed Irene to travel along, as we might say today, virtually.

III

Oceanography, marine geodesy, satellite geodesy, and now space geodesy have transformed the field. Irene can't keep up, and I can do so only as a lay outsider. We get EOS, Transactions of the American Geophysical Union, and I read or summarize the articles of interest to her—the print is too small for her to read, and the technical details are usually not of sufficient use to her for me to enlarge the print for her on a Xerox machine. In the issue for April 22, 2003, there is a fascinating piece entitled "Geodesy Is Not Just for Static Measurements Any More." It reads like an update of O'Keefe's inspiration to use the first observations from the Vanguard satellite in 1958 to reevaluate the geophysical implications of a new understanding of hydrostatics of the earth. Space geodesy has become a new remote sensing tool, "poised to advance geophysical understanding of mass transports in the Earth system's multiple 'fluid' components'" (EOS 84 [16]:145). These fluid components include the atmosphere, hydrosphere, cryosphere, biosphere, lithosphere, and the deep interior of mantle and cores. For example, this article, by Benjamin Chao of the Goddard Space Flight Center, suggests that the all-ocean general circulation models in use today do not correctly conserve the water mass, the atmospheric general circulation models do not correctly conserve the dry air mass, and the large-scale land hydrological and crysopheric mass budget remains poorly understood.

While the technologies are new or improved—satellite laser ranging, very-long-baseline interferometry, land/ice laser altimetry, GPS occultation for atmospheric sounding, satellite-to-satellite tracking, and space-borne accelerometers for precision gravity measurements—one wonders what a young Irene Fischer would accomplish in this new world of instrumentation, as she had done in the early days of the Universal Automatic Computer (UNIVAC) and early satellite geodesy. In those days, she resisted American showoff enjoyment of multiple equations with multiple unknowns when things could be done more simply with fewer equations and fewer unknowns. She worked her desk calculator and her pen and pencil to provide checks on the huge mainframe computers, which generated mistakes that took months to track down. Her firm control of logic and problem formulation cut through many artifacts of signal/noise conundrums that the new space geodesy seems to be multiplying. And yet, each new technology producing new "facts of life," as the Vanguard flattening number did and as satellite techniques did for Irene's South American Datum, also provides new insights, understandings of interconnections, and implications of the earth system.

In the 1970s Irene played a role in making it possible for oceanographers and geodesists to talk to one another across conflicting assumptions and methods, clarifying the differences between the geoid and the "standard ocean" and fusing the techniques of classical geodesy, oceanography, and satellite altimetry into a workable marine geodesy. Oceanographers mysteriously (to a geodesist) argued passionately (Irene used the emotional heat of the debates as initial cues to where crucial issues lay for the oceanographers) about whether or not mean sea level sloped down or up toward north and even more mysteriously admitted that mean sea level was only nearly level; moreover, there were odd bulges in what they insisted were "dynamically parallel" surfaces to the geoid in the ocean.

Initially, Irene thought, since satellite geodesy determined long distances across the waters and established positions of islands and ships with increasing accuracies; since geodetic markers were being placed on the ocean floor to create a marine control net like earlier land control nets; and since bathymetric (ocean depth) data were being collected through increasingly sophisticated methods, satellite altimeters could eventually give marine geoidal undulations and deflections of the vertical as well as monitor wave heights and ocean currents. But the mean ocean surface was not the geodesist's geoid, nor was it a reference surface for oceanographers. While an altimeter in a satellite measures its distance to the nearest surface point on the ocean, to reach the geoid one must make corrections for the variable oceanographic features, including salinity, density, and gravimetric deflections from the vertical. Oceanographers used steric leveling—calculated seawater densities—with reference surfaces at two thousand meters depth, considered to be nearly level, although in some regions there were strong currents even at that depth, and so some oceanographers preferred to use other depths. While oceanographers argued that this isobaric surface two thousand meters down was dynamically parallel to the geoid, Irene demonstrated otherwise and tracked down the historical and conceptual reasons.

Her historical investigation revealed that the tables in use in the 1970s were the ones constructed by V. Bjerkness in 1910, based on twenty-four water samples taken from the surface of the ocean in 1902 during the international exploration of the north European waters and on a single water sample taken at three thousand meters depth off the coast of Portugal in 1908. And while there were criticisms that these samples might not be representative of the whole ocean and that there would be variation in intensity of gravity, Bjerkness argued for a simplified model of a standard ocean, an inherently spherical model, conceptually quite different from the geoid. The eighteenth-century expedition of the French Academy of Sciences, mentioned above, demonstrated that the measured length of a one-degree arc in the north-south direction depended on its geographic location. At the same time, Isaac Newton's law of universal attraction provided the understanding that the rotation of the earth would flatten it at the poles. The theoretical model then was an ellipsoid rather than a spheroid, but such understandings had not been incorporated into the standard ocean. Further, when incorporating the irregular distribution of mass into the Figure of the Earth, Irene pointed out, geodesy measures the differences between the ellipsoid and the geoid, while the oceanographers had no similar procedure, and hence the odd bulges and arguments about local slopes of mean sea level up or down toward north.

The idea of using altimeters in satellites had been talked about in 1964, and in 1971 they were put on board the Skylab, which was launched in 1973, as an experiment. They were successful beyond all expectations in providing a geoidal profile along the satellite path in remarkable agreement with an existing gravimetric profile computed by Manik Talwani of the Lamont Geological Observatory. Altimeters were included in the GEOS-C satellites launched in 1974. Irene integrated satellite techniques with astrogeodetic and gravimetric ones in order to create a useable marine geodesy, initially for the area around Kwajalein Atoll test range and later for the Mid-Atlantic Ridge.

I recently found Kathleen Crane's autobiography, *Sea Legs, Tales of a Woman Oceanographer* (2003). I thought Irene might be fascinated to read an account from the other side, as it were, of her friendly debates with oceanographers in the 1970s, of the struggles of another successful woman scientist who also had to build a career in the 1970s by surmounting various male obstacles—most seriously the refusal of American naval ships to allow women on board, so she did her work on the more friendly Scandinavian and other ships—who also had been interested in midocean ridges, and who worked not only at Scripps and Woods Hole, but also at the renamed Lamont-Doherty Geological Laboratory (renamed again in 1993 the Lament-Doherty Earth Observatory). Lamont's Talwani, as noted, produced the gravimetric profiles Irene had used in the early 1970s in her forays into marine geodesy and was, in 1981, while Crane was there, director of the observatory (I. Fischer 1988: 401; Crane 2003: 184).

Crane was particularly interested in the heat gradients, hot springs, and volcanoes that were discovered in the spreading centers of the midocean ridges. These promised to transform models of ocean circulation, which traditionally had assumed the heat driving the system came only from the sun. Teeming new forms of life were found in these hot springs and vents. Crane helped pioneer side-looking sonar and manned submersibles, working at the Galápagos spreading center with Robert Ballard and the Woods Hole's *Alvin* and later, while at Lamont-Doherty, with Russian colleagues in Lake Baikal with Canadian-built *Pisces* and Finnish-built *Mir* submersibles. Irene was a user of bathymetric charts compiled by such side-looking sonars in multiple beam arrangements which could sweep the areas on both sides of a moving ship out to more than two miles. Such bathymetric charts were not yet available for her Kwajalein studies but became available by the time she

produced her paper in 1977 on the Mid-Atlantic Ridge. She blew up a
newly compiled bathymetric chart of 1976 and by hand outlined in
color the major contours every thousand meters. She was fascinated:

> I took the work home and engaged my husband to help. We were richly
> rewarded when out of the maze gradually a pattern emerged. The color
> scheme brought out an unbelievably dissected landscape of jagged moun-
> tain blocks, separated by deep canyons at right angles to the slightly NNE
> direction of the crest and rift valley. . . . Way back in the first half of [the
> twentieth] century, the Dutch geophysicist F. A. Venig Meinesz and oth-
> ers made gravity measurements in a submarine in an ambitious attempt
> to decipher these messages of what's happening underneath. And way
> back at the start of my career in 1952–53, I had listened to doubts about
> the validity and reliability of such measurements, and had contributed a
> study in the Western Mediterranean Sea dispelling that doubt. Now I had
> come full circle, happy to find a few of Venig Meinesz' gravity measure-
> ments within the area of my map sheet. . . . Venig Meinesz thought there
> must be some isostatic compensation under the ridge. Somewhat to the
> north of our area, unfortunately not within it, there had been two scien-
> tific cruises producing two transoceanic gravimetric and bathymetric
> profiles, from which scientists of the Lamont Geological Observatory had
> deduced that there was indeed some isostatic compensation under the
> ridge; and they had constructed some tentative suboceanic density mod-
> els to account for the discrepancy between the observed gravity and that
> calculated from the bathymetry. (I. Fischer 2005: 321)

Getting oriented in a new book like Crane's with new names and
new career trajectories and institutions is not easy when you can't read
the book yourself. Books like this rarely come in large print, and when
they do they often do not come with enough white around the margins
and paragraphs to make reading easy. Listening to someone else read
takes focus and attention. Becoming familiar with a book is a different
process in old age if you can't flip around in the pages or use the index
yourself, more like exploring a new territory with a cane. And if your
memory is no longer quite so good, things easily get confused. You fill
in hypothetically, sometimes coming to closure about connecting the
dots with false memories that seem so clearly right. So the first couple
of times we tried to read Crane's autobiography, the engagement was
only partially successful. But the book was not forgotten: it was recalled from the library at Irene's request to try again, this time more
successfully not by reading from beginning to end, but by zeroing in
on projects and places, looking for the meat, for the points of attachment, for the personal and social in the science, and skipping the early

childhood and other such points of lesser triangulation. That Crane became a mother was important, as were the expeditions into the Arctic Ocean from Spitzbergen, where "you" (she sometimes confuses me with my father) spent time. Spitzbergen was a very important memory place topos. But so were the oceanographic techniques: side-looking sonar, oh yes, I remember that.

Irene's love has always been geometry (even though the intuitive ability to draw a clock face or visualize geographical relations has been disturbed by, as she puts it, the loss of pieces of her *Gehirn*), and her career was marvelously adapted to the exploration of the Figure of the Earth and the parallax of the moon rather than to geophysics itself. Her scientific career from 1952 to 1977 coincided with the golden age of classical geodesy, and she reveled in her ability to participate and lead.

IV

The geoid for me, as should by now be clear, is a material-semiotic object—hard as rock, fluid as the sea, smooth and distorted as a computational surface, changing as an infrastructural platform for research—and also a transitional object that draws me into mathematics, history, far-away places, and a community of people from Eratosthenes to O'Keefe, mathematicians to astronauts, and always already into the family romance that an immigrant geographer-historian and his mathematician-geodesist wife created. The geoid is—like my mother's career, my ethnicity, and other aspects of my identity—something that most people know little about, something obscure and marginal to most people but preciously constructed over many generations, and in its own minor key is quite central to the harmonics of the worlds we inhabit.

V

The voices—the evocations—of the geoid are a community that Irene and I share in her autumn years, warm memories, incidents, and stories. They help to orient her world, reaffirm her personhood, allow her dignity amidst the indignities of old age. In this community, at this time, it is less important that sometimes fantasy and the dream world intervene, that logic gets confused, that reading cannot be managed, that what was once intellectual challenge is now "too technical." What is important is the self and its relations, the ability to feel oneself as sentient, as having accomplishments, as being recognized. Most of the people she writes about and for are gone or at least retired. The memoir, Irene complains, was not written as a primer, "Geodesy? What's That?," but as a sharing of memories, personal stories, and perspectives for her colleagues. The lovely opening is of her retirement party, when she began to tell stories, and people responded, suggesting she write them down. That opening was cut from the abridgment, as were several of her favorite anecdotes about her family life as it intersected with her career life. And yet, the complaints themselves remain the struggle for control of self, the assertion that she is still here, still engaged, and wanting recognition and engagement.

The geoid is a transitional object. In the past it condensed the geodetic interfaces of surveying and gravimetry, of oceanography and astrogeodetics, and of gender in a man's world, as when a Military Air Transport Service (MATS) plane called passengers by rank and told the little woman who responded to "Fischer, G-12," as the highest-ranked passenger, that women should wait until the higher ranks were called; and as when her name was removed from one of her papers because some bureaucrat thought it improper for a woman's name to appear first on a scientific paper, later to be restored by red-faced higher-ups who knew who this scientist was. The geoid also condensed the interfaces of bureaucracy and science, as when administrators, regarding conferences as vacation perks they appropriated for themselves, refused to allow her to travel to present her papers at conferences, with the consequences thereby of being able neither to provide answers to technical questions about the paper or the larger project at the conferences, nor to bring back to the researchers the useful professional information that are the rationale for scientific meetings. In the 1970s there are increasingly stories even of attempts to sabotage conference presentations, publications, and promotions that reflect on a deteriorating bureaucratic environment at sharp odds with her increasing international recognition and also awards and medals for distinguished service, including election to the National Academy of Engineering. Management courses became obligatory for branch chiefs, and at one point Irene amusingly describes a course she had to sit through based around the faddish theme of why women do not succeed because of fear of success. Might perhaps her retort that an immigrant struggling to rebuild a life did not have the luxury of such fears have contributed to the rejection of her autobiography by feminist editors of a "women and science" series at Rutgers for being insufficiently feminist? (They had eagerly solicited autobiographies of women scientists because they said few such role models existed.) Or perhaps she was simply not enough of a celebrity figure for them.

Although Joseph Dracup's recent history of geodetic surveys notes that "Irene Fischer was long recognized as the U.S. expert on datums, ellipsoids and the geoid . . . [and] anyone who ever heard Mrs. Fischer discuss these elements, among the least understood of geodetic subjects, always came away with a clearer picture of them" (2000: 262); and although she was elected in 2002 to the National Imaging and Mapping Agency (NIMA) Hall of Fame, still, much of her work is little known outside the field.

But now the geoid is a transitional object in another sense, a vehicle for negotiations of old age, a territory for which the geodesy is as complicated as those new geodesies whose technologies outpace their ability to securely tell noise from signal. The geoid is a mutual reference surface. The geoid keeps the two of us in sync and grounded.

Embryonic, zoonic
Techtonic, cyclonic,
We humans are never humane
Explosion, erosion,
Corrosion, implosion—
And back into Chaos again!
—FREDERICK WINSON, *The Space Child's Mother Goose*

Neither right nor morality are ever given in their pure state . . . intertwined
[they] offer to human action its space of playing; its concrete latitude. . . .
neither the level of foundational freedom nor . . . of the rules of right. It is the
appearance of a certain pragmatic freedom, where it is a question of pretension of cunnings, of fishy intentions, of dissimulations, of undisclosed efforts
to influence, of compromises and waiting.—MICHEL FOUCAULT, *Introduction to Kant's Anthropology*

Particle creation in high-energy collisions [are a little like] when two tax-
ies collide, they may both emerge undamaged, accompanied by five or six
other taxis arising from the initial kinetic energy of the former.—BERNARD
D'ESPAGNAT, *On Physics and Philosophy*

Time again to review, rethink, recalibrate. Immanuel Kant did it in
1798, Alfred Kroeber in 1948. Earlier, ibn Khaldun in 1377, al-Biruni in
1000, Fa-hsien in 414, Herodotus in the fifth century BCE, among
others, provided comparative *Prolegomenas*, *Chronicles*, and *Travels*.
Max Weber produced his *Basic Concepts* (in sociology) retrospectively, after he had finished *Economy and Society*; and particular domains of anthropological thought were configured by Emile Durkheim's *Elementary Forms* (of religious life) and *Rules* (of sociological
method), William James's *Varieties* (of religious life), Lévi-Strauss's
Elementary Forms (of kinship) and *Mythologies*, Clifford Geertz's essays on "Cultural Systems" (religion as; moral thought as) and *Inter-*

pretation (of culture). *An Appraisal of Anthropology Today* was an international symposium collection edited by Sol Tax (1953). More recently, *Anthropology as Cultural Critique* (Marcus and Fischer 1986) initiated a new series of reorientations. Even more recently, there have been a series of efforts to account for new globalized assemblages proceeding topographically (*Global Assemblages, Friction*)[1] or methodologically and topically topologically (third spaces, *Emergent Forms* [of life and the anthropological voice]).

The recent "rediscovery" of Kant's Anthropology (Foucault 1961, Jacobs and Kain 2003; Wilson 2006)—both the course he taught for twenty-three years—from 1772–73 to 1795–96, and the final text of 1798, as well as the recent publication of a critical edition of fifteen hundred pages of student notes on seven years of his course (hence Anthropology capitalized but not italicized to indicate the course and the text)—is not only a challenge to the conventional account of Kant's philosophical critiques (of pure reason, of practical reason, and of judgment), reminding us that Kant privileged real-world experience and, like William James after him, knew that reason alone not only had its limits but could be misleading: hence his stress on *Gelahrheit* and *Weltkenntnis* (learning through experience, knowledge of the world) as opposed to the *Gelehrtheit* (scholastic, imitative learning), and his title *Anthropology from a Pragmatic Point of View* [*pragmatischer Hinsicht*]. "The one [*Gelehrt*, scholastic] only understands the play [*Spiel*] of which it has been a spectator, but the other has participated [*mitgespielt*] in it."[2]

It is also a reminder of the broadest intellectual aspirations of the field of anthropology. As Robert Louden writes, "Anthropology was a new academic discipline in the late eighteenth century and Kant played a pivotal role in its creation" (2003: 60). Moreover, Kant's Anthropology "inaugurates the continental tradition of philosophical anthropology out of which numerous twentieth century intellectual movements both grew (e.g. existentialism) and reacted against (e.g. Foucault's early archeology work)." Indeed, among Foucault's first works was a commentary on Kant's Anthropology. And third, "In his writings and lectures on ethics, Kant repeatedly not only invokes the term 'anthropology'" (ibid.), but insists: "In the doctrine of virtue I always consider historically and philosophically what happens before I point out what ought to happen" (Wilson 2006: 13). The Anthropology course grew first within and then separated out of the Geography course that he gave every year from his earliest teaching years (1755–56). Johann Gottfried von Herder's notes as a student in Kant's lectures mention anthropology as a topic as early as 1762–64 (ibid.: 8, 13). Once Kant introduced the Anthropology as a separate course, it alternated with the Geography as a sequence every year (Wilson 2006). The Anthropology was also always taught alongside his course on Ethics. As Werner Stark puts it, "No ethics without anthropology! . . . No anthropology without ethics!" (Stark 2003: 23).

The Anthropology was intended to be popular and attracted some forty students a year, and one year, seventy. It addressed the pedagogical problem that university students did not have the experience and maturity needed to make the knowledge of his philosophical courses applicable to their lives. This was also the rationale for his Geography course: "When I recognized immediately at the beginning of my academic lecture [career] a great negligence existed among young students, that they learned early to reason, without possessing sufficient historical knowledge which could take the place of [lack of] experience: I formed the resolution to make the history of the current condition of the earth or geography, in the broadest sense, into a pleasant and easy summary, which could serve to prepare them for practical reason, . . . I called such a discipline . . . Physical Geography." (*Kant Gesammelte Schriften* [Kant's Collected Writings, KGS], Nachricht 2:312, quoted in Wilson 2006: 10–11). Anthropology for Kant, Wilson argues, was "the best and most efficient way to teach students critical thinking." Scholarly neglect of Kant's Anthropology, she says, evidences "a prejudice amongst philosophers for conceptual philosophy over philosophy that points to experience. . . . This bias is not new. Kant was aware of it too. . . . he didn't agree with it. . . . That is why Kant dedicated his teaching career to doing anthropology" (ibid.: 2).

The program set out by Kant contains within it instabilities and tensions that have remained generative. Indeed, writes Diane Beddoes, "Kant by convention . . . has been welded to reason, law, the categorical imperative, and a reductive view of science. Yet on reading Kant, Kleist [1777–1810] took to wandering through a Europe blasted by the Napoleonic wars, torn between fanatical patriotism and despair; his Kant is the pulverizer, demolishing predictability, progress and faith and leaving only irresolvable ambiguities" (1997: 28). If Beddoes's rhetoric is beautifully (sublimely?) tinged with the trembling of a late twentieth-century world blasted by wars, torn between fanaticism and despair, if she underplays the degree to which degrees of certainty are always built upon ascertaining the limits of knowledge (a Kantian perspective, also a Qur'anic *tafsir* [hermeneutic] and Talmudic one), nonetheless she captures one side of why Kant remains fascinating two centuries after his death in 1804, the other being the efforts, mostly scholastic but some pragmatic, to work out the systematicities in his moral, aesthetic, and practical philosophies, built upon the Enlightenment charge *sapere aude* ("dare to know"; also a charge of Qur'an and hadith and of the Talmud).[3] The great tremors of Kant's lifetime were the American and French revolutions and the violent births of modernities in Europe, the colonies, and the peripheries beyond.

Kant apparently was an avid reader of travelers' reports, and the Geography began as an attempt to turn this reading into cosmopolitan knowledge that would prepare students to become citizens of the world, to develop the faculty of judgment, to exercise freedom within the intrinsic communal nature of human beings, recognizing that people's mores differ in different places and times. Kant's situatedness in Königsberg, as Foucault notes, "administrative capital, university city and commercial center, crossroad, near the sea, [had] a constant educative value in the comprehension of man as citizen of the entire world" (Foucault 1961, Bove trans.: 28).[4]

What difference would it have made had Kant been sitting in Cochin, Kaifeng, Banda Acheh, Constantinople, or Cuzco, nodes in earlier global webs of cultural exchange? That Kant, instead of debating with Mendelssohn and Maimon, would have, in Cochin, been trading the botanical and zoological knowledges that Garcia da Orta and Hendrik von Reede learned (and passed on to Carolus Linnaeus) from the toddy tappers of Kerela while discussing Ayurvedic and Greek (Yunani) medicine with the local (less empirically knowledgeable) Brahmin pandits and Muslim hakims (Grove 1995). The Kant in Cuzco could have learned history with *quipu* aids to historical and political economy accounts of the Inca empire, and perhaps the ecological knowledges embedded in the talmud of Amazon myths that Lévi-Strauss would begin to decipher and annotate a century and a half later.

Kant of Königsberg, of course, is both an innovator and a man of his times. His vocabulary develops within a discourse about human nature and the ways to study human nature in the wake of the scientific revolution in the natural sciences, as well as within a neo-Stoic Christian vocabulary of Providence and final ends (or teleology). In the former, he is in conversation with Christian Thomasius, Christian August Crusius, Alexander Gottlieb Baumgarten, Johann Joachim Spalding, Thomas Abbt, Herder, Gotthold Ephraim Lessing, Moses Mendelssohn, Moses Maimon, Condillac, Condorcet, Voltaire, Montesquieu, Adam Smith, David Hume, Frances Hutchinson, Lord Shaftesbury (Anthony Ashley Cooper), Pietro Verri, and Rousseau.

Building upon and modifying Rousseau, Kant adopts a view of the human species that is, in principle, capable of self-perfecting, or expanding its powers, exercising freedom, and refining its morality through social interaction that is not just a synchronic cosmopolitanism, but also has a historical dimension, and future-oriented and future-shaping dimensions. But this Enlightenment vision, as both Susan Shell and Foucault note, is grounded in conflict, suffering, and the triangulation of faculties. Subjectivity, self-consciousness, and sensibility, Foucault points out, are never given but always reemerging, under construction. E.g.: "The study of sensibility, whilst reworking the great critical opposition of *Schein* (appearance) and *Ersheinung* (phenomenon), does not explore what can be held as well-founded in the phenomenon, but what has something at once fascinating and precarious within the fragment of appearance, since the latter veils what it makes shimmer (dangle), and also comes to transmit what she steals" (Foucault 1961, Bove trans.: 13). Against Rousseau's fantasy of human consciousness as providing a feeling for the wholeness of our experience, Kant recognizes totality as merely "an idea of reason that cannot be felt" except in momentary experiences of the sublime (Shell 2003: 221). "Life involves more pain than pleasure," and "pain is the natural goad by which man is prompted to develop his talents and abilities before reason is ready to take over" (ibid.: 195).

As a stoic, Kant recommends meditation on the insignificance of life, but in terms of analyzing the operations of mind (*Gemüth*) and social being (*Menschenwesen*), Kant stresses triangulation of competing forms and faculties as the basis of judgment. Kant's notion of human freedom (*freihandelndes Wesen*, literally free-handed being) has to do with these exchanges, in the circulation, for instance, of a husband's "pretension to reduce the freedom of the woman in marriage," the husband's moral recognition of his wife as a subject of freedom, and the "woman's pretension to exercise, in spite of [patriarchal laws of] marriage, her sovereignty over man" (Foucault 1961, Bove trans.: 5): "Thus a whole network is created where neither right nor morality are ever given in their pure state; a network where they, intertwined, offer to human action its space of playing; its concrete latitude. This is neither the level of foundational freedom nor the level of the rules of right. It is the appearance of a certain pragmatic freedom, where it is a question of pretension, of cunnings, of fishy intentions, of dissimulations, of undisclosed efforts to influence, of compromises and waiting" (ibid.).

Thus Kant articulates three productive antinomies, aporias, or instabilities: human nature as cultural; methods and critique; problems of evil, human conflict, and the mismatches between individual intentions, system dynamics, and social forces at different scales, between *polis* and *kosmopolis*, nation-state and global competitions.

A first productive instability, oscillation, tension, or chiasmic exchange is the tension between regulative ideals and ethnographic realities (as with competence versus performance in grammatical speech production, *langue* versus *parole*, justice versus law, models or reference rules versus real-world approximations and imperfections, and so on): "I shall always begin by considering historically and philosophically what happens before specifying what ought to happen. . . . my purpose [is] to establish what . . . the rule of [human] behavior is when, transcending the two types of limit, [the human being] strives to attain the highest level of physical or moral excellence, though falling short of that attainment to a greater or lesser degree. This method of moral enquiry is an admirable discovery of our times, which, when viewed in the full extent of its program, was entirely unknown to the ancients" (Kant's course announcement, 1765, quoted by Stark 2003: 23, 34n19). This is true both on the individual and social levels:

> [Pragmatic anthropology] examines what the human being is only far enough to draw out rules concerning what he can make of himself. The determination [*Bestimmung*] of human character depends, not on his drives and desires, but rather solely on the manner in which he modifies these. One also says nothing, if one uses the word "character" to refer to a human being's capacities; [it concerns] how he makes use of them, and what he will do. (Quoted in Stark 2003: 27 – 30; citations omitted)

Human nature is an evolving and emergent combination of technical, pragmatic, and moral predispositions. As Wilson (2006: ch. 4) and Wood (2003) explicate: "Technical" here means manipulating things, including the transition from hunter-gatherer and pastoral economies to urban-agricultural ones as crucial to property relations and forms of the political state (Wood sees striking anticipations of Marx). "Pragmatic" means culture, education, active social organization: civil constitutions, disciplinary cultures, becoming civilized (*gesittet*), progressive changes in marriage, and the possibility of developing prudence (*Klugheit*) as opposed to cunning (*Arglist*). "Moral" means treating oneself and others according to principles of freedom under laws, or governances through self-given rational laws.

A second instability, oscillation, or tension is that of methods and critique. If the *object* of knowledge is in unstable oscillation between the empirical and the effort toward expansion of pragmatic and prudential capacities (the cultural, the moral), the *methods* of self-knowledge (individual and social) are equally unstable or in oscillation between the means and limits of self-knowledge. Here the role of both critical thinking or critique and of experiential knowledge (*Weltkennt-*

nis) is central. *The Critique of Pure Reason,* after all, is about the limits of reason, about the reflexive use of reason to determine its limits. As Wood again explicates, correcting the misunderstandings of philosophers such as Alasdair MacIntyre, "Metaphysically we know that as natural beings we fall under the universal causal mechanism. But our capacity to investigate this causality empirically is virtually nonexistent" (Wood 2003: 45). There follows a catalogue of Kantian difficulties of self-knowledge:

> When our incentives are active, we are not observing ourselves; and when we are observing ourselves, our incentives are at rest.... When a person is observed by others, he wants to represent himself and makes his own person into an artificial illusion.... Without noticing ... we suppose we are discovering within us what we ourselves have put there.... The hard descent into the Hell of self-knowledge usually only produces anguish and despair which unfits them for knowledge and action.... Nothing is more harmful to a human being than being a precise observer of himself.... All self-scrutinizers fall into the gloomiest hypochondria.... (Wood 2003: 50; citations omitted)

Kant's view "that we are psychologically opaque," Wood concludes, "has more to do with a set of ideas more often associated with . . . Nietzsche and Freud": most of our mental life consists of "obscure representations," paradigmatically those in the way people deal with sexual thoughts and desires (ibid.). Deleuze similarly observes that even in *The Critique of Pure Reason,* "Kant constantly returns to the theme that there are *internal illusions* and *illegitimate uses* of faculties. The Imagination sometimes dreams rather than schematizes" (Deleuze 1963: 24).

Crucial here is the role of representations, what in the debates of the nineteenth century will come to be called intersubjectivity, and the role of how different languages divide up the semantic universe differently. The German vocabulary of representation (*Bild, Vorbild, Nachbild, Einbildung, Bildung*) and imagination (*Einbildungskraft, Vorstellung, wahnen, Wahnsinn*) becomes very productive for Kant, Hegel, Dilthey, Simmel, and others, engaged in disambiguating, refining, and justifying the methods of the moral or human sciences (*Geisteswissenschaften*), cultural and social analyses (*Kulturwissenschaften, Sozialwissenschaften*), as well as for twentieth-century followers in phenomenology, existentialism, pragmatism, structuralism, poststructuralism, programming, and modeling.

Third Instability (oscillations and tensions): problems of evil, human conflict, and the mismatch between individual intentions, system dynamics, social forces at different scales, between the *polis* and *kosmopolis*, nation-state and global competitions. While Kant's neo-Stoic Christian language is now archaic, the instabilities and tensions remain. Kant speaks of the human species as the unit toward the perfection of which the human finds its destiny and invokes at various points the logic of the Stoic line, *quem fata non ducunt, trahunt* (whomever the fates do not lead, they drag), like a dog, bound to a cart, running alongside or being dragged along. Wars, floods, conflict, we often say, may turn out "in the end" to have a silver lining, "to be for the good," albeit a good we did not have in mind and causing much suffering along the way. British social anthropology, and especially the Manchester School (Max Gluckman, Victor Turner), wrote powerful ethnographic and analytic case studies of just such conflicts between actors' intentions and the way the social structure overrode the intentions of individuals on all sides. Kant, we might say, did not yet have the mid-twentieth-century notion of complex and open systems and instead relied upon the vocabulary of prudence, pragmatism, drive for species preservation, and providence at the species level.[5]

The crucial term here is "pragmatism," *Anthropology from a Pragmatic Point of View*, from the point of view of human action in its broadest sense—including the body, the living species around us, and the physical environment or Gaia more generally—human *action* as opposed to just human *acts*, as a means of *cosmopolitan* action (*mitspielen*) in the world (*Weltkenntnis*). Pragmatic anthropology is contrasted with physiological anthropology (of the physician Ernst Platner), which attempted to reduce all to the body, as today we might object to the reductionism of sociobiology and evolutionary psychology. Pragmatic anthropology is contrasted with scholastic anthropology and introspective (empirical) psychology. Pragmatic anthropology is intended both to be useful in guiding cosmopolitan action and to teach prudence, the ability to judge actions in the world by reference to global practices and long-term rather than short-term returns.

Pragmatism would, of course, be the term picked up in the nineteenth century and twentieth by William James, John Dewey, George Herbert Mead, C. S. Peirce, and by the wing of logical positivism led by the founder Moritz Schlick and later Charles Morris in Chicago. For the American (and Viennese) pragmatists, observation was a starting point, as it was for Kant. James, like Kant, would write about how difficult it was to disprove parapsychology and how reasoning alone (pure reason) can lead astray, thus requiring some physical evidence for scientific proof (a set of conundrums or oscillations and instabilities explored in the case of Robert Boyle's experiments at the Royal

Society by Steven Shapin and Simon Shaffer [1985] and by a number of science studies investigations thereafter). Dewey would assert the notion of a public as that which the experts cannot see, the unintended consequences of human actions. Mead would expand upon Kant's insistence that the individual's self-fashioning is always routed via others, education, influence of society, what in the later ethnographic version of Barney G. Glass's and Anselm L. Strauss's "grounded theory" would be called symbolic interactionism. The semioticians Peirce and Morris would insist on concepts being *concepts for* someone, along with all the other informational and affective "pragmatics" that speech acts convey, often without the full consciousness of the speaker, and that would become a fundamental feature of anthropological sociolinguistics. Philosophers such as Ian Hacking call themselves pragmatic realists, meaning thereby that objects like electrons are real insofar as human actors can use them or their representational and instrumented forms to effect changes in the world, without further need for impossible ontological verification.

I have picked on Kant's *Anthropology from a Pragmatic Point of View* partly to push back the genealogy begun in chapter 1 and partly because the publication of his students' notes and of several revisionary evaluations of his Anthropology reopens the ambivalent but perennial discussion of the relation between the Enlightenment and contemporary movements both in anthropology and in the human and social sciences generally: poststructuralisms, deconstruction, critical anthropology, interpretative anthropology, postcolonial anthropology, and so on. The Enlightenment was not so ethnocentric and parochial as some detractors suggest (where would the goals and values of postcolonial histories and anthropologies be without it?), and neither are the recent movements so distanced from the procedures, instabilities, and oscillations of the Enlightenment as their detractors on the intellectual right claim, speaking in the name of Truth, Objectivity, Foundationalism, and so on. Particularly for French theory in the late twentieth century, Kant remains an important intertext: for Bourdieu, Deleuze, Derrida, Foucault, Levinas, Lyotard, and others.

Of special interest today are the instabilities or tensions in Kant's articulations, many of which remain generatively productive and in fact require a deconstructive understanding of these fields of discussion as fields of tension or tropes of debate among valid principles and *Gestalt* switches. Derrida's readings of Kant's essays "Religion at the Limits of Reason Alone" and "On a Newly Arisen Superior Tone in Philosophy" are exemplary in this respect. Kant's Anthropology was a major statement of the Enlightenment, both insisting upon the tools of reason, political citizenship, cosmopolitan politics, an international system of constitutional republics, and human rights. He was not always pleased to see the directions in which some of his students took what came to be called German Idealism, nor would he have agreed with the way in which the academic philosophical traditions still are biased in favor of conceptual as opposed to experience-based philosophy, pure reason, or at least reason highly protected from the realities of the world. Wilson and the authors in the Jacobs and Kain volume make the case that the Anthropology has an important function in the overall project of the composition of the Critiques,[6] and I would broaden this claim to one of the important function today of Anthropology for any viable philosophy to have traction in the world.

There was a moment, in fact, in the 1960s and 1970s, when Anthropology seemed poised to take over something like the function of *Anthropology from a Pragmatic Point of View*, in the push to expand the university curriculum to be culturally more inclusive, to perhaps use anthropology to replace classics or national literary canons at the center of general education. (The anthropologist invoked as a figure of speech has taken hold in popular discourse: "an anthropologist would say," meaning a social comparativist and even human species perspective.) Comparative literature departments, centers for cultural studies, postcolonial studies, film studies, and some women's studies programs also were poised to join hands with anthropology in this moment of change. The moment passed, but it may yet return in other guises, perhaps via the vehicles of the new media studies programs and their burgeoning possibilities across the curriculum and their production from many sites across the globe.

One of these is the continuing fascination with Kant among physicists who draw out the implications for our worldview of quantum mechanics and string theory, such as Bernard d'Espagnat's *On Physics and Philosophy*. d'Espagnat notes that

> The question "reality or just model" never comes to light in the articles physicists write. . . . their theoretical constructions, elaborate as they may be at the level of equations and methods are left by them very much "open" regarding concepts [and are] not in the least worried by the fact that some of these principles [of standard quantum mechanics] impart a fundamental role to such notions as "measurement" and "preparation of system states." Now this fact—the occurrence of a reference to human action within the very axioms of physics—. . . implies that the theories built up in this way markedly depart from a principle that was one of the main guidelines of all classical ones. I mean the rule that basic scientific

statements should be expressed in a radically objectivist language, making no reference whatsoever, be it explicit or implicit, to us ("operators" or "measurers"). (2002: 18)

His initial example is the creation of particles in high-energy collisions, which is, he jokes, a little like two taxis colliding, "both emerg[ing] undamaged, accompanied by five or six other taxis arising from the initial kinetic energy of the former" (ibid.: 15). Creation, he notes, is not a scientific notion, and to work with what happens in an accelerator requires reducing it to something we can master: system states and changes. The mathematical formalism that predicts such occurrences (first predicted by P. A. M. Dirac), he continues, "yields not one but three distinct theories, all of them grounded on the general quantum rules, yielding essentially the same observational predications, but widely differing concerning the ideas they call forth. They are called the 'theory of the Dirac sea,' 'Feynman graph theory,' and 'quantum field theory'" (ibid.: 16).

We need not be detained here by the twists and turns of variants of idealism (under which d'Espagnat includes phenomenology, positivism, and pragmatism, i.e., that the relation between representations on the one hand and realities independent of us on the other, in some final ontological sense, is indeterminate or based upon pragmatic epistemological approximations, or as Llewelyn reading Derrida reading Hegel puts it, "Ontology is possible as effect, but impossible as foundation" [2000: 95]) and variants of realism (different ways in which the relation of our representations to such an ontological or independent reality is identified, e.g., mathematical realism, Einsteinian realism, Pythagorianism, ontological realism, near realism, structural realism).

What, however, d'Espagnat wishes to argue is that slowly popular consciousness will absorb what physicists already know: that not only can the human mind "operate well outside the framework of familiar concepts, but also that it absolutely must do so" (2002: 15). He thinks, "Of all sciences, only physics, apparently, yields this message. But it does. And the fact that it does may well be taken to constitute one of its main contributions to the development of thought" (ibid.). Similarly, Kant commented that Anthropology should be of interest to an increasingly enlightened public, one open to pluralist and cosmopolitan reflection. And while quantum physics opens up a seemingly radically other world, the ethnographic projects of anthropology make that claim as well, and for similar philosophical reasons, if on different empirical grounds. In this, as Ernst Cassirer argued, Kant operates as a precursor of both.

In some ways, Kant's Anthropology is more like Durkheim's *Rules* or Bruno Latour's part II of his *Pasteurization of France*: it is a logical prolegomenon to a human science of observation, attentive above all to dilemmas, missteps, paradoxes, and the need to steer a careful passage among the capsizing rocks and shoals of introspection (psychology), common sense of one's own culture (ethnocentrism), pure reason, metaphysics, biological reductionism, and the like. It is neither yet ethnographic (although various cultures are mentioned in passing) nor experimental (although observations on stages of childhood development and linguistic usages are used as illustration, there is not the trial-and-error elicitation of the linguist, or the game-playing, standardized testing of the developmental or clinical psychologist, or the taboo- or convention-breaking experiments of the ethnomethodologist in order to more clearly see tacit social boundaries).

Thus, Kant's Anthropology opens with a diaeresis (or what the Wikipedia nowadays calls disambiguation)[7] between physiological and pragmatic anthropology: what nature makes of the human being versus what the human being as a free actor makes of him or herself or can and should make of herself or himself. Descartes is immediately invoked as a negative example: "He who ponders natural phenomena, for example, what the causes of the faculty of memory may rest on, can speculate back and forth (like Descartes) over the traces of impressions remaining in the brain, but in doing so he must admit that in this play of his representations, he is a mere observer . . . for he does not know the cranial nerves and fibers, nor does he understand how to put them to use for his purposes. Therefore all theoretical speculation about this is a pure waste of time" (1798: 3). If, however, the human being uses his knowledge "to hinder or stimulate memory to enlarge it or make it agile, then this would be a part of anthropology with a pragmatic purpose" (ibid.: 3–4).

Already introduced here are the critical terms of "representations" (opening the various gaps between phenomena and noumena, realities of and realities for, common sense and critical reflection, customs and habits at home and those abroad); the difference between observation and active abstraction (which turns perception into thinking, understanding, reason, but also communication, dissembling, self-deception); and the challenges of determining both capacities and duties ("what the Mensch can and should do").

Moreover, "such an anthropology, considered as knowledge of the world . . . is only called 'pragmatic' . . . when it contains knowledge of the human being as citizen of the world," not just knowing but participating. ("The one [scholastic, imitative, passive knowledge] only lets one understand the play [*Spiel*] of which it has been a spectator, but the other has participated [*mitgespielt*] in it.") The verb "to play" (*spielen*) in German is very productive [*vorspielen, nachspielen, anspielen, ausspielen, vorauspielen, mitspielen, Beispiel*), including the example (*Beispiel*) and the allusion (*Anspiel*). Marx, for instance, begins *The Eighteenth Brumaire of Louis Napoleon* (1852) with several riffs on representations, theatricality, and allusions both among actors and analysts;[8] and he too (more vigorously) insists that the point is not merely to understand, but to change the world.

The text proper begins again in the same vein with an analysis of linguistic forms and three forms of egoism that prevent a pragmatic anthropological perspective. The development of the linguistic subject, the "I," in a childhood stage following self-reference in the third person (Karl wants to eat) is used by Kant to set up a distinction between perception (apprehension of the ideas of sense) and knowledge of those objects of sense (experience) doing the work of abstraction. Abstraction allows perceptions to be united under the concept of an object. (Merleau-Ponty will discuss the failure of abstraction in the psychosis of the patient "Schneider," who cannot make the cut between perception and imagination.)[9] The notion of the "I" can expand in three faulty directions (logical, aesthetic, and moral) with respect to a pragmatic anthropology: (1) presumptions of understanding or the logical egoist who thinks it is unnecessary to test his judgment also by the understanding of others (with political implications for the critical importance of the freedom of the press, against claims of the ruler or experts of knowing what is best); (2) the presumption of taste or the aesthetic egoist isolated in his own judgment; (3) the presumption of practical interest or the moral egoist who only considers his own utility and happiness (and has no thought of duty).

Kant therefore concludes, "The opposite of egoism can only be pluralism . . . [in which one] regards and conducts oneself as a mere citizen of the world.—This much belongs to anthropology." After pausing to note that the solipsist's question about how one knows others exist is not anthropology but "merely metaphysical," Kant goes on with the linguistic example of the royal "we," and the fact that in the feudal system persons were addressed by their station, down to the "point where even human dignity stops," i.e., the serf, who is addressed as "thou" (like a child, who is not permitted to have his own way) (1789: 18).

Apart from today's resonances—with Giorgio Agamben's meditations on "bare life," the German post–World War II constitution's codification of the inviolability of the dignity of life, and the distinction (Aristotle, Arendt, Agamben) between *bios* and *zoe,* mere life and the good life, humanitarian bare existence and political rights—the point is that Kant is proposing what Durkheim, Marcel Mauss, and British social anthropology would stipulate as "social facts." Social facts are not reducible to individuals but are formed social structurally and culturally. Kant identifies culture with the educative, socially self-fashioning, pragmatic ends of the human being. Already in the discussion on egoism, Kant specifies the paradoxical demand that the human being not merely sink into the banality of the *sensus communis* and habits (Pierre Bourdieu's *habitus*) of his time and place, while yet not being so reliant only on his own logic and reason as to become isolated from social and cultural grounds of judgment. Durkheim, a close reader of Kant, particularly in the *Elementary Forms of the Religious Life*, insists on this split in the only partially socialized personhood of the individual, and the coproduction of individualism with the increasing division of labor, specialization, and organically entangled nature of complex societies. Hans-Georg Gadamer in *Truth and Method* provides an account of the intellectual history of thinking about the *sensus communis* (common sense) and the aesthetic faculty of judgment of taste, as Norbert Elias does for the history of the social self in *The Civilizing Process*.

It is again Foucault who astutely summarizes, noting that "in the anthropological research each faculty follows a line/track that is also the path of all possible deviations: Self-consciousness, for example, is not defined as a form of experience and condition of limited but founded knowledge; it appears rather as the always re-emerging temptation of a polymorphous egoism: . . . [And] in a paradoxical return, consciousness will renounce the language of this first person . . . to decline itself in the fiction of the We" (Foucault 1961, Bove trans.: 13). So, too, for mind: "The *Gemüt* is not simply 'that which is' but 'that which it makes of itself'"; "the swarming movement of ideas . . . that are made and remade as so many particles" (ibid.: 10). Sensibility, the way objects are given to us, and understanding, the way they are unified under concepts and thought, are two different sources of representation; without their difference and conjunction there could be no valid synthetic a priori judgments (Caygill 2003). *Einbildungskraft* (imagination) comes from *Ins-eins-bildung* (building into one), part perception, part construction (Lleweyln 2000: 7). There is an inverse structure between the given and the a priori in the Anthropology and the Critique: for the Anthropology, the given is "always already the unconscious synthesis of bits of perception and obscure representations," but one can watch the "I" come into sociolinguistic operation. In the Critique, Foucault writes, "the 'I' can never be object, but only a form of the synthesis; the spoken 'I' marks the passage of feeling to thought without being either the real agent or the simple coming to consciousness—it is the empirical and manifest form within which the synthetic activity of the 'I' appears as a figure already synthesized" (Foucault 1961, Bove trans.: 12).

Just as the a priori synthetic judgments depend upon a conjunction of two different sources of representation (sensibility/perception, understanding/abstaction), so too the analysis of taste depends upon a communicative mediation and upon the triangulation and play of the aesthetic, moral, and rational faculties. Guyer (2003) dissects three key arguments common to the Anthropology and the Critique of Aesthetic Judgment: art may have moral content without sacrificing the freedom of play between imagination and understanding; aesthetic experience can reveal our capacities for morality without sacrificing its aesthetic qualities; and the experience of beauty in nature and art provides evidence of the fit between nature and human objectives. Deleuze notes the double fields of operation of the *sensus communis* among the faculties and as the basis of communication: "Any accord of the faculties between themselves defines what can be called a *common sense* . . . an *a priori* accord of faculties. . . . From this point of view common sense appears not as a psychological given but as the subjective condition of all 'communicability.' Knowledge implies a common sense, without which it would not be communicable and could not claim universality" (Deleuze 1963: 21).

This is not the place to continue to work through Kant's Anthropological prolegomenon, only to recognize, first, that, while one should not expect from it anything approaching the thick description or comparative (statistical or conceptual) standards of contemporary ethnographic, social, linguistic, or cultural analysis, it nonetheless provides a logical prolegomenon to much of that project, and, further, read generously, raises dilemmas and problematics that continue to reverberate in both philosophy and anthropology. Second, by claiming Kant's Anthropology as *one of many* precursors to modern anthropology, I want to insist with Kant that philosophy too is not properly done without anthropology, or rather that anthropology is the proper name for the general questions about human beings, our societies, our cultural forms, our interactions with the world around us and that biologically also constitutes us, historically and in relation to our place in world(s) to come.

How Do the Body Electric, Biological Sensibility,
or Electr(on)ic Technology Age?

Flappity, Floppity, Flip!
The Mouse on the Moebius Strip
The Strip revolved
The Mouse dissolved
In a chrondimensional skip
—FREDERICK WINSON, *The Space Child's Mother Goose*

I picked Kant's Anthropology also out of a palimpsest aesthetics. My own *Bildungsroman,* as it were, began as the son of a geographer-historian and a mathematician-geodesist, and as the only undergraduate majoring in geography at the Johns Hopkins University, where one of the two textbooks in my human geography class was Alfred Kroeber's *Anthropology* (1948), itself evolved through twenty-five years of teaching, the other being George Carter's own *Man and the Land, A Cultural Geography*: geography and anthropology, as in Kant's sequence. My father, trained as a historian, but, in the United States, a professional geographer, taught everything from geomorphology and physical geography to human and political geography. His hometown, Vienna, like Königsberg, was a cultural crossroads (and Königsberg even figures eccentrically in our family stories).[10] Like Kant, he had been known (when he courted my mother) as one of those people by whose regularity you could set your clock. Like Kant, he was fascinated by character. When he took me to museums, I was intrigued by his interest in portrait paintings. It was perhaps both a bourgeois cultivation (one thinks of the portraits in bourgeois homes) and a historian's and human geographer's search for moral and cultural signs. The portrait that hung in his study at home, amidst the family photos, was one of Erasmus.

For Kant, character formed a bridge between the natural and moral conceptions of human nature, the ongoing pragmatic-cultural-moral vocation of being human. Character is both a person's observable behavior and her or his moral way of thinking. Character pivots, as both Freud and Durkheim would expand, between personhood and the development of an autonomous self.

Kant was not only a man of his times, times that can be traced in his vocabulary, citations, references, and debate partners as well as in his efforts to accommodate the new developments in science, especially Lavoisier's chemistry, and thus to view magnetism, electricity, chemistry, and biology as a dynamic system.[11] But he was also an embodied man, aging and suffering the indignities that mock pure reason and exert shifts in the reading of character. Writing in the Anthropology, not about himself, he remarked, "The one universal characteristic of madness is loss of common sense (*sensus communis*) and substitution of logical private sense (*sensus privates*)" (KGS, 7:219; quoted in Wilson 2006: 99). Although some sources claim signs of cognitive changes began as early as age fifty, others say age seventy (he gave his last lectures at age seventy-two in 1796). Initial neuro-ophthalmological symptoms included his migraines, transient visual obscurations (scotomas, amaurosis), bouts of double vision, and a progressive loss of vision in his left eye.

He always had a few peculiarities. He was a gourmand and delighted in nightly conversation-filled dinners, and indeed Foucault recognizes that for Kant the model social group is neither the family nor the state, but the *Tischgesellschaft* (dinner society):

> None of the three great functions of language must be omitted: enunciation of contingent fact [*Erzahlen,* story telling], formulation, exchange, and rectification of judgment (*Raisonieren,* reasoning), free play of language on itself (*Scherzen,* jokes). Round and round . . . in a movement that is the rhythm proper to this form of meeting: initially the *novelty* of the event, then the seriousness of the *universal,* finally the *irony* of the game.[12] . . . The truth that the Anthropology exposes is then not a truth anterior to language and that it will seek to transmit . . . it is in the movement itself of exchange. (Foucault 1961, Bove trans.: 30)

But after dinner, he would walk alone to air his body: alone, so that breathing through his nostrils would not be disturbed by having to converse. To this he attributed his avoidance of colds and other respiratory problems. He also ate breakfast alone, and when De Quincey began to care for him in old age, he asked, with his normal courtesy, that De Quincey sit out of his sight, because he was too old to get used to a different routine. No *Tischgesellschaft* at breakfast! There was also the oddity of his idiosyncratically designed garters. He would not wear normal garters to hold up his socks, presumably because they might also interfere with circulation, and instead devised a windlass contraption around the waist with angler's wheel and spring: "Behold Kant then expounding his philosophy to a select circle of his disciples working the windlass as he walked, 'paying out cable' or 'hauling in the slack'" (De Quincey 1890, quoted in Eaton 1936: 455). By fall 1803, he showed symptoms of restlessness, always wanting to leave as soon as he had arrived, obsessive buttoning and unbuttoning of his clothes, memory loss, periodic language impairment, balance problems, falling frequently, and suffering nocturnal hallucinations. De Quincey reports that Kant developed an obsession with accounting for everything by electricity.

Electricity was in the air (Newton, Ben Franklin, Luigi Galvani, John Wesley, medical electrical experiments, Bancroft's electric eels from Guiana, etc.), and Kant himself had attempted to incorporate new developments in magnetism and chemistry, although he remained only on the verge of a unified theory ("the idea that chemical forces are at bottom electrical in nature never occurred to him" [Friedman 2006: 62]).[13] De Quincey reports that Kant connected electricity to the plague of cats (as electric, static-producing animals) dying in Vienna, Basle, and Copenhagen; electric cloud patterns to his migraines. As the symptoms of dementia (perhaps Lewy body dementia) progressed, he could no longer sign his name or eat properly. As in many elderly people, the symptoms came and went. Henrich reports the poignant image of the elderly Kant working on his final manuscript, "not able to write more than a sentence without losing the thread of his thought" and "for that reason, the manuscript contains many repetitions of the same sentence"; and yet those sentences affirm central intentions of his philosophy (2003: 52).[14] Not being able to maintain conversation isolated him, but recall of his childhood and being able to recite Virgil's *Aeneid* and other poetry learned in school seemed to comfort him. (De Quincey 1890; Guard and Boller 2005; Marchand 1997; Podoll, Hoff, and Sass 2000).

One does not know how much Kant's symptoms of physical failings and dementia upset him, to what extent he was merely stoic, or to what extent he observed himself, or trembled at the thought of an *Aeneid* of *Verücktheit* (madness). In the Anthropology, he remarks on the *Abgrund* (chasm, lack of grounding) that the mentally ill (*einiger Gemüthskranken*) fear. *Wahnsinn* (errant sense, nonsense, imagination, *Sinn* = meaning) operates, Llewelyn notes, in a double direction for Kant: sometimes he identifies the imagination with intuition (perception), sometimes with the understanding (reason). Normally there is a threefold synthesis: "apprehension in intuition, reproduction in imagination, and recognition in a concept" (Llewelyn 2000: 107). But when one mistakes for outside what is only in our mind, a vertigo can happen, as when we look into a chasm (*Abgrund*) (Kant 1798: section 32, quoted in Llewelyn 2000: 118). A similar feeling can attach to the sublime, an oscillation between repulsion and attraction (say before a volcano, an earthquake, sometimes in warfare), a "tremoring" in John Sallis's felicitous term, which can also refer to the religious feeling before the *mysterium tremendum* of the divine (Sallis 1987; Llewelyn 2000: 116). Deleuze puts it this way: "[The Sublime] brings the various faculties into play in such a way that they struggle against one another. . . . Each makes the one go beyond the limit of the other. It is a terrible struggle between imagination and reason, and also between understanding and the inner sense. . . . It is a tempest in the depths of a chasm opened up in the subject" (Deleuze 1963: xii). Kant assigns the triangulating mediations and translations between perceptions, imagination, and reason as reality checks, a procedure (*Verfahren*) by analogy with a legal procedures (Llewelyn 2000: 8); but *Verfahren* also means missing one's way. *Verfahrung, Verücktheit* (madness), Hegel remarks, may not be amenable to reason, yet be susceptible to treatment by rational measures, such as an acting cure or playing along cure, use of a transitional object, or *Herausdrehung* (twisting out).[15]

This may not be the place to enter into Lacanian topologies with their Möbius twistings, things on the surface yet hidden on the other side, knots and folds, but there is one important final conundrum: "the challenge laid down in Hegel's thesis that it is the history of the world that prescribes what is ultimately just" (*die Weltgeschichte ist das Weltgericht*, world history is the world tribunal), which Llewelyn explores through Hannah Arendt (Llewelyn 2000: 140). Kant, of course, has a counterthesis in "the autonomy of the minds of men and their possible independence of things as they are," but Arendt claims that what interests Kant is "the secret ruse of nature that caused the species to progress and develop all its potentialities. . . . Kant is never interested in the past; what interests him is the future of the species. . . . only once [in his essays in political philosophy], almost in passing, in a parenthesis, does Kant state that it is a question of bringing about 'the highest end intended for man, namely, sociability (*Geselligkeit*)'" (Arendt 1982: 8; Llewelyn 2000: 140). The secret ruse may be such things as Adam Smith's hidden hand, but surely the development of sociability is not just conceptually parenthetical.

Levinas and Derrida are better guides: the one tracing out the face that speaks, the demand of the other that gets under one's skin; the other tracking the material realities that facilitate an illusion of philosophy's thinking itself, the writing down that is composed of recombinant bricolages of alphabet, phrases, rhetorical figures, and other assembled and dissembling spare parts, producing the laughter of Silenus,[16] "the eternal burst of laughter of the unconscious or of woman that indefinitely harasses, questions, ridicules, mocks the essence, the truth of man" (Llewelyn 2000: 92). Derrida's cat calls: "How would you ever justify the fact that you sacrifice all the cats in the world to the cat you feed at home every morning for years, whereas other cats die of hunger at every instant? Not to mention other people" (2002: 380; see also 1997, 2003).

A reminder that without anthropology, pragmatic, on-the-ground, empirical exploration (be it political science, economics, history, or other disciplines of research), philosophers are apt to follow their errant procedures (*Verfahren*) and fantasies, as Foucault did with regard to the Iranian revolution. Celebrity punditry, or philosophy's illusions of philosophy's thinking, is little excuse, even if a misrecognized exercise of limits may be found or invoked, even if Iran and the Mediterranean have centuries of cultural exchange.[17]

Cosmopolitanism, Cosmopolitics, and Anthropological Futures

"The unsociable sociability of man."
—Immanuel Kant, Fourth Thesis, "Idea for a Universal History from a Cosmological Point of View"

Vaishnav jan to tada kahayeh /Peer paraiyeh jana re. [A truly realized person is one who recognizes the pain of others.]
—Mahatma Gandhi's favorite hymn, sung in the concluding scene of Deepa Mehta's film *Water*

It is mainly research on transnationalization over the past decade, less in sociology than in cultural studies, ethnology, ethnography, geography, etc., that has effectively questioned the empirical and methodological assumptions of mainstream methodological nationalism.
—ULRICH BECK, *The Cosmopolitan Vision*

Cosmopolitanism, the dialectic between cosmos and polis, lies also on a dialectic between the humanities and the social sciences. Associated with philosophy from Diogenes to Kant, cosmopolitanism can be evaluated only in institutional terms [proposition 1]. These institutional terms, many claim, are newly emergent or transformed today, both as a morality of recognizing and working with difference and as new forms of institutional life that can handle conflict, complexity, and alterity [proposition 2]. Evidence of transformative growth points and cracks in old hegemonic ideologies is often visible first in "minor" loci: the anecdote, the vignette, the ethnographic incident. These can serve the anthropologist as short stories serve the historically minded literary critic [proposition 3]. These minor loci and forms can irritate hegemonic narratives, like a lose pebble causing the foot to wobble. They also can open into labyrinths or loose threads of paths and turns which hegemonic accounts attempt to erase for the ease of narration or generalization or simplified model building. Anthropological fu-

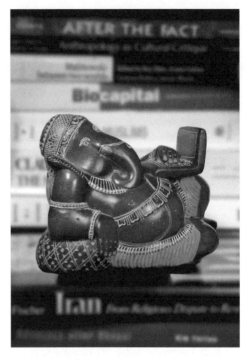

32. Laptop Ganesh with anthropology and anthropology of science and technology books. Ganesh owned by M. Fischer. Photo by Richard A. Chase.

tures need to be keyed to these possibilities, alterities, and ways in which the world around us is simultaneously structured (and emergent) otherwise than in the official stories, discursivities, and institutional formalities.

Aamir Mufti—writing about Saadat Hasan Manto's post-Partition Urdu short stories (*afsana*) and Congress Party President Abdul Kalam Azad's pre-Partition epistolary-style reflections on the nationalist movement—suggests that in contrast to the "major" literary form of the novel (which Fredric Jameson overemphasizes as always allegorizing nation building)[1], such "minor" literary forms "render an account of national modernity inscribed not with affirmations of identity and subjectivity but with displacement and difference" (Mufti 2007: 178). Pebbles and labyrinths.

Pebbles and labyrinths are difficult to abide, sometimes vertigo inducing, upsetting. Cosmopolitical complications are often difficult to manage and always keyed to historical contexts. Anthropological work of the sort described in the preceding chapters can be a critical resource. Anthropology itself, as argued at the outset, will need to be recognized as multiple, to be cultivated as such, itself practicing, modeling, and experimenting with cosmopolitan relations. The geoid might be good to think with in this context as well, as opening to different temporalities, across networks of competition and national identities as well as stages of life and relationships.

Three sorts, or temporal relations, of cosmopolitanism are especially indexical, what one might, as a first approximation, call relations of past, future, and present.

Reflexive, often diasporic, nostalgic cosmopolitanism: First, there is the cosmopolitanism that emerges from nostalgia for mercantile and administrative cities, empires, villages, and towns of mixed populations destroyed by twentieth-century politics; even if everyone did not get along in these places, there were at least regulated institutions that kept private prejudice in check and mainly off the public screen. Unreflexive nostalgia easily becomes romantic, often exclusionary chauvinism ("We tolerate even our minorities"). Self-critical, reflexive nostalgia, by contrast, has potentials for preserving alternative genealogies of the present that can be used as resources for future reorientations.

These nostalgias need not be old: Dharavi, Asia's largest squatter settlement in Bombay/Mumbai, is not only a place of informal economies but also in fact an economic engine of small industry, and it was, until the 1990s, robustly resistant to communal strife. How that resistance was broken is worthy of serious reflection and repair—not merely of restitution and mea culpas or blame pointing. (On Dharavi, see Neuwirth 2005; Sharma 2000; Chatterji and Mehta 2007). The Ottoman empire's millet system is often invoked as a model of a multicultural, multireligious form of cosmopolitanism to which we might look for lessons in our era of renewed ethnic cleansing and religious fundamentalisms; but such comparisons must be done with a realistic eye: few minorities would like to return to second-class citizenship, and European variants like the *zuil* (pillar) structure of Dutch society, in which religious communities had their own institutions so that people could live "apart together" (K. Taussig 2009), have also proved less than utopian. So, too, the nostalgia for the Vienna of modernism in science, music, literature, workers' housing. In both Viennese and Ottoman cases, holocausts turned these examples into painful crucibles for exploring how these polities might have transformed themselves otherwise. The turn against immigrants by many in the Netherlands in the aftermath of the murders of the politician Pim Fortuyn and the filmmaker Theo van Gogh has caused more realistic reexamination of the organization and limits of Dutch pride in their tolerance and liberalism. All these examples require not simple nostalgia but critical reflexivity and contemplation of different reflexive social institutions and discourses, not least being, on the one hand, the very term "tolerance" and its implied grounds of who does the tolerating and who is tolerated, and, on the other hand, how public spheres are to be organized and protected in the increasingly heterogeneous contemporary world.[2]

Like Walter Benjamin, Raymond Williams, George Lipsitz, and other critical theorists, I have long been interested and invested in this kind of cosmopolitianism that dialectically explores new and old media, life histories, ethnicity formations, contestations within (and among) religious formations as well as the ways in which social theories of change and legitimation arise out of historical experiences. At issue in these projects is the juxtaposition of historical settings and cultural framings for comparative perspectives, for exploring changing structures of feelings, for recognizing the "long fetch" of events that seem to come suddenly but upon reflection have buried histories, and for the redemption of anticipations of social justice, that is, envisioning the existing world with not just its actual capacities, but envisioning it otherwise, as reconfigured, as able to negotiate diversity, complexity, and alterity, provide opportunity, hope, and justice.

Future-directed, emergent, and experimental cosmopolitics: Another sort of cosmopolitanism emerges from keen awareness of change—both subtle and dramatic—that is forcing the development of new institutional forms. Experimental sensibilities are critical since established organizations and conventional ways of thinking and doing things no longer work. States, for example, are becoming separated from the ideology of nation-state. States no longer are entirely in control of their economic, environmental (or ecological), foreign, health, or communications policies. The state is only one among the set of competing transnational actors. States compete nowadays with multinational corporations, finance markets, media (CNN, al-Jazeera), international organizations (UN, World Bank, World Court), quasi superstates (EU), treaty- and convention-established arbitration and dispute settlement organizations (WTO, ICH), and transnational NGOs (both those "humanitarian industries" which project power from the metropoles into the third world and those decentralized NGO alliances organizing from the third world upward and outward) figured in the name of the Zapatistas or the World Social Forums, despite their practical internal counterforces and contradictions (see de Sousa Santos 2007; Juris 2008; Stringer 2006).

Cosmo*politics*, in other words, are attentive to "the shifting ground beneath [her, our] feet" (Rushdie 1995: 87; 1999) and to the violence those shifts may provoke. Cosmo*politics* experiments with new "phrasings of legitimacy" (Lyotard 1979, 1983), new "meta-games of power"

(Beck 2002a, 2004a), the syntax of institutional relations that can convert "just gaming" into gaming for justice (Lyotard 1979).

Along with other colleagues, I have long been invested in these shifting grounds too as politics and as a focus for anthropological work. In the interviews conducted as part of the *Late Editions* project (edited by Marcus, 1993–2000), for example, shifting grounds was the privileged ethnographic context and the subject of conversation with interviewees. The challenge there, as in some of the chapters presented here, was to elicit ways in which people were working around radically transformed organizational and conceptual forms, exploring the prevailing sense that once again at the end of the twentieth century emergent forms of life and professional practices were outrunning the pedagogies in which practitioners had been trained (see also Fischer 2003). The anthropological focus remains critical in such conversations.

Consider, for example, the organizational work done around pseudoxanthoma elasticum (PXE). The patient advocacy alliance PXE International is exemplary in showing how the ground can shift beneath our feet, how new infrastructures can be configured into new power relations within the health care industry. PXE, a genetic disorder which causes blindness, is a so-called orphan disease, that is, one that affects too few people to draw major private or public research funding. The parents of two children with PXE turned their (construction industry and nursing) managerial skills toward reconfiguring the profit-driven medical research environment by first locating a worldwide pool of patients willing to donate blood and samples, recruiting research physician-scientists, and creating patent agreements that give PXE International a share of whatever proceeds might come from scientific discoveries, a share that is then redirected into research and therapy. PXE International coordinates Internet-linked patient groups, changes the relations between patients, doctors, and insurance companies, and reconfigures the high-cost research environment.

Third, there is the kind of cosmopolitanism emergent from and concerned with the shifting *circuits and crucibles of globally distributed "republics of science and technology,"* without which none of the above could be instituted, institutionalized, modified, or reconfigured and which increasingly is focused on the means, media, and social modalities of deliberation. Scientific and technological developments have always been conceived of as a kind of global republic open to all who are sufficiently trained. Patronage, political, economic, and other constraints have always reduced the scale of this vision, but it was the commitment to this global republic that often kept channels of communication open across such political divides as the Iron Curtain of the Cold War period, and to which many scientists remain committed across other hostile barriers, both for the love of science (and need for scientific labor) and for the concomitant needs for relatively open spaces of exchange and competition. I have referred to some of these struggles and debates in chapters 2 and 5: the rules of admission to and play in the debates of the Royal Society between Boyle and Hobbes (Shapin and Shaffer 1985), the struggles over state-directed science in the 1930s and 1940s, the role of empires in establishing centers of calculation, mapping, and setting up of research facilities. Today the global terrain has shifted once again to a more distributed and increasingly decentralized one, referred to in the fourth genealogy of chapter 2.

At issue in this shifting of the ground beneath our feet are new technological and social platforms and circuits that are often registered first in "minor locations." They are more generally visible in the so-called teletechnologies of the Internet and blogistans of China and Iran, the Open Course Ware initiatives of MIT and other universities, and most of all in the varied initiatives of open source technologies. These platforms and circuits and the ingenuity of their designers, hackers, and entrepreneurs allow cyber cafes in squatter settlements and wireless kiosks in villages of Indonesia and India to become potential sites of local problem solving and infrastructure creation. Teletechnologies can serve as autoimmune diseases provoking a "frenzy of position taking," as Jacques Derrida put it, as well as providing ways around petrified institutions, decayed educational institutions, and exploitative bureaucracies and middlemen. This is a cosmopolitanism that is concerned with investments in society's means of deliberation, with the processes as much as content, with new ways of enabling adaptations and cooperation, with hacking technologies into useable bits for people, with shifting power ratios, providing access, maneuvering around older brittle institutions, but also with new modes of assembly, of data mining for new modes of scientific sleuthing and new tracking tools to keep such modes of extraction and control transparent and accountable. It is a cosmopolitanism that involves a play of moral demands and institutional experimentalism that conforms to Kant's early modern ideas that the cosmopolitan condition does not just come into existence by itself or maintain itself without challenge and that it is a social endeavor, not something that can be accomplished in the philosophical first person or by the solipsistic ego.

Solutions today, of course, need not be high tech: it is not the high tech but the open source side of the idea of republics of science and technology that is at issue and that requires defense against the incursions of excessive intellectual property enclosures.

For example, in the United States the efforts of Transactional Records Access Clearinghouse (TRAC) provide a medium-tech open source example. By filing Freedom of Information suits, TRAC gains access to public records of the Justice Department, Internal Revenue Service, Federal Bureau of Investigation, Department of Homeland Security, and the like, which it then makes available on the web. Journalists, researchers, and the public can then run comparisons—for instance, by judge, prosecutor, lead charge, outcomes, and penalties—and thereby generate such questions as Why are there so few drug prosecutions in the war on drugs in cities with the highest illegal drug markets? Are there political patronage networks in patterns of prosecution? Why has the budget of the Justice Department's criminal division gone up by 29 percent under President George W. Bush but prosecutions have fallen? Why has the environmental division's budget gone up by 40 percent while prosecutions have fallen by 12 percent? Or in general what are the effects of the 56 percent cut in federal assistance, from $2.5 billion in 1997 to $1.1 billion in the budget request of 2008, on local crime fighting? The goal is to make a recursive public sphere that can hold public servants accountable to their oaths of office, and the democratic processes in a complex world more robust and accountable.

Anthropological Futures

In the margins, as dark undersides and cautions, there have always been the *slurs against cosmopolitanisms*, against transnational mercantile diasporas (Jews, Hadarima or networks from the Yemeni Hadramut, Southeast Asian Chinese, Jains, Chetiars), and against scholars who seriously put into play views contrary to those locally hegemonic: sophists, religious others, once upon a time postcolonialists, perhaps still deconstructionists. In the past century the charges and punishments were the most severe under communist and Nazi regimes in Europe and under nationalist regimes, as in Indonesia's convulsions in 1965, but the destruction of Muslim-Jewish-Christian secular parties in the Middle East (or their turn into totalitarian ones) is also a victim of anticosmopolitan campaigns.

Amidst the pieties of and condemnations of cosmopolitanisms, the anthropologist is challenged to pay attention to the emergent—ethnographically detailed, media-conscious, attentive to political economy,

and philosophically engaged—ways in which cosmopolitanisms in-
stitutionalize themselves.

The troubled histories of debates over cosmopolitanisms, with their
utopian and dystopian legacies, have long taproots. Most theatrically
vivid were the Soviet (and similar recent Russian) allegations against
monetary commerce as economic crimes and against intellectual
commerce as dangerous to civic ideology. But the debates over usury
and rhetoric are also medieval and distributed across the civilizations
of the globe, and, as noted, go back at least to the death of Socrates and
the defense of the domestic oecumene against the traders who were to
be kept at the margins, outside.

The chapters in this volume have attempted to traverse a history
across cosmopolitanisms, cosmopolitics, and anthropologies to come.
In each of the first four chapters attention was paid to the institutional
contexts (the first *proposition above*) within which concepts, heuristics, models, comparisons, and contrasts have arisen around such constellations of inquiry as the cultural, the natural, the body, the scientific, and the technological. In the fifth chapter a slightly different
heuristic of a scientific career across the layers of the twentieth century from Vienna Circle to Mercury and Apollo missions was refracted through a transitional object figuring and stabilizing personhood in old age. The cultural, natural, embodied, personal, scientific,
and technological are among the key words of anthropology, keying to
shifting registers of meaning across cosmopolitanisms, cosmopolitics,
and anthropologies to come.

Chapter 6 explored this dynamic notion of anthropology in its aspirations to become a modern science without losing its humanity, of
keeping its feet firmly planted, not ambivalently but fully ambi-val-
ently, in both the social sciences and the humanities. Such an anthropology has always asked not just what human beings are, but what one
can expect of them, of their "unsocial socialities" that, in principle,
should be capable of exercising freedom and refining social moralities.
These are socialities that are never given but are always under repair
and reconstruction, invention and creation. Nudged by the conflicting
pressures and connectivities of second-order modernity, such socialities are always working through ever-changing and ever-intensifying
challenges of complexity, diversity, and alterity (the second *proposition above*).

The anthropologies to come still need probes to pry open the knots,
complications, and densities of the emergent forms of life within
which we live and work, plan and hope, compete and experiment.
Among the available probes are elaborated ethnographic vignettes,

soundings, mappings, and juxtapositions (the third *proposition above*). In the twenty-first century, cosmopolitanisms and cosmopolitics have become two of a series of slogan terms that primarily revive, rework, and restart the processes that Immanuel Kant observed and promoted, albeit today under transformed conditions of teletechnological globalization or *mondalization,* with its built-in divisions, wars, new stratifications, frenzied position taking, and need for new forms of ethnographic and cultural critique. Post-Kantian anthropologies are postings of Kant into futures he could not imagine, futures that are returns on Enlightenment investments in expanded global portfolios.

Anthropologies to come require ethnographic vignettes that serve as destabilizing pebbles, ethnographic gemwork shifting back and forth between microscope and setting, or baroque pearls (Port. *barroco,* pearls that are irregular in shape)[3], complications for the simplified official stories and disciplinary truths, other ways of recognizing what is going on. And so we begin again to think of anthropological futures.

Postings from Anthropologies to Come

Pebbles, Sparrows, Labyrinths, and Ethnographic Vignettes

As a kind of methodological exercise for anthropologies to come, two initial vignettes may pry open the reflexive, transnational, and diasporic circuits of cosmopolitanism, before considering the varied macro, meso, and micro scales through which lively cosmopolitical worlds compose themselves. The view from Bandung, Tehran, and Istanbul can help open the global portfolios of anthropologies to come, anthropological futures.

These postings back and forth between past and future anthropologies are matters of method, so to speak, that is, nascent, experimental, and musical, not yet routinized, deadened, or subject to mechanical reproduction (though certainly digitally sampleable and reconfigurable). In other words, in good hands, they are culturable, investments and seeds for future returns, anthropological futures from a pragmatic point of view.

I: Reflexive, Transnational Circuits of Cosmopolitanism

The human condition in its plurality.
—HANNAH ARENDT

Vignette One: Reading Hannah Arendt in Tehran, February 2007

Why, in 2007, Hannah Arendt (she died in 1975)? Why in Tehran? A few background sticking points: Invited to give talks at the Institute of Philosophy in Tehran, I was intrigued by a graduate student who was writing a dissertation on Arendt and by others who seemed to find her interesting. Was this, I mused, confirmation of Danny Postel's *Prickly Paradigm* essay, *Reading Legitimation Crisis in Tehran* (2006), in which he noted the interest of Tehran intellectuals in liberal, rather than

33. Cellphone Ganesh.
Photo by Dennis
McGilvray.

revolutionary, political philosophy.[1] Indeed, the previous year at the Iranian Academy of Sciences, Ron Thiemann, a Harvard theologian colleague, and I were engaged by Gholam-Reza A'avani, Director of the Iranian Institute of Philosophy, in a long debate about the philosophy of John Rawls. Before his four-month-long arrest from April to August 2006 and subsequent exile to India and Canada, Ramin Jahanbeglu, the director of the Cultural Research Institute, a small NGO in Tehran, had brought to Iran such liberal luminaries as Jürgen Habermas and Richard Rorty. Given the George W. Bush administration's belligerent announcement of $75 million dollars to support democratic opposition elements within the Islamic Republic of Iran, the Iranian authorities were suspicious of efforts at a "velvet revolution," such as those the United States had supported in eastern Europe. In 2006 and 2007 they arrested Haleh Esfandiari of the Woodrow Wilson International Center for Scholars in Washington, Kian Tajbash, employed by the Soros Foundation, and Ali Shakeri, a founding board member of the Center for Citizen Peace Building at the University of California at Irvine, all of whom eventually were released, as was the Prague-based journalist Parnaz Azima, who works for al-Farda, the U.S. Persian language broadcast of Radio Free Europe and Voice of America. The original arrest of Esfandiari, although she wasn't jailed for several months, came three weeks after President Mahmoud Ahmadinejad was chased from the Amir Kabir Polytechnique University and several students were imprisoned under apparently false charges of disseminating a magazine impugning the Prophet Muhammad, Imam Ali, and Rahbar Khamene'i.

Amidst these sticking points, there was also the boomeranging Danish cartoon circuit, which Tehran seized upon as a propaganda opportunity, as it had years earlier in the Salman Rushdie affair: Khomeini's *fatwa* came in February 1989 (Fischer and Abedi 1990; Fischer 2009). Between the Danish cartoons and the retaliatory Iranian-hosted Holocaust cartoon controversy, there was a domestic cartoon ruckus in which a government-identified Tehran newspaper ill-advisedly published a nine-cartoon attack on the fear of the United States stirring up ethnic conflict using the metaphor of stirring up Turkish-speaking cockroaches. The mischievous Holocaust cartoon competition mobilized a transnational network of cartoonists who recirculated old Nazi tropes against Jews now fitted to U.S.-backed Israelis oppressing Palestinians; these were headlined by President Ahmadinejad's redeployment of an old quote from the Ayatollah Ruhollah Khomeini that the Zionist state would eventually be wiped off the pages of time, and his asking for more research into whether the Holocaust was in fact as bad as claimed and in any case why Palestinians should pay for the misdeeds of Europeans. The day Ahmadinejad was chased off the Amir Kabir University campus by student hecklers was the day of the opening of the Tehran Holocaust conference.

Imagine yourself (say, in a story in the style of Saadat Hasan Manto) in these circumstances as a member of the Tehran Jewish community. Asserting love of country and the long, pre-Islamic roots of Jews in Iran, the leadership of the community wrote an open letter to the president protesting his insinuations about the Holocaust, posted it on the web, and obtained the signatures of many intellectuals in support, including many non-Jewish Iranians, mainly in the diaspora but also some courageously within Iran. Government reaction was not slow: the writer of the letter was told to take it off the web, the council members were replaced, the community magazine was closed, and a Potemkin visit to Jewish sites was organized for foreign ambassadors to demonstrate how well treated Jews are and what pride Iran takes in having the only large Jewish community in the Muslim world (it numbers circa 25,000 persons, down from over 100,000 in 1979). Members of the old leadership were admonished to stay home and not meet with the guests.

In Iran, as elsewhere, however, things are never as simple as they seem. The former council president, a fairly well-known movie producer, was given new state funds to help produce two new film projects. A prominent figure in the community, he had been a student activist in the early 1960s and had met Khomeini in those days. When Khomeini returned, he was among the Jewish community who established contacts and persuaded Khomeini to publicly protect the Jews as long as they disavowed Zionism. The opportunistic slippage back and forth between Iranian officials' use of "Jews" and "Zionists" remains a powerful disciplining tactic, given its built-in deniability, as in "Did I say Jews? I meant Zionists." It is not surprising that this film producer's reaction should also have been nuanced and multiple. On the one hand, "It's not a serious matter; I've been through these things for forty years now." On the other hand, he delivered a lecture on Arendt to the Jewish community in their community center in Sheikh Hadi neighborhood, a once-cosmopolitan neighborhood where no Jews live any longer, to which I will return in a moment.

Hannah Arendt is, of course, a very interesting choice for a Jewish Iranian to select, and it appeared that this was no spur-of-the-moment selection, for she had been a favorite philosopher of the film producer for many years. He was delighted that in the audience was someone who had listened to Arendt as a student at the University of Chicago in the 1960s. The talk was very good, beginning with Arendt's biography, her distinction between just living (as animals do, including migration, seasonal changes, house building, even tool use) and living the life of thought and intentionality. There were passages on the importance of politics and the role of Rosa Luxemburg; Heidegger and the Nazis; Arendt's time in France and the United States; her relations with Israel and her exchange with Gershom Scholem; and a longer passage on the Adolf Eichmann controversy, the point of which was that Nazism, not the miserable functionary, should be on trial.

Only in the question period did he respond directly to the legacy for today, first by nodding, as it were, to the pact with Khomeini, noting that were Arendt alive today she would be talking about the holocaust of Iraqis just as she opposed the Vietnam War, that she rejected defense of the Jews alone, that holocausts have happened throughout history to the Jews and others. But then he spoke also to what was on the audience's mind: what was important about the holocaust issue was that when attacked, one not remain silent but defend oneself and not just allow well-meaning others to say everything would be okay. One needs to answer words with words: *harf-be-harf zadan.* Not remain silent. There was applause, and as he stepped down from the stage the female head of a Jewish hospital stood and gave an emotional tribute to his teaching and leadership over the past three decades. Her emotional tones clearly reflected her shock at having been prevented, as one of the Jewish community's leaders, from going to her hospital during the staged visit for the foreign ambassadors. More applause.

Vignette Two: Exile from Sheikh Hadi

Sheikh Hadi, where this event took place, is a storied neighborhood in Tehran once full of Zoroastrians, Armenians, Jews, Bahais, and Shi-ites. A royal palace and the Institute Pasteur stand on one edge of the neighborhood, the Zoroastrian fire temple and high school on the other side; the best-known Armenian delicatessen, Andre's, is a bit to the northwest, just below the City Theater. Jewish businessmen with Muslim partners, politicians, and notables lived here. In 1953 a little boy watched his mother cry as Muhammad Mossadeqh's front gate was crashed by a jeep carrying the royalist crowd leader and *zur-khaneh pahlavan* (traditional gymnasium athlete-champion) Shaaban Bimokh (Shabaan the Brainless).

That boy, "Perry" Parviz Yashar, went to study in California in the 1970s at the famed Arts Center in Los Angeles, where many well-known automobile designers, industrial artists, and public muralists have been trained and taught. He made a name as a designer for Wedgwood, Rolls-Royce, the levitating train planned in the 1970s, the Bay Area Rapid Transit, and other projects. For a period, he returned to Tehran to teach art at the university. I got to know Perry at the Mehregan, or fall New Year celebrations, in San Diego in 2006, and we have been collaborating ever since. I want to reproduce here two of his paintings and provide a summary reading—more detailed analysis and allusions will appear elsewhere—that highlights the nostalgia for the cosmopolitan Sheikh Hadi neighborhood.

As in many accented works of exiles (Naficy 2001), in these paint-ings by Yashar ethnicity, religion, and nationalism are not explicitly marked, but they are dramatically registered. In the first painting's mise-en-scène sex, lies, politics, passions, facades, and smoke shuffle and reshuffle one another.

Lord of Illusions plays with the tropes of playing cards, magicians, metamorphoses, deceits, desire, and corruption. Butterflies and frogs, snakes and birds, fish and hearts transform into one another. Swords cut unities into duplicities, devilishly swallowed in further deceits. Hearts and matches inflame. Eggs crack, and hands emerge, shuffle, and hide. Birds of peace merge with wolves of war. Nipples, eyes, and,

34. *Lord of Illusions*. Painting by Parviz Yashar. Photo by Parviz Yashar.

perhaps, camera shutters see and distract. Wine and glitter, spades and hearts, pipes and pipe dreams. Salvador Dalí puffs dreams of desire. Princess Diana weeps hearts of tears, wanting to be free (bare legs) but locked up in constraints (chastity belt, zippers that open and close on hearts and mouths). Who is sovereign, as the king cuts the Soldier Jack in two, doubling the illusions? Who manipulates whom, the devilish monkey with his arm on the king's shoulder, producing the sovereign from under his magician's stovepipe hat? Is it the sex that makes the world turn inside out, the dazzling show, cruelty and power, corruption and desire?

The second painting, which the artist calls *Exit from Eden* or *Helter Skelter* (as in the Beatles song, "When I get to the bottom, I go back to the top of the slide") is a riotous carnivalesque variation. The King of Hearts breaks out of the card (television/computer screen, psychiatric asylum, puritanical theocracy), leading or leaving the Queen by the hand. The Queen is still frozen, stuck inside, while the King, who is supposed to provide protection, is himself doing all sorts of devious

35. *Exit from Eden.* Painting by Parviz Yashar. Photo by Parviz Yashar.

things. The punning double exposure of sexual and religious imagery is explicit. The castle asylum is on fire, the Cardinal holds his shepherd's crook spearing a man's head. A fish tail octopus arm masturbates between a pair of legs, while a second snake arm swallows both a fish and a bird, and a third gas station nozzle arm pumps gas. Flights into freedom are no longer just traditional fish, birds, and shoots of new plants but include the automobile and motorcycle. The bawdy visual pun of an industrial cock pours poisons into the fish pool (autoerotic production and warfare generating ever more toxic collateral damage).

Yashar titles the piece *Exit from Eden* or *Helter Skelter,* and while both those biblical and carnival ride figurations are constitutive, the Beatles song *Helter Skelter* (1968) and the Philippe de Broca film *King of Hearts* (1966) provide a generational edge, one that takes on a double exposure for the generation of the Iranian revolution, that of Yashar, now in their fifties and sixties.[2] The Beatle John Lennon was killed in 1980, just as the Islamic Revolution in Iran moved from its moments of euphoria, press freedom, and Terror (always double exposure) to its consolidation as a politically stalemated, theocratically policed, limited republic. A third historical horizon is also braided into *Exit from Eden*, the time of painting, during the struggles between a born-again Christian evangelical American president empowered by a fundamentalist movement and a Twelfth Imam—invoking Iranian one. The importance of the carefully non-Islamic religious imagery becomes clear, standing for an exposure in general of the misuse of religion as repressive, aggressive, and misogynist.

The multiple double exposures, visual puns, and kaleidoscopic allegories of these two Yashar paintings hint at the encyclopedic genres of world-historic transformations like James Joyce's *Finnegans Wake* and Thomas Pynchon's *Gravity's Rainbow*. They show both the dark side and the irrepressible spirit celebrated in Yashar's other paintings as well as in his Wedgwood designs, in which he uses all his technical skills to present the flash of flamenco, the vibrations of the strings, the elegance of modernity, and the modularity of the technical.

The Eden of Yashar's title is, in part, the Sheikh Hadi neighborhood, where the family had a modern villa—now turned into a banal brick facade—whose unusual architectural touches and colors he can still intimately detail as constitutive of his childhood memories.

Sheikh Hadi is but one member in the set of touchstone nostalgic cosmopolitan sites that have been destroyed by the politics of the twentieth century. For me they include Vienna, whose émigrés, including my parents, created a sea change in American and Turkish academia and in the global republics of science more generally (Hughes 1975, Reisman 2006). A second such touchstone for me, as a graduate student in India, was the powerful shock of reading Khushwant Singh's novella *Train to Pakistan* (1956), about a north Indian village determined not to allow the communal fires of Partition to enter but which proved impotent to protect its residents. *Train to Pakistan* was followed by many other accounts, including S. H. Manto's short stories, the film *Garam Hava* from 1973—with script, lyrics, and dialogue by Kaifi Azmi, based on a story by Ismat Chughtai, directed by M. S. Sathyu—and Bapsy Sidhwa's *Ice Candy Man* (1989), made into a film, *Earth,* by Deepa Mehta in 1998, in which there is a structurally identical scene of determination not to allow the Partition fires to separate friends, equally in vain. India's holocaust, only slightly later than and connected with Europe's, is richly analyzed by Aamir Mufti as a continuous problematic of *Enlightenment in the Colony* (2007), pushing accounts of India beyond the postcolonial or subaltern into the very makings of modernity. The two holocausts were, unnervingly for me, intertwined in Anita Desai's *Baumgartner's Bombay* (1989), the story of a German Jewish refugee in Bombay hanging out at one of my haunts, Leopold's Irani (and Zoroastrian) teahouse, one of the sites of my dissertation work on Zoroastrians and Parsis in Iran and India (as well as Jews, Bahais, and Shi'ites in the town of Yazd, Iran).[3] Desai's text is also used by Mufti to tie together his analyses of the minority questions of Europe and India. Sidhwa's ice candy man equally unnervingly, uncannily, reappears in Bapsy Sidhwa's America, where she and I became friends (in Houston).

As if these hauntings and cat's cradle intertwinings were not enough, yet another of these touchstones for me is not merely the Jerusalem of Salim Tamari and Meron Benveniste (Fischer and Misselwitz 2006), which my grandfather visited and wrote a report about in 1911, but even more intensely the joint border patrols between Israelis and Palestinians in the 1990s, described in a remarkable ethnography by Deborah Heifetz-Yahav. These joint border patrols depended upon learning a fragile dance of one another's masculinities, a wrong move igniting violence, but right moves exercising, slowly building, the sinews of possible peace: not only across presumptive nationalities, but also on each side, between, on the Palestinian side, the returned "Tunisian" Fatah leadership and the insiders or between the Hebronites and Nablusis and other localities with their own dialects and alleged behaviors; and, on the Israeli side, between the Druze officers, the fiercely anti-Arab second-generation immigrants from North Africa who become border patrol fighters, and Ashkenazi Jews. It was a microcrucible of the continuing pressure cookers in the Middle East and their transnational circuitries.[4] A confidence building measure, joint patrolling alone could not sustain an extended temporality without other reinforcements. As a microexample it is hardly a romantic site of everyone getting along without friction, but it is a site of Kantian "unsocial sociability" with real possibilities.

Reading Arendt in Tehran and deciphering Parviz Yashar's *Escape from Eden* in Tehrangeles are among the reflexive forms of nostalgic cosmopolitanism that still have, out of their complexities and contradictions, lessons to impart. Arendt is a figure whose star is returning, not so much for her thoughts on totalitarianism or on the banality of evil, but for her important touchstone insistence on the "human condition in its plurality" and her insistence on the difference between just living and living justly.

These vignettes, each pebbled labyrinth openings into anthropological pasts and futures, and into macro-, meso-, and microlevel networks of cosmopolitan and cosmopolitical significances, perhaps can model the possibilities, alterities, and ways in which the world around us is simultaneously structured (and emergent) otherwise than in the official stories and institutional formalities, reinscribing the differences between just living and living justly.

II: Just Gaming and Violence in Cosmopolitics

The ground beneath [her, our] feet.
—SALMAN RUSHDIE, *Midnight's Children*

Electronic networks and the synesthesia of the media are said to be the test beds and infrastructures of cosmopolitan futures, not to be measured by their high-tech nature or engineering efficiency, but by their cultural models, socially recursive publics, open source, people-friendly tools, environments, and enablements. Things are moving on the ground; "the ground beneath our feet" is no longer what it was.

At least three relationships (macro, micro, and meso) are said to have changed in cosmopolitics since Kant's nine theses in search of a global patchwork of confederated republican-style governance ("Idea for Universal Peace from a Cosmological Point of View," 1794). First, at the macro level, states are no longer the largest containers of national economy, health policy, environmental policy, or foreign policy. Second, at the micro or grassroots level what once were called new social movements have morphed into highly mediated networks, able to cope with distance and diversity, and facilitating constant organizational tinkering and experimentation with alliances and bottom-up decentralized decision making. Third, at the meso level, literature, music, and film provide "minor language" displacements of mainstream presumptions. These may be both progressive and retro. Among the retro ones is the "frenzy of position" taking that, as I quoted Derrida earlier, constitutes much of the so-called return to religious fundamentalisms today, returns not to something that once was but more like respirations or returns of breath, after a pause, to a changed state.

Macro: Retooling the Material-Semiotic Operators of Cosmopolitanism

Kant imagined the continued growth of the republican spirit of the American and French revolutions into federations of republics that would provide the checks and balances to leverage humankind's "unsocial sociabilities" into institutional, legal, and juridical means for multiple crosscutting, not always simultaneous equilibria (Höffe 2001). For Kant, cosmopolitanism is a double semantic operator: descriptive of emergent republicanism and experimental goal or task (ibid.: 169; Beck 2004a: 20). In a striking metaphor, Kant analogizes his sketch for cosmopolitanism's lively futures to rumors sown by a Gypsy woman or a whiff of the enthusiasm of the sublime, which might help things along (Fenves 1991: 179; compare to Marx's "in a moment of enthusiasm," and Durkheim's revolutionary moments of "effervescence" that can foster a new *conscience collective*).

Conflicts, unsociable socialilties, for Kant, remain central to human anthropology and to human freedom. Even war can be, as Hegel would insist, spiritually or morally regenerative, albeit not warfare itself but the virtues it fostered, such as courage and renewed commitment to cosmopolitan ideals. The cosmopolitan condition is in permanent danger of decline when not challenged (Fenves 1991: 170). Kant on the one hand demanded the abolition of secrecy in favor of free and public discussion, while on the other hand he insisted that possession of power corrupts the free judgment of reason. His anthropology from a pragmatic point of view, therefore, keeps separate and in productive tension the practice of law from the foundations of justice, the corruptibility of empirical action from the ideals of the rule of law, and in general worldly political experience from the regulatory ideal of the categorical imperative to foster the freedom of every individual insofar as that does not compromise the freedom of others.

The European Union (EU) is perhaps something like the federation that Kant anticipated, neither a macrostate nor just trade agreements, more like a weave of regulations, policy directives, codes of conduct, and monitoring mechanisms to which new member states must agree to conform (e.g. on the Eurogroup of finance ministers, see Puetter 2006; on the Court of Human Rights, Goldhaber 2007). All is not well in the actually existing EU, as conflicts over immigration policies indicate. Even EU proponents and analysts like Ulrich Beck are confused, as when Beck, arguing that the very idea of Europe is an open network, nonetheless insists that Europe, unlike America, is not a land of immigrants and that its diversity stems only from long-rooted local cultures (Beck 2004a: 176). (For a more sophisticated and alternative view invoking the history of "Kant the Jew, Kant the German" or the German-Jewish "couple" as but one of the many dualities in Europeanness, see both Derrida 1991c and Mufti 2007. They focus on the surplus meanings of Jews for the Enlightenment, but one might as easily focus on other dualities and multiple migrations over the centuries in European identity formations, of which the figuration of the Gypsy woman in Kant might be a hint [Fenves 1991: 179]). Thus one might recall not only "Moorish" and Islamic Sicily, Andalusia, and Toledo, about which Ania Loomba (2007) reminds us in her analyses of European obsessions with these cosmopolitian formations and their demise as the literary ideas of Europe formed. One might also recall the "Black Atlantic" ports of England (Gilroy 1993), and the others inherent in Polish identity, figured not only in Jews, Lithuanians, and Ruthenians, but also in the Iranian tribe, Sarmatians, from which Polish aristocrats claim descent, as well as in the Turks, to whom the national hero General Józef Bem fled in 1848, converting to Islam, and in whose city Istanbul the Polish national poet Adam Mickiewicz lived at the end of his life (Fischer and Kocanowicz 1995).

It is not only the overlapping weave of EU, NATO, the Organisation for Economic Co-operation and Development (OECD), UN, the World Trade Organization (WTO), the World Court, and other internationalizing institutions and treaty instruments that continues to help negotiate an emergent new cosmopolitan order within and beyond Europe, along with and interacting with other such networks, such as the Association of Southeast Asian Nations (ASEAN), the Organization of Islamic Countries, the Organization of American States, and so on. More important is the way in which politics is transformed by a new

mix of and changeable relationships among NGOs (transnational, regional, local), the media, capital, states, and international organizations. It is this that Beck calls the new "meta-power games" of cosmopolitics (Beck 2002a).

Beck usefully suggests that we understand Europe as a project born
of the play of four moral demands: a project of resistance (against the
perversion of European values under the Nazis); the struggles for
reconciliation (initiated by the Nuremberg trials and the creation of
crimes against humanity as a new legal category beyond war crimes or
crimes against peace); the institutionalization of self-criticism and experimentalism (the evolving EU); and the separation of state from
nation (allowing for new political "grammars") (Beck 2004a: 168–72;
see also Fischer 2003: ch. 1, on the moral code enforcement in the name
of Europe against the Austrian right-wing coalition government of the
late 1990s).

This play of moral demands and institutional experimentalism expands Kant's notion that the cosmopolitan condition is not something
that simply comes into being or that maintains itself without challenge. It conforms, moreover, to Kant's notion of critique as a social,
rather than solipsistic, endeavor, that is, as a juridical procedure or a
court of justice, in distinction to Cartesian meditations that can be
performed in the first person (Höffe 2001: 210).

The International Court of Justice (ICJ), the International Criminal
Court (ICC), and the negotiations over Turkey's accession to the EU
are three examples of the persuasive, nonviolent nature of this weave.
The ICJ court has no means of enforcement, and yet many of its
decisions do have persuasive effects. The ICC is a response to cross-
state violence, and, where states are incapacitated, it builds on a legacy
going back to the early nineteenth-century international courts in
Freetown, Havana, Rio de Janeiro, Cape Town, and New York that
enforced antislavery treaties, freeing some eighty thousand slaves
(Martinez 2007).[5] Turkey, long a member of Europe by virtue of its
vital role in NATO, its trade with Europe, and its supply of labor to
Germany, is harmonizing its legal codes and practices with those of
Europe, even (or particularly) under the current government, led by
the Islamist party Adalet ve Kalkinma (Justice and Welfare).

Bulgaria, a new member of the EU, has brought into the EU not only
a Muslim population (13 percent of the total, or about one million
people), but also, more importantly, an old conception of *symphoneia*
between state and established religion which subordinates religion to
the state, as it was under the Ottoman caliphate. The Bulgarian state
has won legal cases against the Seventh-Day Adventists over their

refusal of life-saving blood transfusions and against Middle East–supported *salafi* groups over the wearing of headscarfs in school. Appeals by the state were sustained at the EU level, thus denying any absolute right of freedom of religious belief if it violates civil laws for the protection of health or the EU resolution disallowing discrimination against women on grounds attributed to religion.

What is interesting in the context of experimental institution building is the ability to acknowledge different civic epistemologies (*laïcité* in France, *symphoneia* in formerly marxist Bulgaria). This is also true in science policy debates, such as whether to allow stem cell research, where different civic epistemologies in Britain and Germany yield somewhat different outcomes and where EU rules provide primarily additional political resources to deploy in national debates (Jasanoff 2005). As already described, in Germany, the "dignity" of life enshrined in the Basic Law, resonating with a deep *conscience collective* formed in response to the Nazi regime, prevents the production of human embryos for stem cell research, but the parliament compromised by allowing such research on embryos produced elsewhere. The rules of the procedural state were preserved. In England, one solved the issues by naming blastocytes preembryos, as also is the case in the Netherlands. The decision making in England is channeled by "experts" who can make such pronouncements. The presuppositions of civic epistemologies differ and prestructure the ways in which policy debates, even with national competitiveness implications, can play out.

Violence is not absent, as NATO intervention in Kosovo against the Serbian extreme nationalist government of Slobodan Milosevic illustrated (Clark 2001) and as unsettling struggles over immigration policies and discrimination continue to illustrate (Fassin 2002, 2003). Indeed, Beck goes so far as to acknowledge as a constitutive paradox of "realistic cosmopolitanism . . . that, in making recognition of others central to its conception of society and politics, cosmopolitanism makes enemies who can only be checked by force" (2004a: 49). For Beck, this is only one of a series of seeming paradoxes of cosmopolitanism. Beck claims that cosmopolitanism, by obliging us to respect others as equals in principle, "for that very reason . . . does not involve any requirement that would inspire curiosity or respect for what makes others different" (ibid.: 49).

To an anthropologist this is a highly dubious proposition. It is the general danger that Emmanuel Levinas called "reducing the other to the same." It presumes, however, a lack of dialogue and communication. More to the point might be the frequent political claim by Islamist and neo-Confucian cultural exceptionalists against the imposition of Western notions of human rights, usually signed onto by their governments under the UN Declaration of Human Rights. But Muslim counterinsistence on social justice as being more important than individualistic human rights and neo-Confucian insistence on building disciplined socioeconomic structures are hardly outside the debates of modern Enlightenment theory, Western or not. Indeed, as Beck notes, such cultural arguments are themselves a function of, resistance to, or redefinitions of the cosmopolitization of life-worlds.

While there are always power relations, Beck is not persuasive when he opposes universalism and relativism, writing, "the emphasis on context and on the relativity of standpoints springs from an impulse to acknowledge the differences of others; but when it is absolutized in thought and practice it flips over into an incommensurability which results in pre-established ignorance" (2004a: 49). But these are nonsensical alternatives. As Beck himself observes, "Cosmopolitanism without provincialism is empty, provincialism without cosmopolitanism is blind" (ibid.: 7), meaning not provincialism but grounded or ethnographic situatedness. Beck's solution is to invoke minimal substantive norms and universal procedural norms. But such generalization undercuts his efforts to come to terms with the anthropological stress on relationality (not relativism).

Much more interesting but difficult for Beck to handle at his level of abstraction, and hence his interesting acknowledgment of the utility of ethnography (2004a: 26), is his notion that cosmopolitanism will require new grammars, syntax, and semantic elements in new forms of metapower games and recombinant play with semantic elements such as "universalism, relativism, ethnicism, nationalism, cosmopolitanism, multiculturalism, etc." (ibid.: 48–49; also 2002a). This sounds very much like the comments made in 1988 by a close reader of Kant, Jean-François Lyotard.

Lyotard first used Wittgenstein's notion of "language games" and later the vocabulary of "phrases," "linkages," and "passages" in communication *differends,* where different social relationalities make real-time translation difficult or impossible. Time is crucial: the dialectic (*dialéktikè*) of bringing arguments to light so that they can be adjudicated. Unlike Hegel, whose dialectic encloses the play of difference within a totalization, within its own genre of speculative discourse, Lyotard's "language games" and "differends" index standpoints and social differences. The "dialéktikè, the theses, arguments, objections, and refutations . . . is what provides material for paralogisms and aporias." Hegel puts these into the service of a unifying didactic end: "There are [in Hegel] no true discussions" (Lyotard 1983: 86). Here

Lyotard aligns himself with Adorno's and Derrida's notions of negative dialectics and *différance*. Time is constitutive and deferring: one must be *given time*, time to work through and adjudicate.[6]

Europe is now encircled by detention camps of refugees and migrants attempting to gain entry. The aspirations of cosmopolitanism, the claims of hospitality, the notion of freedom are put under pressure (viz. German *frei*, from I.E. *pri*, to care for, mutual help [Höffe 2001: 152]). Assertions of universal human rights and rights of humanitarian intervention can be double-sided, subordinating as well as emancipating. Indeed, from an institutional point of view, the humanitarian industry brings its own political, logistical, and other dynamics, which have complicated interactions with local political hierarchies and ways of doing things and longer term effects (Pandolfi 2002, 2006; Fassin 2002, 2003; Duffield 2007; Ghani and Lockhart 2008; Panourgia 2008a, 2008b).

Nonetheless, Beck, Lyotard, Derrida, Adorno, Haraway, Latour, and others are correct that cosmopolitics involves a shifting terrain of what Haraway calls material-semiotics, the way in which a change in one or more material objects, institutions, or lexemes (e.g., a category such as "stateless" or "crimes against humanity") can rearrange the substantial relationships among them all. Beck uses the language of shifting grammars and metagames of power for handling emergent paradoxes and ambivalences among the nation-states, NGOs, international organizations, and other players on the international stage. Lyotard spoke of the inability to tarry with Hegel's fantasies of a unifying dialectic, and the necessary return to the notion of dialectic as a play of conflicts that do not resolve but continually generate *differends* (of phrases, linkages, and passages) to which we must attend, not just recognize, but work with, work through, attend to with recursively experimental institutional solutions. In such processes of social learning and experimentation lie anthropological futures.

Micro: Honk for Social Change (or the Gypsy Woman)

At the grassroots level, new social movements have morphed into highly mediated networks. Constituting these mediations are the open forms (open source, creative commons, wiki editing), the multi-media dimensionality (visual, music, text), and the legal, normative, and economic defenses against the closing of the commons.

Street theater, activist marching bands, direct action spectacles staged for media dissemination, marches with banners and costumes, symbolic barricades, hunger strikes, information tables, popular music, and many other tactics have long been staples of democratic political action. They were important to the Quit India movement, to the American civil rights movement, to the public square demonstrations that helped precipitate the fall of the Soviet Union as well as more generally to consciousness raising around the globe. What is arguably distinctive today is the media and networking reach of these activities. Speculations by Hardt and Negri (2000), manifestos by artists groups, social histories of music by George Lipsitz (1990, 1994, 2007) and others as well as ethnographic studies by Jeff Juris (2008) and others provide an emergent archive for probing the degree to which these remain small-scale actions or constitute a broader sensibility, a social and cultural experimentation with flexible, open source, interoperable, and socially reflexive forms of social organization.

Jeff Juris's study of antiglobalization protests (Zapatistas, Seattle, Prague, Nice, Quebec, Gothenburg, Genoa, Barcelona), the World Social Forums (Porto Alegre, Mumbai, Caracas, Bamako, Karachi), European, Latin American, and Asian Social Forums (Quito, Hyderabad, Florence, Paris, London, Athens), and similar mobilizations suggests we pay particular attention to a number of features. Social flexibility: these mobilizations compose themselves by loosely layering sets of networks, each with its own histories, visions, and organizational forms, each differently rooted in local circumstances and differently connected to global alliances. These networks include unions, NGOs, and parties as well as small activist groups. The Zapatistas achieved global recognition, but many other "autonomous" groups of squatters, indigenous people's groups, and poor people's movements are more focused on local problems, engaging only strategically, when feasible, in transnational networking. These movements, Juris suggests, point to a "democratic deficit" and to a disembedding of the market from society. They are, he thinks, creating "social laboratories," experimental spaces for learning to address diversity and difference.

A minor node in such networks is the annual Honk! Festival of Activist Marching Bands, held in Davis Square, Somerville, Massachusetts. The second annual Honk! featured three local bands plus bands from New Orleans, Rome, San Francisco, Montreal, Chicago, New Hampshire, Maine, and North Carolina. Workshops discussed how bands negotiated relatively open or closed memberships (representation, diversity, safety, cohesion, how to maintain a sound), how bands work with community groups (whom to play for or to refuse, how to negotiate money, how to use colors, costumes, lyrics, flyers to get messages across), how bands negotiate space at performances, how bands use different sorts of music to calm crowds or to pump them up, how bands liaison with or interact with police.

Cakalak Thunder from Greensboro, North Carolina, had several rich experiences to share, including one about a moral dilemma whether to participate in what turned out to be, they discovered upon arriving, a closed furniture trade show that violated their ecological concerns, another about how to engage gentrification that threatened people they were trying to help yet provide the income for the band to continue their efforts, and one about challenging a college Young Republican group to a public "beat battle" and their mutually videoed interactions with the police.

Perhaps the most interesting cosmopolitan group was the effort by The Himalayas and Lesser Pandas to provide images of Iranian civilization that defuse the belligerent mainstream discourse about Iran, hybridizing and affectionately parodying Zoroastrian, Muslim, Jewish, and Chinese "perpetual New Year rituals" against despair and for hopes of renewal and transformation: "Lesser Panda! Lesser Listen! Lesser Homeland! Lesser Danger! Lesser Torture!"

Meso: Literary Reorientations

In between the macro level of cosmopolitical theory and the micro level of grassroots organizing, there is a meso level in literature, music, and film that provides insistent minor language displacements of mainstream presumptions. I want to return briefly to Aamir Mufti's readings of works by Abul Kalam Azad and Saadat Hasan Manto with an eye to the ethnographic, journalistic, and oral history details that disrupt mainstream political narratives, using here also the recent book by Trita Parsi called *Treacherous Alliance: The Secret Dealings of Israel, Iran, and the U.S.* (2007).

Mufti reads Azad's *Ghubar-e khatir* against Jawaharlal Nehru's *Discovery of India*, both written in the Ahmednagar Fort prison where the All India Working Committee of the Indian National Congress were interned from 1942 to 1945 after they had passed the Quit India Resolution. Nehru's well-studied text is the confident epic of India's progress toward science and rational social policy. Azad deconstructs all this in epistolary form, twenty-four letters, fragmented musings, and meditations. *Ghubar-e khatir* or *dil ka ghubar* (laments of the heart, or mists of interiority) deconstructs Nehru's account, not least by returning repeatedly to the scene of early morning composition disrupted only by Nehru's snoring and bouts of mutterings that are always in

English. The two texts constitute a *differend* in relation to one another, Nehru puzzled by the Muslim leaders' attachments to their traditions even if trained like himself in European erudition, and Azad demonstrating the never-ending cycle of insufficiency of uniform citizenship for the expression of multiple identities. It is, argues Mufti, a mirror image of the Jewish question in Europe and had similar disastrous results. Nehru and Gandhi could never quite understand the resistance to a single script (preferably Devanagari, not Persian) of the vernacular language that Muslims came to call Urdu (and write in the Arabic-Persian script) and Hindus Hindi (and attempt to Sanskritize). Azad's letters to his friend Maulana Habibur Rahman Khan Shervani, the founding vice chancellor of Osmania University, parallel for Mufti the letters between Walter Benjamin and Gershom Scholem and cover similar dilemmas.

At the end Azad writes a parable about the sparrows that come to roost in his barracks, showering his desk and floor with their nesting debris, their intimate dust clouds (*ghubar-e khatir*). Unable to chase off these invaders and enemies (*dushman*)—they always return—Azad is forced to adapt to these neighbors, who become guests even. In this shift in language and attitude, Azad begins to offer food, tempting the birds to come progressively closer. The game is possible only via mutual dissembling, "the man feigning disinterest in the approach of the birds, and the birds . . . feigning disinterest in his offerings of food, as they circle, recircle, and bypass it many times before their final approach." Azad turns himself to stone, and they occasionally sit on his knees and shoulders but fly off at the slightest movement or sound. Though Azad analogizes the mutual approach to a radical other as steps (*maqam*) in the Sufi path of union with God, Mufti comments that there in fact is "no transcendental resolution here, only the prospect of the gradual emergence of trust and the managing of fear . . . the allegory is about the relative alignment of force that structures the life of society into majority and minority domains, and the adjustments called for from the majority [the measures that the larger, more powerful being must undertake in order to allay the fears of that smaller, less powerful creature] in order to achieve an ethical practice of coexistence" (Mufti 2007: 174).

Trita Parsi's story, similarly, has to do with cosmopolitics on a macro level, but the details of his stories provide the ends and stitches of a brocade that can best be understood quite differently from the back. One knows the general pattern of the tapestry of Middle East geopolitics, of how, with Egypt's departure from the Soviet sphere,

Iraq became more of a concern for both Iran and Israel, of how under the shah a tacit alliance was maintained with Israel, and how the geopolitical calculations shifted with the collapse of the Soviet Union and the rise of Iran, seen as a threat by its Arab neighbors. Parsi reminds us to look at the stitches behind the scene: how often Israeli leaders went to Tehran and Iranian officials met Israelis in Europe, or even occasionally Iranians went to Israel, and the degree to which such contacts continued long after the fall of the shah. These stitches, or hidden exchanges, came into view through the Iran-contra scandals of the Reagan White House, which involved Israeli brokering of arms for Iranian money for Reagan's support of the contras in Nicaragua.

It is in these details, fragmentary letters and meditations, diplomatic and military back channels, that alternative requirements and possibilities are registered for understanding the theaters of Parviz Yashar's painting the *Lord of Illusions.*

III. Globally Distributed Republics of Science and Technology: The View from Bandung, Tehran, and Istanbul

Cosmopolitics is at play not only in war industries, resource extraction, communications, medical science, and ecology, but also in most global technologies. It is also at play within the distributed modern sciences. High-energy physics requires costly accelerators built through international cooperation. Teams of investigators negotiate different styles of tinkering with detectors versus reliance on technicians (Traweek 1988). Biology labs in the United States have large numbers of Chinese nationals as postdocs, many of whom return to China to set up research institutes and companies. As the United States, in the second Bush administration issued fewer visas for foreign students and postdocs, and made obtaining them an obstacle course, the networks of scientific mentoring and collaborations began to shift elsewhere. More Indonesians, for example, are taking up scholarships in Japan and Australia. Generally, biological and ecological sensibilities are being rapidly transformed, and many of the key sites of biodiversity research (e.g., Indonesia) and understandings of climate change (e.g., in the Amazon or the Arctic) depend upon physical terrains through obligatory passage points under the control of new national actors.

In both these positive and negative ways, global relations are morphing. Indeed, in his work of the early 1990s, Beck makes the transnational production of risks—toxicities, pandemics, financial crises, Bhopal,

Chernobyl, HIV/AIDS, BSE mad cow disease—central to the creation of second-order modernity: the need for socially reflexive and temporally recursive institutions, and the political consequences of the geographical and class redistribution of costs and benefits. Saskia Sassen's work on global cities similarly makes the new teletechnologies of speed and access central to economic and political reorganization. Of course, science and technology policies long have been central to national competitions, imperial formations, and center–periphery economics.

Arguably, however, the political and ethical terrains of the distributed republics of science and technology are different today, powered as they are by the silicon and molecular revolutions, from what they were even in the 1950s and 1960s, when, for instance, the NASA space programs were conceived as building new infrastructures with participating nations across the globe. India was one of the more interesting exemplars: satellites built in India integrated monsoon tracking, agricultural crop estimation, village education, and filmmaking, with more functionalities anticipated. Such global research projects as the International Geophysical Year began to draw in research communities around the globe in more focused and intensified ways, even while cosmopolitical competition continued.

There are at least two dimensions, perhaps, in which the terrain is different today: the striated global terrain of ethical and political plateaus, and the contrasting civic epistemological terrains of negotiation among interests and values.

Striated Ethical and Political Plateaus

Complexly striated terrains of research, innovation, and practical deployments operate below the aggregate horizons of brain drain, increasing concentration of educational and vocational resources in the first world, increasing inequalities, and the optimistic horizons of hi-tech innovation in capital-intensive biopolises and technopolises in Dubai, Singapore, Korea, Shanghai, and elsewhere.

A microexample from 1957, alluded to in chapter 5, during the competitions of the Cold War might serve as a resonator. Geodesy, the study of the shape and size of the earth, with practical consequences for mapping, military, and space trajectories, is a global science. Irene Fischer, one of the leading U.S. geodesists, in 1957 needed to know which of two methods the Russians had used in 1939 to calculate a long east–west geoid profile: "Since no new numerical information was let out of the U.S.S.R., this 1939 profile was very important and I wanted to be sure to apply it correctly. My question was: was this profile computed according to the 'projection' or the 'development' method? In the latter case, I would have to apply the Molodensky Correction to it; this would make a non-negligible difference of about twenty-five meters in geoidal height at the east end, where I would have to connect it to the Manchurian geoid" (I. Fischer 2005: 55–56). At the international meetings in Toronto, Fischer tried a ploy to extract the information:

> I could not expect an answer to a letter or an informal question to an individual, so I tried a public question by presentation and publication in addition to an attempt at personal contact. . . . I had computed my paper for both cases with alternative solutions. . . . Then I tried Mr. A. A. Izotov, who also at first said that he did not know or remember, but I did not buy that since I knew Izotov from the literature as being in that very field. Eventually a meeting was arranged, with Dr. F. Bros from Czechoslovakia to be Izotov's interpreter. It seemed prudent at this point to have my own interpreter and I found the Israeli geodesist, Mr. B. Goussinsky, whose mother tongue had been Russian, willing to help me. I also brought the English translation of Dubovskoy's article, to be as technically specific as possible. When Izotov saw this report he was clearly upset and wanted to know how I got it and where the Russian original was. I said: "On my desk in my office." Then he said that if he could have seen my original he would have known where it came from and could have answered my question. That did not not make much sense to me with respect to my question but it illuminated the circumstances. The impression that he was afraid to say anything was underlined when later on he did not even want to answer questions about his own paper, presented and distributed at the meeting. A statemate! But not quite. Several months later I received a letter from Goussinsky with a translation of Isotov's report on the Toronto Assembly, mentioning both of my papers in detail. He reported that my Russian source material was taken from Dubovskoy and he gave my numerical results, quoting the numbers . . . not even mentioning that two sets of solutions had been computed and published. So here was my answer, loud and clear: Dubovskoy's work was done with the development method and needed the correction that I had inserted on page 6a. . . . Just to be quite sure, I asked [Brig. Bombford] to use his good offices as President of an International Association of Geodesy Study Group to double check with Dr. I. D. Zhogolovich, who was now Secretary of the IAG Section V (Geoid Section). The answer was a clear confirmation. (I. Fischer 2005: 56–57)

A microexample, mentioned briefly in chapter 2, from telecommunications within Indonesia today, situated on a vertical national

cross-section rather than a horizontal cross-national one. At the Institute of Technology of Bandung (ITB), an innovative generation of
computer scientists has tackled the challenges of networking the vast
rural areas of the Indonesian archipelago with extreme low-cost wireless technology, guerilla education, and moving into the Ministry of
Technology and Research. Building open access to communication
networks requires overcoming regulatory as well as technical and social challenges. All three tactics of low-cost, open-source technology,
guerilla expansion of user base and demand, and leverage from within
the government are required. The struggle to get regulatory legislation
which would cover the lowest bandwidth (or third layer of Information and Communication Technology [ICT]) and make it available to
the public the scientists argue, should generate, not subtract, demand
and users for the telcommunications industry. The first Internet gate-
way was at the University of Indonesia in 1993. Onno Purbo at ITB set
up a used 286 computer and a ham radio 2-meter band to connect to
the Aerospace Agency in Bogor. The system was 1.2 kilobytes per
second, packet technology, radio network, an old Pentium 1 and 2 as
server, all self-funded and built by ITB students. By 1995 they had
upgraded the system a bit, but the army came and threatened to jail
Purbo. The director-general of telecommunications asked Purbo to
move the frequency, which he did, in the process expanding coverage.

Soon there were too many people doing this network building for
the police to control. It was, says Purbo with a grin, a successful guerilla campaign. Meanwhile, the then rector of ITB saw no need for the
Internet and refused funding requests. Purbo says one needs three
ingredients to win the fight for expanded access: power, money, and
mass activity. It is the last that he uses for leverage. He paid for a
telecom link and then began showing people how to put free telephony switches on top. For this he briefly went to jail, in the process
generating more positive publicity both domestically and internationally. He resigned from ITB, arguing that he could reach only two
hundred students at a time there, but by doing his guerilla demonstrations and workshops and by participating in some 170 mailing lists he
is able to reach thousands.

His guerilla activity is designed to create public pressure for the
creation of legalized regulatory structures for the third-layer ICT. (The
first layer is fixed-line telecommunications, the second is cellphones,
both controlled by companies and regulated as utilities. It is illegal to
operate without a license.) There are technical, social, and, above all,
regulatory challenges. The effort, as his former colleagues at ITB say, is

to create a third-layer communication network that villagers, schools, and communities can maintain themselves, creating content for their own needs, using low-cost assemblies and open-source technologies, and building infrastructures linked via standard protocols that a high school student can deploy. Technical problems include designing platforms assembled of low-cost radio links, satellite links, and routers that can support voice transmission. Take a Chinese cooking wok (costing four dollars), attach a wireless universal serial bus (USB) (twenty-four dollars) which gives a range of four to five kilometers, and with a few other cheap pieces you have a Wokbolic assembly for thirty-five dollars, like a satellite dish. Social problems include how to do updating for seventy-thousand villages using peer-to-peer technology, and how to create business models for rich, poor, and extremely poor villages.

But the primary problem at the moment is regulatory. Self-assembly has been spreading, and there have been police raids of cybercafes to take away computers. The government has agreed not to tax (license) 2.4 gigabyte equipment, but the fight now is to make it 5.6 gigabytes and to remove the language in the regulatory agreement that still, in principle, requires all equipment to be licensed. It is a joke, Purbo says, to require the government to approve a wok-based piece of equipment. When his son's high school Internet collapsed, running a hundred computers on two slow DSL lines, he helped them set up their own mailman on a Linux server. While Purbo purses a strategy of growing the user base to pressure the government for regulatory reform, his former colleagues at ITB are pursuing the technical problems and lobbying inside the system for changes with the regulators. One of these former colleagues, a different former ITB rector, is now state minister of technology and research and is trying to manage the countervailing political and bureaucratic pressures from the government side.[7]

Examples could be multiplied. At the Institute of Physics and Mathematics (IPM) in Tehran, a remarkable group of scientists helped keep the scientific culture of Iran alive through a period of cultural revolution when the universities were closed and Islamically purged.[8] It was the first site in Iran to be connected to the Internet and is home to a world-class string theory group. Often accused of maintaining world-class credentials at the expense of being an enclave with little social multiplier effect, members of this group have in fact produced high school science textbooks by using newly coined Persian vocabulary to make science more accessible. One of their members, Reza Mansuri, in addition to serving as a deputy minister for research in the Ministry of

Science and Higher Education under the Mohammad Khatami govern-ment, has pioneered a popular astronomy magazine linked to astronomy clubs around the country. Iran has developed Bt rice and industrial-scale tissue-engineered propagation of date palms and other fruit trees and has experimented with new social models for paying donors for kidneys and providing transplants free and for WHO-designated best-practices pro-grams of HIV/AIDS triangular clinics.[9]

In Turkey, a state-of-the-art good manufacturing practice (GMP) stem cell therapy production unit for human therapies like bone mar-row transplants, cancer vaccines, and organ and tissue engineering has been set up at Karadeniz (Black Sea) Technical University in Trabzon by two hematologist-oncologists and a microbiologist, with funding from fifty-three private investors. On the wall hangs a picture of a Turkish veterinarian who was an early pioneer of stem cell research (see figure 8 in chapter 2). Turkey is not only the leader in the Islamic world of scientific output but has now engaged in a new generation of private universities, of which three seem to be stabilizing as small but world-class research and teaching facilities to supplement the genera-tion of state universities initiated under Mustafa Kemal Atatürk with the input of a generation of refugees from Germany and Austria. Sedar Omay, one of the three founders of the stem cell production facility, affirms that hematology was begun in Turkey by Emil Franck. Omay himself was educated in Japan, the microbiologist in Sheffield.

In Egypt an experimental farm built with technosavvy combined with Rudolph Steiner and Sufi ideology not only has proved it can grow and market organic crops, but also has maneuvered the Egyptian government into banning cotton pesticide crop dusting and support-ing healthier growing techniques.[10] In Taiwan, a cadre of biostatisti-cians has inserted itself as power brokers in the disputes over the International Convention on Harmonization for global clinical trials (Kuo 2005). In Brazil, tower experiments in the Amazon to determine whether the tropical forests are carbon sources or carbon sinks are interpreted differently by U.S., European, and Brazilian scientists. The international effort of the six hundred plus scientists who contribute to the Large-Scale Biosphere Atmosphere Experiment Program is in-tended to chart the sustainability of the Amazon ecology and the role of the Amazon forests in the global carbon cycle and thus in regulating the global environment. They are also training a new generation of Brazilian global environmental scientists who can work independently of the currently hegemonic American and European assumptions about how forests work, one of the contentious North–South divisions over the global political economy (Lahsen 2001, 2004, 2005; Lahsen and Pielke 2002).

These and numerous other initiatives constitute a cosmopolitical terrain of competition and struggle, but one that is a quite different problematic from those generated merely as aggregate pictures of brain drain or postcolonial subordination to imperial hierarchies. The latter problematics have not disappeared, but the ground is shifting beneath our feet.

Civic Epistemological Terrains

It is worth underscoring again, for the contemporary world, Fleck's demonstration that there is no epistemology without history, and Jasanoff's demonstration that policy outcomes are affected by the historically embedded presuppositions of different traditions of civics. Jasanoff's examples are genetically modified organisms and stem cell research (Jasanoff 2005). In Germany, as noted, the absolute inviolability of the dignity of human life is inscribed in the Basic Law and in the conscience collective, so that it proved impossible to pass legislation allowing embryonic stem cell research; and yet stem cell research has such economic promise and such medical promise to heal and protect the dignity of human life that it also proved impossible not to allow stem cell research. The solution to this dilemma had to be one that affirms the procedural integrity of the Rechtstaat. The current compromise was to allow stem cell research as long as the extraction of cell lines from blastocysts was not initiated in Germany. And there would be an oversight regulatory commission. In the United Kingdom, things played out differently. There, as I discussed earlier, the House of Lords was able to declare blastocysts to be preembyos and therefore allow the issues to be regulated by expert committees. Although public confidence in government regulatory committees was shaken in the aftermath of the mad cow disease scandals, and a brief period of experimentation with more open public participation in policy matters was allowed, the open processes became so subject to delaying tactics that the United Kingdom soon returned to regulation by expert commissions. Jasanoff sums up the three quite different civic epistemologies as follows: in Germany, procedure rules; in England, "experts know best"; and in the United States, skepticism prevails, that is, litigation using "better science."

Such civic epistemological differences become increasingly important as efforts proceed at harmonization of standards in quality control, safety, health, environmental protection, and trade. These are only in part technical issues in which scientists and engineers are involved; equally they are social organizational, cultural, and historical issues for which a social anthropological sensibility is required.

Conclusions: Pebbles, Sparrows, Labyrinths, and Ethnographic Vignettes, Postings from Anthropologies to Come

The cosmopolitan and cosmopolitical challenges of the twenty-first century will require that attention be increasingly focused on the ways in which technologies are peopled—creators, designers, users, hackers, nonconforming patients and doctors, alternative networks for leveraging medical research and care—and resistances are negotiated into new ways of doing things. "Resistance" will no longer be a blunt, catchall term but will be broken down into various kinds of transducers, synapses, reactions, expansions, contractions, titrations, filterings, translations, displacements, rescalings, twists of topology, and emergent forms of life.

The three temporal and spatial relations of cosmopolitanism—reflexive nostalia; experimental cosmo*politics*; attention to current peopling of technologies, sciences, and technoscientific policy decision making—need to interact as differential critiques of one another, juxtaposing trifocal sensibilities: the humanistic textures of literature, film, music, and philosophy; the social anthropologies of living with diversity and alterity across differing historical and cultural experiences; and technoscientific knowledges and infrastructures that facilitate and constrain flexibility, creativity, and freedom.

We need to enjoy and explore the synaptic density of connections, interferences, and allusions captured in multisited or multilocale ethnographically elaborated vignettes to both find strategic switches and pressure points and to reveal unanticipated displacements and multiplicities within emergent worlds of macro cosmopolitics, meso institution building, and grassroots constituting capillary powers.

Azad's sparrows and the Palestinian–Israeli joint patrols are microexamples (sometimes *Beispiel*, sometimes *Muster*) of this jeweler's-eye work of ethnography and social anthropology, the back and forth of detail work and sitting back to view the settings. Both hospitality to sparrows and the civic confidence building of patrols depend upon fragile, yet life-critical negotiations of emotions, trust, and calculations across diversities, alterities, and differends. Each of the vignettes and microexamples are windows, doors, labyrinths, rabbit holes that open into other worlds full of the unsocial sociability of precursor and emergent forms of life. What makes them useful is not their never-ending capacities for complexity or following out new threads, though that is one of their important features. What makes them useful is their capacity to probe how micro, meso, and macro levels of analysis and reflection do and do not fit, keeping scales, explanations, structures, cultural meanings, and social forces in play and renewing anthropological futures from a pragmatic point of view.

Prologue

1. "Even Mathematics, Natural Philosophy and Natural Religion are in some measure dependent upon a science of Man; since they lie under the cognizance of men, and are judged of by their powers and faculties." David Hume, *A Treatise of Human Nature*, 2d ed., ed. L. A. Selby-Bigge and P. H. Nidditch (Oxford: Oxford University Press, 1978), xv; cited by Jacobs 2003: 108, 130n13.

2. See Flory 1987, Forsdyke 2006, Lang 1984, Long 1987, Stadler 2006; and on the continuation of arguments about empire, money, power, and cultural thought in Thucydides, Kallet 2001, Sahlins 2004.

Chapter 1. Culture and Cultural Analysis as Experimental Systems

1. Parts of this and the following introductory paragraphs and parts of sections 5–7 have been excerpted under "Culture and Cultural Analysis" in *Problematizing Global Knowledge: Special Issue, of Theory Culture Society* 23(2–3) (March-May 2006): 360–64.

2. There have often been suggestions that the culture concept is exhausted, is used too thinly by nonanthropologists, or is so misused that it should be abandoned by anthropologists. Cultural thinness was an idea proposed by Robert Levy in his study of Tahitian culture (1973) as a way of characterizing certain of its cultural accounting procedures in contrast to cultures that did such accounting in more complicated and detailed ways. This comparative contrast was similar to the contrast that Terence Turner described between his frustrating experience talking to the Kayapo of the Brazilian Amazon and that of Victor Turner holding rich "seminars" on symbolism with his Ndembu informants. George Marcus would much later adopt the usage "thin ethnography" to characterize strategies of rapid ethnography in business schools, among cultural studies writers claiming to do ethnography, or the many others who think doing a few interviews is what anthropology means by ethnography. These have their uses, but they are usually instrumental ones that are rather different from traditional "thick description" (Clifford Geertz's

term) or in-depth ethnography that seeks to get at webs of meaning and interconnections among institutions. Multilocale or multisited ethnography (Marcus and Fischer 1986) often requires a strategic mix of thin and thick ethnographic modalities to characterize large, globally distributed processes that work themselves locally in different ways.

Abu-Lughod (1991) suggested we drop the term "culture" because it has been misused to stereotype Arabs and others; and indeed, my phrasing here is meant to cover not just this, but locutions of the sort that ascribe special aptitude for "soul," "spirit," ecological wisdom, and other markers of romantic, less-alienated culture as if compensation for lack of wealth and power, reason and hegemony. For a recent example of the effort to immobilize culture into variables and scales of universal measures of achievement-orientation in a revival of 1950s modernization theory, see the book *Culture Matters: How Values Shape Human Progress* by Lawrence Harrison and Samuel Huntington (2000). Though claiming to be scientific, these often fall into similar pejorative tactics (as well as misrepresentations of earlier social theorists cited as foundational, particularly in the case of Max Weber). For a more interesting debate on the uses of culture in the worlds of commerce, business management, organizational behavior, and anthropology in corporations, also revolving around whether culture can be approximated for practical purposes as fixed variables or needs to be more relational, see Cefkin 2009, and Ortlieb 2009.

For an older debate about the utility of the term "culture" and the scientific nature of anthropology, one might look again at A. L. Kroeber's *The Nature of Culture* (1952) as well as Radcliffe-Brown's arguments about the nature of theory (1952). It has been popular to simply dismiss these awkward discussions, but they can be read today as halting steps toward an interpretive or symbolic anthropology in Kroeber's case, and toward structuralism in Radcliffe-Brown's case, but with many other interests that cannot simply be collapsed into those later paradigms. Kroeber, while invoking Herbert Spencer, Gabriel Tarde, and Durkheim, strikes a stance of pragmatic empiricism. He likes the notion of emergence and recognizes culture as its own level of organization, for which he used Spencer's awkward label the "superorganic," which he says grows historically and contextually, concluding, "Causation should not be denied because it is hard to determine, but to put its isolation into the forefront of the endeavor, as if we were operating in old-fashioned mechanics, is naïve." Leslie White, reviewing Kroeber's "Configurations of Culture Growth" in the *American Anthropologist* in 1946, thought Kroeber had no place for individuals, while, inversely, Kroeber's teacher Franz Boas had no "vision of a science of culture" and so elevated the individual to supreme importance. This is a crude and unfair reading of both but it reflects the reductive polemics of the time posing the individual versus society.

Meanwhile, Radcliffe-Brown, in his introduction to a set of his collected essays, *Structure and Function in Primitive Society* (1952), went back to Montesquieu as the first to formulate the notion of a *social system,* defined as a "set of relations," and to Auguste Comte for distinguishing social statics versus social dynamics. Like Kroeber, he goes back to consider Spencer's theory of social evolution (while distancing himself from the specifics of Spencer's speculations) but draws a distinction between social structures (composed of roles), social processes, and social functions. He begins a tradition of recognizing that there can be differences between individual purposes and system requirements, a tradition that would be elaborated by E. E. Evans-Pritchard and the Manchester School (Max Gluckman, Victor Turner, Abner Cohen). In concluding, he notes that he no longer uses the term "culture" as he did in many of his earlier essays ("as a general term for a way of life, including the way of thought, of a particular locally defined social group"), but that he wants to create a theory from the concepts process, structure and function, in the two-hundred-year-old cultural tradition of Montesquieu, Comte, Spencer, and Durkheim. Following Radcliffe-Brown, British social anthropology would privilege the terminology of the "social," while American cultural anthropology would privilege the word "cultural," but meaning by these terms quite overlapping endeavors (particularly once the University of Chicago had become colonized by Radcliffe-Brown).

3. The second world, or socialist bloc, was more explicitly interested in changing identities and in sharply breaking with the past: forging a New Socialist Man; a rationalized, industrial, and welfare society; and a socialist-modernist culture, with hostility toward religion, kinship relations, and other modes of social and cultural tradition. Even where concessions were made to nationalities, e.g., in Muslim Central Asia, the Arabic alphabet was replaced with Cyrillic specifically to break historical ties, and family clan and lineage structures were broken up to foster socialized production. Nonetheless, new Soviet cultural forms (civic rituals, socialist realism in the arts) as well as pursuit of high artistic forms (such as ballet and philharmonic music), valorizing engineering and the sciences, and development of mass culture forms from propaganda to input-output national planning models, large-scale agriculture and industrial organization—all these were fostered in a complicated dialectical relationship with the first world in which catching up as well as ideas of an alternative modernity played key roles. Indeed, debates before and immediately after the Bolshevik revolution revolved around blockages to creating socialism in one country and in a semimonetized economy, apart from the industrialized first world, which was supposed to lead the revolution, according to earlier Marxist models of how new social formations would arise out of accumulations of contradictions between social relations (property ownership laws, class conflicts) and forces of production (including science and technology).

4. Sir Edward Burnett Tylor (1832–1917) is known for his articulation of the anthropological notion of culture, for a celebrated article on the comparative method that blocked easy claims of evolutionary progress, and for his efforts to make anthropology a tool for social reform (part of the social reform acts and debates of the nineteenth century in England, led by the increasing

political strength of the entrepreurial middle classes and Dissenting Sects). Remembered for his lines, "Theologians to expose, 'Tis the mission of primitive man'" (which he contributed to Andrew Lang's "Double Ballad of a Primitive Man"), Tylor's "omnibus" definition of culture opens his two-volume work *Primitive Culture: Researches in the Development of Mythology, Philosophy, Religion, Language, Art and Custom* (1871), toward the end of which he reaffirmed that anthropology was "essentially a reformer's science" (2:410).

Tylor's concept of culture is often contrasted with that of Matthew Arnold in *Culture and Anarchy*, originally published as essays in 1867–68 in *Cornhill Magazine*, and the pair are often seen as founders of the difference between literary accounts of high Culture (with a capital C, as it were) versus anthropological understandings of culture. George Stocking (1968: ch. 4) makes a case for a general commonality between Arnold and Tylor of Victorian notions of evolutionary progress, but even he acknowledges that Arnold could never have written a book entitled *Primitive Culture* because it would have been a contradiction in terms for Arnold. Arnold, as Stocking also acknowledges, was alienated from the liberal, nonconformist middle classes with which the Quaker Tylor was identified. Tylor, not being of the established Anglican church, could not go to "Arnold's Oxford," though eventually, thanks to the liberal reforms gained by the ascendant middle classes and Dissenting Sects, he taught there, rising from keeper of the University Museum, to reader and eventually professor, becoming a member of the Royal Society in 1871, and being knighted in 1912. Central to Tylor's generation of comparativist ethnologists was the struggle for a systematic understanding of cultural development that could become a guide for such reforms as the British public was debating throughout the nineteenth century, reforms involving not just extension of suffrage, but also marriage reform, penal codes, and whether religion and its dogmas could be sustained as the basis for scientific investigation.

Tylor's most important methodological article, "On a Method of Investigating the Development of Institutions Applied to the Laws of Marriage and Descent" (1889), was an effort to use statistical correlations to establish functional relations between, for instance, exogamous dual organization and classificatory terminologies of kinship or between parent-in-law taboos and matrilocal residence. One thing he caustically noted was that no index of moral progress among nations could be established beyond arbitrarily simply putting ourselves at the top. Kroeber could still, in 1935, in an article entitled "History and Science in Anthropology" in the *American Anthropologist*, cite this article with some admiration. Couched in the now-archaic terms of "adhesions" and efforts to distinguish between cultural diffusion and endogenous development, Tylor's theories can easily be dismissed as only of historical interest. Alternatively (the glass half full rather than half empty), one might recognize here the beginnings of what in the next generation would become a methodological functionalism, the obligation to ask, if one thing changes in a culture or society, what else also changes? (the systems or ecological rule: "you cannot change only one thing").

Tylor was one of a generation of remarkable comparativists that included Sir Henry Maine (1822–88), a scholar of comparative jurisprudence (*Ancient Law: Its Connection with the Early History of Society, and Its Relation to Modern Ideas*, 1861) who also worked in India on land settlement in the Punjab and civil marriage codes and became a vice chancellor of Calcutta University; Louis Henry Morgan (1818–81), who worked with the Seneca in New York State (*The League of the Iroquois*, 1851) and pioneered the comparative study of classificatory kinship systems and their jural import (*Systems of Consanguinity and Affinity of the Human Family*, 1868–70; *Ancient Society*, 1877), on which Marx and Engels drew; Max Müller (1823–1900), the German comparative philologist and religion scholar who edited (and translated some of) the fifty-volume *Sacred Books of the East* (1879–1910); Friedrich Ratzel (1844–1904), the German human geographer who wrote about urbanism, habitat, *Lebensraum*, and the critical importance of physical geography; William H. R. Rivers (1864–1922), the experimental psychologist and ethnographer who went on the Torres Strait expedition in 1898 and during World War I became a psychiatrist at Craiglockhart Military Hospital to the shell-shocked, including, famously, to the poet Siegfried Sassoon; William Robertson-Smith (1846–94), the Scottish scholar of Semitic languages and comparative religion who famously was dismissed from his chair at the Free Church College in Aberdeen for his writings in the *Encyclopedia Britannica*, eventually becoming professor of Arabic at Cambridge and editor of the *Encyclopedia Britannica* (*Kinship and Marriage in Early Arabia*, 1885; *Religion of the Semites*, 1889); Wilhelm "Pater" Schmidt (1868–1954), the Viennese comparative linguist, ethnologist, and student of Australian aboriginal languages (who earned Freud's jealous hostility); Charles Gabriel Seligman (1873–1940), the ethnologist on the Torres Strait expedition in 1898 and on expeditions to New Guinea, 1904, Ceylon, 1906–8, and the Sudan 1909–12 and 1921–22, and chair of ethnology at the University of London, 1913–34; Edward Westermarck (1862–1939), the Finnish ethnographer of Morocco who taught at the London School of Economics, 1907–30.

Again, while one can dismiss this generation as too Eurocentrically evolutionist, it produced not only a wealth of comparative materials that were made available to challenge European and Christian parochialisms, but also a rich history of social and political struggle over self-governance and social policy both for the creation of modern nation-states and for the construction of colonial empires (of which Maine and the Utilitarian philosopher John Stuart Mill are obvious examples, as are missionary ethnologists and explorers, but which becomes more fine grained in the next generation of anthropologists trained for the administrative service).

5. Anthropologists conventionally cite *The Persian Letters* (1721) of Montesquieu and even Herodotus's *Histories* (440 BCE) as examples of the rhetoric of critiquing one's own society by reference to other cultures, using an anthropological trope of first-person witnessing. The French literature scholar Michele Longino analogously argues in *Orientalism in French Classical*

Drama (2002) that Oriental others, especially Ottomans, were important figures in the public theatrical construction of French nationalism both at the time of its formation and in continuing interpretations of such plays, suggesting why some versions of these stories became canonical while others did not. Edward Said's *Orientalism* (1978) is a similar such argument about the construction of colonial-era discourses and their legacies in the present. Henry Mayhew's *London Labour and the London Poor: The condition and earnings of those that will work, cannot work, and will not work* (1861) was often cited by early twentieth-century anthropologists as a parallel rhetoric of distinguishing the cultured classes from the world of the poor. In all these examples, the social scientists argued, what escapes is the *in situ* social and cultural organizations, perspectives, knowledges, and self-representations of the peoples ostensibly being described, represented, and deployed.

6. An integrated history has yet to be written, although fragments of labor histories, constitutional and legal histories, urban planning, religious and social reform movements do exist. Less well mapped is the circulation, reinterpretation, adaptation, and refunctioning of ideas, and of course reform and institutional development. Hindu and Buddhist ideas were common among European Romantics and American Protestant Transcendentalists, informing, for instance, some of the public service ideology and asceticism of New England savants, elites, and philanthropists like Ralph Waldo Emerson and Alfred Harlow Avery, an important funder of Syracuse and Boston universities. Inversely, leaders of reform movements in India adopted and adapted European Enlightenment, utilitarian, and social reform ideals as part of nationalist and anticolonialist struggles. B. R. Ambedkar (Ph.D. Columbia University, father of the Indian constitution, and leader of the Buddhist movement among *dalits*, tribals, and untouchables) was a contemporary of Malinowski: both intervened in domestic debates about what is reformable in the cultural assumptions of societies as different as England, Russia, and India. On two centuries of Islamic modernisms and reform movements in the Muslim world, see M. Fischer 1982.

7. The notion of experimental systems has taken on renewed saliency in recent years, especially in science studies, and particularly the notion that what at one point is an unstable and experimental object to be discovered can be stabilized and turned into a tool for the construction of further experiments and surprises (Rheinberger 1997; see also, in *Anthropology as Cultural Critique: An Experimental Moment in the Human Sciences* [1986], the double genealogy we draw upon from the sciences and the avant-garde in the arts). Various notions of systems, as I trace in this chapter, have played important roles in both general intellectual thought and the social sciences over the past hundred and fifty years, from machines and large-scale or networked technological systems (Marx on machines; Hughes 1983, 1998, on railroads, electrification), structure and function in the early twentieth century (linguistics, biology, social anthropology, but also the interest in models, both how their elements can be varied, and how they change as they scale, and in anthropology with the recognition that actors might operate with cultural models that

do not conform to reality, native models versus analysts models, competence versus performance in speech, lineage models that are stable while actual genealogies are adjusted to fit) to more information and cybernetic notions in midcentury (open and closed systems; Parsons and Schneider and Geertz's cultural systems), to more targeted experimental systems (*Drosophila*, yeast, *C. elegans*, knock-out mice, and tools such as pcr). See also "Four Haplotype Genealogical Tests for an Anthropology of Science and Technology for the Twenty-First Century" (Fischer 2006b).

8. E. P. Thompson (1968) retrieves the contending strategies and perspectives of working-men's groups and their struggles against industrial discipline and for political reform, seeing them as actors and cultural formulators, not just social categories. Nimtz (2000) similarly, while focusing on Marx's career, situates Marx's efforts at political organizing and strategizing against the contemporary array of movements in England, France, and Germany. Sewell (1980) reminds that while the French Revolution of 1789 created a system of private property, the struggles of 1830 and 1848 were under the banner of demands that labor be recognized as property, as a basis of wealth production, and of protection in national workshops, even creating in effect in the Luxembourg palace, as a body parallel to the National Assembly, a kind of workers' social republic that lasted for four months.

9. Ringer (1969) provides an account of Weber's generation, elaborating the cultural social markers of the German educational and class system—learning Greek and Latin, for instance, as higher status than vocational skills, not dissimilarly to the training in England, where training in the classics was also a social badge that allowed entry to the administrative elite, whether in the Home, Foreign, or Colonial offices. Readings (1996), writing almost two centuries after Fichte, describes a new transformation of the educational system due to the breakdown of the cultural markers of the nation-state that were codified in canons of national language literatures as the basis for a common state culture. Wolf Lepinies (2006) has recently revived the discussion of the role of *Bildung* in Germany as the locus of a trust for Germans that the state itself does not possess and, he argues, in Germany never in the past possessed. Culture as a shield against slipping back into savagery in some ways reminds one of Geertz's account of Javanese decorum ("Person, Time and Conduct in Javanese Society"), and indeed Geertz's essay is mediated by Alfred Schutz's phenomenological sociology, an effort to extend Weber's "interpretive sociology." Norbert Elias's *The Civilizing Process* (1939) traces how forms of sensibility and cultural behavioral norms have changed over cultural-historical time, of which the German *Bildung* is a particular bourgeois and philosophical formation. *Bildung* generates in German an important array of forms that have shaped thinking about culture: Geertz's "models of and models for," for instance, comes from Dilthey's and Simmel's *Nachbild und Vorbild*, a weaving of meaning by constructing concepts to fit social interactions as well as by shaping those interactions to conform with cultural concepts.

10. Habermas argued that in the eighteenth century coffeehouses became

the locus of a public sphere, a space of rational argumentation, a space between the state and civil society from which public opinion could be organized and used to call the state to account. This public sphere was mediated by newspapers and face-to-face argumentation. In the course of the nineteenth century and twentieth these public spheres came to be colonized and manipulated by industrial and political interests, via commodification, advertising, and other mechanisms of the culture industry. Gellner argued that literacy was a requirement for industrial labor forces, and industrialization policies for the consolidation of European and East-European nation-states required literacy in national languages. Benedict Anderson made a similar argument for the rise of nationalism in colonial arenas, namely, that newspapers and other print media allowed for readers to imagine themselves as part of an interconnected political arena.

11. While the revolution of 1789 had introduced private property and abolished property held for the common good or given by the king for temporary use (capitalist relations replacing feudal ones in agriculture), it had led by 1848 to fragmentation and indebtedness. Both clerics and mayors, the parish and local administrative systems, were harnessed to Louis Bonaparte's (Napoleon III) Party of Order campaign. Urban working-class organizers had failed to organize peasants. Peasants had, Marx argues, no means of self-representation and were thus persuaded to vote for Napoleon as their representative and protector against urban creditors. Marx consequently cites their structural situation as one of having neither class-consciousness nor any means of organizing such a consciousness or alliance with urban artisans or wage laborers.

12. A school of Indian historians formed around Ranajit Guha and the annual series Subaltern Studies, which attempted to read against the grain of the colonial archives in order to recover the voices, motivations, and organizations of the workers, peasants, and others. Among the contributors are Shahid Amin, Partha Chatterjee, Dipesh Chakrabarty, Gyandra Pandey, and Sumit Sarkar. Gayatri Spivak provides a useful introduction in the volume of *Selected Subaltern Studies* that she edited with Guha (1988).

13. The dangers of such scapegoating hardly need to be spelled out for Germany in the decades leading up to the Nazi period, but they hold also for mercantile groups elsewhere in the world, for example, the Chinese in Southeast Asia and Jains, Marwaris, and Chettiars in India and East Africa. Werner Sombart's *The Jews and Modern Capitalism* (1911) intended to engage Weber's thesis. The work was received at the time as too philo-Semitic by the right and too anti-Semitic by many Jews and liberals, and Sombart himself moved from a left-wing identity as an interpreter of Marx to ultimately a right-wing nationalist association with the Nazis. Weber's thesis has generated a rich literature of both criticism and elaboration, both via Ernst Troeltsch's sparking of a rich literature on the sociology of Protestant sectarianism and, via R. H. Tawney and R. K. Merton, a rich literature on rationalization, science, and capitalism.

14. See Laura Snyder's recent account (2006) of the debates over utilitarianism between John Stuart Mill and William Whewell, in which Mill modified

"the greatest good for the greatest number" by recognizing that the good is differentiated by qualities of pleasure and cultural character, that knowledge of moral truth progressively expands. In this he follows Plato's *Republic*, in which Socrates distinguishes between lovers of wisdom, lovers of honor, and lovers of gain and gives the highest regard to the first.

15. Meaningful sounds in a language (phonemes) are generated by *binary distinctions* (voiced versus unvoiced) at particular points in the oral cavity (bilabial or lips, the tongue at the top of the palate, near the glottis). Languages use differing sets of distinctions; they have different phonemic systems or meaningful sounds selected out of the possible range of sounds, phonetics, the human voice can in principle make. Some similar sound segments occur in mutually exclusive environments: where one occurs, the other never occurs (this is called *complementary distribution*). In similar fashion, as F. de Saussure formulated it, semantic meaning is generated through a *system of differences*, again, contrasts between the members of a lexicon or semantic field. Thus French *mouton* does not have the same value as—is not an exact equivalent of—its English cognate "mutton" because *mouton* also means sheep. So too, more generally, information theory uses a binary logic or coding.

16. Ernst Cassirer (1874–1945) was a philosopher of the cultural sciences born in the German town of Breslau (now the Polish town of Wroclaw). Turning down a job at Harvard, he was professor of philosophy at Hamburg until 1933, when he fled the Nazis, for Oxford, Göteborg, Yale, and Columbia. He is best known for his three-volume *Philosophy of Symbolic Forms* (1923–29), to which the *Essay on Man* was both a summary introduction and a sketch for a fourth volume under the urgency of combating the ideas that had facilitated the Nazis. Already in 1929 Cassirer debated Heidegger in what was seen as a debate between historical humanism and ahistorical phenomenology. Cassirer warned that Heidegger's approach could be easily used by political leaders. And in *The Myth of the State* he would make this criticism even stronger.

17. Oswald Spengler (1880–1936) was a German philosopher best known for his book *The Decline of the West* (1918), which combined a cyclical conception of rise and decline of civilizations with a cultural pessimism. Although he voted for the Nazis in 1932 and hung a swastika flag on his house, and although the Nazis took him as a precursor, he refused the Nazi racial ideology and thought Hitler vulgar; ultimately his *Hour of Decision* got him expelled from the party. His name is often used as an iconic marker for cultural pessimism. Talcott Parsons famously and rather unkindly begins his *The Structure of Social Action* (1939) by asking who now reads Spengler, reinscribing his name but asserting that we have moved on to more scientific methods.

18. Martin Heidegger (1889–1976) was a philosopher in Germany who became entangled in Nazi politics. Even before the Nazi rise to power, his thought was criticized by both humanists (such as Cassirer), the Vienna Circle (Neurath, Carnap), and the Frankfurt School (Adorno and, after the war, Habermas) as irrational and easily appropriable for political mischief. Appar-

ently a mesmerizing teacher, he claimed to refound philosophy on ontology rather than metaphysics and epistemology. His first major work was on "Being" (*Sein und Zeit*, 1927), and his later work was on framing (*Gestell*) and the poetics of thought (*Dichtung*). After World War II, French intellectuals incorporated him as a major predecessor, though much of their work taking up his attentiveness to poetics serves as a sharp critique of other aspects of his work. He was appointed rector of Freiburg University by the Nazis in 1933 and during his tenure there were book burnings and forced resignation of Jewish professors. His inaugural address continues to draw negative comment. He resigned a year later, but he never resigned from the Nazi party. His views on modernity and technology are fairly standard reactionary conservatism but were given some heightened notoriety after the war by his analogizing the gas chambers to industrial agriculture, by which, of course, he meant to criticize the latter, but the context was his continued refusal to in any way apologize for his role in the Nazi period. Some people find his notion that nature is turned by technological society into a "standing reserve" that can be appropriated by mathematizing calculation to be innovative rather than fairly obvious or a standard antimodernist complaint. His removal of the dedication of *Sein und Zeit* to his teacher, Husserl, who, as a Jew, was forced to resign from Freiburg, was in part reciprocated by Husserl's late work *The Crisis in the European Sciences*, in which he introduced the concept of the "life-world" (picked up and elaborated by the French phenomenologist Merleau-Ponty) as a counter to Heidegger's ahistoricism.

19. Two of the best introductions to the Frankfurt School remain Martin Jay (1973) and David Held (1980). (For the post–World War II period, when Adorno returned to Germany and hosted the famous conferences on Weber and on the logic of scientific discovery, see Müller-Doohm 2003.) One often makes a distinction between the prewar Frankfurt School (closed immediately by the Nazis when Hitler came to power), the dispersal of that group of scholars eventually mainly to the United States, the postwar return of Adorno and his troubled relationship with the radical students of Germany's New Left, and the postwar generation of scholars led and influenced by Jürgen Habermas, who proved a strong voice for open democracy and against normalizing the Nazi period.

20. "Emic" and "etic" were shorthand terms introduced by the linguist Kenneth Pike from the linguistic terms phoneme and phonetics. Phonemes are the sounds selected in a given language as meaningful sounds, from the range of phonetic sounds that the human voice can make. Thus /bit/ and /pit/ are differentiated in English by the phoneme /b, p/, while the German phoneme "ch" (*Ich*) is not recognized and is hard for many English speakers to say. Analogously, then, it was proposed that there might be many semantic fields in which there was an objective natural grid against which cultural terms could be measured and compared across languages, such as colors against the spectrum.

21. I take this paragraph from chapter 6 of my *Emergent Forms of Life* (2003),

where I use it to explore ethnic autobiographies and multiple alternatives that narrators such as Maxine Hong Kingston explore in efforts to articulate the fragments of "talk stories" that go into the formation of their "identities."

22. For a moment, the interest in James Joyce by Lacan, Derrida, and others in France, seemed to dovetail with the explosion of Salman Rushdie's *Midnight's Children* (1981) and the use of a linguistic style that expanded English with linguistic elements from other languages, cultural perspectives, and presuppositions. Similar expansions were happening to other world languages, including Arabic. But this potential as a vehicle for multilingual cultural studies waned, although there was talk about starting journals that would simultaneously publish in, say, Chinese, Japanese, and English to draw their audiences into the possibilities of enriched cross-cultural discourses.

23. The allusions here are to Fleck (1935) and Emily Martin (1994) on immunology and to Foucault's and Deleuze's notions of modernist disciplinary societies (constructed around such sites as schools, clinics, and penitentiaries and around discourses—particularly the foundational disciplines of linguistics, economics, and biology, or language, labor, and life that Foucault argues are characteristic of the modern era), now being transformed into more diffusely and pervasively organized modes of control via codes and flows (Deleuze 1990). The liquidity created by derivatives and similar financial instruments is a powerful concrete example of flows that depend upon the mathematical abstraction of different kinds of risk and classificatory processes.

24. The Wikipedia and Web 2.0 refer to tools that allow collaboration and sharing of information. Wikipedia cofounder Ward Cunningham is credited with pushing the idea of "moving to the edge of your competence on purpose." (On the evolution of the Wikipedia toward registration and passwords for authors and on the study by *Nature* magazine of its reliability as compared with that of the *Encyclopedia Britannica*, see http://en.wikipedia.org.) Derek Powazek uses the metaphor of company towns for Web 1.0 sites such as the Well, Salon, and such gaming-derived sites as BuildingBuzz (on which you spend buzz bucks). In contrast, Web 2.0 sites such as Technorati (for which he used to be creative director), Boing Boing, Flikr, MySpace, YouTube, blogads.com, and sina.com aggregate and rank links, and use robot spiders and crawlers as accountants. They thereby can position themselves as "thought leaders," or places to which people come to find other links or services. (On Web 2.0 entrepreneurs, see Jones 2008. On the ways the world is "blown to bits," data disperses and is recoverable, changing privacy, identity, and personal control, see Abelson, Ledeen, and Lewis 2008.)

The "butterfly effect" is the popular tag for the feature of dynamical systems by which, when initial conditions are slightly changed, large effects can be propagated over generations (the flap of a butterfly wing or a seagull's wing in China or Mexico can affect a weather pattern). The tag is associated with Edward Lorenz, though the idea is older and is now important in chaos theory and the study of complex systems, including especially what is now called the Lorenz attractor, which derived from atmospheric convection equations, takes the shape, under certain values when the plots are drawn, of butterfly wings, or under some values of a torus knot.

25. China is the most interesting country to watch (followed by Iran) for its attempts to both have and control the Internet, a veritable test bed of hardware and software innovations. China is attempting to install an ambitious new system of controls, leaving behind the failing so-called Great Wall of China strategy and building a Golden Shield (launched in Beijing in 2000). The massive upgrade, CN2 or China Next Carrying Network, is supposed to incorporate next-generation routers in a three-tier system that combines Internet surveillance with smart cards, credit records, speech and face recognition, and close-circuit television capabilities. Internet service providers in 2004 were supposed to have installed monitoring devices that track individual e-mail accounts. The hardware upgrades are being supplied by Cisco, Juniper, Alcatel, and Huwavei. The routers are supposed to make possible increased filtering and also tracking of e-mail message content. Various reports on Internet surveillance and censorship and on the cat-and-mouse games played by dissidents and others to avoid these controls have been produced by the Rand Corporation (Chase and Mulverson, 2004), Freedom House (Esaray 2006), Reporters without Borders annual reports by country (www.rsf.org), and He Qinglian's *Media Control in China* (2008). Another element of control may be the shifting flow of Internet traffic bypassing the United States (Markoff 2008).

26. Poetry comes with historical contexts and analogies to the present. "Night letters" (*shabnameh*) of the Constitutional Revolution (1905–11) have become famous exemplars of modern poetry, and the classical poetry of Iran is rich with anticensorship contexts and meanings. The Persian Weblogistan is one of the most active languages on the Internet, and while again most is diaries and trivia, it is a space of cultural genre development in new language forms that mix written and spoken Persian and that create new female genres of writing, and it is occasionally a space for real-time journalism of unfolding events, organizing tools, and a determined site of feminist solidarity and consciousness-raising. (I thank Orkideh Behrouzan and Alireza Doostdar for their astute commentaries on Persian blogs.)

27. The introduction of the gun is often said to be a cultural destroyer of cultural ideals of heroic warriors in tests of honor because one does not see those one shoots (see Meeker 1979, on the transformation of Arabian battle poetry): the airplane gunner targeting through computerized imagery on a screen high above the ground is this process intensified.

28. On the Algerian example—Algeria winning independence after the French had effectively won militarily—see Connelly (2002).

29. This and the next two paragraphs are taken from Fischer 2007b, which focuses on Palestine and Israel as one borderland site of these now almost paradigmatic situations of conflict and asymmetric struggle.

30. On this, see my "Cultural Critique with a Hammer, Gouge and Woodblock: Art and Medicine in the Age of Social Retraumatization" (Fischer 2003:

ch. 4), the notion of "ethnographic psychotherapy" attributed to W. H. R. Rivers in his dealings with World War I shell shock by Kleinman (2006: 214), and the history of post-traumatic stress disorder (PTSD) as a *Harmony of Illusions* (Young 1995).

31. Foucault, like Adolphe Quetelet and Durkheim before him, looked to disciplinary sites (including the collection of social statistics) inculcating self-disciplining subjectivities and subjectivations, as tools by which states could regulate populations and who should live and who should be let die, who should thrive and who be restrained. Agamben updates these eighteenth- and nineteenth-century technologies to make central moral issues addressed in the mid-twentieth century by Carl Schmidt (the challenges to liberal democracy of those who would use the ballot box to destroy it) and Walter Benjamin (the fantasies, ideologies, and haunted histories carried by industrial and commercial objects). Agamben makes the camp as a space of exclusion—defining who is or is not a legal person—central to the foundations of contemporary governance regimes, including liberal democracy (beginning with the concentration camps in the Boer War, reaching their full evil with the Nazis, becoming routinized in the long-term UN Relief and Works Agency (UNRWA) camps for Palestinians and as refugee and migrant camps in Southeast Asia and Africa and now again as controls on immigration into Europe). Camps of those trying to get into Europe now are situated around the peripheries (North Africa, eastern Europe, Canary Islands) as well as within Europe (Sangatte in France, Campsfield, Oxford), as there were camps, prisons, and holding areas in the United States for Central Americans and waves of Haitian refugees and their successors (these are the subject of work by the anthropologists Didier Fassin, and Mariella Pandolfi and her students). Slums, *banlieue*, and ghettos are other forms of camps, in which the people are often treated as reserve labor and biopolitical subjects (kept alive but stripped of chances for equality).

32. Max Horkheimer's and Theodor Adorno's *Dialectic of Enlightenment* (1944) is perhaps the best known of a series of discussions by the Frankfurt School on the ways in which hyperrationality can transform from liberatory to straightjacketing ideology if there are not countervailing checks. They had in mind the rise of fascism, mass party politics, and unfettered industrial and commercial rationalities. Heidegger too worried, in a more directly anti-modernist mode, that science and technology were to blame for turning nature into a standing reserve for production and the world in general into a "world picture" that could be exploited.

33. A historian of the financial reconstruction of the Austro-Hungarian empire in the late nineteenth century and early twentieth and an innovator in Vienna in introducing the history of the United States as distinct from British history, he argued, on the basis of migration statistics, intermarriage, and reverse influence to Europe, that regardless of who won World War II the centers of cultural creativity had already passed outside the boundaries of Europe. In the revised edition in 1948 he found reason to confirm his earlier argument. It would, of course, soon become commonplace to speak of an

American century. But he also foresaw a growing influence from Latin America, especially Brazil.

34. Joe Dumit (forthcoming) writes of "patients-in-waiting" as the global population that the pharmaceutical industry is attempting to recruit as consumers of its products through genomic individualized medicine, and before then by drugs taken for life prophylactically (such as Lipitor for cholesterol).

35. See Sunder Rajan (2006) and Fortun (2008) on the legal protections (of entrepreneurs, of patients) in life science "promises," as, for instance, written into Security and Exchange Commission requirements for public disclosure in corporate documents.

36. See Sunder Rajan 2006, Waldby and Mitchell 2006 on biocapital; and LiPuma and Lee 2004, Lepinay 2005a, 2005b, MacKenzie 2006 on new material-semiotic forms of derivatives that transform particular risks into liquidity, which in turn undermines national sovereignties, a process located in what LiPuma and Lee call *"cultures* of financial circulation" (2004: 31; emphasis added), in which the mathematical physicists and statisticians who design the stochastic models and trading algorithms are quite separate from those who know about the substance of markets and commodities.

37. One of the most serious problems for liberal democracies that again has come to the fore is how to protect themselves from forces among their citizens (and other residents) who wish to destroy them. Again, it does not follow that there should be no defense against the use of "one man, one vote" slogans when they would elect dictatorships: liberal democracies are more than voting; they include division of powers, checks and balances. It is precisely against such simplistic reductionism of claims (and for analysis of social and cultural systems, implications, consequences, and transductions) that anthropology arose in the first place. The UN Declaration of Human Rights is sometimes demeaned as being grounded in Western Enlightenment ideas and Western individualism. But if one listens to the arguments by, say, Iranian Shi'ite intellectuals, one quickly realizes that their alternative call for social justice rather than individual rights might not be so different from the arguments of nineteenth-century German intellectuals that the free trade economics propounded by the British was a tool to keep Germany in a subordinate position; and the goal of social justice is hardly exterior to Enlightenment values. (See LiPuma and Lee, 2004, for similar arguments about South Africa, Brazil, and Indonesia and the *cultures* of financial circulation as threats to nation-state sovereignty in general.)

38. Akbar Ganji is a celebrated Iranian journalist who began as a fundamentalist follower of Khomeini, but in the 1990s, particularly after a series of extrajudicial assassinations of intellectuals in Tehran, used his journalism to hold the state to account. He was jailed for six years, during which time he wrote two republican manifestos, and upon his release he refused to remain silent. He is an associate of the philosopher Abdul Karim Soroush, who trained in the philosophy of science in London, becoming a disciple of Karl Popper; Soroush has been attempting to argue within Islamic terms for a

separation of religion and politics. Haghighatjoo is a lawyer who was elected to the Iranian parliament and while still a Majlis representative was sentenced to prison for speaking out. The sentence was postponed but still can be implemented. She now argues that the way the Islamic Republic's constitution has evolved, it can no longer be reformed but needs total rewriting, a position Ganji also takes.

39. Negative utilitarianism, instead of "the greatest good for the greatest number"—which could easily be prejudicial to minorities—calls for reforms that harm the fewest.

40. Such scholars as Michel Serres, Donna Haraway, Jacques Derrida, and Avital Ronell are expert in deploying such lively languages, which at their best bring together different reference frames in illuminating ways. Dead metaphors are those that no longer cause listeners or speakers to attend to the gaps in meaning between the tenor and vehicle or the carrying across fields of comparison and contrast. They become conventionalized and dead. Lively metaphors, by contrast, are those that take on new meanings and cause listeners and speakers to attend to the work they perform. In symbolic anthropology of the 1970s much was made, in a similar vein, of key symbols and constellations of symbols, which were central to cultural codes and systems, and how they were kept alive and growing or how they began to fade and die and lose vibrant connectivity.

Chapter 2. Four Cultural Genealogies for a Recombinant Anthropology of Science and Technology

1. This chapter originated for a panel convened by the editors of *Cultural Anthropology* on genealogies of anthropology and STS at the Society for Cultural Anthropology meetings in Milwaukee in spring 2006. Many thanks to Kim and Mike Fortun and to Kaushik Sunder Ranjan for critical readings and suggestions during the several redraftings and to members of the panel and audience as well as a workshop with Sheila Jasanoff's students at Harvard's Kennedy School for questions and feedback. I also would like to acknowledge the Carnegie Corporation's support, which enabled some of the fieldwork referred to in the fourth section.

2. I adapt the term from Ulrich Beck (1986) but intend also the notions of "mode two" knowledge (Gibbons et al. 1994) or "post-normal" science (Funtowicz and Ravetz 1992). Other allied notions include "communities of enunciation" (Fortun 2001), civic epistemologies (Jasanoff 2005), biology as civics (Haraway 1997), and "matters of concern" (Latour 2005a).

3. Suchman led a famous group of anthropologists, linguists, and others at XeroxParc which spawned the field of "work practices" studies. It was the beginning of work by anthropologists in corporations, now with its professional organization, Ethnographic Practice in Industry Conference (EPIC). Sheila Jasanoff, the founder of the Science and Technology Studies Department at Cornell, trained as a linguist and lawyer and has been important in keeping the

field focused on politics, power, policy, and the law. In recent work (2005) she has explicitly taken up anthropological ethnography as a tool of the trade.

4. On genealogies, think of the many studies of genealogies in segmentary lineage systems where gaps in the genealogies three to seven generations back from the speaker, or "ego," function to allow their adjustment to present political and demographic realities; also Michel Serres's (1983) brilliant deconstruction of myths of foundation in his book on Rome into their multiplicities of alternative narrative foreclosures and potentials; and Stefan Helmreich's (2003, 2009) amusingly wry and accurate demolition of the logics of biological genealogical tree maps.

5. In metaphor, the vehicle or source is the subject from which the attributes are borrowed; the tenor or target is the subject to which attributes are ascribed. Tenor-vehicle is the vocabulary of I. A. Richards (1936), while target-source is the more recent colloquial vocabulary adopted by George Lakoff and Mark Johnson, e.g. (1980).

6. On previous such relatively large molecular biology large-science projects (the Human Genome Project, the Human Genome Diversity Project, the SNP Consortium), see M. Fortun (2003), Reardon (2004), Sunder Rajan (2006); and on the HapMap project: in Houston, Jennifer Hamilton and Deepa Reddy (in process), and in five sites across the United States, Joan Fujimura et al. (in process). The International HapMap Project is a collaboration of scientists and funding agencies in Japan, the United Kingdom, Canada, China, Nigeria, and the United States, and all the information generated is to be released into the public domain (www.hapmap.org; www.nxature.com). On how public domain repositories became necessary for corporations to shift entangling patent rights to more remunerative downstream products, see Sunder Rajan (2006).

7. These affective as well as rationalist debates are not limited to the 1930s but constitute a style or tradition from the nineteenth century to the present. They include the gay sciences of Nietzsche-Derrida-Ronell, twisting the wires of the sciences and poetic arts together, and of the undersongs and oversongs, the dystopias and utopias, of technologies; embedding ethnographies of science and technology within alternating currents of cultural and epistemic worlds from Luther-Weber's *Beruf*, Bacon's purifications, back to Plato's *hypotheon* and *logon didonai*, and forward to normal accidents, and from Foucault-Lyotard-Beck's first-order (classical discursive) to second-order (post)modernities, from actuarial control to risk society, from Rousseau's *vox populi* to Spinoza-Virno multiplicities, and from sequestered labs to the earth as laboratory. These abstractive, generalizing, macroaccounts are *beta testing* or *test drives* in that they are affective (libidinal) as well as attempts at generalizing (rational).

8. Crucial to the techniques of writers such as Adorno and Benjamin was the notion of mimesis, of using the terms of an opponent but then showing how they can be exploded through their internal contradictions, how they lead to absurdities, or how they can be leveraged into quite other directions

than the opponent intended. Adorno repeatedly used this tactic against Heidegger (see Hullot-Kentor 2006 for some beautiful readings and explications). Michael Taussig (1993) has expanded upon Benjamin's ideas about the "mimetic faculty," a faculty that has often been connected with mimetic faculties in animal and pedagogical worlds. It remains an important tactic of the poststructuralists in the continuing strategy of dismantling the naïve neologistic mythos of the Heidegger cult and similar legacies of the neo-ontological movement of the 1920s (see Hullot-Kentor 2006: 236 and passim).

9. Magic words or slogan terms, as Fleck pointed out, are rhetorical ways in which intellectual sparring teams mark out enemies. They are often constructed as caricatures with a grain of truth that radicalizes an opponent's position often to an absurd position that no one would own. Among some of the most important such terms of abuse in science studies are "positivism," "postmodernism," and "relativism" (mischaracterizing a methodological obligation to attend to "relations" among elements, or, in anthropology, the obligation to understand a point of view and relate it to its sociological and historical context). Inversely "antihumanist" and "anti-Enlightenment" are jaunty flags of temporary self-distinction, to make a point, that have mutated into distorting labels taken literally.

"Humanism" is used in a variety of ways: (1) The slogan that Nietzsche, Derrida, or Ronell are "antihumanist" strikes me as peculiarly parochial and philosophically indefensible. The slogan came about in the 1960s–80s to characterize irrationalism (and so Nietzsche, if one reads him not as a critique of false pieties of normal religion and morality); sometimes psychoanalysis (insofar as it shows we are not in control of our unconscious), and linguistic or rhetorical analyses (structuralism, poststructuralism) that show that we operate within codes that precede and exceed our intentions. It was a flag of structuralism and Foucault's "death of the author" against the failures of the Soviet Union (*The Gulag Archipelago* came out in French in 1974) and the Nazis (Heidegger's "Letter on Humanism") as false claims to fulfill "humanist" hopes; and a warning against mere claims of good intention in waving the flag of human rights and humanitarianism. In his argument with Sartre, Lévi-Strauss said Sartre's classical humanism of social consciousness needed to be replaced with a new form of humanism. One can argue (Christopher Norris has done so admirably in many books) that Derrida is a defender of reason and is not antihumanist; ipso facto for Ronell; and that the fact that the world is not simply mechanical, that our reason and our social systems are constantly under redirection is only to make what is human more precise and less illusory. (2) Humanism, as I understand it, is a philosophical project of basing ethical, epistemological, and scientific arguments on human capacities, sensibilities, affect, and reason, rejecting supernatural *dei ex machina*, divine revelation, arguments from mere authority or mere tradition. (3) Historically, in the Renaissance humanism took the form of rediscovery of classical knowledge, which often had metaphysical foundations such as the notion of *ousia* (substance) or *psukhê* (mind). A figure such as Erasmus was able to satirize and criticize Catholicism while remaining Catholic, and he remained a friend of Luther while refusing to become Lutheran; but with Galileo's condemnation and the burning of his books, the humanist crisis came to the fore, shocking such figures as Descartes into recognizing that humanist freedom had lost out against a flow of history that was no longer in favor of bourgeois, civic, and humanist ideals and would need the absolutist state as defense against both the nobles and revolts from below (Negri 1970). (4) The eighteenth-century projects of Kant and Fichte attempted to straighten out the metaphysics as well as the insufficiencies of Humean empiricism. Fichte attempted to start again with "drive structures—of longing, of dreaming, of striving and so on" (Henrich 2003: 18). While the idea of universal human morals and modes of thought was part of these projects, and "Enlightenment" was meant to help humankind educate itself, universality was challenged by anthropologies of different cultures and the emergence of the notion of cultures in the plural (*Sittlichkeit, Bildung, Kultur, Zivilisation*) and cultures as experimental systems (each of the preceding terms in fact being a slightly differing epistemic object). In no way does this compromise the larger project of humanism. (5) Modern humanist societies and movements included the pragmatists William James and John Dewey, the scientists Julian Huxley and Albert Einstein, the writers Thomas Mann and Kurt Vonnegut (who was until his death in 2007 the honorary president of the American Humanist Association).

10. William James's *Varieties of Religious Experience* (1902) remains an interesting exercise in parsing parapsychological phenomena as something that cannot be technically disproved and yet cannot be acceptable as scientific. The milieu of séances is vividly revived in Avital Ronell's (1989) study of Alexander Graham Bell. The Vienna Circle of philosophers, mathematicians, physicists, and social scientists attempted to clarify scientific language as being that which in principle can be subject to empirical testing, verification, and falsification. They had close relations with American pragmatists: logicians such as C. S. Peirce and Charles Morris, philosophers of the public such as John Dewey, physicists such as Percy Bridgeman, who developed similar ideas under the name operationalism.

11. Paul Lazarsfeld, founder of Columbia University's Bureau of Applied Social Research (the successor to the wartime Radio Project), hired Adorno to help with the Authoritarian Personality project and studies of wartime propaganda. Lazarsfeld was trained in Vienna in mathematics (with a dissertation on the mathematics of Einstein's gravitation theory), was a junior student in the penumbra of the Vienna Circle, and also cowrote a pioneering ethnography, *Marienthal: The Sociography of an Unemployed Community*, with his wife, Maria Jahoda, and Hans Zeisel (Jahoda, Lazarsfeld, and Zeisel, 1933). A pioneering force in sociology as a statistically informed discipline, he also trained Barry Glaser, the founder of so-called grounded theory or qualitative methods in sociology, very close to anthropological ethnographic methods.

12. *Essai sur la connaissance approchée* (1928), Paris: Vrin 1987, S.13, 284; cited by Rheinberger 2006: 25.

13. The formulation "differential reproduction" has become familiar in Rheinberger's work on experimental systems in molecular biology (1997), in Derrida's literary-philosophical deconstructions and reconstructions (from "Structure, Sign and Play" [1966] on), in Gilles Deleuze's philosophies of new concept formation (from *Difference and Repetition* [1968] on).

14. The physicist Ludwig Boltzman, among others, saw evolutionary biology (Darwin) as proving that life could be reduced to mechanical-physical principles. Others, drawing on organicism and vitalist ideas, insisted that the complexity of biology could not be reduced to atoms and biochemicals. See Rheinberger 2006: ch. 1 for a brief overview.

15. See David Lloyd's "Kant's Examples" (1989) for a lovely account not only of the difference between *Beispiel* and *Muster*, but also of the circular temporality, pedagogical imperatives, and the bourgeois political historicity of Kant's "pragmatic anthropology." Scientific opinion is a *sensus communis* or *doxa* (common sense, both physical sensing and a community of achieved sensibility and authority) that is created in a dynamic, dialectical temporality of anticipation (a "project," as Sartre would express it in existentialist language), a "happy union" (a *glücklichen Vereinigung*, happy union) between a future better understanding yet to come and a present preparation (suspended between *das Zeitalter... ein späteres Zeitalter*), and in a collective democratic endeavor of freedom that Hannah Arendt would specify as a condition of the human condition of plurality, a gradual building of a political space in which all are equal citizens, whatever their inequalities outside that space, a space which is, moreover, responsive to their (individual as well as in the aggregate) different perspectives and situated experiences. The hierarchical laboratory is a pedagogical space in which the graduate student is trained to become a mature scientist, the equivalent of Arendt's mature citizen. It is the lab head who speaks as the free citizen of the republic of science.

16. *Essai sur la connaissance approchée* (1928), S. 297; Rheinberger 2006: 29.

17. Two kinds of meaning were included as scientifically valid: analytic or structural or combinatorial logic; and in principle verifiable or falsifiable representations of the experiential world. Otto Neurath combined these discussions with the need for them to be grounded not only in "the practical contingencies of inquiry" but also in "the social dimension of knowledge production and transmission within the framework of historical materialism" (Uebel 1992: 20). Uebel (1992) provides a useful review of the various positions debated in the Vienna Circle as a rebuttal to what he calls the traditional view of their position (i.e., the canonic view propagated through the various attacks on them). There are useful accounts of the historical and sociological context of the Vienna Circle in Uebel (1991) and Nemeth and Stadler, eds. (1996). All three volumes focus on Neurath but serve to give a more balanced account of the group's debates, agreements and disagreements, and historical horizons. Among these, it is worth recalling the rejection of Kant by the Austrian church and court as products of the French Revolution (Haller 1991: 43), and the affinities in Vienna of, on the one hand, political Catholicism, natural law, and authori-

tarian structure of government and, on the other, the antimetaphysical enlightenment philosophy of the Vienna Circle with the theoretical foundations of
social democracy (Stadler 1991: 53). A case is also made for seeing Neurath as a
precursor of Kuhn; and Kuhn's famous essay "The Structure of Scientific
Revolutions" was part of Neurath's and Carnap's project of the International
Encyclopedia of Unified Science. Neurath is known for his interest in using
visual means of conveying information accurately to broad audiences (Neurath
1939).

18. The struggle morphs into debates over basic and applied science as the
best way to generate new knowledge; large-scale engineering versus decentralized initiatives. At the beginnings of molecular biology in the Berkeley,
University of California at San Francisco, and Stanford consortium in the
1940s and 1950s the determination was to pursue basic science; by contrast,
MIT's Health, Science and Technology Program (HST) has prospered by pursuing a combined basic and applied science approach. MIT pursued a science-
based engineering curriculum, while Germany built its industrial might
through vocational engineering schools (see Lash and Urry 1994 on differences between Germany, England, and the United States). On the disastrous
effort to replicate the Tennessee Valley Authority in southwestern Iran and
the Helmand Valley of Afghanistan, see Fischer 1980b; Goodall 1986. On
large-scale engineering projects in the United States and Russia, see Graham
1998; Hughes 1998.

19. Polanyi is known for his articulation of tacit knowledge, which would be
ethnographically detailed by Harry Collins (1974). Polanyi's "The Republic of
Science" (1962) is interesting as well for its account of science as a community
of trust, beliefs, and passing down of knowledge by authority, a position
worked out in historical ethnographic detail for the seventeenth-century
Royal Society by Steven Shapin and Simon Shaffer (1985). Polanyi compares
the republic of science to the double-handedness of British politics: on the one
hand is the dominance of utilitarianism in British political theory, on the other
is the actual dominance of Edmund Burke's "partnership of those who are
living, those who are dead, and those to be born"—"The voice is Esau's but the
hand is Jacob's" (Polanyi 1962: 22–23).

20. The vocabulary of (un)veiling, clearings, getting beyond appearances
and representations, facticity (quiddity in scholastic language), and the turn to
poesis and self-awareness, all partake of a family resemblance which is, as one
says, the metaphysical tradition of the philosophies that define themselves in
terms of the ancient Greeks. Illuminationism (*ishraqi*) is a school of Iranian
mystical philosophy stemming from the work of the twelfth-century Suhravardi; it was popularized in the West by Henri Corbin (1960) and S. Husain
Nasr (1964). Corbin is also an early translator of Heidegger into French. More
technical and rationalist and less mystical accounts of Suhravardi are provided by Hossein Ziai (1990, 1992, 1996), which might prove a fascinating way
to critique Heidegger and place him even more firmly within a scholastic
metaphysical tradition than is usually recognized by merely noting the Chris-

tian theological traces and the legacies of his interest in mysticism (in his dissertation), his revolt against Catholicism, his turn to radical Lutheranism (searching for a "free Christianity," first in Meister Eckhart and Luther, then in Dilthey, Kierkegaard, and Schleiermacher as Christian Protestants), and finally to a folk religion built around his own interpretation of Nietzsche and Hölderlin's poetry, complete with his own rituals around the fire (and with Hitler salute) and now posthumously with Heideggerians annually pilgrimaging to Freiburg and building forest huts in *imitatio* of the master. Iranian illuminationism has a fascinating Neoplatonic account of symbolic forms (*alam al-khayal*, translated by Corbin as *mundus imaginalis*). It also has a fascinating technical deconstruction of Aristotelian logic and a counter-development of logic and semantics building upon the Stoics and Megarian Neoplatonists. It also takes positions against Aristotle and Ibn Sina (Avicenna) in the discussions of the priority of essence (Being) over existence (viz. Heidegger's ontology versus ontics) and develops a way to think about prerepresentational knowledge, which "results in attempts to unravel the mysteries of nature not through the principles of physics but through the metaphysical world and the realm of myths, dreams, fantasy, and truths known through inspiration. The distinction between scientific knowledge and knowledge-by-presence is crucial for al-Suhrawardi, just as it is for Heidegger (in speech), who claims that the essence of human beings lies in their self-awareness, through the luminosity of their own inner existence" (Ziai and Leaman 1998). Although it is often claimed that Heidegger was secularizing Christianity, in fact he was seeking out an originary experience of religious being in the world, and for him phenomenology is about the speech that lets phenomena come to presence for the experiencing of self. As Theodore Kisiel (1993) and Christopher Rickey (2002) show in detail, for Heidegger Aristotle's *phronesis* (insight for action) becomes via authentic religiosity the *Augenblick* (instant of vision, blink of an eye), the lightning flash of authenticity, the "clearing" for presence to manifest. (Walter Benjamin would use the notion of images flashing up in a moment of dialectical insight to quite different ends [Buck-Morss 1991] as also the notion of intoxication [Bolz and van Reijen 1996: 57–58]; Theodor Adorno would devote a small volume, *The Jargon of Authenticity: On German Ideology* [1964], to debunking Heidegger's notion of authenticity; and Jacques Derrida tirelessly showed how speech is *not* originary presence.)

21. Bayh-Dole mandated that universities make their research available to the private sector by patenting and licensing, on pain that federally funded research results not so pushed into innovation development be reappropriated for patenting and licensing by the federal government itself. The idea was to stimulate the pace of innovation. The Chakrabarty decision allowed the patenting of an oil-eating bacterium, which then opened the patenting gates to a wide variety of process and materials patents that had not thought to be patentable before. The effect is both to stimulate private entrepreneurial innovation and to privatize information in the form of intellectual property rights. Theoretically the patent system is supposed to make processes public

in exchange for earning licensing fees; in fact it operates to make some information less open as proprietary.

22. Isotype (International System of Typographic Picture Education) was a general pictogram method. Basic (British American Scientific International Commerical) was intended to teach English as the most widespread international language. Neurath worked with graphic artists like Gerd Arntz, Peter Alma, Bruno Zuckermann, and W. Sandberg. Neurath was involved in housing projects and efforts at economic reform. He, along with the Vienna Circle figures Hans Hahn, Philipp Frank, and Rudoph Carnap, was close to the leadership of the social democratic government of "Red Vienna" (1920–34) with its successes in municipal housing, providing not only running water and toilets, but light and, in new housing estates, green spaces. Neurath helped establish the Cooperative Housing and Allotment Association, working with Adolf Loos, Josef Frank, Josef Hoffman, and other architects, and collaborated with members of the Bauhaus in Germany. During World War I, Neurath had been head of the General War and Army Economics section of the War Ministry, and afterward he was involved in economic planning for the socialist movements in Saxony and Bavaria. With the crushing of the Bavarian movement, he was jailed but then released through the intervention of the Austrian government, Otto Bauer, and Max Weber on the grounds that he was an economic technician (Leonard 1999; see also Galison 1990).

23. The myth and symbol school that helped establish American Studies provided a powerful way to establish the credibility of American culture in contrast to European culture, and I do not mean to belittle their contributions. Leo Marx's *Machine in the Garden* (1964) remains a popular text (the pastoral as a critique of the industrial world), and Richard Slotkin's more recent books on violence in the American mythos provide another well-received body of work (e.g., 1973). That Leo Marx should have written a sympathetic account of Heidegger (1984) is perhaps a token of affinity between Protestant transcendentalism, often with an Orientalist mystical tinge, in New England and mystical searchings in Europe that influenced Heidegger. But Heidegger's trajectory ought to provide a cautionary note, as the philosophical and ethnographic metabolizing of his legacy, I will argue here, has demonstrated. In any case, American Studies itself has divided into a popular culture approach descending from the myth and symbol school and an ethnographic, anthropological, and social-historic approach associated with such authors as Roger Abrahams (1964), Jose Limon (1994), George Lipsitz (2001), and Kathleen Stewart (1996).

24. Idioms of the 1990s have displaced the simplistic older debates about technological determinism. From computer programming we have become accustomed to talking of technological fixtures as either bugs or features: the same item seen as a negative or a positive. From business strategies, similarly, we talk of problems as providing new business opportunities, as in toxic waste providing opportunities for green technologies. Notions of constraints morph into leveraging, redirecting, and reconstructing.

25. There is a family of resemblances among narratives of alternative modernities (Gaonkar 2001), postcolonial analyses, and the dialectics among hegemonic grand narratives of history (Lyotard 1979, White 1973) and irrepressible counter or dissident "minor languages" (Deleuze 1975) of those minorities and small societies (much of the literature of central Europe, such as Jaroslav Hašek's *The Good Soldier Schweik* [1926]) whose members feel they have been run over by History, Reason, and Progress. Ethnographers have worked in all three of these traditions, and with a bit of recontextualization more can be translated into these traditions.

26. *The Dialectic of Enlightenment* is a critique by "mimesis with a difference" of Heidegger's approach. Heidegger's essay of 1954 is a response based on lectures from 1949–54 (see, for instance, McCormick 2002, whose account I follow here). For Adorno and Horkheimer, a key feature of the development of technology is the exploitation of others' work and capital, the production of appropriable and redistributable surplus value. State capitalisms of the 1930s extract surplus value from workers' labor, as did classical eighteenth- and nineteenth-century industrial capitalisms, but their imaginaries are no longer structured only around fantasies of individuals selling their labor freely or under coerced conditions to the disciplining invisible hand of the market, enforcing brutal competition among capitalists who cannot afford to be kinder to their workers lest they go bankrupt. Instead, a political logic has become incorporated through the work of mass parties, mass advertising, mass rituals, and the transformation of subjectivities from Oedipal family forms to ones governed by peer groups or projections of charismatic, perfect role models (political leaders, movie stars), what Freud similarly analyzed in his essay on "group psychology" and Adorno famously analyzed in his contributions to *The Authoritarian Personality* (1950). Patriarchal (monarchies) or patrimonial (imperial) forms of governance have been transformed by massification and new kinds of communication and control technologies, as have subjectivities.

27. In *Psychology from the Empirical Standpoint* (1874), Brentano distinguished mental acts as having intentionality, as being directed toward some object. The problems of human agency were central to discussions about the differences between the physical and social sciences (and their methods) and were taken up in various ways by Dilthey (intersubjectivity, *Nachbild und Vorbild*, which Geertz would turn into English as "models of, and models for"), Husserl (all concepts are concepts for someone), Weber (one can construct "as if" ideal types to account for observed patterns of social action), C. S. Peirce (indexicality, iconicity, and symbolization; firstness [speaker], secondness [addressee], and thirdness [indexicals]), and linguists (messages and sociolinguistic pragmatics).

28. See the similar thought about Husserl expressed by Sha Xin Wei (2005: 79 fn 4), and Barbara Stafford's effort to retrieve a genealogy of thinking about preverbal cognitive images or to deal with the "brain-in-the-vat" problem, namely, "that the material world we live in is both real and unreal: a plausible

fiction set up—imposed, as it were—by something more basic and prior to what we see, yet mysteriously corresponding to it" (Stafford 2004: 315–48). She tweaks this genealogy of "ontologically enriched formalism" in the direction of neurobiology. Douglas Hofstadter (2007) does something similar in trying to model neurobiology in terms of self-referential loops and emergence. Sha, a consummate explorer of mathematics, electronic-sensor environments, and socialities, tweaks A. N. Whitehead's " 'lures for feeling' made from measure theory and topological dynamical systems" (and the work of others such as Husserl, Gilles Deleuze, Alain Badiou, and René Thom) in the direction of "an archeology of mathematics" and mathematical physics.

29. On the puzzle of Heidegger's charisma, Levinas, explaining his youthful enthusiasm for Heidegger, recalled that Heidegger's "firm and categorical voice came back to me frequently when I listened to Hitler on the radio" (Moyn 2005: 95). Habermas as well, on a visit to Rice University, said he cannot read Heidegger without hearing the sound of Nazi rhetoric. The French philosopher Maurice de Gandillac wrote in 1934 of the contrast in debate at Davos between "[Ernst] Cassirer . . . 'so circumspect, so discreet,' and the 'woodsman' Heidegger, paradoxical, lyrical, passionately one-sided" and of his surprise at "seeing . . . the mass of German students fall under the spell [subir la charme] of the vehement philosopher in somewhat the same way as the German audiences today experience the Führer's magnetism" (ibid., 95).

30. One can, of course, distinguish between transcendental and existentialist phenomenology (as Paul Ricoeur usefully suggested), and this was one of the axes along which Jean-Paul Sartre attacked Heidegger. Sartre's "cogito" becomes a "moment of responsibility," structured by a series of aporias (see Rajan 2002: 58 and passim). But for Riceour, Merleau-Ponty, and other existentialist phenomenologists, Husserl is seen as having both tendencies.

31. See Bernstein (2002) for a nice account of how Arendt criticizes, by transforming, Heidegger's tropes, insisting upon working toward a political realm of freedom that is constituted by the inherently different perspectives of human beings debating and thereby establishing their *doxa* (public opinions, worked out in public forums, ideally between institutionally equal citizens working through their inherently differently situated perspectives), working thus against Heidegger's solipsistic Selves for whom *Mitsein* and *Mitdasein* is only a generic or pregiven background and not an actual agon of social action historically and socioculturally located. Her grounding of the human being in speech and action "in-between" plural human beings and her Kantian notion of doxa parallel the anthropological development of the notion of culture. In relation to the mass technologies of totalitarian movements, she characterizes (thereby criticizing) Heidegger's account of *Offentlichkeit*, or publicness (distancing, leveling, reduction to the common denominator, even *Das Licht de Offentlichkeit verdunkelt alles* (the light of publicness obscures everything)—just the opposite of hers—as a description of a degraded public arena in the administered state, one constituted, as the Frankfurt School analyzed, by mass advertising and mass politics as well as mass industrial production. It is in the

plurality of the human condition, even under such conditions, that Arendt argues possibilities always exist for initiatives of organizing otherwise. (Philosophically Arendt is reacting against her earlier adoption of the theological notion that freedom resides in fighting against fate and the desire to atone for sins that one could not help committing, so called innocent guilt. See Leonard 2005: ch 1 on Schelling and Oedipus, and the tragic tropes of German philosophy.)

32. This insistence on relations and relations of relations was already central to so-called British anthropology's functionalism or structural-functionalism, particularly as voiced by A. R. Radcliffe-Brown. The proximate source was Durkheimian sociology, but the more general source was the interdisciplinary language of structure and function in describing organisms and physical processes, including an effort to employ the notion of variance in mathematical functions. These were productive ideas for comparative studies of kinship and marriage systems (Radcliffe-Brown and Forde 1958, Schneider and Gough, 1961, Lévi-Strauss 1949), political structures (Fortes and Evans-Pritchard 1958), and the like. Marcel Mauss was taken as a founding ancestor both by British social anthropology (his *The Gift* [*Essai sur le don*] was the very first text I was given as a student at the London School of Economics in 1965) and by Lévi-Strauss, who reconstructed him in terms of his own structuralism (1950). The effort, on the other hand, to specify a set of functional equivalents of different cultural and social solutions to a basic set of human needs quickly proved a biologically reductionist dead end, since there is no way to specify an exhaustive list either of needs or of the functional equivalents said to be whole or partial solutions to any of them (Aberle et al. 1950).

33. I take the phrase from the testimonial by David A. Nock about how he was directed to Kuhn by his teacher, the sociologist Arthur K. Davis, in his obituary of the latter (Nock 2002).

34. Tilottama Rajan (2002) makes a distinction between affirmative poststructuralism (Barthes, Deleuze and Guattari, Gregory Ulmer) and a negative poststructuralism, which is more philosophical and continues to be concerned with the "loss of phenomenology," with the loss of either a transcendental ego (the possibility of universal apriori forms of thought), direct apprehension or intuition of reality, or a metaphysics of being. It is this philosophical traumatic core that, as a Lacanian Real, he traces in Sartre, Derrida, Foucault, and Baudrillard, all of whom in his reading worry a "doubly barred" subject, barred from subjectivity (the Imaginary, phenomenology) and barred from objectivity (the Symbolic, Lévi-Straussian structuralism). This explains the rhetoric of dismissing Kantian or contemporary pragmatic anthropology as merely positivist, empirical, or ontic, and the fear that the integrity of philosophy as a discipline is threatened by the rise of the human sciences. But it is only one side of a rich set of inquiries into the structuring of discourses, which perhaps is a way of recuperating even negative poststructuralist meditations for affirmative poststructuralist readings. Indeed, Rajan himself suggests that deconstruction and postmodernism functioned in the 1960s as a return of the unfinished project of phenomenology of the 1930s and plots his account as phenomenol-

ogy and structuralism being the unconscious of each other (ibid.: 90). He cites Derrida's comment that Husserl's phenomenology "in its style and its objects is structuralist" because "it seeks to stay clear of psychologism and historicism" (*Writing and Difference*, 159, cited in Rajan, 100). Similarly, he cites Derrida's assertion that deconstruction is always epistemic and affirmative, always concerns systems with a view to opening onto other "possibilities of arrangement" (Derrida, *Points*, 83, 212, cited in Rajan, 94). Similarly again, Rajan notes that Foucault's early essay on Kant's "Anthropology from a Pragmatic Point of View" is the seed of *The Order of Things* (Rajan, 95). In this context, Deleuze's and Guattari's revision of machinic imagery as assemblages and the shift from representation to mediality (also in Barthes, Ulmer, and Derrida) help free the discussion of technology (as machinic, inhuman) from the state apparatus and make poststructuralism "available for a postmodern pragmatic anthropology" (Rajan, 36).

35. The examples are from Latour's *The Pasteurization of France* (1988), the italicized terms are the object-oriented protocols, which now are widely used for many other examples.

36. They defined themselves in the 1980s as new in distinction to older Mertonian sociologies of science that were more concerned with the institutions and ideals of science (organized skepticism, universalism, disinterestedness, common ownership of discoveries), by investigating the practices of how scientific work is actually done.

37. Berger's and Luckman's popular re-presentation in English of the German tradition of the sociological phenomenology of Simmel, Schutz, and others, titled *The Social Construction of Reality: A Treatise in the Sociology of Knowledge* (1966), provided an archaic ring to the anthropological ear for claims that social construction is an innovation of the 1980s. Indeed, what is interestingly dissonant is the invocation, by SSK, of a German philosophical tradition of social analysis grounded in the debates over method in the late nineteenth century (Dilthey, Weber) while being seemingly hostile to, or oblivious to, their Continental philosophical descendants (phenomenology, hermeneutics) drawn upon by anthropologists. It is as if the universe of SSK were constituted by philosophies of science grounded in British analytic philosophy and its restricted interpretation of logical positivism.

38. Key terms of thought collectives have symbolic/magical properties as slogans that turn people into enemies or friends. Fleck's formulation highlights the affect of accusatory terms, "you evil positivist, postmodernist, relativist" and so on, which often have little to do with the actual commitments of the accused. The so-called science wars of the 1990s are a good example. Deleuze's and Latour's formulations stress the more positive mechanisms, while Fleck also includes the possible dysfunctional effects.

39. The most prominent exceptions, none of whom belong to this genealogy but who converse in sub-version, dialect, or minor language translation with them, are, on the one hand, German language–based scholars (Hans-Jörg Rheinberger's interest in Derrida and Husserl; Friedrich Kittler's mate-

rialist structuralism; and Avital Ronell's interest in psychoanalytic theory); and, on the other hand, the long-standing interest of medical anthropologists in the French traditions of phenomenology (Bergson on duration, Merleau-Ponty on embodiment, Canguilhem on the normal/pathological, Foucault on discursive effectivity, madness, subjectivation). These more pragmatist, phenomenological, psychosocial, and psychoanalytic approaches have long been in conversation with, or have been tested and contested by, medical and other ethnographies of the production of epistemic objects, sociocultural assemblages and institutions, and explanatory systems: e.g., Byron Good's *Medicine, Rationality, and Experience* (1994), Mary-Jo DelVecchio Good's *American Medicine: The Quest for Competence* (1995), and the work of Arthur Kleinman (1988, 2006), engaging phenomenology on the one hand and narrative theory on the other; Allan Young (1995), Tanya Luhrman (2000), Margaret Lock (2002), Andrew Lakoff (2005), João Biehl (2005, 2007), and Good et al. (2008) engaging Lacanian topology and Foucaultian discipline on the one hand and science studies' "epistemic objects" on the other; Veena Das's work (2007) engaging Wittgenstein and Cavell on the one hand and violence and poisonous knowledge on the other; the list could be extended.

40. From the notes I took at Weinberg's speech before the Fifth Annual Meetings of the National Association of Scholars, held at the Marriott Hotel in Cambridge, Massachusetts, in November 1994, on the theme "Truth and Objectivity in the Natural Sciences, Social Sciences and the Humanities."

41. There is a deeper history of some scientists' visceral negative reaction to science studies, one which has to do with earlier strata of political interference with science both from the Left and the Right of European politics and the felt need to preserve a degree of autonomy for the "republic of science." Isabelle Stengers reminds that scientists *loved* (her word and emphasis) Kuhn's notion of paradigm shifts (1962), ignoring the sociology of Fleck that inspired it, because it did not challenge their autonomy and because it flattered their sense that scientific discovery was able to break with or transcend past habits of thought (Stengers 1993: 5). By contrast, earlier Bolshevik and Nazi interference in science generated considerable debate. Nikolay Bukharin's defense of political guidance of scientific production within a planned economy at the Second International Congress on the History of Society and Technology in London in 1931 was greeted with enthusiasm by J. D. Bernal and Joseph Needham but was vigorously opposed by Michael Polanyi both in his organizing of the Society for Freedom in Science and in his essay "The Republic of Science" (1962). It is the "irrationalism" of Heidegger and the Nazis' effort to purge "Jewish science" that still informs Gerald Holton's (displaced but understandable) visceral distaste for anything called postmodern. These earlier political debates were sanitized and internalized in the history of science, in which they are called, respectively, internalist and externalist histories.

42. Indeed, in his effort to dethrone Durkheimian sociology and to locate Gabriel Tarde as the relevant ancestor to ANT, Latour claims that in Tarde's effort to find a solution to the bifurcation of nature into two vocabularies of

agents and causes, Tarde came upon a unifying notion of folding, the topological trope that Deleuze stresses in his *Foucault* (1986), the trope of subjectivation as a matter of folding forms and forces back upon themselves (Latour
2001d). For a different spin on Tarde, see Maurizio Lazzarato's *La politica
dell'evento* (2004) cited by Terranova (2007: 139–41). This is a Tarde tuned to
a telemedia environment. The public is a dispersed crowd (or "deterritorial-
ized socius") constituted as a public by "affective capture" through relays and
feedback among a patchwork of Internet, television, print news, and advertising media. Unsettling of the regulative ideals of rational public sphere debate,
these affective publics are regulated through ways of life rather than through
argument or belief, as in "keep shopping" (after 9/11) and "we won't allow the
suicide bombers to disrupt our way of life" (London, Israel). Intervention here
occurs by controlling attention and memory, leveraged through the hiring of
public relations firms and through norms for news coverage.

43. See also Barbara Herrnstein Smith's essay on Fleck and Latour (2005:
46–84). She places Latour in direct succession to Fleck and opposes them to
the tradition of seeing sharp discontinuities, which she associates with Kuhn
and Foucault. She also accepts the stereotype that Fleck's approach is broadly
("point by point") opposed to Karl Popper and the logical positivists (ibid.: 48,
72). Fleck himself disagrees, explicitly locating himself halfway between the
logical positivists and the Durkheimians. Smith is correct that Fleck does not
think logical reconstruction is the way to do history or sociology of science (or
epistemology). But that is quite different from the problem of demarcating
science, and Popper himself always insisted (like Fleck) that you do not start
with definitions but definitions arise out of practical scientific work and the
need to make discriminations ("diaresis"). Smith is on sounder ground when
she notes that Fleck's thinking has affinities with social theorists (she men-
tions Simmel, Mannheim, Durkheim) and with Gestalt theory (on which see
Harrington 1996) and that in retrospect older science often seems like a
"harmony of illusions" (which the medical anthropologist Allan Young takes
as the title for his book on the history of making post-traumatic stress disorder (PTSD) into a medical category recognized in the Diagnostic and Statistical Manual of Mental Disorders (DSM IV) and thus covered by insurance). In
sum, she too agrees that analytic philosophers of science have not served
themselves well by divorcing themselves from the sociologies and anthropologies of science over the past century. As an immunologist and biochemist
himself, she notes that Fleck's "lab-instructed accounts are more attentive to
the significance of technical practices" than are Foucault's, even when Foucault pays attention to transformations across more heterogeneous processes
and effects than she thinks Kuhn does. Unfortunately, in her effort to combat
such misleading "magical words" of enemy making as "relativist" and "postmodernist," she ultimately yields to those terms and calls Fleck a "radical
relativist" rather than sticking to the need to track multiple relations among a
network of factors in most sciences.

44. By contrast, a text like Peter Redfield's otherwise evocative book (2000)

on the location of the European satellite launch site in French Guiana as part of a tropical development syndrome continuous with the French penal colonies in the same area (decadence, unfulfilled promises of welfare for the locals) does not have such an interest, and he quite rightly refused to consider himself part of the anthropology of science and technology project. One learns little, if anything, aside from the geographical reasons for locating the launch site, about the building of satellites and rockets, their scientific payloads, or the training of the scientists or engineers.

45. A striking example is the work of Nathan Greenslit on how people on medications relate to a double sense of who they are in relation to the drugs that allow them to function, incorporating often quite sophisticated understandings of the workings of hormones, pharmaceuticals, and even their own enrollment in marketing seductions (Greenslit 2007).

46. Rapp's (1999) study of how families received amniocentesis indications of Down syndrome contradicted secular middle-class assumptions that most people would choose to terminate the pregnancy; her data forcefully remind of the strong religious strain of those who reacted by preparing family support systems for a disabled child, understanding the meaning of life to reside in the moral tests and trials provided by God, which had their own rewards. Sherin Hamdy has found something similar in the refusal of dialysis patients in Egypt to opt for kidney transplantation that would put family or others at risk (Hamdy 2006). Sanal's studies of an African American kidney donor showed a structure of rich religious meaning that allowed the donor to feel she had turned her life as well as that of her brother around; on the other hand, patients in Turkey could feel social displacement and quite deep reworking of affiliational socialities. More profound were the challenges to belief systems of doctors, who attempted to use a ritual structure to redress the novel handling of corpses, and the competition between deeply held beliefs about organ networks being privatized or socialized. Fox's and Swazey's studies (1974, 1992) involve heart transplant experiments and the tyranny of the gift that patients and donors felt, and how these feelings were regulated by rules of anonymity. Cohen (1999, 2001, 2004) shows how organ harvesting can exacerbate gender, class, and caste inequalities. Petryna (2005) explores how global clinical trial organizations attempt to deal with different levels of medical care in different parts of the world, and how ethical criteria and justifications are invoked to rationalize nonuniversal procedures.

47. Rabinow 1996a, 1999, on venture capital biotech startups in the aftermath of the legal changes of the Bayh–Dole Act and the Chakravarty Supreme Court decision of 1980 and on patient groups raising funds and providing blood for research. Sunder Rajan's *Biocapitalism* (2006) and *Lively Capital* (forthcoming) on novel relations between biotech startups, especially as many changed from producing molecules to producing genomic data, and pharmaceutical companies; between large-scale public consortia and private research companies; between government laboratories and pharmaceutical companies in India; and more generally between the promissory structures of

capital investment in the life sciences and shorter-term reorganizations and redirections.

48. I take the phrases "problematic of emergence" and "epistemologies of encounter" from Chris Kelty (2008). They participate in a family of resemblance with a tradition of concern with "emergent forms of life" (Fischer 2003), and cultural critique by epistemological juxtaposition (Marcus and Fischer 1986).

49. See epilogue.

50. Based on my interviews with Reza Mansuri, Hessamaddin Arfaei, Cumrun Vafa, Yusuf Sobuti, and others in 2006 and 2007.

51. Based on my interviews with Arash and Kamran Alaee in 2006 and 2007 as well as reports by Broumand (1997), Ghods (2004), Zargooshi (2001).

52. Kiki Papageorgiou at the Department of Anthropology, University of California, Irvine, is writing her dissertation on Sekem, and I am indebted to her work, presented at the American Anthropological Association meetings, 2006. Sekem's activities can be accessed by googling their web site.

Sekem, the transliteration of an Egyptian hieroglyph meaning "vitality," is the name of a growing set of enterprises founded by Ibrahim Abouleish in 1977 in the desert sixty kilometers northeast of Cairo. Abouleish was named a Distinguished Social Entrepreneur by the Schwab Foundation, received the 2003 Right Livelihood Award, and is recognized for his pioneering of models for sustainable modes of life that pay attention both to good science, and cultural and spiritual needs. Born in 1937, Abouleish went to university in Graz, Austria to study chemistry and medicine, and earned a Ph.D. in pharmacology in 1969. After a visit to Egypt in 1977, he decided to return to his country of origin. He designed and built a 125 acre organic farm, and in 1984 started the Sekem Development Foundation with a kindergarten through secondary school, vocation training, medical clinic, adult education, arts and sports center, and an academy for applied arts and sciences in Heliopolois (Cairo). Some 2000 people are employed in Sekem companies. Sekem Holding company was formed in 2001 for long-term planning and investment. Six associated companies process and distribute herbs, spices, natural medicines, organic cotton, and vegetable and fruit produce. Products are sold through Organic Farm Food in England, EOSTA in Holland, and Sekem's own Nature's Best Shops in Egypt.

The architect Ibrahim F. Karim, a developer of BioGeometry™ has a similar trajectory. Trained at the Zurich Institute of Technology (Eidgenössische Technische Hochschule Zürich, ETH), Karim returned to Egypt to apply resonance and harmonic relations of energy to his architectural designs in tourism, health care, and other projects, combining radiesthesia, biofeedback, perception, and Pythagorian theories. Radiesthesia (dowsing, diagnostic pendulism) is said to be an ancient Egyptian temple practice and is explored by a group of interested Egyptians in the Imanhotep Science Society (founded in 1986) along with biotronics and homeopathy. An earlier Parapsychology Group was active in the 1960s.

What I find interesting in these examples is the application of scientific and pragmatic skills and connections pursued with an accent on identity or cultural heritage. By themselves the identity and heritage speculations are nothing new. However, their sociocultural functioning as parts of technoscientific worlds is interesting both for the founders and practitioners, and for making worried villagers open to technoscience. This is not always easy: the villagers near the first Sekem farm did not recognize the ancient Egyptian symbols as connected to them, and at one point aggressively accused the cosmopolitans of satanic belief and practice. They did not understand them as ecological scientists, community builders, and spiritual seekers. The villagers did not appreciate the fusion of ancient and modern cosmologies as vehicles for education, culture, health, diet, mental agility, and curiosity.

53. A mosaic of ethnographies of Central American tropical biology research is gradually emerging, although primarily written from North American perspectives. Perhaps the best introduction is the account of the research community at the Smithsonian Tropical Research Institute (STRI) in the rain forest on Barro Colorado Island, Panama, by the journalist Elizabeth Royte (2001), based on a visit in 1990 and a year's on-and-off ethnographic stay in 1999. She provides accounts of a dozen researchers, their modes of work, their inspirations, their mentors and lineages, their subjects (army ants, leafcutter ants, bats, tungara frogs, spiny rats, spider monkeys, spiders, beetles, bees, hummingbirds, lianas, forest respiration, stream biogeochemistry, the first fifty-acre experimental plot now replicated in a dozen places around the world, mutualism and coevolution, creation of an herbarium, etc.). She presents a history both of the STRI and of the changes in field biology from descriptive to quantitative to experimental field methods. She notes that in 1799 Alexander von Humboldt, exploring the Venezuelan rain forest, expressed his frustration at being able to recognize so little. "Naturalists setting out for the tropics a century and a half ago needed to be mapmakers and anthropologists, sketch artists, general practitioners, marksmen, survivalists, and linguists. . . . Today's scientists' skills are almost entirely different . . . instead of looking at what an organism eats, where it lives, and how it reproduces—yesterday's brief—today's researcher might examine that organism's neurobiology, its genetic relationship, and chemical arsenal" (Royte 2001: 160). Barro Colorado Island holds "one of the deepest troves of environmental baseline data in the tropics" (ibid.: 28).

William Allen's (2001) complementary account of the establishment of transformative research in the largely tropical dry forest of Guanacaste, Costa Rica, focuses almost exclusively on the role of the biologist Dan Janzen (but with fascinating side stories about President Oscar Arias's biology advisor, Rodrigo Games; Janzen's wife, Winnie Hallwachs, also a biologist; and a few others). Janzen's career provides a wonderful transect across changes in ecological understanding and frameworks from his father's career as director of the U.S. Fish and Wildlife Service, through the butterfly specialist Paul Ehrlich's and the botanist Peter Raven's important formulation of coevolution to new strategies for biological corridors and ways to charge for ecological or environmental services. Dan Janzen provided the classic study of ant–acacia tree "coevolution"; helped establish the Organization of Tropical Studies and its eight-week boot camp for tropical biology; advised the Costa Rican government on what to do about the invasion of gold miners into Corcovade National Park during the unemployment and economic crisis of the 1980s and thereby established the principle that one cannot defend nature reserves by treating the human beings who live around the park as if they were the aliens; overturned the conservationist dogma that one had to buy forests because once gone they could not be revived by showing how the forest could be restored; pioneered the understanding that nature reserves cannot be isolates but needs corridors for animal, bird, and seed migration as well as forest patches in cultivated land and that one can use livestock in forests. He helped create new economic roles for rural young people as parataxonomists (helping inventory flora and fauna) and as trained nature guides for ecotourists. He was involved in helping evolve the debt-for-nature exchanges of the late 1980s (Costa Rica was third after Bolivia in 1987, then Ecuador, and was followed by the Philippines and Malaysia). Allen provides a clear account of how the four-party exchange works. There is a similar innovative domestic way of raising support through contracts to provide environmental services. A major juice producer signed a long-term contract when shown why orange groves near forest reserves are provided a degree of natural biological pest control and require less pesticide. There is a good account of the struggles between the National Park and the Forestry bureaucracies and how that was resolved as well as a brief account of the establishment of INBio (Instituto Nacional de Biodiversidad), and of the role of Rodrigo Games, the Costa Rican plant pathologist who worked on plant viruses, became a key advisor to President Arias, and helped create INBio as well as Costa Rica's national research council.

A third complementary ethnography is by Luis Vivanco (2006), based on a year of fieldwork in 1995 and another in 2004, about the cloud forest reserves in Monteverde, Coata Rica, on the continental divide between the Atlantic and Pacific, above the Lake Arenal irrigation project. This is less a complement for the biology than a careful account of the many conflicts that went into the creation of the several reserves, including the contestations over such slogans as "sustainable development" and "community participation," the decline in international support for the reserves and thus the increased dependence on ecotourism and environmental services, the fears that a quarter million ecotourists a year may be too many (fifty-seven thousand to the Monteverde Cloud Forest Reserve alone in 2004), particularly given that hotels and workers' housing do not always follow the government's ecological certification rules, and socioeconomic inequalities are increasing. (On a visit in 2008, my wife and I were impressed by the number of hotels that did have such certification, which requires biodigesters, recycling water, and other measures as well as direct benefits to the local community [buying locally, supporting schools and other community institutions], and outreach on ecology to both visitors and employees. On the coasts, there are gated communities of time shares that threaten the creation of a dual society. We spoke about this to young Costa Ricans who work in the ecotourism industry and found that they worry about these social effects and the complicity they may be forced into by their providing tourist services.) Marc Edelman's (1999) *Peasants against Globalization* unfortunately ends in the 1980s, before ecotourism became one of Costa Rica's leading economic sectors, but he provides some useful background to the extraordinary political pressures the Costa Rican state has negotiated through very changeable economic fortunes and its acceptance of structural adjustment in those years in part to offset the Reagan administration's anger at Arias's refusal to allow a landing strip in what became the Guanacaste reserves to be used by the CIA and contras for the war in Nicaragua. One of the CIA planes is now a restaurant near the Manuel Antonio reserve in southern Costa Rica.

The Arenal artifical lake, Costa Rica's largest reservoir, which supplies a quarter of the country's electricity and irrigates thirty thousand hectares, is itself a site of ecological, regulatory, and economic struggles. Once the watershed was declared a national hydroelectric reserve in 1977, land became frozen: one could still own the land but could not freely sell it or use it for collateral or cut the forest, and so incentives rose to sell to the reserves. Farmers resisted paying for water that used to be free and complained that they were second in line for water at the time of year when they needed it most, which coincided with the time when the state electric monopoly wanted to refill the reservoir. Arenal is one of the case studies that constitutes the web-based "Tool Box"of the Global Water Partnership, a technical network for sharing experiences about integrated water management, headquartered in Sweden, supporting case studies and technical formulas supplied from around the world.

These studies so far only occasionally allude to climate change indicators (but see Pounds et al. 1999 on the decline of amphibians in Monteverde), and they introduce only a small fraction of the scientific publications generated (some 253 articles on Monteverde between 1966 and 1993; more generally see the compendium by Nadkarni and Wheelwright 2000; and Leigh's *Tropical Forest Ecology: A View from Barro Colorado*, 1999). *The Last Flight of the Scarlet Macaw* (Barcott 2008) is a picaresque cautionary tale of a zoo in Belize for injured and cast-off tropical animals run by the American Sharon Matolo, a mushroom, tapir, and macaw biologist, former circus animal trainer, and Air Force veteran trained in jungle survival in Central America in the Vietnam era. Barcott notes that even high-powered environmental and economic impact studies may be insufficient to prevent the destruction of a fauna-rich valley by a dam built by a coalition of local politicians and international electricity companies. All the more reason for experiments such as Costa Rica's to be attended to.

54. From Al-Kharazmi as the father of algebra; the Kerela toddy tappers as informants to da Orta's and von Reede's and thence Linnaeus's botanies; Chi-

nese, Ayurvedic, Galenic/Yunani, and Ibn Sina (Avicenna)'s medicines; ibn
Khaldun's sociology, Brahminic roots of Ramanujan's mathematical virtuos-
ity; Jesuit contributions to Chinese mathematics; madrassa and yeshiva backgrounds to some scientists' argumentative and calculative skills; Protestant
roots of the purificatory preparations for demarcating, pursuing, and verifying
science (viz. Bacon and Popper in Ronell 2005; more generally Weber); colonial accounts of restricted access to scientific jobs, or postcolonial accounts of
brain drain and dependency

55. The Indian satellites were to be multifunctional: monsoon tracking,
crop prediction, dissemination of information to farmers and villages, educational television. The program even had resident anthropologists to track the
impact and provide feedback to the designers of programming. It also produced several prominent filmmakers, such as Ketan Mehta. A community
science center set up nearby by the physicist Vikram Sarabai and his assistant
E. V. Chitnis (director of the Center for Space Applications Research) provided hands-on laboratory equipment for after-school experimentation and
helped produce a group of now-prominent scientists, including the malaria
biophysicist Chetan Chitnis (M.A. Rice University, Ph.D. Berkeley, postdoc
NIH), now a Howard Hughes Medical Institute investigator at the International Center for Genetic Engineering and Biotechnology in New Delhi. Tata
Institute for Fundamental Research (TIFR) is a world-class research institute
set up by the physicist Homi Bhabha and known for its units of physics,
molecular biology (established by Oveid Sidhiqqi), and mathematics. (Based
on my interviews with Chitins's father and son, Sidhiqqi, and others at TIFR
and ICGEB in the 1990s.) India today has more civil earth remote sensing
satellites than any country in the world (DeNicola 2007). On Indonesia, see
Barker 2005.

56. C. K. Tseng, the father of modern seaweed biotechnologies in China and
the founder of China's Marine Biology Laboratory and other ocean science
institutions, was educated at the University of Michigan and spent the World
War II years at the Scripps Institute of Oceanography (Neushul and Wang
2000). Tsien Hsue-shen, the father of the Chinese missile program, got his
start as a leading figure at the California Institute of Technology (Caltech) and
the Jet Propulsion Laboratory in Pasadena (Chang 1995). He trained briefly at
MIT but transferred to Caltech to work with the Göttingen-trained Theodore
von Karman, who had consulted at Beijing's Tsinghua University, where MIT-
trained aeronautics professors sent Tsien to MIT.

57. B. J. Habibie rose to be a lead engineer and designer of the European
Airbus before returning to Indonesia to head up an effort to build, first, an
aeronautics industry, and then ships, trains, and automobiles as well as to
stimulate technological development more generally. The troubled story of
these endeavors under the Suharto regime is a fascinating mix of transnational politics, domestic organization, and technical success. The Surabaya
shipbuilding industry (tankers and grain transport) continues to be a success.
Airplanes and a high-speed train were built, but the marketing of the former

foundered on international certification issues, compounded by structural adjustment retrenchments. The automobile project foundered on corrupt demands made by the Suharto family. One often-overlooked success was the reinvigoration of the Eijkman Institute for Molecular Biology under the Melbourne-trained and -professionalized biologist Sangkot Marzuki. Based on my interviews with Habibie, Marzuki, and others in September 2006 as well as at ITB and the Institut Pertanian Bogor (IBP), the Bogor agricultural university. On Habibie, see Amir 2005.

58. Nodal facilitators include, at ITB, Sulfikar Amir (2005); in Taipei, Wen-Hua Kuo (2005) and Fu Daiwie; at the National University of Singapore, Gregory Clancey (2006); at Sharif University, A. N. Mashayekhi; at the Institute of Philosophy, Shapour Etemad; in Bogota, Aleixis de Greiff. In India there is a variety of literature: Chouhan 1994, Nandy 1980, 1988, Visvanathan 1985, 1997, Raj 2000, Rajora 2002, Ramanna 1991, Sarai Reader 1, 2 (2001, 2002), Shiva 2005, Shiva and Bhar 2001, Shiva, Bhar, and Jafri 2002; the series of scientists' biographies by Venkataraman 1992a, 1992b, 1994; the work on vaccine development by Veena Das and students at the Delhi School of Economics as well as cosmopolitan or diasporic Indian interventions from Europe and America associated with both the Subaltern History collective and postcolonial studies (e.g., Prakash 1999, Chakrabarty 2002), and more specifically science studies (e.g., Abraham 1998, Jasanoff 1994, Sunder Rajan 2006).

59. Based on my interviews with Reza Mansuri, Yusef Sobouti, Prenzan Premadi, and others in Iran and Indonesia, 2006–7.

60. The transformation of Infosys and Wipro, both based in Bangalore, are interesting stories of how companies were able to work up the value chain from back office work for foreign firms to body shopping to developing their own products. Nayaran Murthy, the founding director of Infosys was trained initially at an IIT (Kanpur), then at the Indian Institute of Management (IIM, Ahmedabad), where he was trained at the moment of transition from mainframes to personal computers by MIT-trained guru J. G. Krishnayya, who himself went on to found a pathbreaking public sector servicing company, Systems Research Institute (Pune, www.sripune.org) that helped computerize auditing tools and specializes in GIS applications. Murthy is somewhat unusual in having forgone advanced degree training abroad but gained experience in large-scale projects by working for the Paris subway before joining SRI and then founding Infosys. Krishnayya and Murthy are generational hinges between older state-sponsored and mainframe-based computer services pioneered at TIFR and the National Center for Software Technology (NCST, led by S. Ramani, whose postgraduate training was at Carnegie Mellon University). Often unnoticed in the enthusiastic accounts of the software industry in India is the long-standing role of Tata Consultancy Services, which trained much of the software labor force and continues to be a major player both domestically and internationally. (Based on my interviews with N. Murty, J. G. Krishnayya, S. Ramani, F. C. Kohli, and others in the 1980s and 1990s.)

Chapter 3. Emergent Forms of Un / Natural Life

1. Cornell West sardonically uses New Orleans blues and jazz to underscore the meaning structures of the long-term deep play:

New Orleans has always been a city that lived on the edge. The white blues man himself, Tennessee Williams, had it down in *A Streetcar Named Desire*—with Elysian Fields and cemeteries and the quest for paradise. When you live so close to death, behind the levees, you live more intensely, sexually, gastronomically, psychologically. Louis Armstrong came out of that unbelievable cultural breakthrough unprecedented in the history of American civilisation. The rural blues, the urban jazz. It is the tragi-comic lyricism that gives you the courage to get through the darkest storm. . . . This kind of dignity in your struggle cuts both ways, though, because it does not mobilise a collective uprising against the elites (West 2005).

It is a repetitive deep play. In 2001 the play *An Evening with* [Hurricane] *Betsy* dramatized the bitter conspiracy rumors that arose during the floods in New Orleans in 1965, as they did again during and after Katrina, rumors about sacrificing the poor neighborhoods and trying to rid the city of them, rumors that while literally untrue nonetheless express a certain kind of truth and reality (Remnick 2005: 48, 53; see below).

2. There has been speculation about whether the Ground Wave Emergency Network (GWEN) might have had something to do with the unusual weather pattern involved in the floods in 1993. GWEN is said to be an emergency communications network using extremely low frequency (ELF) radiation of 72–80 Hertz. Both the Soviet Union and the United States experimented with geophysical warfare techniques that leverage instabilities in the environment. The speculation is that "an 'electronic dam' can be set up using ELF generators —a magnetic field is created which stalls or blocks a weather front, therefore causing a torrential rain over an area" (Bertell 2001: 136). The Benjaminian World War I image that "new constellations rose in the sky" is here echoed in the airglow reported over the Midwest on September 23, 1993, during the flooding. An unusual lightning flash rising from the clouds upward instead of downward was reported, possibly part of a larger series of such events, such as the airglow before the Tangshan earthquake in China in 1976 (in which 650,000 died) and mysterious ELF-pulsed waves before the quake in California in 1986–87, the one in Armenia in 1988, the ones in Japan and northern California in 1989, and the one in Los Angeles in 1994 (ibid.: 131–32). Such speculations are hard to evaluate given military secrecy. All the more reason for determined monitoring and sleuthing by civilian groups and investigative journalists, as part of a civil society checks and balances and as a way of exploring the theoretical possibilities of ecological interconnections.

3. The climate change debate, when seen in relation to local or regional patterns, becomes sociologically even more interesting. In addition to concerns about the effect on coastal areas of rising ocean levels, the Amazon and

the Arctic are touchstones of research and debate about climate warming. Even more than the politically tinged debate in the United States of contrarians to the Intergovernmental Panel on Climate Change (IPCC) consensus on global warming, largely paid for by oil companies, the debate in the Amazon has high political stakes for Brazil in terms of economic growth versus more conservative ecological sustainability policies, and also in terms of sovereignty and freedom from global pressures on national policies and in terms of the development of a scientific establishment independent of European and U.S. interests. The Large-Scale Biosphere Atmosphere Experiment (LBA) has been internationally funded to determine the role of the Amazon in the global carbon cycle: Is it a carbon sink (removing greenhouse gases)? What is the Amazon's role in regulating the global environment and its sustainability? The LBA is also a capacity-building project to train Brazilian environmental scientists. Most U.S. scientists assume the Amazon is a large *source* of carbon, while EU scientists try to prove that it is a small *sink* (Lahsen 2001, 2004; Lahsen and Pielke 2002). (U.S. scientists think that the new-growth forests in the northern hemisphere are carbon sinks and argue that countries with sinks would be allowed to emit more greenhouse gases under Kyoto style protocols.) If the Amazon is a sink, deforestation would be more of a problem, and Brazil could seek funds to preserve the forest from developed countries. Tower experiments in Manaus (by the University of Edinburgh) and Para (by Harvard) provide contending results and disagreements over method and interpretation. The Manaus experiment seems to show the Amazon is a sink; the Harvard experimenters claim it is closer to a steady state (as one might expect from traditional theory about old-growth forests). Satellite data provided by NASA are viewed with suspicion by Brazil as tainted by American interests in using international controls on environmental policy as a way to control Brazil's growth. Brazil's ability to provide its own scientific analyses is hampered, it is felt by some government policy makers, by the training and ongoing networks of influence that Brazilians acquire in the United States and Europe.

In the Arctic, the Inupiaq near Barrow Point, Alaska, and the Inuit of Canada are on the front lines. It is quite evident that the climate is warming, the tundra is softening, the whale and caribou migrations are changing, and sea levels are rising. Barrow Point, along with other research stations around the Arctic, has been a major climate research station for over a hundred years. But correlating Inuit observations and ecological knowledge with scientific runs of data and complex general circulation models is not seamless. Indeed, while general physics laws have convinced many scientists of the validity of the IPCC's claims about anthropogenic causes of climate warming, the general circulation models are far too complex, too abstract, and too general to make the argument on their own. It appears that "massive [climate] changes could come from inputs much smaller than the models' margins for error" (Wohlforth 2004: 167). Some policy analysts now understand that responses to climate change will proceed from local decisions, the slow, adaptive way in which complex systems adjust. Local governments and states have adopted carbon reduction standards, and some corporations are cutting carbon emissions. Ron Brunner, a policy analyst at the University of Colorado, writes that some climate modelers think of their work as writing an "operator's manual . . . for Spaceship Earth." But, as Wohlforth puts it, "the whole enterprise rests on a logical fallacy: events in an infinitely complex world, full of constantly adapting people and natural systems, cannot be predicted reliably by a mathematical code. Understanding climate change, as well as responding, must happen inside individual human beings, in their minds and in their bones, through judgment and trial and error, in the way the Inupiat, and all people, learn the truth by living it. We need modern science, Ron wrote, but we also needed a ten-thousand year old science based on the human experience of concrete places and events" (ibid.: 278).

A recent new turn in the Inuit story is the preparation of legal grounds for filing suit in international courts against the United States, or against U.S. corporations in federal court, on human rights grounds, not so much individual human rights as the rights of a culture to survive. The Inuit seek a ruling by the Inter-American Commission on Human Rights (an investigative organ of the Organization of American States), which has a history of treating environmental degradation as a human rights issue. The acknowledgment by the United States of anthropogenic sources of climate warming in offical reports and the signing of the Rio and Kyoto treaties provide legal grounds. Whatever the legal consequences, it is a sophisticated publicity ploy enrolling both the media and established NGOs with legal expertise such as the Center for International Environmental Law in Washington, D.C., and EarthJustice in San Francisco.

4. One could elaborate a "deep play" account of each of these chemical and toxic disasters. Perhaps Richard Power's (1998) novel *Gain* is precisely that. It deals with the growth of a chemical corporation which provides employment and valued commodities and perhaps on the side causes breast cancer. The investigative journalist Colin Crawford's (1996) *Uproar at Dancing Rabbit Creek: Battle Over Race, Class and the Environment* deals with the political competitions that on the side allow or block the siting of toxic waste facilities. Much more is culturally at stake than just waste disposal.

5. The following few paragraphs draw from the sections of chapters 1, 2, and 9 of my *Emergent Forms of Life* (2003).

6. In a fascinating legal case that got much publicity and several law review articles in 1997 and the following years of appeals, Newman, with the financial backing of Jeremy Rifkin, filed for a patent on making a chimp-human chimera to try to clarify the "nature" of the human being. Chimeras are mosaics of cells of two species and do not reproduce: they reproduce one or the other species or hybrids but not themselves. Still, he thought presenting people with the idea of a part-human, part-chimp would give many people pause and generate discussion about the regulation of biological experimentation and commercialization. He had no intention of actually making such a

chimera and thought that disclosing the process in a patent would prevent others from such patenting and commercializing efforts. He did want to stop experimentation on human cloning and germ line modification but was not opposed to medical experiments with transgenic animals. The point was to generate public discussion and not allow experimentation or commercialization to proceed without such legitimation. What percentage of cells makes an organism human? And are organisms really "inventions" that can be defined by "compositions of matter" patent descriptions? Human embryonic stem cell research was clearly on the horizon, and even today Newman remains concerned about the claims made for "nuclear transfer" cloning and genetic engineering since so often the repair mechanisms work partially at best. Still he admits that he cannot always tell what is natural but argues that there are complex biological interactions that we still know very little about that should temper experimentation. In 1997, the Patent and Trademark Office (PTO) commissioner rejected Newman's patent application on the grounds that the PTO did not issue patents for things that violate public morality. That was hardly a satisfactory definition (the OncoMouse had been patented in 1984, in 1998 human embryonic stem cells would be identified, and within a decade human-mouse chimeric embryos would be made but not brought to term). Newman filed appeals, and each time the court could uphold the PTO only on technicalities or by delaying requests for more specification, and eventually just that it was inappropriate subject matter, that it was not the intent of the Constitution or Congress to allow patents on part-human organisms, but no statute could be cited. At that point, Newman and Rifkin ran out of money.

7. The Cortesia congregate wasp, like many Hymenoptera, lays eggs in the host, in this case the tobacco sphinx caterpillar, which dies when the larva bursts out to morph, first, into pupas and then into flying wasps. Along with the eggs come virus particles which manipulate the physiology of the caterpillar so that the wasp larva can develop (webmasterúnoscope,cnrs.fr; Espagne et al. 2004). More generally see the work of Lynn Margulis on symbiosis, Serres on parasites, Deleuze and Guattari on rhizomes, and Helmreich on the breakdown of genealogical or arboreal models in marine biology.

8. She is thinking of Massachussetts's release of thirty-seven turkeys in 1972. In 2007 there were an estimated twenty thousand wild turkeys, and they have increasingly become part of the urban and suburban scene. For Thanksgiving dinner, one might buy a mass-produced free range turkey while fending off a wild turkey in the backyard. *Boston Globe* November 16, 2007: A 17.

9. For the rich literature on animals as tropes, see, for instance, on ironic markings by and other uses of animals in recent art, Baker 2000; on animals as figures of transference, Lippit 2000, Wolfe 2003; on anthropomorphism, Daston and Mittman 2005; on melancholia, Kuzniar 2006. The Daston and Mittman volume does acknowledge some historical changes, such as the sentimentalization of pets in urbanizing England and intense resistances to not anthropomorphizing animals (in reflex physiology experiments with frogs, in

the National Geographic magazine's insistence on anthropomorphizing in a documentary about rehabilitating abandoned pet orangutans; the use of celebrity animals in protection campaigns and in enhancing ethologists' own celebrity). Lippit engagingly suggests that in the late nineteenth century and early twentieth the figure of the animal shifts from ritual sacrifice and communication with the next world to circuits of spectral communication in anticipation and response to a parallel function of psychoanalysis and the cinema operating as supplements of the subject. "Everywhere animals disappear," Lippit quotes John Berger, leading to a sense of panic. "Animals never entirely vanish," says Lippit. "Rather they exist in a state of perpetual vanishing. Animals enter a new economy of being," the spectral, the undead, the mourned, in which the zoo is one melancholy site. Hadot (2004) surveys Western tropes of nature from ancient Egypt to modern France and notes how repetitive they are.

10. See Lévi-Strauss's comparative epistemological investigation of how names of birds, dogs, cattle, and racehorses form contrastive sets (1962: 203–8), and Leach's (1964) essay on animal categories and verbal abuse. Lévi-Strauss's *Mythologies* is a compendium of mythically restructured ecological knowledges.

11. Take for instance the antimicrobial "grammar" of peptides being used to explore ways of combating drug resistant pathogenic bacteria. The grammar was recognized by a pattern recognition algorithm from language research. Patterns in amino acid sequences include wordlike sequences that can be swapped without changing the functioning of the peptide. New peptides that differ from all known peptides can thus be constructed. These can attach to membranes of bacteria that are otherwise resistant to drugs (Loose et al. 2006). Whether this is merely a fancy metaphor for a variant of standard computational methods or not, the point here is that algorithms and information technologies are the tools of discovery and manipulation.

12. Two examples already mentioned are the suggestion that trees might be given standing in environmental conservation lawsuits; and the Inuit's and other indigenous people's lawsuits under human rights law on grounds of destruction of traditional habitats and cultural ways of living.

13. In discussing the different dog-training traditions of Vicki Hearne, Susan Garrett, and others, Haraway provides a lovely anecdote about her six-year-old godson's first puppy training lesson. He was taking karate lessons at the time and had learned the ritual of facing an opponent eye to eye and bowing before a match. "Marco," Haraway writes, "at first treated [Cayenne] like a microchip implanted truck for which he held the controls." Cayenne learned the cues and sat for him. "Marco, I said, Cayenne is not a cyborg truck: she is your partner in a martial art called obedience. You are the older partner and the master here, you have learned how to perform with your body and eyes. Your job is to teach the form to Cayenne. Until you can find a way to teach her how to collect her galloping puppy self calmly and hold still and look you in the eye, you cannot let her perform the 'sit' command."

14. Haraway, unlike Greek and Greek (2000), does not accept the argument that animal experimental systems are no longer scientifically necessary or are all too often misleading.

15. Washoe died on October 30, 2007, aged forty-two. Born in West Africa and adopted at ten months by the cognitive scientists R. Allen and Beatrix T. Gardiner, by age five she had learned some American Sign Language and became a celebrity. In 1980 she was adopted by Deborah and Roger Fouts and moved to Central Washington University. The degree of chimpanzees' language-learning capacities remains controversial. Washoe's obituary appeared, among other places, in the *New York Times* on November 1, 2007.

16. Recalling for him momentarily both Odysseus's dog in Ithaca, "the last true Greek in Ithaca," and the dogs in Exodus who participated in the miracle through the holding of their barking while the Egyptians mourned their first-born: "Not a dog shall growl."

17. "But enough of allegories! We have read too many fables and we are still taking the name of a dog in the figurative sense" [152] . . . Bobby and I are not like [Odysseus's] dog and his master" (quoted in Clark 1997: 168).

18. Derrida's term for a global world dominated by western European Christianized forms of public discourse.

19. Scott Gilbert, in "Reconstructing the Body in the Intercultural University" (1993), suggestively linked the four bodies of four scientific research domains with different metaphorical transductions to the social world. The *neural body*, deriving from nineteenth-century divisions between brain and body, has adapted to computer-friendly visions of science as acultural. (As suggested by the references in the present chapter to Simmel, Durkheim, Freud, Benjamin, Taussig, Ronell, and Milun, the history of the social and physical nervous system is much more complex and less acultural than suggested by Gilbert here.) The *immune body* and the lymph system before the 1960s was a popular metaphor for defense of the body, albeit technically already misleading, as Fleck argued in 1935, and of distinguishing self from nonself; after the 1960s, obsessions with cancer transformed the immune body into metaphors of the body out of control. The *genetic body*, Gilbert suggests, parallels the medieval view of the soul which survives the death of the body and is the body of potentials, of repertoires of phenotypes. It is a separate culture in which most ordinary people are illiterate. While this formulation yields too much to the oft-misleading and quite old trope of the book of life, critiqued by Lily Kay (2000), it is the case that we are learning to write new biologies (Rheinberger 1997). The *phenotypic* body is increasingly seen as epiphenomenal to the other three bodies. Gilbert's point is not really to insist on the legacy correlations between ethnicity and the metaphors of the genetic body, defense and the metaphors of the immune body, or cultural "memes" and the neural body. Rather, he was reacting against intercultural studies existing apart from the contemporary sciences and symmetrically suggesting that there is waiting time in biology labs that could be used to read the accounts of Fleck or Emily Martin (1994), or in molecular biology labs to

write grant proposals for non-Western cultures, or to take regular field trips to see and experience real animals.

Chapter 4. Body Marks (Bestial / Natural / Divine)

1. On this reading of Benjamin, see Koch (1994).

2. Simian immunodeficiency syndrome in chimpanzees, thought to have mutated into HIV-1 human immunodeficiency syndrome, may itself be a hybrid of monkey viruses (http://news.nationalgeographic.com).

3. Emergence is modeled in "artificial life," or a-life, experiments with genetic algorithms, agent-based flocking rules, bottom-up robotics, and cellular autonomata (Cariani 1992; Helmreich 1998; Resnick 1994; Whitelaw 2004), metal alloys, biochemical reactions; and is thought out in philosophies of relations between the physical, chemical, and biological (Žižek 2004). Philosophically, both Whitelaw and Žižek draw on the discussions of causality initiated by G. H. Lewes and J. S. Mill, proceeding through Hegel and Kant, to Nagel (for Whitelaw) and via Weismann, Freud, Lacan, Deleuze, and bodies without organs (for Žižek). Ansell-Pearson (1997) attempts to trace out a Nietzschean lineage. Both Whitelaw and Žižek comment on the idea that emergence has to do with accumulation of causes which can be understood only retrospectively as a form of feedback loop, or causes whose relations surpass those of actuality (and thus can be understood as a form of virtuality). I would add to this the Wittgensteinian notion of the social consequences of decisions and actions in the evolution of technoscientific worlds (see M. Fischer 2003, 2005).

4. Vincent Crapanzano's analysis of Moroccan Muslim circumcision is remarkable for the way it traces anxiety structures and gender bifurcation across both life histories and histories of the colonial and independence periods. Derrida's (and Cixous's) account of circumcision also is marked by colonial histories, as is, in another register, Victor Turner's account of the schisms and continuities as well as rites of affliction of the Ndembu. Obeyesekere's account of the dreadlocked ecstatic priests is not just an account of the historical emergence of a new religious form in Sri Lanka but a reflection of a worldwide growth in the post–World War II period of religions of the oppressed (Lanternari 1963).

5. On the teleprompter and its genealogy of experiments on eye movements, from Helmholtz on, to probe the relation between physiology and mind, or between the gaze and desire as elaborated by Jacques Lacan, see von Hilgers (forthcoming). See also Haraway's play with techno-eyes in "Situated Knowledges" (Haraway 1991).

6. Bataille, with Andre Breton, founded the antifascist group Contre-Attaque in 1935. For a slightly different but complementary reading of Bataille's and Hans Bellmer's work on the Eros/Thanatos thematics of fascism, see Laura Frost (2002: ch. 3). Bataille's obsessions with the eye, grossness of life, bodily loss of control, and deathly transition is plausibly rooted in his experiences as the child

of a syphilitic (blind and paralytic) father and suicidal, eventually demented mother (Surya 1992). The pornography of the eye has not only to do with sex, but also the stigmata of the syphilitic: "The weirdest thing was certainly the way he looked while pissing . . . his pupils . . . pointed up into space, shifting under the lids . . . with a completely stupefying expression of abandon and aberration" (*The Story of the Eye*, 72; Surya 1992: ch. 1). The loss of inhibition around sex is a commonplace of dementia as well as a highly charged (anxious nervous system) transgression of the sacred constituted as a (nonstable) function of the social. Bataille's own body and corpus, thus, are also suggestive in relation to bodily marks: a Nietzschean, post-Catholic (converting to Catholicism, and later abandoning it), depressive, sufferer of at least two bouts of tuberculosis, and, toward the end of his life, of cerebral arteriosclerosis. Other key influences were his interest in dreaming, and the photographs of the execution of Fu Chou Li by being cut to pieces while alive, injected with opium to extend the torture. The pictures that he saw in 1925 were still occupying him when he published them in 1961 and have a hallucinatory quality with the eyes rolled back in an undecidable expression of either pain or demented ecstasy. Not only involved with (and against) the surrealists, he founded a number of journals (*Documents, La critique sociale, Acephale, Actualite, Critique*) and was an early publisher of Barthes, Foucault, Derrida, and others. With Michel Leiris and Roger Callois in 1939 he founded the Collège de Sociologie. Pablo Picasso, Max Ernst, and Joan Miró auctioned paintings to raise money for him when he was in financial straits toward the end of his life. His first wife, the actress Sylvia Makles Bataille, later married the psychoanalyst Jacques Lacan, who himself was a friend; their daughter Julie took her mother's name, Bataille.

7. Michael Grace, a biologist at the Florida Institute of Technology, is a leader in this work, reported by Lee Dye, ABCnews.com.

8. See Roosth (2006) on Jim Gimzewski's use of ATM to listen to the vibrations of yeast cells, and his hopes for this in cancer detection, since cancerous cells metabolize adenosine triphosphate (ATP) more quickly and would therefore vibrate at a higher frequency than healthy cells. Roosth describes this as a series of transductions:

> The yeast/atomic force microscope/human assemblage that performs sonocytology is a series of vibrations traveling through different material media and converted by mediating transducers into sound and signals. The kinetic motion of motor proteins becomes a cytoplasmic rumble that vibrates the cell wall, which exerts pressure on a cantilever, causing the piezoelectric crystal to convert the deflection into an electrical output, creating a graphic trace of its deflection, which is then converted using a computer program into an electrical signal that exits a pair of speakers as mechanical wave oscillation, creating a periodic turbulence in the air that vibrates the tympanum, that vibrates the ossicles, that vibrates the fluid of the cochlea, that triggers hair cells to send electrical signals to nerves that travel to the brain, in which each time the signal travels from one neuron to another it must be transduced from electrical to

chemical energy while traveling through the intercellular synapse. . . . Sound triangulates between space and time. . . . If traditional light microscopy with its staining and fixing techniques offers a vision of flat surfaces frozen in time, and microcinematography animates these cellular landscapes, then sonocytology promises a volumized science . . . creating an acoustic space (ibid.: 25–26).

9. On the work of MIT's Mrganka Sur, see Brakeslee (2000) and Sharma, Andalucci, and Sur (2000).

10. www.seeingwithsound.com; www.nytimes.com.

11. Cartwright and Goldfarb (2006: 141–43), and Geary (2002: ch. 2) describe current research on retinal implants which also rely on an external camera to send signals to electrode arrays that activate retinal cells to send signals to the optic nerve; with somewhat less image quality William Dobelle experimented with putting the electrode arrays in the visual cortex. A man with a Dobelle eye has had the implant since 1978. Both epiretinal and subretinal implants have been tried. Much still needs to be learned about nerve conduction, hopes for "wet chips" that match the body's conduction of chemical charges, and nanomanufacturing. Experiments in nanoknitting by Rutledge Ellis-Behnke and his colleagues at MIT have shown promise in restoring sight in rats by injecting nanofibers into damaged portions of the brain that act as scaffolds for axons to regrow (Goldberg 2006).

12. On the history of microcinematography, see Landecker (2002, 2007).

13. The classic film, based on H. G. Wells's story "The Island of Dr. Moreau" (1896), was made in 1927: *Island of Lost Souls,* with Charles Laughton as Dr. Moreau. The film focused on surgery and blood transfusion technology to create humans from lower animals; remakes under the original title, *The Island of Dr. Moreau,* in 1977 (with Burt Lancaster) and in 1996 (with Marlin Brando) shifted the technologies to genetics and neuroscience.

14. Although a number of biologists and computer scientists have publicly invoked this fantasy, it is attributed originally to Harvard's Walter Gilbert in his enthusiasm for the information lingua franca of genetics and genomics. See Kay (1993) on the way the "code of life" metaphor became inserted into the language of biology, its misrecognitions, and its functionality as a lingua franca across disciplines.

15. Born in 1920 in Dallas, Griffin was educated in France, doing a medical internship at the Asylum in Tours experimenting with music therapy for the criminally insane, studying at the Conservatoire de Fontainebleau (with Nadia Boulanger, Robert Casadesus, and Jean Batalla) as well as studying Gregorian chant with Benedictines at the Abbey of Solemnes. At nineteen he became a medic with the French Resistance, evacuating Austrian Jews to the port of St. Nazaire. He served thirty-nine months with the U.S. Army Air Corps in the South Pacific, where he was injured. From 1946 to 1957 he lost his sight but wrote five novels in that time. He converted to Catholicism in 1952 and became a Third Order Carmelite. www.tsha.utexas.edu.

16. Without chemically altering his skin, the Israeli David Grossman per-

formed a Griffin-like exploration of the lives of Palestinians in the Occupied Territory in *Yellow Wind* (1987). In an interview reflecting on his childhood, he comments on the Nazi tattoos: "In my neighborhood, you saw people with numbered tattoos. People used to cry out in their nightmares, and we heard them. But what was strange was that people did not talk about it. In those years, it was as if they didn't want to interfere with the momentum of building up the myth of a strong state. As children we got all the contradictory radiation of strength and fragility. This manic-depressive wave went through us all the time" (Grossman, interviewed by Mark Sorkin in *The Nation*, July 11, 2005: "Reflections on the Body Politic").

17. Temporary tattoos inscribed with the words "Justice for Jessica" were distributed in India in March 2006 by a Brazilian cosmetics company in support of a protest campaign against the acquittal of an alleged (and confessed) murderer of a barmaid and model, Jessica Lal. A less entangled mixing of cosmetics, commerce, and politics, Jenny Holzer's art action issued in *Lustmord-Zyklus* (1993), which contains thirty color photographs about rape and murder in the former Yugoslavia, with sudden shifts of perspective among perpetrators, victims' families, and victims. Texts are written on the skin with a felt-tip pen, photographed, enlarged, filling the visual space so as to be "menacingly close to the viewer" (Benthien 2002: 3).

18. I follow here the lovely reading of Dennis Patrick Slattery 2000: ch. 9.

19. From a letter of O'Conner cited in ibid., 199.

20. For the notion that in the late nineteenth century American Protestants had so deprived themselves of multisensory ritual that in their tourism to Europe they sought out cathedrals and Catholic ritual, see W. Lloyd Warner's *Family of God* (1961) and T. J. Jackson Lears's *No Place of Grace* (1981).

21. As Turner correctly notes, Maimonides explained this proscription as one against the temptation of idolatry, and other rabbis also explained that since man is created in the image of God that perfection should not be profaned or marred; both are explanations used by Muslims as well, and in the proscription by the Roman Catholic Church. On the paradoxes of circumcision rites, see below.

22. Many Muslims in North Africa and elsewhere have traditional tattoos, as people notice especially during the hajj. Temporary henna tattooing is part of wedding and some circumcision ceremonies, but even permanent tattoos are not *haram* if done in ignorance or before one has converted and need not be removed. It is a topic discussed on a number of Muslim web sites today (e.g. www.islamonline.net). Among Jews, the famed Moskowitz family of tattoo artists—beginning in 1918 with Willie, an immigrant from Russia, to his grandson Marvin (retired 2000)—kept the business going, despite a health department ban in Manhattan in the 1960s, by moving to Long Island, and watched the tattoo move from a sign of rebellion to an insignia against the Holocaust ("never again" and star of David tattoos) to gentrification.

23. Liminal periods in the ritual process, as Victor Turner elaborated, fuse together, con-fuse, emotion (fear, anxiety), bodily pain, and bodily substances

(blood, milk) with the cognitive (ideology, rationale, explanation), moral (social affiliation, status) and symbolic. The most powerful symbols, Turner argued, had this bipolar structure, viscerally grounding social understandings and expectations, so that the socially obligatory is transformed into something internalized and viscerally sacralized such that transgressions cause unnerving physical reaction. The transgressive thereby becomes itself ritually powerful, as in trance curing rituals in which Muslims, for instance, in the Zar cults of East Africa and the Persian Gulf, are made to drink prohibited blood and in which separation, drumming, and hyperventilation also make the body pliable, and diets and prohibitions continue the cultic discipline.

24. For a somewhat similar, and brilliantly elaborated Jewish reading of circumcision, see Derrida's "Circonfession" and Cixous's *Portrait of Jacques Derrida as a Young Jewish Saint*, which draw upon an array of Jewish, Catholic, North African, French, male and female thematics of "too young to sign, he could only bleed" (Cixous 2001: viii), the stigmata of 1940 (and other "dates of Passovers, transfers, expulsions, naturalizations, de-citizenships, exinclusions, blacklistings, doors slammed in your face, . . . the archives of what he calls 'my nostalgeria' and that I call my 'algeriance'" [ibid.: 5]), scarification/mortification ("what happens to the skin and flesh of the text, incision, graft of a fragment lifted from another segment of time"), the hidden name of substitution/superstition of new identity "dissociated from this initial hallmarking" (Elie, qu'on elit, the Elie's of the dead, the name of election), male names with female endings (Jackie, Elie), North African inflections (Ali Baba, Baba Elie), a prince whose parentage is provisionally concealed to keep him alive (dead elder brother Paul Moses), Oedipus of El-Biar, and more.

25. "With milk dripping from her breasts, her back in bloom, her womb about to give birth, and her feet wrapped in nature's substance, Sethe is reminiscent of the great goddess of fertility, of the earth goddess, of life itself insisting on finding an aperture into the world" (Slattery, 2000: 215).

26. I draw here upon and tweak Paula Willoquet-Maricondi's reading (1999) of the film. Cixous invokes the Greenaway film on the first page of her essay "The Laugh of the Medusa" (1975), and Bersin (2001) traces out the parallels and differences between Cixous's and Greenaway's search for the father as a source of writing. Cixous's feminine writing need not be done by a woman. Joyce's writing is feminine for Cixous. But Bersin argues that while Greenaway's version of Cixous's search for enabling feminine writing is instructive, it is not fully worked out in these terms.

27. See Giuliana Bruno's comments on the "assemblage of three screen ratios—one widescreen and color; one of smaller dimensions in black and white; and the last a tiny videographic window screen" (Bruno 2002: 286).

28. For more examples of prosthetic and sensory rewiring experiments, organized by the five senses, see Geary (2002), and on the early exploration of the body electric (i.e., the stimulation of muscles by electrical impulses), see Becker and Selden (1985).

29. A metaphor transferred from pharmacokinetics by Lawrence Cohen for

how state policies impact bodies, for instance, in regulations for markets in transplantation and requirements for sterilization before donating of organs is allowed, and the pattern of surgeries that tends to form (1999, 2004).

30. On November 27, 2005, Isabelle Dinoire, thirty-eight, underwent the world's first partial facial transplant in Amiens, France, with tissues, muscle, arteries, and veins from a brain-dead donor in Lilles. She had lost her nose, lips, and chin from a dog bite. http://news.bbc.co.uk.

31. The term "material-semiotic objects" is taken from Haraway (1997). These are objects that not only reconfigure the material world (sensors, transducers, newly created objects) but also simultaneously configure semantic relationships.

32. Sanal recounts how in one dramatic incident heavily covered by the media a young woman who had shot her husband and then herself was redeemed by having her organs distributed to save the lives of six people. In a subsequent case, amidst anxieties about young women committing suicide, a young woman left a suicide note that forbade the transplantation of her organs as a transgressive rejection of the patriarchal and Islamic constraints on women.

33. On these and similar technologies, see Geary 2002: ch. 6.

34. Biocybernetics was launched with Defense Department funding in the 1970s, and now is funded also by the National Institute of Neurological Disorders and Stroke. Some devices are implanted in the brain. In 2003, Miguel Nicolelis, a neurobiologist at Duke, put eighty-six microwires into a monkey brain, taught him to use a joystick, then unplugged the joystick, and the monkey learned to do the same tasks merely with his brain waves, dropping the joystick and not using his hands. Cyberkinetics Neurotechnology Systems, Inc. has a "BrainGate™" in a four-person clinical trial and hopes to have the device on the market in two to three years. The chip was adapted by John P. Donoghue, chairman of Brown University's neuroscience department, and Dick Normann from a microarray chip Normann designed in Utah (where the chips are still manufactured) to send signals into the brain as part of a visual prosthetic; Donoghue realized it could also be an uplink. They tested it first on a cat and then on twenty-two monkeys before asking FDA for permission to run a human clinical trial. Nicholas Hatsopoulos, formerly at Brown and Caltech and now at the University of Chicago and a founder and director of Cyberkinetics, explains that although the one hundred electrodes massively undersample the 1.6 million neurons under the chip, prediction of motion seems to work because to some degree the cells are redundant, and for that reason need to be studied collectively rather than cell by cell. Donoghue is convinced that implants will be required to get the signal clarity to transform noisy signals into something that a patient can use. But others are experimenting with noninvasive methods. The cap being tested by Wolpaw, and the engineers from the Altran Foundation for Innovation and its subsidiary, Cambridge Consultants, in Boston, has sixty-four electrodes, electro-gel, and an amplifier that does not require implantation into the brain. It is being tested with a medical scientist

with ALS "who is losing control of his eyes, the last part of his body he can move," to "replace an older system that let him use a computer through eye movement." He is able to use it to send e-mail messages. (The small market for the device, well under 170,000, is a constraint.) (Heuser 2006: A16; Martin 2005; *University of Chicago Magazine*, June 2006: 20–21.)

35. The revolt against Catholic corporeal theology and iconography included posing iconically as the Virgin Mary with one breast exposed, the use of crosses and skulls, bloodied facial imprints on gauze cloths (like the shroud of Turin), and reliquaries of her fat. The first of the surgical series was called *The Reincarnation of Saint Orlan.*

36. Blood was also part of the facial imprints on gauze and partakes of Orlan's intertwined symbolism (blood/wine and grapes) of both Christianity and Dionysus/Bacchus.

37. Adams takes Hans Holbein's "The Ambassadors" as a classic anamorphosis, where, depending upon the angle, you see a blur or a skull (produced by drawing the image projected from a cylinder mirror). She then suggests that isomorphically to subject any oppositional pair (male/female, mind/body, subject/object, essence/appearance) to an anamorphic process "is to reveal the extent to which each term of the pair is *not* in contradiction to the other term," but "the relations between them . . . are strewn with strange thresholds and hybrid forms" (1996: 142), a point made long ago by Lévi-Strauss in arguing that the generativity of category and mythic oppositions lies in the thirds that they produce as mediators, each mediation in turn producing more. In Lacanian terms, this is also generated in the gap between signifier and signified, one that here Adams suggests is also invested with a foundational anxiety.

38. The word "circus"—carnival might be better—reminds of Ray Bradbury's *The Illustrated Man* and the role of tattoos in carnivals.

39. Invoking the metaphor of a door which opens but cannot be entered as well as the unhinging of a door, a body part, or a mind.

40. On the dissociations experienced in anatomy dissection classes, see B. Good (1994: ch. 3) and Avery quoted in Fischer (2003); for a denial of this, see Arnold (2004).

41. On the film *Journey to Qandahar* (or *Kandahar*) by Mohsen Makhmalbaf and its powerful image of prostheses being dropped by Red Cross helicopters to Afghan men running on crutches to receive them, see M. Fischer 2004. On the silencing of survivors of the massacres and rapes on Bali in 1965 and their continuing effects, see Dwyer and Santikarma (2003: 298–99). Walter Benjamin observed that soldiers returning from World War I were impoverished rather than empowered in storytelling abilities, and indeed the trauma of war has silenced generations of soldiers. There is a transposition of the public inscriptions of regimes of "truth" on the body of torture victims in the premodern period described generally by Rusch and Kirchheimer (1939), for France by Foucault (1975), and for Iran by Fischer (1989) and Rejali (1994) to a hidden disciplinary and rehabilitation system in the modern period, with

today a reversion to public torture and rape, but on a population basis, as in Bali in 1965, the Balkans and Rwanda in the 1990s, and today in Darfur and elsewhere. Fanon (1961) pointed out the psychological damage inflicted upon the torturers as well as the tortured; today we have the effects of Agent Orange and PTSD on Vietnam veterans and Gulf War Syndrome (chemical and possible radiation effects) on veterans from the first Gulf War.

42. Made by the Israeli company Given Imaging, this capsule endoscopy was available in nearly three hundred hospitals by 2002 (Chase 2002).

43. See Parvin Adam's (1996) analysis above for a more astute feminist take, one grounded in the splits of the speech act or enunciative effects, indeed, one that rejects a simple masculine–feminine split, asserting instead in Orlan's case a woman–woman inscription of sexual difference.

44. Clynes and Kline coined the word "cyborg" in 1960 in an article titled "Cyborgs & Space," published in the journal *Astronautics*. Stelarc proposed to work on cyborgs at NASA.

45. Habermas's disappointing (philosophically, scientifically, politically) essay *The Future of Human Nature* (2002) must be seen in this older light, as indeed its German subtitle makes clear: "auf dem Weg zu einer liberalem Eugenik" (On the Way to Liberal Eugenics). For more informed accounts of the philosophical, scientific, and political debates on biological technologies, see Jasanoff (2005) on Germany and K. Taussig (2009) on Holland.

46. The compilation of criminal tattoos from the Soviet period by Batlaev, Plutser-Sarno, and Vesiliev (2003) suffers precisely from an insufficiently described account of which tattoos are voluntary, which forcibly imposed and under what conditions, and how particular meanings of a more general code are negotiated.

47. See Martin (2004) on the making visible and counting of chromosomes ("colored bodies") by staining, and after the 1950s by other means of generating micrographs.

48. See Geary 2002: chs. 3 and 7 for a review of sociable and affective robotics technologies.

49. *Gattaca* (1997), written and directed by Andrew Niccol, describes a world in which DNA identification can be done from any scrap of the body (a strand of hair, shed skin cells) and in which probabilistic predispositions to illness read from the genome disqualify one for jobs that require educational and other investment. In this world parents thus strive for preimplantation of genetically perfect mixes of sperm and eggs (making "love children" both antiquated and disadvantaged), which sets up a surveilled caste society. One understands the intricacies of the implications through the story of a love child with tremendous will power and intelligence who tries to game the system by using a genetically superior sibling who lacks the same drive to provide him with biological covers. The film's title is a pun on the Attica prison in the state of New York and the prisoners' revolt there in 1971, as well as sequences of genetic code using the acronyms for guanine (G), adenine (A), thymine (T), and cytosine (C).

50. "Will you still need me,/will you still feed me,/When I'm sixty-four" (Beatles, "When I'm Sixty-Four").

51. Catacoustis, the inner echo "of a musical order," the return, in very precise circumstances, of a melodic fragment, like "the psychopathology of everyday life," of a "tune in one's head" that "keeps coming back," like the Kol Nidre, the haunting melody of the Jewish prayer on Yom Kippur, the day of atonement ("The Echo of the Subject," in Lacoue-Labarthe 1989). Lacoue-Labarthe's reference to the Kol Nidre is perhaps not so surprising given his work on Derrida, Paul Celan, and criticism of Heidegger.

52. One thinks of the diaries of pioneers in the American West who, unable to articulate directly what they saw, drew upon more familiar tropes of castles and paradise. Or more to the point of the body is the art of the physician-artist Eric Avery, who sees in an autopsied skull the face of Edvard Munch's "The Scream," in a patient being lifted by nurses "Lazarus arising from the Dead," in the fingers of the surgeon reattaching a hand Michaelangelo's image of God's hand touching man, and the stigmata of St. Sebastian in the Rio Sumpul massacre of 1981 in El Salvador (see Fischer 2003).

53. Emmanel Levinas's formulation of ethics as the response to the face of the other has become a useful shorthand in contemporary discussions of ethics as well as a counter to the metaphysics of being in philosophy.

54. Jacques Derrida's *Given Time (Donner le temps)* (1991b) is both a contribution to the growing literature begun by Marcel Mauss's *The Gift (Essai sur le don)* (1925) and a meditation on the time given before death (volume 2 was titled *Given Death* [*Donner le mort*, translated by its American publisher as *The Gift of Death*] 1995).

55. Dumit, *Drugs for Life* (forthcoming).

56. "I had only to look at a picture or an anatomical specimen, and its image would remain both vivid and stable . . . for hours. I could mentally project the image onto the paper before me—it was as clear and distinct as if projected by a camera lucida—and trace its outlines with a pencil. My drawings were not elegant, but they were, everyone agreed, very detailed and accurate. . . . I had only to think of a face, a place, a picture, a paragraph in a book to see it vividly in my mind" (Sacks 2005: 39).

Chapter 6. Ask Not What Man Is But What We May Expect of Him

1. Ong and Collier 2005, Tsing 2005

2. Akademie Kant 7:120, cf. 25:9, 854−55, 1209−10, quoted in Wood 2003: 41.

3. Contemporary Muslims frequently cite the *hadith* (saying of the Prophet) "Seek knowledge even if it is in China," but the first verse of the Qur'an is even stronger when interpreted through the critical apparatus of its hermeneutics: "Taught Man that he knew not" (see Fischer and Abedi: 1990: 97−122). The critical apparatuses of the Jewish hermeneutic tradition developed along with those of the Islamic ones, e.g., the frequently cited midrash of B. Metzia 59a,

59b, in which all judgment is left by God to Man. Jews, of course, took part in the European Enlightenment, and the struggle for the modern soul of Islam is not so unlike that of Christians and Jews at the time of Kant. Kant was suspected of Spinozism and atheism, though to a modern eye his language remains tinged with Christian claims and formulas.

4. Dieter Henrich notes, however, that from a German point of view, "although Königsberg was a center of learning for the Baltic states and for Russia which owned them, it was exceedingly difficult to reach. Fichte once walked there to visit with Kant, but Kant had only occasional visits from other young colleagues and followers. Twice he refused invitations to universities in the center of Germany. It is thus tantalizing to imagine how post-Kantian philosophy might have developed had Kant been able to exert his personal influence on it" (2003: 123). Indeed, since Kant rejected the efforts of Jacobi, Reinhold, Fichte, and Hegel as forms of unacceptable mysticism, his presence as a more direct interlocutor in Jena (where Reinhold, Fichte, Schelling, and Hegel succeeded one another) might have had interesting effects—or perhaps not, given that philosophers seem to have a drive to systematize and efface the instabilities and "needle points" that Kant insisted upon.

5. The "species level" formulation, awkward as it is today, was picked up by Spencer, Kroeber (who called it by Spencer's term, the super-organic), and even Lloyd Warner (viz. *The Family of God*).

6. See especially Paul Guyer's tracing of (i) how the aesthetic and moral spheres are articulated by Kant so that they provide the grounds for the expansion of freedom; and (ii) how the growth of these formulations can be tracked over the years of the teaching of the Anthropology (Guyer 2003). Similarly, see Howard Caygill's account (2003) of how the Anthropology (especially section 8–11, "Apology for Sensibility") was a crucible for working out how the different rules of sensibility and those of the understanding can in conjunction lead to valid judgments, an argument central to the *Critique of Pure Reason*. Susan Shell traces how Kant begins with Rousseau but then, after reading Pietro Verri, recognizes pain as the goad to human development and the need for a stoic development of equanimity, in which happiness and totality are not the ends or goals not of life but are themselves only notions of reason that cannot be completed or experienced (except through moments of the sublime); and how these developments can be tracked in the Anthropology. See also Foucault (1961) on the similarities regarding moral sentiments in the Anthropology and Kant's "Observations on Beauty and the Sublime" (1764), and more generally on the ways in which the Anthropology is like "half-seeing" the Critique through a negative.

7. Perhaps for biographical reasons, I rather like the increasingly archaic term "diaeresis." Karl Popper was fond of insisting that philosophy (or critical thought) should never begin with definitions, but only produce them as they become necessary to differentiate meanings in the course of an argument, demonstration, or construction of a theory. For this he always invoked the term "diaeresis," introduced into seventeenth-century English from the Greek

verb "to divide" (he would have known Greek from his school days). In or-thography it means a diacritical mark to shift a normal pronunciation of a letter (as with the umlaut in German), to pronounce each letter separately when vowels are written next to each other (as in "naïve"), to pronounce a letter that otherwise would be silent (as in the "Brontë sisters")

8. The preface to the second edition speaks of "a grotesque mediocrity to play [*Spiel*] a hero's part," and of how this allusion-filled (*Anspielen*) represen-tation of social forces and strategic actions, failures, and missteps differs from those of Victor Hugo (great man in history narrative) and Proudhon (objec-tive, historically determinist narrative). Like Walter Benjamin's later analysis of baroque tragic dramas (with their stock buffoon and evil minister charac-ters), Clifford Geertz's more sedate analyses of involuted theater states in Bali, and the newspapers' and Jon Stewart's *Daily Show* accounts of the Bush ad-ministration, Marx casts Napoleon ("the old crafty roué") as the *Hanswurst*, a stock character in the *Haupt-und-Staatsaction* (capital city and state action) genre, as orchestrating "performances of state as comedy in the most vulgar sense, as a masquerade, where the grand costumes, words and postures merely serve to mask the pettiest knavery" and with thousands of "rascally fellows [*Lumpenkerl*]" playing "the part of the people, as ['the mechanical'] Nick Bottom that of the lion" [in Shakespeare's *Midsummer Night's Dream*]. Marx hopes that eventually the old mole will do his work ("Well grubbed, old mole"), an allusion via Hegel to Schlegel's translation of Shakespeare's *Hamlet*. For Hegel, the valiant mole is the subterranean reworking of self-control and cultivation of rational consciousness that will allow the Spirit to achieve abso-lute knowledge. For Marx, it is the subversion by the workers who will build new political consciousness, organization, and strategies in the future, align-ing representations with evolving social realities in a self-fashioned, increas-ingly democratic praxis. *Hamlet*, of course, is concerned with usurpation, legitimacy, and ghostly agency in history. "*Hic et ubique?*" ([you are] here and everywhere?) queries Hamlet to the ghost under the stage (backstage, behind the scenes), "then we will shift our ground"; but at the ghost's third cry de-manding Hamlet swear, Hamlet responds, "Well said, old mole! Canst work i' th' earth so fast?" Marx plays on the pun "*Brav gewühlt*," well burrowed, well subverted, old mole (*Maulwurf*).

9. Cited by Llewelyn (2000: 23) from Merleau-Ponty's *Phenomenology of Perception*. Schneider has difficulty responding to the request to point with his finger and is no good at pretending, play acting, experimenting, or dealing with the subjunctive (what is contrary to fact).

10. My mother's Tante Bertha married into a merchant family in Königs-berg and received a double dowry (double sets of dinnerware, cutlery, linens, etc.) because it was felt to be so far away they might never see her again. By the time of the next generation, it was not so far away, and my mother's younger brother spent some time with that family learning enough about business to know he didn't want to do it.

11. "So one must know of the human being, whether he can also do what is

required of him" (notes from his ethics course of 1774–75, 27:244, quoted in Stark 2003: 24) rings biblical in its cadence; What is man that Thou are cognizant of him, what is required of him? At the same time he was of the generation forging a secular cosmopolitan discourse. And for most of the theologically derived terms, we now can easily substitute other terms, including "teleology," whose last serious discussions in the 1950s have now been replaced by systems and information theory language (open systems, *gaia*).

The remark about the "Palestinians living among us," i.e., the Jews, a "nation of merchants," is primarily a historical and social characterization of a mercantile ethos, less anti-Semitic than an antimercantile complaint, ostensibly viewing merchants as living by the buyer beware credo and thus being cheaters and unproductive members of society. It seems to be an isolated comment, reflecting perhaps the kinds of chronic social conflicts that Marx would also explore. Kant acknowledges that the constitution of this nation of merchants cannot be abolished "since we have certain sacred writings in common with them" (*Anthropology from a Pragmatic Point of View*, E. T. Mary, J. Green, 77, E. T. Louden 2006: 100). It's an odd comment also given that he acknowledged Salomon Maimon as his most astute critic and that he was engaged in debate with Moses Mendelssohn.

12. The rhythm and cycle are similar to those invoked in Hayden White's account of nineteenth-century histories moving through an effort at holistic compositions, trying unsuccessfully to harmonize emplotment, argument, and ideological implication, and by the end of the cycle of romantic, tragic, comic, and ironic beginning anew to break the irony (White 1973).

13. See Delbourgo 2006. At the end of the eighteenth century, many physiologists experimented with the idea that all animal life was electrical and electricity could heal diseased bodies. Edward Bancroft experimented with electric eels from Guiana, where he lived in 1763–67. Newton's *Opticks* (published in 1704) speculated about light, fire, and electricity as modifications of the ether that mediates between divine and material worlds. In America, T. Gale, one of many itinerant electrotherapists, wrote about a republic of individuals emancipating themselves by electrotherapy, activating their bodies and making their souls ecstatic. Humanist societies in England had similar programs. John Wesley, the English founder of Methodism, practiced similar electrical autotherapy. Still, De Quincey found Kant's speculations to be a sign of his weakening intellectual acuity. For the way in which scientific developments after Kant interacted with various kinds of neo-Kantian philosophies (*Naturphilosophie*, Gestalt theories, the "return to Kant" of the Marburg neo-Kantians such as Ernst Cassirer and Herman Cohen, Alois Riehl's Kantian realism, Helmholtz, logical positivists), see the essays by Frederick Beiser, Robert DiSalle, Michael Friedman, Michael Heidelberger, Tim Lenoir, Helmut Pulte, Robert Richards, and Alan Richardson in Friedman and Nordmann (2006). Lenoir's essay is particularly good in attempting to correlate experimental instrumentation and developments in both psychology and philosophy.

14. "Nevertheless, the elderly Kant, working on his final manuscript that he

never managed to complete, the so-called *Opus postumum,* defined philosophy as the theory of, first, the principle of the intellectual world; second the sensible world; and third, what conceives both in a real relationship—namely, the subject as a rational being in this world. He repeated this programmatic formula in the manuscript many, many times. . . . and one of those sentences is the one I just quoted: 'The self is the connecting link between the two worlds' " (Henrich 2003: 52).

15. Hegel's example (in section 408 of the *Encyclopedia*) is of a person who imagines he is dead. One should not tell him he is mad but humor him. Such a person was taken to a coffin, where a third person was already in his coffin. After a while the third person sits up and asks for something to eat, and the first person is induced to do the same and is cured (Llewelyn 2000: 106). A similar example occurs in Mani Haghighi's film *Men at Work* (2006). A buddy gone berserk in the freezing cold is coaxed into the car for some hot coffee, after which, his buddies promise, they will not interfere in his berserk task. He too is cured.

16. The shrill laugh of Silenus, the wise companion of Dionysus, as he responds to King Midas's question, "What is the best and most desirable of all things to man?" "Not to be born, not to be, to be nothing. But the second best for you is to die soon" (Sophocles, *Oedipus at Colonus,* line 1224). See M. Fischer (2004: 196) on this trope as it reverberates in ancient Greek, medieval Persian, and nineteenth-century European discussions on the "middle world" of art, and Nietzsche's response (and that of Sadegh Hedayat) that art can momentarily overcome the terror of the world. The philosophical play is with "appearance" (existence, illusion as transfiguring into perfection, deceitful illusion as mere appearance; viz. German *Schein* and *Erscheinung,* Sanskrit *maya*). Nietzsche cites Schopenhauer's criterion of the philosophical ability, "the occasional ability to view men and things as mere phantoms or dream images" (*Birth of Tragedy* 1872, sec 1), to explore the ambiguous and interprenetrating relations between the incompletely intelligible everyday world, the perfections of ideas and imaginings, and the deceits and corruptions of illusions, appearances.

17. "Afary and Anderson . . . link Foucault's intellectual intoxication with the Muharram rituals he witnessed to his fascination with what he called 'limit experiences' that pushed the boundaries of life by flirting with death. . . . [They] read Foucault's articles on Iran in tandem with his *History of Sexuality* —which they point out, he was writing during the period of his travels to Iran. He imagined in Iranian sexuality—particularly in the Muharram passion plays—precisely the kind of homoerotic openness that he venerated in the classical Mediterranean world" (Postel 2006: 67–68).

Conclusions and Way Ahead

Hymn sung in Deepa Mehta's film *Water* quoted in Devyani Saltzman's account of the shooting of her mother's film (2006: 248). The film, about the plight of Hindu widows, is set in Benares but had to be shot in Sri Lanka because the state of Uttar Pradesh could not protect the filmmakers, even though they had national government permission to film. The welcoming state government of Bengal could not provide sufficient protection either during the period of ascendant Hinduvata fervor. The Bharatiya Janata Party (BJP) lost the national elections just as the film shooting was being completed in Colombo, although the government of Gujarat remained in BJP hands.

1. See Aijaz Ahmad's (1994) criticism of Jameson (1991).

2. See my "Iran and the Boomeranging Cartoon Wars: Can Public Spheres at Risk Ally with Public Spheres Yet to be Achieved?" (*Cultural Politics*, 2009), and "Purity, Danger and Violence: Torn Religions in the Contemporary World," Berkeley Center, Georgetown University, lecture, December 3, 2007. On Holland, see the films *Antonia's Line* (1996), analyzed by K. Taussig (2009), and *The Black Book* (2007).

3. George Marcus (2007: 1129) supplies this Portuguese observation, so apt to his own "collaborative ethnography" with a Portuguese aristocrat (Marcus and Mascarenhas 2005). "Baroque," for my work, has long been a favored term of cultural critique, following Walter Benjamin's *Origin of German Tragic Drama* on the Lutheran and Spanish baroque allegorical dramas which served as a partial intertext for my analysis of Persian passion plays. This "intertext" worked for me both as a parallel in dramatic genre, in similar political and affective circumstances, and also as an analogue for drawing "ethnocentrically cosmopolitan" European and American scholars and pundits into the rich worlds of Iranian discourses and modalities of cultural critique. Thus what is assumed to be exotically different turns out to be historically, civilizationally, and theologically deeply entangled. As Marcus would now say, these are "emerging communicative spaces in tension that require expertises to be ethnographic themselves" (2007: 1142). A baroque footnote that should not be dismissed as returning to the archive rather than to the scene of fieldwork, since both facets are important to the ability of the ethnographic to explore the resonances and highly charged natures of emergent communicative spaces, unless, of course, one believes that the postmodern has no historical depth or resonances (a highly unlikely speculation).

Epilogue: Postings from Anthropologies to Come

1. In its turn, an allusion to the controversial *Reading Lolita in Tehran* by Azar Nafisi, controversial both for its depiction of the unrelieved hostility to the lives of women under the Islamic Republic of Iran, and for the way it was passed out by agencies of the U.S. government as a coffee-table book, at least in Indonesia if not elsewhere in the Islamic world. A former student in the reading group described in the book notes that, upon Nafisi's return to Iran from the Beijing (UN) Women's conference—where she networked with other feminist activists such as the Moroccan anthropologist Fatima Mernisi —Nafisi was energized about such a reading group. That is, aside from what-

ever jealousies of others in *dowreh*s or discussions groups (a widespread social form in Iran, both among the modern and the traditional literate classes), or self-promotion or not on Nafisi part, what is quite interesting is the transnational network of women's workshops and reading groups, especially in the Mediterranean region, run also by such figures as the sociologist Nilüfer Göle.

2. The de Broca comedy, which famously played for thirteen years in the Central Square Theater in Cambridge, Massachussets, became an antiwar mascot film of the generation that tried to adopt the slogan "Make love, not war." Set at the end of World War I, as a British unit prepares to reenter a French town where German and British soldiers had killed each other off, a scout is sent ahead to evaluate conditions and deactivate any German bombs. The town is abandoned by all expect an odd collection of whimsical people who dub him their savior, the King of Hearts. Realizing they are inmates of the local insane asylum, the soldier attempts to lead them out of town to safety. Brightly costumed, they gaily visit the places they knew before being locked up, but at the edge of town they refuse to leave, asking if it is any safer or crazier out there in the war. Celebrating the innocence and wisdom of the insane, the film was read as asking who the mad really are.

3. Yazd has become both less cosmopolitan, in that there are fewer Jews and Bahais, and even the last Anglicans (who ran the lovely Point Four Hotel) have gone; and more cosmopolitan, in that with the floods of refugees from the Iraq war and from Afghanistan, the town has exploded in population and kinds of people, no longer quite as self-enclosed. It has always exported population (to the Gulf, to India, to Tehran), and many have become prominent in these expanded worlds, including former president Khatami of Iran and former president Katsav of Israel.

4. Israelis and Palestinians both had some prior experience with joint patrols, although not with each other. Set up as a confidence building device and to put security cooperation on public display, they were an effort to turn a theater of war into a theater of peace, though at times, she writes, it was more like a theater of the absurd, a game of pretend friendships. At issue in the daily tasks was a constant negotiation of different conceptions of masculinity, nuances of nonverbal behavior, emotion management, choreography of movement and touch, mirroring of posture and gesture, and acquiring the moves of the other's masculinity. Performing these moves builds functioning work units; getting them wrong sets off conflict and violence. The exercise was in turn ritual, game, and dramaturgy. It was a ritual process of transformation: of physically embodying the as-if equality that was to be modeled and built up over time. It was a male game of provocations and score keeping, attempting to shift relations of control but always attempting to keep the loser of any particular interaction in the continuing tournament. It was a serious game of "face." Both personal and national honor were the stakes, with respect, reproduction of honor, and the need to avoid unanswerable humiliation of the other as the moves and countermoves. The game was one of mobilizing and leveraging the contradictory struggles of equality and inequality to realign

power among not just dyads of men, but men in groups, the groups themselves set within larger structural contexts.

5. On the ICC as well as the tribunals for the former Yugoslavia and Rwanda,
see Moreno-Ocampo 2007.

6. On time, see Lyotard 1983: 6–7.

7. Based on my interviews with Onno Purbo, Kusmayanto Kadiman, Ar-
mein Langi, Budi Rahadjo, and others, in September 2006.

8. Based on my interviews with Reza Mansuri, Hessamaddin Arfaei, Cumrun Vafa, Yusuf Sobuti, and others in 2006 and 2007.

9. Based on my interviews with Arash and Kamran Alaee in 2006 and 2007
as well as on reports by Broumand (1997), Ghods (2004), Zargooshi (2001).

10. Kiki Papageorgiou at the Department of Anthropology, University of
California, Irvine, is writing her dissertation on Sekem, and I am indebted to
her work, presented at the American Anthropological Association Meetings,
2006. Sekem's activities can by accessed by googling their web site.

Abelson, Hal, Ken Ledeen, and Harry Lewis. 2008. *Blown to Bits: Your Life, Liberty and Happiness after the Digital Explosion.* Boston: Addison-Wesley.

Aberle, David.F., A. K. Cohen, A. K. Davis, M. J. Levy Jr., F. X. Sutton. 1950. "The Functional Prerequisites of a Society." *Ethics* 60: 100–111.

Aboulafia, M. Y. 1996. *Making Markets: Opportunism and Restraint on Wall Street.* Cambridge: Harvard University Press.

Abraham, Itty. 1998. *The Making of the Indian Atomic Bomb: Science, Secrecy and the Postcolonial State.* London: Zed.

Abrahams, Roger D. 1964 [2006]. *Deep Down in the Jungle: Black American Folkore from the Streets of Philadelphia.* New Brunswick: Transaction Books.

Abu-Lughod, Lila. 1991. "Writing Against Culture." In R. Fox, ed., *Recapturing Anthropology.* Santa Fe: School of American Research.

Adams, Parveen. 1996. "Operation Orlan." In *The Emptiness of the Flesh: Psychoanalysis and Sexual Difference.* London: Routledge.

Adorno, Theodor. 1964 [1973]. *The Jargon of Authenticity.* Translated by Knut Tarnowski and Frederic Will. London: Routledge and Kegan Paul.

——. 1950. *The Authoritarian Personality.* New York: Harper.

——. 2006. *Current of Music: Elements of a Radio Theory.* Frankfurt am Main: Suhrkamp.

Adorno, Theodor, and Max Horkheimer. 1944 [1972]. *The Dialectic of Enlightenment.* Translated by John Cumming. New York: Herder and Herder.

Agamben, Giorgio. 1995 [1998]. *Homo Sacer: Sovereign Power and Bare Life.* Stanford: Stanford University Press.

——. 1997 [1999]. *Remnants of Auschwitz: Archives and Witnesses.* New York: Zone Books.

——. 2003 [2005]. *States of Exception.* Chicago: University of Chicago Press.

Agee, James, and Walker Evans. 1941. *Let Us Now Praise Famous Men.* Boston: Houghton Mifflin.

Ahmad, Aijaz. 1994. *In Theory: Classes, Nations, Literatures.* New York: Verso.

Allen, Barbara L. 2003. *Uneasy Alchemy: Citizens and Experts in Louisiana's Chemical Corridor Disputes.* Cambridge: MIT Press.

Allen, William. 1964. *The African Husbandman.* London: Oliver and Boyd.

Allen, William. 2001. *Green Phoenix: Restoring the Tropical Forests of Guanacaste, Costa Rica.* New York: Oxford University Press.

Amir, Sulfikar. 2005. "Power, Culture and the Airplane: Technological Nationalism in New Order Indonesia (1966–1998)." Ph.D. diss., Rensselaer Polytechnic Institute.

Anderson, Benedict. 1983. *Imagined Communities: Reflections on the Origin and Spread of Nationalism.* London: Verso.

Ansell-Pearson, Keith. 1997. *Viroid Life: Perspectives on Nietzsche and the Transhuman Condition.* New York: Routledge.

Appadurai, Arjun. 2006. *Fear of Small Numbers.* Durham: Duke University Press.

Arendt, Hannah. 1958. *The Human Condition.* Chicago: University of Chicago Press.

———. 1982. *Lectures on Kant's Political Philosophy.* Chicago: University of Chicago Press.

Arnold, Eugene A. 2004. "Autopsy: The Final Diagnosis." In Elizabeth Klaver, ed., *Images of the Corpse: From the Renaissance to Cyberspace.* Madison: University of Wisconsin Press.

Arnold, Matthew. 1867–68 [1883]. *Culture and Anarchy.* New York: Macmillan.

Ayers, Robert. 1999. "Serene and Happy and Distant: An Interview with Orlan." *Body and Society* 5(2–3): 171–84.

Baker, Steve. 2000. *The Postmodern Animal.* London: Reaktion Books.

Barcott, Bruce. 2008. *The Last Flight of the Scarlet Macaw.* New York: Random House.

Barker, Francis. 1995. *The Tremulous Private Body: Essays on Subjection.* Ann Arbor: University of Michigan Press.

Barker, Joshua. 2005. "Engineers and Political Dreams: Indonesia in the Satellite Age." *Current Anthropology* 46(1): 703–27.

Barry, John M. 1997. *The Rising Tide: The Great Mississippi Flood of 1927 and How It Changed America.* New York: Simon and Schuster.

Bataille, Georges [pseud. Lord Auch]. 1928 [1987]. *Story of the Eye.* San Francisco : City Lights Books.

———. 2006. "Critique of Heidegger." *October* 117:25–34.

Bateson, Gregory. 1972. *Steps to an Ecology of Mind.* New York: Random House.

Batlaev, Danzig, Alexei Plutser-Sarno, and Sergei Vesiliev. 2003. *Russian Criminal Tattoo Encyclopedia.* Saint Petersburg: Steidl Fuel.

Bayly, C. A. 1996. *Empire and Information: Intelligence Gathering and Social Communication in India, 1780–1870.* New York: Cambridge University Press.

Beck, Ulrich. 1986 [1992]. *Risk Society: Towards a New Modernity.* London: Sage Publications.

———. 1997 [2000]. *What Is Globalization?* London: Blackwell.

——. 2002a [2005]. *Power in the Global Age: A New Global Economy*. Malden, Mass.: Polity Press.

——. 2002b. "The Cosmopolitan Society and Its Enemies." *Theory, Culture and Society* 19(1–2): 17–44.

——. 2002c "The Terrorist Threat: World Risk Society Revisited." *Theory, Culture and Society* 19(4): 39–55.

——. 2004a [2006]. *The Cosmopolitan Vision*. Malden, Mass.: Polity Press.

——. 2004b. *Kosmopolitische Europa : Gesellschaft und Politik in der zweiten Moderne*. Frankfurt am Main: Suhrkamp.

Becker, Robert O., and Gary Selden. 1985. *The Body Electric: Electromagnetism and the Foundation of Life*. New York: Morrow.

Beddoes, Diane. 1997. "Deleuze, Kant and Indifference." In Keith Ansell-Pearson, ed., *Deleuze and Philosophy: The Difference Engineer*. New York: Routledge.

Beidelman, Thomas O. 1959. *A Comparative Analysis of the Jajmani System*. New York: Association for Asian Studies.

Bellah, Robert. 1985. *Tokugawa Religion: The Cultural Roots of Modern Japan*. New York: Free Press.

Ben-Ari, Eyal. 1989. "Masks and Soldiering: The Israeli Army and the Palestinian Uprising." *Cultural Anthropology* 4(4): 372–89.

Bendix, Rheinhold, and Seymour Lipset. 1951. "Social Status and Social Structure: A Re-Examination of Data and Interpretations." Pts. 1 and 2. *The British Journal of Sociology* 2(2): 150–68; 2(3): 230–54.

Benedict, Ruth. 1934. *Patterns of Culture*. Boston: Houghton Mifflin.

——. 1946. *The Chrysanthemum and the Sword: Patterns of Japanese Culture*. Boston: Houghton Mifflin.

Benjamin, Walter. 1928 [1979]. *One-Way Street*. Translated by Edmund Jephcott and Kingsley Shorter. London: New Left Books.

——. 1931 [1999]. "The Lisbon Earthquake." In M. W. Jennings, H. Eiland, and Gary Smith, eds., *Selected Writings*, Volume 2, *1927–1934*. Cambridge: Harvard University Press.

——. 1936 [1968]. "The Work of Art in the Age of Mechanical Reproduction." In Harry Zohn, trans., *Illuminations*. New York: Harcourt, Brace and World.

Benthien, Claudia. 2002. *Skin*. New York: Columbia University Press.

Berger, Peter L., and Thomas Luckmann. 1966. *The Social Construction of Reality: A Treatise in the Sociology of Knowledge*. New York: Doubleday.

Berman, Marshall. 1982. *All That Is Solid Melts into Air: The Experience of Modernity*. New York: Simon and Schuster.

Bernal, John Desmond. 1939. *The Social Function of Science*. London: G. Routledge.

Bernauer, James. 2004. "Michel Foucault's Philosophy of Religion: An Introduction to the Non-Fascist Life." In J. Bernauer and Jeremy Carrette, eds., *Michel Foucault and Theology*. Burlington, Vt.: Ashgate Press.

Bernstein, Richard J. 2002. "Arendt's Response to Heidegger." In John McCormick, ed., *Confronting Mass Democarcy and Industrial Technology.* Durham: Duke University Press.

Bersin, Alissa. 2001. "My Father's Pen: Writing, the Body, and Female Pleasure in Helene Cixous's *Inside* and Peter Greenaway's *The Pillow Book of Nogiko.*" B.A. thesis, Harvard University.

Bertell, Rosalie. 2001. *Planet Earth: The Latest Weapon of War.* London: The Women's Press.

Bettelheim, Bruno. 1983. *Freud and Man's Soul.* New York: Knopf.

Beunza, Daniel, and Raghu Garud. 2005. "Securities Analysts as Frame-Makers." Manuscript.

Beunza, Daniel, and David Stark. 2003. "The Organization of Responsiveness: Innovation and Recovery in the Trading Rooms of Lower Manhattan." *Socio-Economic Review* 1(2): 135–64.

———. 2004. "Tools of the Trade: The Socio-Technology of Arbitrage in a Wall Street Trading Room." *Industrial and Corporate Change.* 13(2): 369–400.

Biagioli, Mario. 1993. *Galileo Courtier: The Practice of Science in the Culture of Absolutism.* Chicago: University of Chicago Press.

Bianci, Robert. 2006. "Islamic Finance and the International System." Paper presented at the Seventh Harvard Islamic Finance Project Conference, April 23.

Biehl, João. 2005. *Vita: Life in a Zone of Social Abandonment.* Berkeley: University of California Press.

———. 2007. *The Will To Live: AIDS Therapies and the Politics of Survival.* Princeton: Princeton University Press.

Biehl, João, Arthur Kleinman, and Byron Good, eds. 2008. *Subjectivities.* Berkeley: University of California Press.

Bijker, Wiebe. 2002. "The Oosterschelde Storm Surge Barrier: A Test Case for Dutch Water Technology, Management, and Politics." *Technology and Culture* 43:569–84.

Birkner, Gabrielle. 2003. "Tracing a Tattoo Dynasty Back to Its Bowery Days." *Forward*, Sept. 19. www.forward.com.

Bohannan, John, and Martin Enserink. 2005. "Scientists Weigh Options for Rebuilding New Orleans." *Science* 309:1808–9.

Boje, David M. 1998. "Wiley Coyote Meets Roadrunner: Nike's Postmodern Encounters with Entrepreneurial Activists." http://business.nmsu.edu/mg.

Bolz, Norbert, and Willem van Reijen. 1996. *Walter Benjamin.* Translated by Laimdota Mazzarins. Atlantic Highlands, NJ: Humanities Press.

Bourne, Joel K. 2004. "Gone with the Water: The Louisiana Bayou, Hardest Working Marsh in America." *National Geographic* (October).

Bowker, Geoffrey. 2005. *Memory Practices in the Sciences.* Cambridge: MIT Press.

Bowker, Geoffrey, and Susan Leigh Star. 1999. *Sorting Things Out: Classification and Its Consequences.* Cambridge: MIT Press.

Brakeslee, Sandra. 2000. "'Rewired' Ferrets Overturn Theories of Brain Growth." *New York Times*, April 25, 2000.

Brandt, Reinhart. 2003. "The Guiding Idea of Kant's Anthropology and the Vocation of the Human Being." In B. Jacobs and P. Kain, eds., *Essays on Kant's Anthropology.* New York: Cambridge University Press.

Breazeal, Cynthia. 2004. *Designing Sociable Robots.* Cambridge: MIT Press.

Brentano, Franz. 1874 [1973]. *Psychology from an Empirical Standpoint.* Translated by Antos C. Rancurello, D. B. Terrell, and Linda L. McAlister. New York: Humanities Press.

Broad, William. 2005. "High Tech Flood Control, With Nature's Help." *New York Times,* Sept. 6, D1, 4.

Brooks, Peter. 1984. *Reading for the Plot.* New York: Knopf.

Broumand, B. 1997. "Living Donors: The Iran Experience." *Nephrology, Dialysis, Transplantation* 12:1830–31.

Brown, Phil, and Edwin J. Mikkelson. 1990. *No Safe Place: Toxic Waste, Leukemia, and Community Action.* Berkeley: University of California Press.

Bruno, Giuliana. 2002. "M Is for Mapping: Art, Apparel, Architecture Is for Peter Greenaway." In *Atlas of Emotion: Journeys in Art, Architecture, and Film.* New York: Verso.

Buck-Morss, Susan. 1991. *The Dialectics of Seeing: Walter Benjamin and the Arcades Project.* Cambridge: MIT Press.

——. 1992. "Aesthetics and Anaesthetics: Walter Benjamin's Artwork Essay Reconsidered." *October* 62:3–41.

Buell, Lawrence. 2005. *The Future of Environmental Criticism: Environmental Crisis and Literary Imagination.* Cambridge: Harvard University Press.

Bürger, Peter. 1984. *The Theory of the Avant-Garde.* Minneapolis: University of Minnesota Press.

——. 2002. *The Thinking of the Master: Bataille between Hegel and Surrealism.* Evanston, Ill.: Northwestern University Press.

Burke, Kenneth. 1941. *The Philosophy of Literary Form: Studies in Symbolic Action.* Baton Rouge: Louisiana State University Press.

——. 1945. *A Grammar of Motives.* Englewood Cliffs, NJ: Prentice-Hall.

——. 1950. *A Rhetoric of Motives.* Englewood Cliffs, NJ: Prentice-Hall.

——. 1968. *Language as Symbolic Action.* Berkeley: University of California Press.

Butler, Judith. 2004. *Precarious Life: The Powers of Mourning and Melancholia.* New York: Verso.

Caldeira, Teresa. 2000. *City of Walls: Crime, Segregation and Citizenship.* Berkeley: University of California Press.

Callison, Candis. 2002. "A Digital Assemblage: Diagramming the Social Realities of the Stikine Watershed." M.A. thesis, MIT.

——. 2007. "Spinning Climate Change: How Social Groups Use Media, Science and PR to Engage the American Public." Research proposal, MIT.

Callon, Michel, ed. 1998. *The Laws of the Markets.* Malden: Blackwell.

Callon, Michel, Yuval Millo, and Fabian Muniesa, ed. 2007. *Market Devices.* Malden: Blackwell.

Cambrosio, Alberto, and Peter Keating. 1995. *Exquisite Specificity: The Monoclonal Antibody Revolution.* New York: Oxford University Press.

Cariani, P. 1992. "Emergence and Artificial Life." In C. G. Langton, C. Taylor, J. D. Farmer, and S. Rasmussen, eds., *Artificial Life II*. Redwood, Calif.: Addison-Wesley.

Carson, Rachel. 1962. *Silent Spring*. New York: Houghton Mifflin.

Carton, Evan. 2004. "The Holocaust, French Poststructuralism, the American Literary Academy, and Jewish Identity Poetics." In Peter Herman, ed., *Historicizing Theory*. Albany: State University of New York Press.

Cartwright, Lisa, and Brian Goldfarb. 2006. "On the Subject of Neural and Sensory Prostheses." In Marquard Smith and Joanne Morra, eds., *The Prosthetic Impulse*. Cambridge: MIT Press.

Cassirer, Ernst. 1923–29 [1953]. *The Philosophy of Symbolic Forms*. New Haven: Yale University Press.

——. 1944. *An Essay on Man: An Introduction to the Philosophy of Human Culture*. New Haven: Yale University Press.

——. 1946. *The Myth of the State*. New Haven: Yale University Press.

Castells, Manuel. 1996. *The Rise of the Network Society*. Cambridge: Blackwell.

——. 1998. *End of Millennium*. Cambridge: Blackwell.

Castoriadis, Cornelius. 1999 [2007]. *Figures of the Thinkable*. Translated by Helen Arnold. Stanford: Stanford University Press.

Caygill, Howard. 2003. "Kant's Apology for Sensibility." In B. Jacobs and P. Kain, eds., *Essays on Kant's Anthropology*. New York: Cambridge University Press.

Cefkin, Melissa, ed. 2009. *Ethnography and the Corporate Encounter: Reflections on Research in and of Corporations*. New York: Berghahn.

Chakrabarty, Dipesh. 2002. *Habitations of Modernity: Essays in the Wake of Subaltern Studies*. Chicago: University of Chicago Press.

Chan, Anita. 2008. "The Promiscuity of Freedom: Development and Governance in the Age of Neoliberal Networks." Ph.D. diss., MIT.

Chang, Iris. 1995. *Thread of the Silkworm*. New York: Basic Books.

Chase, Marilyn. 2002. "To Avoid Surgery, Eat This Camera." *Wall Street Journal*, August 15.

Chase, Michael S. C., and James C. Mulverson. 2004. "You Got Dissent! Chinese Dissident Use of the Internet and Beijing's Counterstrategies." Santa Monica: Rand Corporation.

Chatterji, Roma, and Deepak Mehta. 2007. *Living with Violence: An Anthropology of Events and Everyday Life*. New Delhi: Routledge.

Chayanov, Alexander. 1966. *On the Theory of Peasant Economy*. Edited by Daniel Thorner, Basile Kerblay, and R. E. F. Smith. Homewood, Ill.: R. D. Irwin.

Chomsky, Noam. 1957. *Syntactic Structures*. The Hague: Mouton.

Chouhan, T. R. 1994. *Bhopal, The Inside Story: Carbide Workers Speak Out on the World's Worst Industrial Disaster*. New York: Apex Press.

Chovitz, Bernard, and Irene Fischer. 1956. "A New Determination of the Figure of the Earth from Arcs." *Transactions, American Geophysical Union* 37(5).

Cixous, Hélène. 1975 [1976]. "The Laugh of the Medusa." Translated by Keith Cohen and Paula Cohen. *Signs* 1(4): 875–93.

——. 2001 [2004]. *Portrait of Jacques Derrida as a Young Jewish Saint.* New York: Columbia University Press.

Clancey, Gregory. 2006. *Earthquake Nation: The Cultural Politics of Japanese Seismicity, 1868–1930.* Berkeley: University of California Press.

Clark, David. 1997. "On Being 'The Last Kantian in Nazi Germany': Dwelling with Animals after Levinas." In Jennifer Ham and Matthew Senior, eds., *Animal Acts: Configuring the Human in Western History.* New York: Routledge.

Clark, Wesley. 2001. *Waging Modern War: Bosnia, Kosovo, and the Future of Combat.* New York: Perseus.

Clarke, Julie. 1999. "The Sacrificial Body of Orlan." *Body and Society* 5(2–3): 185–207.

——. 2005. "A Sensorial Act of Replication." In Marquard Smith, ed., *Stelarc, the Monograph.* Cambridge: MIT Press.

Classen, Constance. 2005. "McLuhan in the Rainforest: The Sensory Worlds of Oral Cultures." In David Howes, ed., *The Empire of the Senses.* New York: Berg.

Clifford, James. 1981 [1988] "On Ethnographic Surrealism." In *The Predicament of Culture: Twentieth-Century Ethnography, Literature, and Art.* Cambridge: Harvard University Press.

Clifford, James, and George Marcus, eds. 1986. *Writing Culture: The Poetics and Politics of Writing Ethnography.* Berkeley: University of California Press.

Coates, Peter. 1998. *Nature: Western Attitudes since Ancient Times.* Berkeley: University of California Press.

Coetzee, J. M. 1999. *The Lives of Animals.* Princeton: Princeton University Press.

Cohen, Alex, Arthur Kleinman, and Benedetto Saraceno, eds. 2002. *World Mental Casebook: Social and Mental Health Programs in Low Income Countries.* New York: Kluwer Academic/Plenum.

Cohen, David William. 1994. *The Combing of History.* Chicago: University of Chicago Press.

Cohen, Lawrence. 1999. "Where It Hurts: Indian Material for an Ethics of Organ Transplantation." *Daedalus* 128(4): 135–66.

——. 2001. "The Other Kidney: Biopolitics beyond Recognition." *Body and Society* 7(2–3): 9–29.

——. 2004. "Bioavailability, Commitment and the Order of Debt: Sacrifice and the History of Organ Transplantation." Paper presented at the Lively Capital Workshop, Irvine, California.

Coleman, Gabriella. 2005. "The Social Construction of Freedom in Free and Open Source Software: Hackers, Ethics, and the Liberal Tradition." Ph.D. diss., University of Chicago.

Collins, Harry. 1974. "The TEA Set: Tacit Knowledge and Scientific Networks." *Science Studies* 4:165–86. Reprinted in *Science in Context,* ed. Barry Barnes and David Edge. Cambridge: MIT Press.

Comaroff, Jean, and John Comaroff. 1991. *Of Revelation and Revolution.* Chicago: University of Chicago Press.

Connelly, Matthew. 2002. *A Diplomatic Revolution: Algeria's Fight for Independence and the Origin of the Post–Cold War Era.* New York: Oxford University Press.

Corbin, Henri. 1960 [1990]. *Spiritual Body, Celestial Earth: From Mazdean Iran to Shi'ite Iran.* Translated by Nancy Pearson. London: I. B. Tauris.

Crane, Kathleen. 2003. *Sea Legs: Tales of a Woman Oceanographer.* Boulder: Westview Press.

Crapanzano, Vincent. 1980. "Rite of Return: Circumcision in Morocco." In Warner Meunsterberger and L. Bryce Boyer, eds., *Psychoanalytic Study of Society* 9. New York: Library of Psychological Anthropology.

———. 2004. "Body, Pain and Trauma." In *Imaginative Horizons.* Chicago: University of Chicago Press.

Crary, Jonathan. 1990. *Techniques of the Observer: On Vision and Modernity in the Nineteenth Century.* Cambridge: MIT Press.

Crawford, Colin. 1996. *Uproar at Dancing Rabbit Creek: Battle Over Race, Class and the Environment.* Reading, Mass.: Addison-Wesley.

Creager, Angela. 2002. *The Life of a Virus: Tobacco Mosaic Virus as an Experimental Model, 1930–1965.* Chicago: University of Chicago Press.

CRIT (Collective Research Initiatives Trust, Mumbai). 2006. Mumbai Free Map: Community Geographic Information System. www.crit.org.in.

Daniel, Valentine. 1997. *Charred Lullabies: Chapters in an Anthropology of Violence.* Princeton: Princeton University Press.

Daniel, Valentine, and John Knudsen, eds. 1996. *Mistrusting Refugees.* Berkeley: University of California Press.

Das, Veena. 1990. *Mirrors of Violence: Communities, Riots and Survivors.* New Delhi: Oxford University Press.

———. 1995. *Critical Events: An Anthropological Perspective on Contemporary India.* New Delhi: Oxford University Press.

———. 2007. *Life and Words: Violence and the Descent into the Ordinary.* Berkeley: University of California Press.

Das, Veena, Arthur Kleinman, Margaret Lock, Mamphela Ramphele, and Pamela Reynolds, eds. 2001. *Remaking a World: Violence, Social Suffering and Recovery.* Berkeley: University of California Press.

Daston, Lorraine and Gregg Mitman. 2005. *Thinking with Animals: New Perspectives on Anthropomorphism.* New York: Columbia University Press.

Davis, Mike. 1998. *Ecology of Fear: Los Angeles and the Imagination of Disaster.* New York: Metropolitan/Henry Holt.

———. 2006. *The Monster at Our Door: The Global Threat of Avian Flu.* New York: Henry Holt.

Deetz, Charles Henry, and Oscar Sherman Adams. 1945. *Elements of Map Projections with Applications to Map and Chart Construction.* 5 ed., rev. 1944. Washington: U.S. Government Printing Office.

Delbourgo, James. 2006. *A Most Amazing Scene of Wonders: Electricity and Enlightenment in Early America.* Cambridge: Harvard University Press.

Deleuze, Gilles. 1963 [1983]. *Kant's Critical Philosophy: The Doctrine of the Faculties.* Translated by Hugh Tomlinson and Barbara Habberjam. Minneapolis: University of Minnesota Press.

——. 1968 [1994]. *Difference and Repetition.* Translated by Paul Patton. New York: Columbia University Press.

——. 1975 [1986]. *Kafka: Towards a Minor Literature.* Translated by Dana Polan. Minneapolis: University of Minnesota Press.

——. 1983 [1986]. *Cinema I. The Movement Image.* Minneapolis: University of Minnesota Press.

——. 1985 [1989]. *Cinema II. The Time Image.* Minneapolis: University of Minnesota Press.

——. 1986 [1987]. *Foucault.* Translated by J. G. Merquior. Berkeley: University of California Press.

——. 1990 [1992]. "Postscript on the Societies of Control." *October* 59:3–7.

Deleuze, Gilles, and Félix Guattari. 1980 [1987]. *A Thousand Plateaus.* Minneapolis: University of Minnesota Press.

DeNicola, Lane A. 2007. "Techniques of the Environmental Observer: India Earth Remote Sensing Program in the Age of Global Information." Ph.D. diss., Rensselaer Polytechnic Institute.

De Quincey, Thomas. 1890. "The Last Days of Immanuel Kant." *Collected Works.* Edinburgh: Adam and Charles Black.

Derrida, Jacques. 1967a [1974]. *Of Grammatology.* Baltimore: Johns Hopkins University Press.

——. 1967b [1978]. "Structure, Sign and Play in the Discourse of the Human Sciences." In *Writing and Difference.* Chicago: University of Chicago Press.

——. 1991a [1992]. "Circonfession." In *Jacques Derrida.* Collaboration with Geoffrey Bennington. Chicago: University of Chicago Press.

——. 1991b [1992]. *Given Time.* Chicago: University of Chicago Press.

——. 1991c [1992]. *The Other Heading: Reflections on Today's Europe.* Translated by Pascale-Anne Brault and Michael B. Nass. Bloomington: Indiana University Press.

——. 1992a [2002]. "The Aforementioned So-Called Human Genome." In *Negotiations: Interventions and Interviews, 1971–2001.* Edited by Elizabeth G. Rottenberg. Stanford: Stanford University Press.

——. 1992b [1993]. *Raising the Tone of Philosophy: Late Essays by Immanuel Kant, Transformative Critique by Jacques Derrida.* Edited by Peter Fenves. Baltimore: Johns Hopkins University Press.

——. 1993 [2002]. "Nietzsche and the Machine." In *Negotiations: Interventions and Interviews, 1971–2001.* Edited by Elizabeth G. Rottenberg. Stanford: Stanford University Press.

——. 1995. *The Gift of Death.* Chicago: University of Chicago Press.

——. 1996a [1998]. "Faith and Knowledge: The Two Sources of 'Religion' at the Limits of Reason Alone." In Jacques Derrida and Gianni Vattimo, eds., *Religion.* Stanford: Stanford University Press.

———. 1997. *The Animal That Therefore I Am*. New York: Fordham University Press.

———. 1996b [1998]. *Resistances to Psychoanalysis*. Stanford: Stanford University Press.

———. 2001. "Above All, No Journalists!" In Hent de Vries and Samuel Weber, eds., *Religion and Media*. Stanford: Stanford University Press.

———. 2002. "The Animal That Therefore I Am (More to Follow)." *Critical Inquiry* 28(2): 369–418.

———. 2003. "And Say the Animal Responded?" In Cary Wolfe, ed., *Zoontologies: The Question of the Animal*. Minneapolis: University of Minnesota Press.

Desjarlais, Robert. 1992. *Body and Emotion: The Aesthetics of Illness and Healing in the Nepal Himalayas*. Philadelphia: University of Pennsylvania Press.

Dewald, Carolyn, and John Marincola, eds. *The Cambridge Companion to Herodotus*. New York: Cambridge University Press.

Dewey, John. 1927. *The Public and Its Problems*. New York: Henry Holt.

Dolgin, Janet, David S. Kemnitzer, and David M. Schneider, eds. 1977. *Symbolic Anthropology: A Reader in the Study of Symbols and Meanings*. New York: Columbia University Press.

Douglas, Mary. 1966. *Purity and Danger*. London: Routledge and Kegan Paul.

Douglas, Mary, and Aaron Wildavsky. 1982. *Risk and Culture: An Essay on the Section of Technical and Environmental Dangers*. Berkeley: University of California Press.

Downey, Gary Lee, and Joseph Dumit, eds. 1997. *Cyborgs and Citadels: Anthropological Interventions in Emerging Sciences and Technologies*. Santa Fe: School of American Research.

Doyle, Richard. 1997. *On Beyond Living: Rhetorical Transformations of the Life Sciences*. Stanford: Stanford University Press.

———. 2003. *Wetwares: Experiments in Postvital Living*. Minnesota: University of Minnesota Press.

Dracup, Joseph. 2000. "A Brief History of Geodetic Surveys in the United States, 1807–2000." Manuscript.

Du Bois, Cora. 1944. *The People of Alor: A Social Psychological Study of an East Indian Island, with analyses by Abraham Kardiner and Emil Oberholzer*. Minneapolis: University of Minneapolis Press.

Duffield, Mark. 2001. *Global Governance and the New Wars: The Merging of Development and Security*. London: Zed.

———. 2007. *Development, Security and Unending War: Governing the World of Peoples*. Cambridge, U.K.: Polity Press.

Dumit, Joe. 2004. *Picturing Personhood: Brain Scans and Biomedical Identity*. Princeton: Princeton University Press.

———. Forthcoming. *Drugs for Life*. Durham: Duke University Press.

Dumont, René. 1957. *Types of Rural Economy: Studies in World Agriculture*. London: Methuen.

Durkheim, Emile. 1893 [1933]. *The Division of Labor.* Translated by George Simpson. New York: Free Press.

——. 1912. *The Elementary Forms of the Religious Life.* Translated by J. W. Swain. New York: Free Press.

Dwyer, Leslie, and Degung Santikarma. 2003. "'When the World Turned to Chaos': 1965 and Its Aftermath in Bali, Indonesia." In Robert Gellately and Ben Kiernan, eds., *The Specter of Genocide: Mass Murder in Historical Perspective.* Cambridge: Cambridge University Press.

Eaton, Horace Ainsworth. 1936. *Thomas De Quincey: A Biography.* New York, Oxford University Press.

Edelman, Marc. 1999. *Peasants Against Globalization: Rural Social Movements in Costa Rica.* Stanford: Stanford University Press.

Edney, Matthew H. 1997. *Mapping an Empire: The Geographical Construction of British India, 1765–1843.* Chicago: University of Chicago Press.

Edwards, Paul N. 1996. *The Closed World: Computers and the Politics of Discourse in Cold War America.* Cambridge: MIT Press.

Elias, Norbert. 1939 [1968]. *The Civilizing Process.* London: Blackwell.

Ellen, Roy, et al., eds. 1988. *Malinowski in Two Worlds: The Polish Roots of an Anthropological Tradition.* New York: Cambridge University Press.

Eller, Jonathan, and William F. Touponce. 2004. *Ray Bradbury: The Life of Fiction.* Kent: Kent State University Press.

Emanuel, Kerry. 2005. "Living on Earth," Sept. 2. www.loe.org.

Engel, Karen. 2001 "From Skepticism to Embrace: Human Rights and the American Anthropological Association from 1947–1999." *Human Rights Quarterly*, 23(3): 536–59.

Engels, Friedrich. 1887. *The Condition of the Working Class in England in 1844 with an Appendix Written in 1886 and a Preface Written in 1887.* Translated by Frances Kelly Wischnewtzky. New York: Lovell.

Epstein, Steven. 1996. *Impure Science: AIDS, Activism, and the Politics of Knowledge.* Berkeley: University of California Press.

Esarey, Ashley. 2006. *Speak No Evil: Mass Media Control in Contemporary China.* New York: Freedom House.

Espagnat, Bernard d'. 2002 [2006]. *On Physics and Philosophy.* Princeton: Princeton University Press.

Espagne, E., et al. 2004. "Genome Sequence of a Polydnavirus: Insights into Symbiotic Virus Evolution." *Science* 306:286–89.

Evans-Pritchard, E. E. 1937. *Witchcraft, Oracles and Magic among the Azande.* Oxford: Clarendon Press.

——. 1940. *The Nuer.* Oxford: Clarendon Press.

Fabian, Johannes. 1996. *Remembering the Present: Painting and Popular History in Zaire.* Berkeley: University of California Press.

——. 1998. "The History of Zaire as Told and Painted by Tshibumba Kanda Matulu in Conversation with Johannes Fabian." *Archives of Popular Swahili* 2(1) (Nov. 6).

Fa Hsien. c. 339–414. "A Record of Buddhistic Kingdoms, Being an Account by the Chinese Monk Fa-Hien of His Travels in India and Ceylon (AD 399–414) in Search of the Buddhist Books of Discipline." Translated and annotated by James Legge. etext.library.adelaide.edu.

Fanon, Frantz. 1961 [1963]. *The Wretched of the Earth.* New York: Grove Press.

——. 1967. *Black Skin, White Masks.* New York: Grove Press.

Farmer, Paul. 1990. *AIDS and Accusation: Haiti and the Geography of Blame.* Berkeley: University of California Press.

——. 1999. *Infections and Inequalities: The Modern Plagues.* Berkeley: University of California Press.

——. 2003. *Pathologies of Power: Health, Human Rights, and the New War on the Poor.* Berkeley: University of California Press.

Farnell, Ross. 1999. "In Dialogue with 'Posthuman' Bodies: Interview with Stelarc." *Body and Society* 5(2–3): 129–47.

Fassin, Didier. 2002. "Politics of Suffering and Policies of Order: The Moral Economy of Immigration in France." Paper presented at the American Anthropological Association meetings, New Orleans, November.

——. 2003. "L'espace moral de l'action humanitaire: a propos de quelques epreuves recentes." Paper presented at the International Conference on Intervention, University of Montreal, October 24.

——. 2006. *When Bodies Remember: Experience and Politics of AIDS in South Africa.* Berkeley: University of California Press.

Featherstone, Mike, ed. 1999. *Body Modification.* London: Sage.

Feld, Steven. 1982. *Sound and Sentiment.* Philadelphia: University of Pennsylvania Press.

——. 2005. "Places Sensed, Senses Placed." In David Howes, ed., *Empire of the Senses.* New York: Berg.

Fenves, David Peter. 1991. *A Peculiar Fate: Metaphysics and World History in Kant.* Ithaca: Cornell University Press.

Ferry, Luc. 1992 [1995]. *The New Ecological Order.* Chicago: University of Chicago Press.

Festinger, Leon, Henry Riecken, and Stanley Schachter. 1956. *When Prophecy Fails.* Minneapolis: University of Minnesota Press.

Fischer, Eric. 1943. *The Passing of the European Age.* 2d ed. Cambridge: Harvard University Press, 1948.

Fischer, Irene. 1954. "The Deflection of the Vertical in the Western and Central Mediterranean Area." *Bull. Geod.,* no. 34.

——. 1959a. "A Tentative World Datum from Geoidal Heights Based on the Hough Ellipsoid and the Columbus Geoid." *J. Geophys. Res.* 64(1).

——. 1959b. "The Impact of the Ice Age on the Present Form of the Geoid." *J. Geophys. Res.* 64(1).

——. 1960. "An Astrogeodetic World Datum from Geoidal Heights Based on the Flattening f = 1/298.3." *J. Geophys. Res.* 65(7).

——. 1962. "The Parallax of the Moon in Terms of a World Geodetic System." *Astron. J.* 67(6).

——. 1963. "The Distance to the Moon." *Bull. Philosophical Soc. of Washington* 16(2).

——. 1965a. "How Far Is it from Here to There?" *Mathematics Teacher* 58(2).

——. 1965b. "A Study of the Geoid in South America." Translated into Spanish for publication by the Panamerican Institute of Geography and History (PAIGH) as "Un Estudio del Geoide en Sud America." *Revista Cartográfica*, no. 14.

——. 1967. "The Shape and Size of the Earth." *Mathematics Teacher* 60(5).

——. 1971. *Basic Geodesy, An Initiation into the Mysteries of Geodetic Concepts* (with colored slides, viewgraphs, and narrator tape). Washington, D.C.: U.S. Army Topographic Command.

——. 1972. *Basic Geodesy, Student Pamphlet.* Fort Belvoir, Va.: U.S. Army Engineer School.

——. 1972/73. "The Role of Africa in the History of Geodetic Concepts." *Festschrift for the 70th Birthday Celebration of Acad. Prof. Dr. V. K. Hristov*, Bulgarian Academy of Sciences, Sofia.

——. 1975a. "Does Mean Sea Level Slope Up or Down Towards North?" *Bulletin Géodésique*, no. 115.

——. 1975b. "Another Look at Eratosthenes' and Posidonius' Determination of the Earth's Circumference." *Quarterly Journal of the Royal Astronomical Society* 16(2).

——. 1975c. "A Mnemonic Verse for π." *Canadian Surveyor* 29(3).

——. 1976. "On the Mystery of Mean Sea Level Slopes." *International Hydrographic Review* 53(2).

——. 1977. "Marine Geodesy: A New Discipline or the Modern Realization of an Ancient Endeavor?" *Marine Geodesy* 1(2): 165–75.

——. 1979. "The Effect of the Mid-Atlantic Ridge in Terms of Gravity Anomalies, Geoidal Undulations and Deflections of the Vertical." *Marine Geodesy* 2(3).

——. 1982. "Geodesy." *McGraw-Hill Encyclopedia of Science and Technology.* Volume 6. 5th ed. New York: McGraw-Hill.

——. 1998. "The Size of the Earth." In Gregory A. Good, ed., *Sciences of the Earth: Encyclopedia of Events, People and Phenomena.* New York: Garland.

——. 2004–5. "Geodesy? What's That?" *American Congress of Surveying and Mapping (ACSM) Bulletin*, nos. 207–18.

——. 2005. *Geodesy? What's That? My Personal Involvement in the Age-Old Quest for the Size and Shape of the Earth, With a Running Commentary on Life in a Government Research Office.* Lincoln: iUniverse.

Fischer, Irene, and Dunstan Hayden, S.J. 1965. *Geometry.* Boston: Allyn and Bacon.

Fischer, Michael M. J. 1980a. *Iran: From Religious Dispute to Revolution.* Cambridge: Harvard University Press.

——. 1980b. "The Khuzistan Irrigation Development." In *The Social Impact of Development on Ethnic Minorities: Iran, Afghanistan, the Sudan, Brazil,* with D. Maybury-Lewis, T. J. Barfield, J. Clay, R. Huntington, B. Pajackowski. Cambridge: Cultural Survival.

——. 1982. "Islam and the Revolt of the Petite Bourgeoisie" *Daedalus* 111(1): 101–25.

——. 1986. "Ethnicity and the Postmodern Arts of Memory." In J. Clifford and G. Marcus, eds., *Writing Culture: The Poetics and Politics of Ethnography.* Berkeley: University of California Press.

——. 1989. "Legal Postulates in Flux: Justice, Wit and Hierarchy in Iran." In D. Dwyer, ed., *Law and Politics in the Middle East.* New York: J. F. Bergin.

——. 2001."Filmic Judgment and Cultural Critique: The Work of Art, Ethics, and Religion in Iranian Cinema." In Hent de Vries and Samuel Weber, eds., *Religion and Media.* Stanford: Stanford University Press.

——. 2003. *Emergent Forms of Life and the Anthropological Voice.* Durham: Duke University Press.

——. 2004. *Mute Dreams, Blind Owls and Dispersed Knowledges: Persian Poesis in the Transnational Circuitry.* Durham: Duke University Press.

——. 2005. "Technoscientific Intrastructures and Emergent Forms of Life: A Commentary." *American Anthropologist* 107(1): 55–61.

——. 2006a. "Changing Palestine–Israel Ecologies: Narratives of Water, Land, Conflict and Political Economy, Then, Now and Life to Come." *Cultural Politics* 2(2): 159–91.

——. 2006b. "Four Haplotype Genealogical Tests for an Anthropology of Science and Technology for the Twenty-First Century." Paper presented to the Society for Cultural Anthropology, Milwaukee.

——. 2007a. "To Live With What Would Otherwise Be Unendurable: Returns to Subjectivities." In João Biehl, Byron Good, and Arthur Kleinman, eds., *Subjectivities: Ethnographic Investigations.* Berkeley: University of California Press.

——. 2007b. "To Live With What Would Otherwise Be Unendurable II: Caught in the Borderlands of Palestine-Israel." In Mary-Jo DelVecchio Good et al., eds., *Postcolonial Disorders.* Berkeley: University of California Press.

——. 2009. "Iran and the Boomeranging Cartoon Wars: Can Public Spheres at Risk Ally with Public Spheres Yet to be Achieved?" *Cultural Politics* 5(1): 27–63.

Fischer, Michael M. J., and Mehdi Abedi. 1990. *Debating Muslims: Cultural Dialogues in Postmodernity and Tradition.* Madison: University of Wisconsin Press.

Fischer, Michael M. J., and Leszek Koczanowicz. 1995. "Working Through the Other: The Jewish, Spanish, Turkish, Iranian, Ukrainian, Lithuanian, and German Unconscious of Polish Culture; or, One Hand Clapping: Dialogue, Silences, and the Mourning of Polish Romanticism." In G. Marcus, ed., *Perilous States.* Vol 1 of *Late Editions.* Chicago: University of Chicago Press.

Fischer, Michael M. J., and Philip Misselwitz. 2006. "Dialogue with Meron Benveniste and Salim Tamari." In Philip Misselwitz and Tim Reiniets, eds., *City of Collision: Jerusalem and the Principles of Conflict Urbanism.* Basel: Birkhauser.

Fleck, Ludwik. 1929. "Zur Krise der 'Wirklichkeit.'" *Die Naturwisseschaften* 17:425–30.

——. 1935 [1979]. *Genesis and Development of a Scientific Fact.* Translated by Fred Bradley and Thaddeus J. Trenn. Chicago: University of Chicago Press.

Flory, Stewart. 1987. *The Archaic Smile of Herodotus.* Detroit: Wayne State University Press.

Forsdyke, Sara. 2006. "Herodotus, Political History, and Political Thought." In C. Dewald and J. Marincola, eds., *The Cambridge Companion to Herodotus.* New York: Cambridge University Press.

Fortes, Meyer, and E. E. Evans-Pritchard. 1958. *African Political Systems.* Oxford: Oxford University Press.

Fortun, Kim. 2001. *Advocacy After Bhopal: Environmentalism, Disaster and New Global Orders.* Chicago: University of Chicago Press.

——. 2003. "Ethnography in/of/as Open Systems." *Reviews in Anthropology* 32(2): 171–90.

——. 2004. "From Bhopal to the Informating of Environmental Health: Risk Communication in Historical Perspective." *Osiris* 2nd ser., 19:283–96.

——. Forthcoming. "Information Technologies, Practices and Economies in Contemporary Environmentalism: Shifting Knowledge Formations, Shifting Politics." In Kaushik Sunder Rajan, ed., *Lively Capital: Directions in the Anthropology of Science.* Durham: Duke University Press.

Fortun, Kim, and Michael Fortun. 2007. "Experimenting with the Asthma Files." Paper presented at Lively Capital III, University of California, Irvine, April 13–14, 2007.

Fortun, Michael. 2003. "Mapping and Making Genes and Histories: The Genomics Project in the United States, 1980–1990." Ph.D. diss., Harvard University.

——. 2008. *Promising Genomics: Iceland and deCODE Genetics in a World of Speculation.* Berkeley: University of California Press.

Foster, Robert J. 2002. *Materializing the Nation: Commodities, Consumption and Media in Papua New Guinea.* Bloomington: Indiana University Press.

Foucault, Michel. 1961. *Introduction to Kant's Anthropology from a Pragmatic Point of View.* Translated by Arianna Bove. http://www.generation-online.org/p/fpfoucault1.htm.

——. 1963 [1973]. *The Birth of the Clinic: An Archeology of Medical Perception.* Translated by A. M. Sheridan Smith. New York: Pantheon.

——. 1966 [1971]. *The Order of Things: An Archeology of the Human Sciences.* New York: Pantheon.

——. 1975 [1977]. *Discipline and Punish: The Birth of the Prison.* Translated by Alan Sheridan. New York: Vintage.

——. 1981–82 [2005]. *The Hermeneutics of the Subject: Lectures at the Collège de France.* New York: Palgrave Macmillan.

Fox, Rene, and Judith Swazey. 1974. *The Courage to Fail: A Social View of Organ Transplants and Dialysis.* Chicago: University of Chicago Press.

——. 1992. *Spare Parts: Organ Replacement in America.* New York: Oxford University Press.

Franklin, Sarah. 2007. *Dolly Mixtures: The Remaking of Genealogy.* Durham: Duke University Press.

Franklin, Sarah, and Helena Ragoné, eds. 1998. *Reproducing Reproduction: Kinship, Power, and Technological Innovation.* Philadelphia: University of Pennsylvania Press.

Franklin, Sarah, and Celia Roberts, eds. 2006. *Born and Made: An Ethnography of Preimplantation Genetic Diagnosis.* Princeton: Princeton University Press.

Frazer, James. 1890. *The Golden Bough.* 2 vols. London: Macmillan.

——. 1915. *The Golden Bough.* 12 vols. London: Macmillan.

Friedman, Michael. 2006. "Kant—*Naturphilosophie*—Electromagnetism." In M. Friedman and Alfred Nordmann, eds., *The Kantian Legacy in Nineteenth-Century Science.* Cambridge: MIT Press.

Friedman, Michael, and Alfred Nordmann, eds. 2006. *The Kantian Legacy in Nineteenth-Century Science.* Cambridge: MIT Press.

Frost, Laura. 2002. *Sex Drives: Fantasies of Fascism in Literary Modernism.* Ithaca: Cornell University Press.

Fujimura, Joan. n.d. "Japanese Biotechnology: Robotics and System Biology." Draft ms.

Funtowicz, S. O., and J. R. Ravetz. 1992. "Three Types of Risk Assessment and the Emergence of Post-Normal Science." In S. Krimsky and D. Golding, eds., *Social Theories of Risk.* Westport, Conn.: Praeger.

Gadamer, Hans-Georg. 1960 [1975]. *Truth and Method.* Translated by Garrett Barden and John Cumming. New York: Sheed and Ward.

Galison, Peter. 1990. "Aufbau/Bauhaus: Logical Positivism and Architectural Modernism." *Critical Inquiry* 16 (summer): 709–52.

——. 1997. *Image and Logic: The Material Culture of Microphysics.* Chicago: University of Chicago Press.

Galison, Peter and David J. Stump, eds. 1996. *The Disunity of Science: Boundaries, Contexts, and Power.* Stanford: Stanford University Press.

Gaonkar, Dilip, ed. 2001. *Alternative Modernities.* Durham: Duke University Press.

Garfinkle, Harold. 1967. *Studies in Ethnomethodology.* Englewood Cliffs, NJ: Prentice-Hall

Gazit, Chana. 2001. *Fatal Flood.* PBS video.

Geary, James. 2002. *The Body Electric: An Anatomy of the New Bionic Senses.* London: Weidenfeld and Nicholson.

Geertz, Clifford. 1963. *Agricultural Involution.* Berkeley: University of California Press.

——. 1960. *The Religion of Java.* Glencoe, Ill.: Free Press.

——. 1973. *The Interpretation of Culture.* New York: Basic Books.

Geison, Gerald. 1995. *The Private Science of Louis Pasteur.* Princeton: Princeton University Press.

Gellner, Ernest. 1959. *Words and Things: A Critical Account of Linguistic Philosophy and a Study in Ideology.* London: Gollancz.

——. 1983. *Nations and Nationalism.* London: Blackwell.

——. 1988. " 'Zeno of Cracow' or 'Revolution at Nemi' or 'The Polish Revenge': A Drama in Three Acts." In Roy Ellen et al., eds., *Malinowski Between Two Worlds: The Polish Roots of an Anthropological Tradition.* Cambridge: Cambridge University Press.

Gennep, Arnold van. 1960. *The Rites of Passage.* Chicago: University of Chicago Press.

George, Timothy. 2001. *Minamata: Pollution and the Struggle for Democracy in Postwar Japan.* Cambridge: Harvard University Press.

Geroulanos, Stefanos. 2006. "Anthropology of Exit: Bataille on Heidegger and Fascism." *October* 117:3–24.

Gershon, Michael. 1998. *The Second Brain.* New York: HarperCollins.

Ghamari-Tabrizi, Sharon. 2001. "Why Is Validation of Defense Military and Simulation So Hard to Do?" Paper presented at the Society for the Social Studies of Science, Nov. 1–4.

——. 2005. *The Worlds of Herman Kahn: The Intuitive Science of Thermonuclear War.* Cambridge: Harvard University Press.

Ghani, Ashraf and Clare Lockhart. 2008. *Fixing Failed States: A Framework for Rebuilding a Fractured World.* New York: Oxford University Press.

Ghods, A. J. 2004. "Changing Ethics in Renal Transplantation: Presentation of Iran Model." *Transplantation Proceedings* 36(1): 11–13.

Gibbons, Michael, Camille Limoges, Helga Nowotny, Simon Schwartzman, Peter Scott, and Martin Trow. 1994. *The New Production of Knowledge: The Dynamics of Science and Research in Contemporary Societies.* London: Sage.

Gibson, William. 2005. "Introduction to 'the Body.' " In Marquard Smith, ed. *Stelarc, the Monograph.* Cambridge: MIT Press.

Gilroy, Paul. 1993. *The Black Atlantic: Modernity and Double Consciousness.* Cambridge: Harvard University Press.

Goffman, Erving. 1956. *The Presentation of Self in Everyday Life.* Edinburgh: University of Edinburgh Press.

——. 1961. *Asylums.* Garden City: Anchor Books.

——. 1974. *Frame Analysis.* New York: Harper and Row.

Goldberg, Carey. 2006. "Ultra-Tiny Knitting Thread Helps Restore Brain Function." *Boston Globe,* March 20, C1, 4.

Goldhaber, Michael D. 2007. *A People's History of the European Court of Human Rights.* New Brunswick, NJ: Rutgers University Press.

Good, Bryon. 1994. *Medicine, Rationality and Experience.* New York: Cambridge University Press.

Good, Mary-Jo DelVecchio. 1994. "Oncology and Narrative Time." *Social Science and Medicine* 38(6): 855–62.

——. 1995. *American Medicine: The Quest for Competence.* Berkeley: University of California Press.

——. 1996. "L'Abbraccio biotechnico: Un invito al trattemento sperimentale." In Pino Donghi, ed., *Il spaere della quarigole.* Spoleto: Laterza.

——. 1998. "Metaphors for Life and Society in Health and Illness and the Biotechnical Embrace." Paper presented at the International Symposium on Health and Illness, Bologna, Italy.

——. 2001. "The Biotechnical Embrace." *Culture, Medicine, and Psychiatry* 25(4): 395–410.

——. 2004. "Narrative Nuances on Good and Bad Death: Internists' Tales from High Technology Medicine." *Social Science and Medicine* 58(5): 939–53.

Good, Mary-Jo DelVecchio, and Byron Good. 2008. "'Indonesia Sakit' and the Subjective Experience and Interpretive Politics of Contemporary Indonesian Artists." In Mary-Jo DelVecchio Good et al., eds., *Postcolonial Disorders*. Berkeley: University of California Press.

Good, Mary-Jo DelVecchio, Byron Good, Sarah Pinto, and Sandra Hyde, eds. 2008. *Postcolonial Disorders*. Berkeley: University of California Press.

Goodall, Jane. 1999. "An Order of Pure Decision: Un-Natural Selection in the Work of Stelarc and Orlan." *Body and Society* 5(2–3): 149–70.

——. 2005. "The Will to Evolve." In Marquard Smith, ed., *Stelarc, the Monograph*. Cambridge: MIT Press.

Goodell, Grace. 1986. *The Elementary Structure of Political Life: Rural Development in Pahlavi Iran*. New York: Oxford University Press.

Goodman, Alan, Deborah Heath, and M. Susan Lindee, eds. 2003. *Genetic Nature/Culture: Anthropology and Science Beyond the Two-Culture Divide*. Berkeley: University of California Press.

Goodman, Ellen. 2007. Op-Ed Column. *Boston Globe*, November 16, A17.

Goody, Jack. 1977. *The Domestication of the Savage Mind*. New York: Cambridge University Press.

Gottweis, Herbert. 1998. *Governing Molecules: The Discursive Politics of Genetic Engineering in the United States and Europe*. Cambridge: MIT Press.

Graeber, David. 2004. *Fragments Towards an Anarchist Anthropology*. Chicago: Prickly Paradigm Press.

Graham, Loren. 1998. *What Have We Learned About Russian Science and Technology from the Russian Experience?* Stanford: Stanford University Press.

Graham, Loren, and Jean-Michel Kantor. 2007. "'Soft' Area Studies versus 'Hard' Social Science: A False Opposition." *Slavic Review* 66(1): 1–19.

Graziano, Frank. 1992. *Divine Violence: Spectacle, Psychosexuality, and Radical Christianity in the Argentine "Dirty War."* Boulder: Westview Press.

Greek, C. Ray, and Jean Swingle Greek. 2000. *Sacred Cows and Golden Geese: The Human Cost of Experiments on Animals*. New York: Continuum.

Greenslit, Nathan. 2007. "Pharmaceutical Relations: Intersections of Illness, Fantasy, and Capital in the Age of Direct-to-Consumer Marketing." Ph.D. diss., MIT.

Gregorio, Michael. 2006. *The Critique of Criminal Reason*. New York: St. Martin's Press.

Griefe, Edward, and Martin Linsky. 1995. *New Corporate Activism*. New York: McGraw-Hill.

Griffin, John Howard. 1961. *Black Like Me.* Boston: Houghton Mifflin.

Gross, Paul, and Norman Leavitt. 1994. *The Higher Superstition: The Academic Left and Its Quarrels with Science.* Baltimore: Johns Hopkins University Press.

Grossman, David. 1987 [1988]. *Yellow Wind.* Translated by Haim Watzman. New York: Farrar, Strauss, and Giroux.

Grove, Richard. 1995. *Green Imperialism.* New York: Oxford University Press.

——. 1997. *Ecology, Climate and Empire: Colonialism and Global Environmental History, 1400–1940.* Cambridge, Mass.: White Horse Press.

Grunwald, Michael. 2000. "An Agency of Unchecked Clout, Water Projects Roll Past Economic, Environmental Concerns: Engineers of Power, Inside the Army Corps." *Washington Post,* 10 September, A1.

——. 2001. "Disasters All, But Not As Natural As You Think." *Washington Post,* May 6, B1.

——. 2005a. "Money Flowed to Questionable Projects." *Washington Post,* Sept. 8.

——. 2005b. "Canal May Have Worsened City's Flooding." *Washington Post,* Sept. 14, A21.

——. 2007. "Reigning in the Corps of Engineers." *Time,* Sept. 20. http://www.time.com.

Guard, Olivier, and Franiços Boller. 2005. "Immanuel Kant: Evolution from a Personality 'Disorder' to a Dementia." In J. Bogousslavsky, and F. Boller, eds., *Neurological Disorders in Famous Artists.* Basel: Karger.

Guha, Ranajit, and Gayatri Spivak, eds. 1988. *Selected Subaltern Studies.* London: Oxford University Press.

Guillemin, Jean. 1999. *Anthrax: The Investigation of a Deadly Outbreak.* Berkeley: University of Chicago Press.

Gusfield, Joseph. 1963. *Symbolic Crusade: Status Politics and the American Temperance Movement.* Urbana: University of Illinois Press.

Guyer, Paul. 2003. "Beauty, Freedom, and Morality: Kant's Lectures on Anthropology and the Development of His Aesthetic Theory." In B. Jacobs and P. Kain, eds., *Essays on Kant's Anthropology.* New York: Cambridge University Press.

Habermas, Jürgen. 1962 [1989]. *The Structural Transformation of the Public Sphere: An Inquiry into a Category of Bourgeois Society.* Cambridge: MIT Press.

——. 1973 [1975]. *Legitimation Crisis.* Boston: Beacon.

——. 2002 [2003]. *The Future of Human Nature.* Malden, Mass.: Blackwell.

Hacking, Ian. 1975. *The Emergence of Probability.* Cambridge: Cambridge University Press.

——. 1982. "Biopower and the Avalanche of Printed Numbers." *Humanities in Society* 5:279–95.

——. 1995. *Rewriting the Soul: Multiple Personality and the Sciences of Memory.* Princeton: Princeton University Press.

——. 1998. *Mad Travellers: Reflections on the Reality of Transient Mental Illnesses.* Charlottesville: University of Virginia Press.

Hagens, Gunther von. 2004. *Body Worlds: The Anatomical Exhibition of Real Human Bodies*. Heidelberg: Institute for Plastination.

Haller, Rudolf. 1991. "On Austrian Philosophy." In T. Uebel, ed., *Rediscovering the Forgotten Vienna Circle*. Dordrecht: Kluwer Academic.

Hamby, Wilfrid D. 1925. *The History of Tattooing and Its Significance*. London: H. F. & G. Witherby.

Hamdy, Sherine. 2006. "Our Bodies Belong to God: Islam, Medical Sciences and Ethical Reasoning in Egyptian Life." Ph.D. diss., New York University.

Hammonds, Evelynn. 1999. *Childhood's Deadly Scourge: The Campaign to Control Diphtheria, 1800–1930*. Baltimore: Johns Hopkins University Press.

Haraway, Donna. 1985. "Manifesto for Cyborgs: Science, Technology and Socialist Feminism in the 1980s." *Socialist Review* 80:65–108.

——. 1989. *Primate Visions: Gender, Race and Nature in the World of Modern Science*. New York: Routledge.

——. 1991. *Simians, Cyborgs and Women: The Reinvention of Nature*. New York: Routledge.

——. 1997. *Modest_Witness@Second_Millennium.FemaleMan©_Meets_OncoMouse™: Feminism and Technoscience*. New York: Routledge.

——. 2003. *The Companion Species Manifesto: Dogs, People and Significant Otherness*. Chicago: Prickly Paradigm Press.

——. 2008. *When Species Meet*. Minneapolis: University of Minnesota Press.

Hardot, Pierre. 2004 [2006]. *The Veil of Isis: An Essay on the History of the Idea of Nature*. Translated by Michael Chase. Cambridge: Harvard University Press.

Hardt, Michael, and Antonio Negri. 2000. *Empire*. Cambridge: Harvard University Press.

Harman, Graham. 2007. *Heidegger Explained: From Phenomenon to Thing*. Chicago: Open Court.

Harr, Jonathan. 1995. *A Civil Action*. New York: Vintage.

Harrington, Anne. 1996. *Reenchanted Science: Holism in German Culture from Wilhelm II to Hitler*. Princeton: Princeton University Press.

Harrison, Lawrence, and Samuel Huntington. 2000. *Culture Matters: How Values Shape Human Progress*. New York: Basic Books.

Hartouni, Valerie. 1997. *Cultural Conceptions: On Reproductive Technologies and the Remaking of Life*. Minneapolis: University of Minnesota Press.

Hayden, Cori. 2003. *When Nature Goes Public: The Making and Unmaking of Bioprospecting in Mexico*. Princeton: Princeton University Press.

Heath, Deborah, Rayna Rapp, and Karen-Sue Taussig. 2004. "Genetic Citizenship." In D. Nugent and J. Vincent, eds., *Companion to Anthropology of Politics*. Oxford: Blackwell.

Hedayat, Sadegh. 1939 [1967]. *The Blind Owl*. Translated by D. P. Costello. London: J. Calder.

Heidegger, Martin. 1929 [1962]. *Being and Time*. Translated by John Macquarrie and Edward Robinson. New York: Harper.

——. 1954 [1977]. *The Question Concerning Technology and Other Essays.* Translated by William Lovett. New York: Garland.

Heidelberger, Michael. 2006. "Kantianism and Realism: Alois Riehl (and Moritz Schlick)." In M. Friedman and Alfred Nordmann, eds., *The Kantian Legacy in Nineteenth-Century Science.* Cambridge: MIT Press.

Held, David. 1980. *Introduction to Critical Theory: Horkheimer to Habermas.* Berkeley: University of California Press.

Helmreich, Stefan. 1998. *Silicon Second Nature: Culturing Artificial Life in a Digital World.* Berkeley: University of California Press.

——. 2003. "Trees and Seas of Information: Alien Kinship and the Biopolitics of Gene Transfer in Marine Biology and Biotechnology." *American Ethnologist* 30(3): 341–59.

——. 2009. *Alien Ocean: Anthropological Voyages in Microbial Seas.* Berkeley: University of California Press.

Henrich, Dieter. 2003. *Between Kant and Hegel: Lectures on German Idealism.* Cambridge: Harvard University Press.

He Qinglian. 2008. *The Fog of Censorship: Media Control in China.* N.p.: Human Rights in China.

Herman, Peter E. 2004. *Historicizing Theory.* Albany: State University of New York Press.

Herring, Ronald J. 2007. "Political Ecology from Landscapes to Genomes: Science and Interests." In Jules Pretty, ed., *Sage Handbook on Environment and Society.* Thousand Oaks, Calif.: Sage.

Heuser, Stephen. 2006. "A Case of Mind Over Matter: Mind-reading Devices Show Promise." *Boston Globe,* April 2, A1, 16.

Hill, Diana. 1995. "Trust but Verify: Science and Policy Negotiating Nuclear Testing Treaties—Interviews with Roger Eugene Hill." In George Marcus, ed., *Late Editions, 2: Technoscientific Imaginaries.* Chicago: University of Chicago Press.

Ho, Enseng. 2006. *The Graves of Tarim: Genealogy and Mobility Across the Indian Ocean.* Berkeley: University of California Press.

Ho, Karen. 2005. "Situating Global Capitalisms: A View from Wall Street Investment Banks." *Cultural Anthropology* 20(1): 68–96.

——. 2009. *Liquidated: An Ethnography of Wall Street.* Durham: Duke University Press.

Höffe, Otfried. 2001 [2006]. *Kant's Cosmopolitan Theory of Law and Peace.* New York: Cambridge University Press.

Hofstadter, Douglas. 2007. *Am I a Strange Loop?* New York: Basic Books.

Hogle, Linda. 1999. *Recovering the Nation's Body: Cultural Memory, Medicine, and the Politics of Redemption.* New Brunswick, NJ: Rutgers University Press.

Holmes, Douglas. 2006. "Central Bankers Unto Themselves: Semiotic Experiments in Monetary Policy." Manuscript.

Hoodbhoy, Perviz. 1991. *Islam and Science: Religious Orthodoxy and the Struggle for Rationality.* London: Zed.

Hooglund, Eric. 1982. *Land and Revolution in Iran 1960–1980*. Austin: University of Texas Press.

Horkheimer, Max, and Theodor Adorno. 1944. *The Dialectic of Enlightenment*. Translated by John Cumming. New York: Herder and Herder.

Hughes, H. Stuart. 1975. *The Sea Change: The Migration of Social Thought, 1930–1965*. Middletown, Conn.: Weslyan University Press.

Hughes, Thomas P. 1983. *Networks of Power: Electrification in Western Society, 1880–1930*. Baltimore: Johns Hopkins University Press.

——. 1998. *Rescuing Prometheus*. New York: Pantheon.

Hullot-Kentor, Robert. 2006. *Things Beyond Resemblance: Collected Essays on Theodor W. Adorno*. New York: Columbia University Press.

Hume, David. 1739 [1978]. *A Treatise of Human Nature*. Oxford: Clarendon Press.

Husserl, Edmund. 1936 [1970]. *The Crisis of European Sciences and Transcendental Phenomenology: An Introduction to Phenomenological Philosophy*. Translated by David Carr. Evanston, Ill.: Northwestern University Press.

Hyde, Sandra. 2007. *Eating Spring Rice: The Cultural Politics of AIDS in Southwestern China*. Berkeley: University of California Press.

Ihsanoglu, Ekmeleddin. 2004. *Science, Technology and Learning in the Ottoman Empire: Western Influence, Local Institutions, and the Transfer of Knowledge*. Burlington, Vt.: Ashgate Variorum.

Ivy, Marilyn. 1995. *Discourses of the Vanishing: Modernity, Phantasm, Japan*. Chicago: University of Chicago Press.

Jacob, Francois. 1987 [1988]. *The Statue Within: An Autobiography*. New York: Basic Books.

Jacobs, Brian. 2003. "Kantian Character and the Problem of a Science of Humanity." In B. Jacobs and P. Kain, eds., *Essays on Kant's Anthropology*. New York: Cambridge University Press.

Jacobs, Brian, and Patrick Kain, eds. 2003. *Essays on Kant's Anthropology*. New York: Cambridge University Press.

Jahoda, Maria, Paul F. Lazarsfeld, and Hans Zeisel. 1933 [1971]. *Marienthal: The Sociography of an Unemployed Community*. Translated by the authors with John Reginall and Thomas Elsaesser. Chicago: Aldine.

James, C. L. R. 1986. *Cricket*. Edited by Ann Grimshaw. New York: Schocken.

James, Erica. 2004. "The Violence of Misery: 'Insecurity' in Haiti in the 'Democratic' Era." Ph.D. diss., Harvard University.

James, William. 1902. *The Varieties of Religious Experience*. London: Longmans Green.

Jameson, Fredric. 1991. *Postmodernism, or the Cultural Logic of Late Capitalism*. Durham: Duke University Press.

Jasanoff, Sheila. 1990. *The Fifth Branch: Science Advisors as Policy Makers*. Cambridge: Harvard University Press.

——, ed. 1994. *Learning from Disaster: Risk Management After Bhopal*. Philadelphia: University of Pennsylvania Press.

——. 1995. *Science at the Bar: Law, Science and Technology in America*. Cambridge: Harvard University Press.

——. 2005. *Designs on Nature: Science and Democracy in Europe and the United States.* Princeton: Princeton University Press.

Jay, Martin. 1973. *The Dialectical Imagination: A History of the Frankfurt School and the Institute of Social Research, 1923–50.* Boston: Little, Brown.

Jeans, James. 1937. *Science and Music.* New York: Dover.

Jenkins, Henry. 2006. *Convergence Culture: Where Old and New Media Collide.* New York: New York University Press.

Jenneman, David. 2007. *Adorno in America.* Minneapolis: University of Minnesota Press.

Johnson, Christopher. 1993. *System and Writing in the Philosophy of Jacques Derrida.* New York: Cambridge University Press.

Jones, Amelia. 2005. "Stelarc's Technological 'Transcendence'/Stelarc's Wet Body: The Insistent Return of the Body." In Marquard Smith, ed., *Stelarc, the Monograph.* Cambridge: MIT Press.

Jones, Bradley S. 2008. *Web 2.0 Heroes: Interviews with 20 Web 2.0 Influencers.* Indianapolis: Wiley Publishing.

Jones, David S. 2004. *Rationalizing Epidemics: Meanings and Uses of American Indian Mortality since 1600.* Cambridge: Harvard University Press.

Juris, Jeff. 2008. *Networked Futures: The Movements Against Corporate Globalization.* Durham: Duke University Press.

Kalar, Brent. 2004. "Review of Brian Jacobs and Patrick Kain, eds., *Essays on Kant's Anthropology," Notre Dame Philosophical Reviews.*

Kallet, Lisa. 2001. *Money and the Corrosion of Power in Thucydides: The Sicilian Expedition and its Aftermath.* Berkeley: University of California Press.

Kant, Immanuel. 1781. *Critik der reinen Vernuft.* Riga: J. F. Hartknoch.

——. 1784 [1983]. "Idea for a Universal History with a Cosmopolitan Intention." Translated by T. Humphrey. In *Perpetual Peace and Other Essays.* Minneapolis: Hackett.

——. 1788. *Critik der praktischen Vernuft.* Riga: J. F. Hartknoch.

——. 1790. *Critik der Urteilskraft.* Berlin: Bey Lagarde und Friederich.

——. 1796 [1983]. "Perpetual Peace." Translated by T. Humphrey. In *Perpetual Peace and Other Essays.* Minneapolis: Hackett.

——. 1798 [2006]. *Anthropology from a Pragmatic Point of View.* Translated by Robert Louden. New York: Cambridge University Press.

Kantorowicz, Ernst. 1957. *The King's Two Bodies: A Study in Mediaeval Political Theology.* Princeton: Princeton University Press.

Kardiner, Abraham, Cora Du Bois, and Ralph Linton. 1945. *The Psychological Frontiers of Society.* New York: Columbia University Press.

Kay, Lily. 1993 *The Molecular Vision of Life: Caltech, the Rockefeller Foundation, and the Rise of the New Biology.* New York: Oxford University Press.

——. 2000. *Who Wrote the Book of Life?: A History of the Genetic Code.* Stanford: Stanford University Press.

Keating, Peter and Alberto Cambrosio. 2003. *Biomedical Platforms: Realigning the Normal and the Pathological in Late Twentieth-Century Medicine.* Cambridge: MIT Press.

Keller, Evelyn Fox. 1995. *Refiguring Life: Metaphors of Twentieth-Century Biology.* New York: Columbia University Press.

——. 2000. *The Century of the Gene.* Cambridge: Harvard University Press.

Kelty, Christopher. 2008. *Two Bits: Free Software and the Social Imagination after the Internet.* Durham: Duke University Press.

Kennedy, Ellen. 2004. *Constitutional Failure: Carl Schmidt in Weimar.* Durham: Duke University Press.

Kim, Dong-Won, and Stuart W. Leslie. 1998. "Winning Markets or Winning Nobel Prizes? KAIST and the Challenges of Late Industrialization." *Osiris* 2nd ser., 13:156–85.

King, Cabell, and David Albertson, eds. Forthcoming. *Without Nature: A New Condition for Theology.* New York: Fordham.

Kisiel, Theodore. 1993. *The Genesis of Heidegger's Being and Time.* Berkeley: University of California Press.

Kittler, Friedrich. 1985 [1990]. *Discourse Networks 1800/1900.* Translated by Michael Metter with Chris Cullens. Stanford: Stanford University Press.

——. 1986 [1999]. *Grammaphone, Film, Typewriter.* Translated by Geoffrey Winthrop-Young and Michael Wutz. Stanford: Stanford University Press.

——. 1997. *Media, Literature, Information Systems.* Amsterdam: Overseas Publishers Association.

Klein, Rick. 2005. "Ex-FEMA Chief Spreads the Blame." *Boston Globe,* Sept. 28.

Kleinman, Arthur. 1988. *The Illness Narratives.* New York: Basic Books.

——. 2006. *What Really Matters: Living a Moral Life Amidst Uncertainty and Danger.* New York: Oxford University Press.

Kleinman, Arthur, Veena Das, and Margaret Lock, eds. 1997. *Social Suffering.* Berkeley: University of California Press.

Knorr-Cetina, Karin. 1999. *Epistemic Cultures: How the Sciences Make Knowledge.* Cambridge: Harvard University Press.

Knorr-Cetina, Karin, and U. Bruegger. 2002. "Global Microstructures: The Virtual Societies of Financial Markets." *American Journal of Sociology* 107(4): 905–50.

Koch, Gertrud. 1994. "Cosmos in Film: On the Concept of Space in Walter Benjamin's 'Work of Art' Essay." In Andrew Benjamin and Peter Osborne, eds., *Walter Benjamin's Philosophy.* London: Routledge.

Kohler, Robert. 1994. *Lord of the Fly: Drosophila Genetics and the Experimental Life.* Chicago: University of Chicago Press.

Krache, Waude. 1978. *Force and Persuasion: Leadership in an Amazonian Society.* Chicago: University of Chicago Press.

Krall, Hanna. 1977 [1986]. *Shielding the Flame: An Intimate Conversation with Dr. Mark Edelman, the Last Surviving Leader of the Warsaw Uprising.* New York: Henry Holt.

Krimsky, Sheldon. 2000. *Hormonal Chaos: The Scientific and Social Origins of the Environmental Endocrine Hypothesis.* Baltimore: Johns Hopkins University Press.

Kristeva, Julia. 1987 [1989]. *Black Sun: Depression and Melancholia.* New York: Columbia University Press.

——. 1995. *New Maladies of the Soul.* New York: Columbia University Press.

Kroeber, Alfred L. 1935. "History and Science in Anthropology." *American Anthropologist* 37(3): 539–69.

——. 1948. *Anthropology: Race, Language, Culture, Psychology, Pre-History.* New York: Harcourt, Brace.

——. 1952. *The Nature of Culture.* Chicago: University of Chicago Press.

Kroeber, Alfred L., and Clyde Kluckhohn. 1952. *Culture: A Critical Review of Concepts and Definitions.* Cambridge, Mass.: Peabody Museum.

Kuhn, Thomas. 1955. *The Structure of Scientific Revolutions.* Volume 2 of the *International Encyclopedia of Unified Science,* edited by Otto Neurath, Rudolph Carnap, and Charles Morris. Chicago: University of Chicago Press.

Kuo, Wen-Hua. 2005. "Japan and Taiwan in the Wake of Bioglobalization: Drugs, Race and Standards." Ph.D. diss., MIT.

Kuzniar, Alice A. 2006. *Melancholia's Dog: Reflections on Our Animal Kinship.* Chicago: University of Chicago Press.

Lacan, Jacques. 1954–55 [1988]. *The Seminar of Jacques Lacan: The Ego in Freud's Theory and in the Technique of Psychoanalysis, 1954–55.* Bk. 2. Translated by Sylvana Tomaselli. New York: W. W. Norton.

Lacoue-Labarthe, Philippe. 1989. *Typography: Mimesis, Philosophy, Politics.* Cambridge: Harvard University Press.

Lahsen, Myanna. 2001. "The Invisible Hand Comes to Japan: Competition and Global Welfare versus Japanese Global Change Science." Paper presented at the American Anthropological Association meetings, Washington, D.C.

——. 2004. "Transnational Locals: Brazilian Experiences of the Climate Regime." In Sheila Jasanoff and Marybeth Long, eds., *Earthly Politics: Local and Global in Environmental Politics.* Cambridge: MIT Press.

——. 2005. "Seductive Simulations? Uncertainty Distribution Around Climate Models." *Social Studies of Science.* 35(6): 895–922.

Lahsen, Myanna, and Roger Pielke. 2002. "'Our' Science, 'Their' Science: Conflicting Agendas and Disputed Theories Concerning Amazonia." Proposal to the U.S. National Science Foundation.

Lakoff, Andrew. 2005. *Pharmaceutical Reason: Knowledge and Value in Global Psychiatry.* New York: Cambridge University Press.

Lakoff, George, and Mark Johnson. 1980. *Metaphors We Live By.* Chicago: University of Chicago Press.

Lakshmanan, Indira A. R. 2006. "In Colombia, a Race to Count the Dolphins." *Boston Globe,* Oct., A1, 6.

Landecker, Hannah. 2002. "New Times for Biology: Nerve Cultures and the Advent of Cellular Life in Vitro." *Studies in History and Philosophy of Biological and Biomedical Sciences* 33(4): 667–94.

——. 2007. *Culturing Life: How Cells Became Technologies.* Cambridge: Harvard University Press.

Landzelius, Kyra. 2005. *Going Native on the Net: Indigenous Cyber-Activism and Virtual Diasporas over the World Wide Web.* New York: Routledge.

Lang, Mabel L. 1984. *Herodotean Narrative and Discourse.* Cambridge: Harvard University Press.

Lange, Dorothea, and Paul Taylor. 1939. *An American Exodus.* New York: Reynal and Hitchcock.

Langer, Susanne. 1942. *Philosophy in a New Key.* Cambridge: Harvard University Press.

——. 1967–82. *Mind: An Essay on Human Feeling.* 3 vols. Baltimore: Johns Hopkins University Press.

Lanternari, Vittorio. 1963. *Religions of the Oppressed.* Translated by Lisa Sergio. New York: Knopf.

Laroui, Abdullah. 1976. *The Crisis of the Arab Intellectual.* Berkeley: University of California Press.

Lash, Scott, and John Urry. 1994. *Economies of Signs and Space.* Thousand Oaks, Calif.: Sage.

Latour, Bruno. 1987. *Science in Action: How to Follow Scientists and Engineers through Society.* Cambridge: Harvard University Press.

——. 1988. *The Pasteurization of France.* Cambridge: Harvard University Press.

——. 1990. "Postmodern? No, Simply Amodern! Steps Towards an Anthropology of Science." *Studies in History and Philosophy of Science* 21(1): 145–71.

——. 1993. *Aramis, or The Love of Technology.* Cambridge: Harvard University Press.

——. 1996. "The Trouble with Actor-Network Theory." *Soziale Welt* 47:369–81.

——. 1998. "For Bloor and Beyond—A Reply to David Bloor's 'Anti-Latour.'" *Studies in History and Philosophy of Science.* 30(1): 113–29.

——. 2001a. "Regeln für die neuen wissenschftlichen und sozialen Experimente." Darmstadt Colloquium: Plenary, March 30.

——. 2001b. "Objectivity [in Le Coneil de Etat]." Harvard History of Science Colloquium, April 17.

——. 2001c. "Politics of Nature and Anthropological Analysis." Brown Bag Seminar, STS Program, MIT.

——. 2001d. "Gabriel Tarde and the End of the Social." In Patrick Joyce, ed., *The Social in Question.* London: Routledge.

——. 2004. *Politics of Nature: How to Bring the Sciences into Democracy.* Cambridge: Harvard University Press.

——. 2005a. "From Realpolitik to Dingpolitik—or How to Make Things Public." In *Making Things Public, Atmospheres of Democracy.* Cambridge: MIT Press.

——. 2005b. *Reassembling the Social: An Introduction to Actor Network Theory.* Oxford: Oxford University Press.

Latour, Bruno, and Steve Woolgar. 1979. *Laboratory Life: The Social Construction of Scientific Facts.* Thousand Oaks, Calif.: Sage.

Leach, Edmund R. 1964. "Animal Aspects of Language: Animal Categories and Verbal Abuse." In E. H. Lenneberg, ed., *New Directions in the Study of Language.* Cambridge: MIT Press.

Lears, T. J. Jackson. 1981. *No Place of Grace: Antimodernism and the Transformation of American Culture, 1880–1920.* New York: Pantheon Books.

Lefebvre, Henri. 1967. *Position: Contre les Technocrates.* Paris: Gonthier.

Leigh, Egbert Giles. 1999. *Tropical Forest Ecology: A View from Barro Colorado Island.* New York: Oxford University Press.

Leonard, Miriam. 2005. *Athens in Paris: Ancient Greek and the Political in Post-War French Thought.* New York: Oxford University Press.

Leonard, Robert J. 1999. "'Seeing Is Believing': Otto Neurath, Graphic Art, and the Social Order." In Neil De Marchi and Craufurd D. W. Goodwin, eds., *Economic Engagement with Art.* Annual Supplement to volume 31, *History of Political Economy.* Durham: Duke University Press.

Lepinay, Vincent-Antoine. 2005a. "Derivative: Sociology of a Parasitic Formula." Manuscript.

——. 2005b. "Markets-in-Law: Legal Outactionism in Securities Markets." Manuscript.

——. 2005c. "Articulating Mathematics in a Trading Room." Manuscript.

——. 2006. "Modern Silos: Finance, Biobanks, and the Technologies of Preservation." Colloquium, STS Program, MIT, March 22.

Lepinies, Wolf. 2006. *The Seduction of Culture in German History.* Princeton: Princeton University Press.

Leslie, Esther. 2000. *Walter Benjamin: Overpowering Conformism.* London: Pluto Press.

Lessig, Lawrence. 1999. *Code and Other Laws of Cyberspace.* New York: Basic Books.

——. 2001. *The Future of Ideas: The Fate of Commons in a Connected World.* New York: Random House.

——. 2004. *Free Culture: How Big Media Uses Technology and the Law to Lock Down Culture and Control Creativity.* New York: Penguin University Press.

Lévi-Strauss, Claude. 1949 [1963]. "The Effectiveness of Symbols." In *Structural Anthropology.* New York: Basic Books.

——. 1950 [1987]. *Introduction to the Work of Marcel Mauss.* Translated by Felicity Baker. London: Routledge, Kegan Paul.

——. 1962 [1966]. *The Savage Mind.* Chicago: University of Chicago Press.

——. 1963. *Structural Anthropology.* New York: Basic Books.

——. 1964 [1970]. *The Raw and the Cooked.* New York: Harper and Row.

——. 1967. "The Story of Asdiwal." In Edmund Leach, ed., *The Structural Study of Myth and Totemism.* London: Tavistock.

——. 1971 [1981]. "Finale." In *The Naked Man.* New York: Harper and Row.

Levinas, Emmanuel. 1935–36 [2003]. *On Escape.* Stanford: Stanford University Press.

LeVine, Robert A. 1973. *Culture, Behavior and Personality.* Chicago: Aldine.

Levy, Robert I. 1973. *Tahitians: Mind and Experience in the Society Islands.* Chicago: University of Chicago Press.

Limon, Jose. 1994. *Dancing with the Devil: Society and Cultural Poetics in Mexican-American South Texas.* Madison: University of Wisconsin Press.

Lippit, Akira Mizuta. 2000. *Electric Animal: Toward a Rhetoric of Wildlife.* Mineapolis: University of Minnesota Press.

Lipsitz, George. 1990. *Time Passages: Collective Memory and American Popular Culture.* Minneapolis: University of Minnesota Press.

——. 1994. *Dangerous Crossroads: Popular Music, Postmodernism, and the Poetics of Place.* New York: Verso.

——. 2001. *American Studies in a Moment of Danger.* Minneapolis: University of Minnesota Press.

——. 2007. *Footsteps in the Dark: The Hidden Histories of Popular Music.* Minneapolis: University of Minnesota Press.

LiPuma, Edward, and Benjamin Lee. 2004. *Financial Derivatives and the Globalization of Risk.* Durham: Duke University Press.

Llewelyn, John. 2000. *The Hypocritical Imagination: Between Kant and Levinas.* New York: Routledge.

Lloyd, David. 1989. "Kant's Examples." *Representations* 28:34–54.

Lock, Margaret. 2002. *Twice Dead: Organ Transplants and the Reinvention of Death.* Berkeley: University of California Press.

Long, Timothy. 1987. *Repetition and Variation in the Short Stories of Herodotus.* Frankfurt am Main: Athenaum.

Longino, Michele. 2002. *Orientalism and Classical French Drama.* New York: Cambridge University Press.

Loomba, Ania. 2007. "Cosmopolitan Legacies." Paper presented at the Cosmopolitanism and Globalization Conference, Humanities Institute, State University of New York at Stony Brook, Oct. 13.

Loose, Christopher, Kyle Jensen, Isidore Rigoutsos, and Gregory Stephanopoulos. 2006. "A Linguistic Model for the Rational Design of Antimicrobial Peptides." *Nature* 443 (October 19): 867–69.

Lord, Nancy. 2004. *Beluga Days: Tracking a White Whale's Truths.* New York: Counterpoint.

Lotfalian, Mazyar. 2004. *Islam, Technoscientific Identities, and the Culture of Curiosity.* Lanham, Md.: University Presses of America.

Louden, Robert B. 2003. "The Second Part of Morals." In B. Jacobs and P. Kain, eds., *Essays on Kant's Anthropology.* New York: Cambridge University Press.

Low, Morris, ed. 1998. "Beyond Joseph Needham: Science, Technology, and Medicine in East and Southeast Asia." Special issue, *Osiris* 2nd ser., 13.

Low, Morris, Shigeru Nakayama, and Hitoshi Yoshioka. 1999. *Science, Technology and Society in Contemporary Japan.* New York: Cambridge University Press.

Lowe, Celia. 2006. *Wild Profusion: Biodiversity Conservation in an Indonesian Archipelago.* Princeton: Princeton University Press.

Luhrmann, Tanya. 2000. *Of Two Minds: The Growing Disorder in American Psychiatry.* New York: Knopf.

Lynch, Marc. 2006. *Voices of the New Arab Public: Iraq, Al-Jazeera, and Middle East Politics Today.* New York: Columbia University Press.

Lynch, Michael. 1993. *Scientific Practice and Ordinary Action: Ethnomethodology and Social Studies of Science.* New York: Cambridge University Press.

Lynch, Michael, and Steve Woolgar, ed., 1988. *Representation in Scientific Practice.* Cambridge: MIT Press.

Lyotard, Jean-François. 1974 [1993]. *Libidinal Economy.* Translated by Iain Hamilton Grant. Bloomington: University of Indiana Press.

——. 1979 [1984]. *The Postmodern Condition: A Report on Knowledge.* Translated by Geoff Bennington and Brian Massumi. Minneapolis: University of Minnesota Press.

——. 1983 [1988]. *The Differend: Phrases in Dispute.* Translated by Georges Van Den Abbeele. Minneapolis: University of Minnesota Press.

Macdonald, A. 2000. "Two Continents, One Meridian, Two Visionaries, One Goal." *Survey Review* 35(275): 307–19.

Macfarlane, Allison, and Rodney Ewing. 2006. *Uncertainty Underground: Yucca Mountain and the Nation's High-Level Nuclear Waste.* Cambridge: MIT Press.

MacKenzie, Donald. 2001. *Mechanizing Proof: Computing, Risk, and Trust.* Cambridge: MIT Press.

——. 2006. *An Engine, Not a Camera: How Financial Models Shape Markets.* Cambridge: MIT Press.

Macksey, Richard, and Eugenio Donato, eds. 1970. *The Structuralist Controversy: The Languages of Criticism and the Sciences of Man.* Baltimore: Johns Hopkins University Press.

MacLeish, Archibald. 1937. *Land of the Free.* New York: Harcourt Brace.

Maine, Henry. 1861. *Ancient Law: Its Connection with the Early History of Society, and Its Relation to Modern Ideas.* London: John Murray.

Malinowski, Bronislaw. 1922. *Argonauts of the Western Pacific.* London: G. Routledge.

——. 1935. *Coral Gardens and Their Magic: A Study of Methods of Tilling the Soil and of Agricultural Rites in the Trobriand Islands.* New York: American Book Company.

——. 1937. *Sex and Repression in Savage Society.* New York: Harcourt Brace.

——. 1948. *Magic, Science, and Religion, and Other Essays.* Boston: Beacon Press.

Malkki, Liisa. 1995. *Purity and Exile: Violence, Memory and National Cosmology among the Hutu Refugees in Tanzania.* Chicago: University of Chicago Press.

Mann, Steve. 2001. *Cyborg: Digital Destiny and Human Possibility in the Age of the Wearable Computer.* New York: Random House Doubleday.

Mannheim, Karl. 1922. *Die strukturanalyse der erkenntnistheorie.* Berlin: Reuther and Reichard.

——. 1936. *Ideology and Utopia.* New York: Harcourt, Brace.

Marchand, J. C. 1997. "Was Emmanuel Kant's Dementia Symptomatic of a Frontal Tumor?" *Rev Neurol* (Paris) 155(1): 35–39.

Marcus, George, ed. 1993–2000. *Late Editions: Cultural Studies for the End of the Century.* 8 vols. Chicago: University of Chicago Press.

——. 2007. "Ethnography Two Decades After Writing Culture: From the Experimental to the Baroque." *Anthropological Quarterly* 80(4): 1127–45.

Marcus, George, and Michael M. J. Fischer. 1986 [1999]. *Anthropology and Cultural Critique: An Experimental Moment in the Human Sciences.* 2d ed. Chicago: University of Chicago Press.

Marcus, George, and Fernando Mascarenhas. 2005. *Ocasião: The Marquis and the Anthropologist, a Collaboration.* New York: AltaMira Press.

Marcus, George, and Erkan Saka. "Assemblage." *Theory, Culture, and Society* 23(2): 101–6.

Marcus, Steven. 1974. *Engels, Manchester, and the Working Class.* New York: Random House.

Markoff, John. 2002. "Japanese Computer Is World's Fastest, as U.S. Falls Back." *New York Times,* April 20, A1, B14.

——. 2008. "Internet Traffic Begins to Bypass the United States." *New York Times,* August 28, B1, 4.

Marks, Jonathan. 1995. *Human Biodiversity: Genes, Race, and History.* New York: Aldine de Gruyter.

——. 2002. *What It Means To Be 98% Chimpanzee: Apes, People, and their Genes.* Berkeley: University of California Press.

Martin, Aryn. 2004. "'Can't Anybody Count?' Counting as an Epistemic Theme in the History of Human Chromosomes." *Social Studies of Science* 34(6): 923–48.

Martin, Emily. 1987. *The Woman in the Body.* Boston: Beacon Press.

——. 1994. *Flexible Bodies: Tracking Immunity in American Culture from the Days of Polio to the Age of AIDS.* Boston: Beacon Press.

——. 2007. *Bipolar Expeditions: Mania and Depression in American Culture.* Princeton: Princeton University Press.

Martin, Richard. 2005. "Mind Control: Matthew Nagle Is Paralyzed: He's also a Pioneer in the New Science of Brain Implants." *Wired* 13(3). www.wired.com.

Martinez, Jenny S. 2007. "The Slave Trade on Trial: Lessons of a Great Human Rights Law Success." *Boston Review* (September/October): 12–17.

Marx, Karl. 1852 [1963]. *The Eighteenth Brumaire of Louis Bonaparte.* 2nd ed. 1869. New York: International Publishers.

Marx, Leo. 1964. *The Machine in the Garden: Technology and the Pastoral Ideal in America.* New York: Oxford University Press.

——. 1984. "On Heidegger's Conception of 'Technology' and Its Historical Validity." *Massachusetts Review* 25 (Winter 1984): 638–52.

Masco, Joseph. 2004. "Mutant Ecologies: Radioactive Life in Post–Cold War New Mexico." *Cultural Anthropology* 19(4): 517–50.

——. 2006. *The Nuclear Borderlands: The Manhattan Project in Post–Cold War New Mexico.* Princeton: Princeton University Press.

Massumi, Brian. 2005. "The Evolutionary Alchemy of Reason." In Marquard Smith, ed., *Stelarc, the Monograph.* Cambridge: MIT Press.

Mathur, Anuradha, and Dilip da Cunha. 2001. *Mississippi Floods: Designing a Shifting Landscape.* New Haven: Yale University Press.

Maurer, Bill. 2005a. "Due Diligence and 'Reasonable Man,' Offshore." *Cultural Anthropology* 20(4): 474–505.

——. 2005b. *Mutual Life, Limited: Islamic Banking, Alternative Currencies, Lateral Reason.* Princeton: Princeton University Press.

——. 2006. *Pious Property: Islamic Mortgages in the United States.* New York: Russell Sage Foundation.

Mauss, Marcel. 1925 [1954]. *The Gift: Forms and Functions of Exchange in Archaic Societies.* Glencoe, Ill.: Free Press.

——. 1979. *Sociology and Psychology.* Translated by Ben Brewster. London: Routledge and Kegan Paul.

Mayhew, Henry. 1861. *London Labour and the London Poor: The Condition and Earnings of Those that Will Work, Cannot Work, and Will Not Work.* London: C. Griffin.

Mbembe, Achille. 2001. *On the Postcolony.* Berkeley: University of California Press.

McCabe, Michael. 1997. *New York City Tattoo: The Oral History of an Urban Art.* Honolulu: Hardy Marks.

McCormick, John C. 2002. "A Critical versus Genealogical 'Questioning' of Technology: Notes on How Not to Read Adorno and Horkheimer." In J. McCormick, ed., *Confronting Mass Democracy and Industrial Technology.* Durham: Duke University Press.

Mead, Margaret. 1928. *Coming of Age in Samoa: A Psychological Study of Primitive Youth for Western Civilization.* New York: William Morrow.

——. 1935. *Sex and Temperament in Three Primitive Societies.* London: G. Routledge.

Mead, Margaret, and Rhoda Metraux. 1953. *The Study of Culture at a Distance.* Chicago: University of Chicago Press.

Meeker, Michael. 1979. *Literature and Violence in North Arabia.* New York: Cambridge University Press.

Mehlman, Jeffrey. 1993. *Walter Benjamin for Children: An Essay on His Radio Years.* Chicago: University of Chicago Press.

Melucci, Alberto. 1996. *Challenging Codes: Collective Action in the Information Age.* New York: Cambridge University Press.

Merleau-Ponty, Maurice. 1945 [1962]. *Phenomenology of Perception.* Translated by Colin Smith. New York: Humanities Press.

Merton, Robert K. 1938. *Science, Technology and Society in Seventeenth-Century England.* Bruges, Belgium: Saint Catherine Press.

——. 1973. *The Sociology of Science: Theoretical and Empirical Investigations.* Edited by Norman W. Storer. Chicago: University of Chicago Press.

Meyer, Stephen. 2006. *The End of the Wild.* Cambridge: MIT Press.

Mialet, Hélène. 1999. "Do Angels Have Bodies? Two Stories About Subjectivity in Science: The Cases of William X and Mister H." *Social Studies of Science* 29:551–81.

——. 2006. "Hawking Hawking: Or How to Do Things with Words." Lecture, MIT.

Miller, Clark, and Paul N. Edwards, eds. 2001. *Changing the Atmosphere: Expert Knowledge and Environmental Governance.* Cambridge: MIT Press.

Milun, Kathryn. 2006. *Pathologies of Modern Space: Empty Space, Urban Anxiety and the Recovery of the Self.* New York: Routledge.

Mitchell, Timothy. 1988. *Colonizing Egypt.* New York: Cambridge University Press.

——. 2002. *Rule of Experts: Egypt, Techno-Politics, Modernity.* Berkeley: University of California Press.

Miyazaki, Hirokazu. 2003. "The Temporalities of the Market." *American Anthropologist* 105(2): 255–65.

——. 2005. "The Materiality of Finance Theory." In Daniel Miller, ed., *Materiality.* Durham: Duke University Press.

——. 2006. "Economy of Dreams: Hope in Global Capitalism and Its Critique." *Cultural Anthropology* 21(2): 147–72.

——. Forthcoming. *Arbitraging Japan: The Economy of Hope in the Tokyo Financial Markets.* Berkeley: University of California Press.

Montoya, Michael. 2007. "Bioethnic Conscription: Genes, Race, and Mexicana/o Ethnicity in Diabetes Research." *Cultural Anthropology* 22(1): 94–128.

Moreno, Jonathan D. 2005. "In the Wake of Katrina: Has 'Bioethics' Failed?" *American Journal of Bioethics* 5(5): W18.

Moreno-Ocampo, Luis. 2007. "Massive Crimes Are Never Simply Domestic: They Cross Borders and Affect Other States." *Boston Review* 32(5): 11–12.

Morgan, Lewis Henry. 1851. *The League of the Iroquois.* New York: M. H. Newman.

——. 1868–70. *Systems of Consanguinity and Affinity of the Human Family.* Washington, D.C.: Smithsonian Institution.

——. 1877. *Ancient Society.* Chicago: C. H. Kerr.

Morris, Rosalind. 2000. *In Place of Origins: Modernity and Its Mediums in Northern Thailand.* Durham: Duke University Press.

Mosse, George. 1975. *The Nationalization of the Masses: Political Symbolism and Mass Movements in Germany from the Napoleonic Wars through the Third Reich.* New York: H. Fertig.

Moyn, Samuel. 2005. *Origins of the Other: Emmanuel Levinas Between Revelation and Ethics.* Ithaca: Cornell University Press.

Mufti Aamir R. 2007. *Enlightenment in the Colony: The Jewish Question and the Crisis of Postcolonial Culture.* Princeton: Princeton University Press.

Müller, Max, ed. 1879–1910. *The Sacred Books of the East.* Oxford: Oxford University Press.

Müller-Doohm, Stefan. 2003 [2005]. *Adorno: A Biography.* Malden, Mass.: Polity Press.

Myers, Natasha. 2006. "Animating Mechanism: Animation and the Propagation of Affect the Lively Arts of Protein Modeling." *Science Studies* 19(2): 6–30.

——. 2007. "Modeling Proteins, Making Scientists: An Ethnography of Pedagogy and Visual Culture in Contemporary Structural Biology." Ph.D. diss., MIT.

Nadkarni, Nalini, and Nat Wheelwright, eds. 2000. *Monteverde: Ecology and Conservation of a Tropical Cloud Forest.* New York: Oxford University Press.

Naficy, Hamid. 2001. *An Accented Cinema: Exilic and Diasporic Filmmaking.* Princeton: Princeton University Press.

Nandy, Ashis. 1980. *Alternative Sciences: Creativity and Authenticity in Two Indian Scientists.* New Delhi: Allied.

——, ed. 1988. *Science, Hegemony, and Violence: A Requiem for Modernity.* Delhi: Oxford University Press.

Nash, June. 1979. *We Eat the Mines and the Mines Eat Us: Dependency and Exploitation in Bolivian Tin Mines.* New York: Columbia University Press.

Nasr, S. Hossein. 1964. *Three Muslim Sages.* Cambridge: Harvard University Press.

Negri, Antonio. 1970 [2006]. *Political Descartes: Reason, Ideology and the Bourgeois Project.* Translated by Matteo Mandarini and Alberto Toscano. New York: Verso.

Nemeth, Elisabeth, and Friedrich Stadler, eds. 1996. *Encyclopedia and Utopia: The Life and Work of Otto Neurath (1882–1945).* Dordrecht: Kluwer Academic.

Neurath, Otto. 1937. *Basic by Isotype.* London: Kegan Paul, Trench.

——. 1939. *Modern Man in the Making.* New York: Alfred A. Knopf.

Neushul, P. and Z. Wang. 2000. "Between the Devil and the Deep Sea: C. K. Tseng in Mariculture and the Politics of Science in Modern China." *Isis* 91:59–88.

Neuwirth, Robert. 2005. "Mumbai: Squatter Class Structure." In *Shadow Cities: A Billion Squatters, a New Urban World.* New York: Routledge.

Newman, Stuart. 2006. "Renatured Biology: Getting Past Postmodernism in the Life Sciences." Paper presented at Without Nature: A New Condition for Theology, Chicago, October 26–28. Forthcoming in Cabell King and David Albertson, ed. *Without Nature: A New Condition for Theology.* New York: Fordham University Press.

Nietzsche, Friedrich. 1872 [1967]. *Birth of Tragedy.* Translated by Walter Kaufmann. New York: Random House.

——. 1886 [2002]. *Beyond Good and Evil: Prelude to a Philosophy of the Future.* Translated by Judith Norman. New York: Cambridge University Press.

Nimtz, August. 2000. *Marx and Engels: Their Contribution to the Democratic Breakthrough.* Albany: State University of New York Press.

Nock, David A. 2002. "The Sociological Legacy of Arthur Kent Davis." *Society/Société,* 26(1) (April).

Norin, Erik. 1967. *Sven Hedin Central Asia Atlas: Memoir on Maps.* Stockholm: Ethnografiska Museet.

Norris, David O., and James A. Carr. 2006. *Endocrine Disruption: Biological Basis for Health Effects in Wildlife and Humans.* New York: Oxford University Press.

Obeysekere, Gananath. 1981. *Medusa's Hair.* Chicago: University of Chicago Press.

——. 1984. *The Cult of the Goddess Pattini.* Chicago: University of Chicago Press.

——. 1992. *The Apotheosis of Captain Cook: European Mythmaking in the Pacific.* Princeton: Princeton University Press.

O'Keefe, J. A., Ann Eckels, and R. K. Squires. 1959. "Vanguard Measurements Give Pear-Shaped Component of Earth's Figure." *Science,* New Series, 129(3348): 565–66.

Okin, Susan Moller. 1999. *Is Multiculturalism Bad for Women? Susan Moller Okin with Respondents.* Edited by Joshua Cohen, Mathew Howard, and Martha Nussbaum. Princeton: Princeton University Press.

Ong, Aihwa, and Stephen Collier, eds. 2005. *Global Assemblages: Technology, Politics and Ethics as Anthropological Problems.* Malden, Mass: Blackwell.

Ong, Walter. 1982. *Orality and Literacy: The Technologization of the Word.* New York: Methuen.

Ophir, Adi. 2003. "The Contribution of Global Humanism to the Transformation of Sovereignty." Paper presented at the International Workshop on Catastrophes in the Age of Globalization. Neve Ilan, Israel. January.

——. 2004. "The Role of the E.U." Paper presented at the Third Faculty for Israel Palestine Peace Conference, Brussels, July 3–4.

Ophir, Adi, and Azoulay, Ariella. 2004. "The Israeli Ruling Apparatus in the Palestinian Occupied Territories." Van Leer Jerusalem Institute, April 20–21.

Orlan web page: www.orlan.net.

Orlan, Carnal Art Manifesto: http://www.dundee.ac.uk/transcript/volume2/issue2–2/orlan/orlan.htm.

Ornston, Darius Gray Jr., ed. 1992. *Translating Freud.* New Haven: Yale University Press.

Ortlieb, Martin. 2009. "Emergent Culture, Slippery Culture: Conflicting Conceptualizations of Culture in Commercial Ethnography." In Melissa Cefkin, ed., *Ethnography and the Corporate Encounter: Reflections on Research in and of Corporations.* New York: Berghahn.

Ozkan, Esra. 2007. "Coaching as an Emerging Form of Professional Expertise." Ph.D. diss., MIT.

Pálsson, Gísli, and Paul Rabinow. 1999. "Iceland: The Case of a National Human Genome Project." *Anthropology Today* 15:5 (1999): 14–18.

Pandolfi, Mariella. 2002. "Right of Interference, Temporality of Emergency, Necessity of Action: The Triangle of Humanitarian Biopower." Paper presented at the American Anthropological Society meetings, New Orleans, November.

——. 2006. "Laboratories of Intervention." Paper presented at the Canadian Anthropology Society meetings, Montreal, May.

Panourgia, Neni. 2008a. "Desert Islands: Ransom of Humanity." *Public Culture* 20(2): 395–421.

——. 2008b. *Dangerous Citizens: The Greek Left and the Terror of the State.* New York: Fordham University Press.

Panourgia, Neni, and George Marcus, eds. 2008. *Ethnographica Moralia.* New York: Fordham University Press.

Parsi, Trita. *Treacherous Alliance: The Secret Dealings of Israel, Iran, and the U.S.* New Haven: Yale University Press.

Parsons, Talcott. 1937. *The Structure of Social Action.* New York: McGraw-Hill.

——. 1951. *The Social System.* Glencoe: Free Press.

Pascarelli, Gia. 2002. "The Geist in the Machine: Freud, the Uncanny, and Technology." In John P. McCormick, ed., *Confronting Mass Democracy and Industrial Technology.* Durham: Duke University Press.

Perin, Constance. 2004. *Shouldering Risks: The Culture of Control in the Nuclear Power Industry.* Princeton: Princeton University Press.

Perrow, Charles. 1999. *Normal Accidents: Living With High Risk Technologies.* 2d ed. Princeton: Princeton University Press.

——. 2007. "The Next Catastrophe: Reducing Our Vulnerabilities to Natural, Industrial, and Terrorist Disasters." Arthur Miller Lecture in Science and Ethics, MIT, October 22.

Petryna, Adriana. 2002. *Life Exposed: Biological Citizens after Chernobyl.* Princeton: Princeton University Press.

——. 2005. "Ethical Variability: Drug Development and Globalizing Clinical Trials." *American Ethnologist* 32(2): 183–97.

Petryna, Adriana, Andrew Lakoff, and Arthur Kleinman, eds. 2006. *Global Pharmaceuticals: Ethics, Markets, Practices.* Durham: Duke University Press.

Pickering, Andrew. 1995. *The Mangle of Practice: Time, Agency, and Science.* Chicago: University of Chicago Press.

Piore, Michael, and Charles Sabel. 1984. *The Second Industrial Divide: Possibilities for Prosperity.* New York: Basic Books.

Pitts, Victoria. 2003. *In the Flesh: The Cultural Politics of Body Modification.* New York: Palgrave Macmillan.

Podoll, K, P. Hoff, and H. Sass. 2000. "The Migraine of Immanual Kant." *Fortschr. Neurol. Psychiatr.* 68(7) (July): 332–37.

Polanyi, Michael. 1962. *The Republic of Science.* Chicago: Roosevelt University.

——. 1966. *The Tacit Dimension.* New York: Doubleday.

Pope, Liston. 1958. *Millhands and Preachers: A Study of Gastonia.* New Haven: Yale University Press.

Porter, Theodore. 1986. *The Rise of Statistical Thinking 1820–1900.* Princeton: Princeton University Press.

——. 1995. *Trust in Numbers: The Pursuit of Objectivity in Science and Public Life.* Princeton: Princeton University Press.

Postel, Danny. 2006. *Reading Legitimation Crisis in Tehran: Iran and the Future of Liberalism.* Chicago: Prickly Paradigm Press.

Poster, Mark. 1990. *The Mode of Information*. Chicago: University of Chicago Press.

———. 2001. *What's the Matter with the Internet?* Minneapolis: University of Minnesota Press.

Pounds, Alan, et al. 1999. "Biological Response to Climate Change on a Tropical Mountain." *Nature* 398:611–15.

Povinelli, Elizabeth. 2002. *The Cunning of Recognition: Indigenous Alterities and the Making of Australian Multiculturalism*. Durham: Duke University Press.

Powers, Richard. 1998. *Gain*. New York: Farrar, Straus, and Giroux.

Prakash, Gyan. 1999. *Another Reason: Science and Imagination of Modern India*. Princeton: Princeton University Press.

Preis, Ann-Belinda S. 1996. "Human Rights as Cultural Practice: An Anthropological Critique." *Human Rights Quarterly* 18(2): 286–315.

Puetter, Uwe. 2006. *The Euro Group: How a Secretive Circle of Finance Ministers Shape European Economic Governance*. New York: Manchester University Press.

Pyenson, Lewis. 1989. *Empire of Reason: Exact Sciences in Indonesia, 1840–1940*. Leiden: E. J. Brill.

Rabaté, Jean-Michel, ed. 2003. *The Cambridge Companion to Lacan*. New York: Cambridge University Press.

Raber, Karen. 2004. "Michel Foucault and the Specter of War." In Peter Herman, ed., *Historicizing Theory*. Albany: State University of New York Press.

Rabinow, Paul. 1989. *French Modern: Norms and Forms of the Social Environment*. Cambridge: MIT Press.

———. 1996a. *Making PCR: A Story of Biotechnology*. Chicago: University of Chicago Press.

———. 1996b. *Essays on the Anthropology of Reason*. Princeton: Princeton University Press.

———. 1999. *French DNA: Trouble in Purgatory*. Chicago: University of Chicago Press.

———. 2003. *Anthropos Today: Reflections on Modern Equipment*. Princeton: Princeton University Press.

———. 2007. *Marking Time: On the Anthropology of the Contemporary*. Princeton: Princeton University Press.

Rabinow, Paul, and Talia Dan-Cohen. 2005. *A Machine to Make a Future: Biotech Chronicles*. Princeton: Princeton University Press.

Radcliffe-Brown, A. R. 1933. *The Andaman Islanders*. Cambridge: Cambridge University Press.

———. 1952. *Structure and Function in Primitive Societies*. London: Cohen and West.

Radcliffe-Brown, A. R., and Daryl Forde. 1958. *African Systems of Kinship and Marriage*. Oxford: Oxford University Press.

Rader, Karen. 2004. *Making Mice: Standardizing Animals for American Biomedical Research, 1900–1955*. Princeton: Princeton University Press.

Ragland, Ellie, and Dragan Milovanovic, ed. 2004. *Lacan: Topologically Speaking*. New York: Other Press.

Raj, Gopal. 2000. *Reach for the Stars: The Evolution of India's Rocket Programme*. New Delhi: Viking.

Rajan, Tilottama. 2002. *Deconstruction: The Remainders of Phenomenology: Sartre, Derrida, Foucault, Baudrillard*. Stanford: Stanford University Press.

Rajora, Rajesh. 2002. *Bridging the Digital Divide: The Model for Community Networks*. New Delhi: Tata McGraw-Hill.

Ramanna, Raja. 1991. *Years of Pilgrimage*. Delhi: Viking.

Ramos, Alcida Rita. 1995. *Sanumá Memories: Yanomami Ethnography in Times of Crisis*. Madison: University of Wisconsin Press.

———. 1998. *Indigenism: Ethnic Politics in Brazil*. Madison: University of Wisconsin Press.

Rampton, Sheldon, and John C. Stauber. 2001. *Trust Us, We're Experts*. New York: Penguin.

Rapp, Rayna. 1999. *Testing Women, Testing the Fetus: The Social Impact of Amniocentesis in America*. New York: Routledge.

Readings, Bill. 1996. *The University in Ruins*. Cambridge: Harvard University Press.

Reardon, Jenny. 2004. *Race to the Finish: Identity and Governance in the Age of Genomics*. Princeton: Princeton University Press.

Redfield, Peter. 2000. *Space in the Tropics: From Convicts to Rockets in French Guiana*. Berkeley: University of California Press.

Reich, Michael. 1991. *Toxic Politics: Responding to Chemical Disasters*. Ithaca: Cornell University Press.

Reisman, Arnold. 2006. *Turkey's Modernization: Refugees from Nazism and Atatürk's Vision*. Washington D. C.: New Academic Press.

Rejali, Darius. 1994. *Torture and Modernity: Self, Society and State in Modern Iran*. Boulder: Westview Press.

Remnick, David. 2005. "High Water: How Presidents and Citizens React to Disaster." *New Yorker*, October 3.

Resnick, Mitchell. 1994. *Turtles, Termites, and Traffic Jams: Explorations in Massively Parallel Microworlds*. Cambridge: MIT Press.

Revkin, Andrew. 2004. "Eskimos Seek to Recast Global Warming as a Rights Issue." *New York Times*, Dec. 15.

Rheinberger, Hans-Jörg. 1997. *Toward a History of Epistemic Things: Synthesizing Proteins in the Test Tube*. Stanford: Stanford University Press.

———. 2006. *Epistemologie des Konkreten: Studien zur Geschichte der moderne Biologie*. Frankfurt am Main: Surhamp.

Ribeiro, Gustavo Lins. 1994. *Transnational Capitalism and Hydropolitics in Argentina: The Yacyreta Hydroelectric High Dam*. Gainesville: University of Florida Press.

———. 2005. "Comment." *Current Anthropology* 46(5): 722.

Riceour, Paul. 1970. *Freud and Philosophy: An Essay on Interpretation*. New Haven: Yale University Press.

Richards, Audrey. 1939. *Land, Labor and Diet in Northern Rhodesia: An Economic Study of the Bemba Tribe.* London: Oxford University Press.

Richards, I. A. 1936. *The Philosophy of Rhetoric.* London: Oxford University Press.

Rickels, Lawrence. 1991. *The Case of California.* Baltimore: Johns Hopkins University Press.

———. 2002. *Nazi Psychoanalysis.* Minneapolis: University of Minnesota Press.

Rickey, Christopher. 2002. *Revolutionary Saints: Heidegger, National Socialism, and Antinomian Politics.* University Park: Pennsylvania State University Press.

Riles, Annelise. 2004. "Real Time: Unwinding Technocratic and Anthropological Knowledge." *American Ethnologist* 31(3): 392–405.

Ringer, Fritz. 1969. *The Decline of the German Mandarins: The German Academic Community 1890–1933.* Cambridge: Harvard University Press.

Rodney, Walter. 1972. *How Europe Underdeveloped Africa.* London: Bogle-L'Ouverture Publications.

Rolland, Jacques. 1981 [2003]. "Getting Out of Being by a New Path." Introduction to E. Levinas, *On Escape.* Stanford: Stanford University Press.

Ronell, Avital. 1989. *The Telephone Book: Technology—Schizophrenia—Electric speech.* Lincoln: University of Nebraska Press.

———. 2005. *The Test Drive.* Urbana: University of Illinois Press.

Roosth, Sophia. 2006. "Sonic Eukaryotes: Sonocytology, Cytoplasmic Milieu, and the Temps Interieur." Siegel Prize Paper. STS Working Paper, MIT.

Rose, Nikolas. 2006. *The Politics of Life Itself: Biomedicine, Power, and Subjectivity in the Twenty-First Century.* Princeton: Princeton University Press.

Royte, Elizabeth. 2001. *The Tapir's Morning Bath: Solving the Mysteries of the Tropical Rain Forest.* New York: Houghton Mifflin.

Rusche, Georg, and Otto Kirchheimer. 1939. *Punishment and Social Structure.* New York: Columbia University Press.

Rushdie, Salman. 1981 [1995]. *Midnight's Children.* New York: A. A. Knopf.

———. 1999. *The Ground Beneath Her Feet.* New York: Henry Holt.

Ryan, Allan J. 1999. *The Trickster Shift: Humor and Irony in Contemporary Native Art.* Vancouver: University of British Columbia Press.

Ryan, Susan. 2006. "New FX Series Has Families Trading Races." *Boston Globe,* March 4, C1, 5.

Sacks, Oliver. 2005. "The Mind's Eye: What the Blind See." In David Howes, ed., *The Empire of the Senses.* New York: Berg.

Sa'edi, Gholam Hossein. 1345 Shamsi [1966]. *Ahl-e Hava.* Tehran: Chapkhaneh-ye Daneshgah.

Safinejad, Javad. 1351 Shamsi [1972]. *Boneh.* Tehran: Sayeh.

Sahlins, Marshall. 1972. *Stone Age Economics.* Chicago: Aldine-Atherton.

———. 1976. *Culture and Practical Reason.* Chicago: University of Chicago Press.

———. 1981. *Historical Metaphors and Mythical Realities.* Ann Arbor: University of Michigan Press.

———. 1995. *How "Natives" Think: About Captain Cook, For Example.* Chicago: University of Chicago Press.

———. 2004. *Apologies to Thucydides: Understanding History as Culture and Vice Versa.* Chicago: University of Chicago Press.

Said, Edward. 1978. *Orientalism.* New York: Pantheon.

Sallis, John. 1987. *Spacings of Reason and Imagination in Texts of Kant, Fichte, Hegel.* Chicago: University of Chicago Press.

Saltzman, Devyani. 2006. *Shooting Water: A Mother-Daughter Journey and the Making of a Film.* New Delhi: Penguin.

Sanal, Aslihan. 2005. "Flesh Yours, Bones Mine: The Making of the Biomedical Body in Turkey." Ph.D. diss., MIT.

Sanders, Clinton. 1989. *Customizing the Body: The Art and Culture of Tattooing.* Philadelphia: Temple University Press.

Santner, Eric L. 1996. *My Own Private Germany: Daniel Paul Schreber's Secret History of Modernity.* Princeton: Princeton University Press.

Sarai: the New Media Initiative. 2001. *Sarai Reader 01: The Public Domain.* New Delhi: Sarai.

———. 2002. *Sarai Reader 02: The Cities of Everyday Life.* New Delhi: Sarai.

Sarno, John E. 2006. *The Divided Mind: The Epidemic of Mindbody Disorders.* New York: Reagan Books.

Sassen, Saskia. 2006. *Territory, Authority, Rights: From Medieval to Global Assemblages.* Princeton: Princeton University Press.

Saussure, Ferdinand de. 1916 [1959]. *Course in General Linguistics.* Translated by Wade Baskin. New York: McGraw-Hill.

Schienke, Erich. 2006. "Greening the Dragon: Ecological Information in the Environmental Governance of China." Ph.D. diss., Rensselaer Polytechnic Institute.

———. Forthcoming. "Ecological and Ethnographic Movement-Images: Scale, Site, Map and Montage." In Casper Bruun Jensen and Kjetil Rödje. eds. *Deleuzian Intersections in Science, Technology and Anthropology.* Oxford: Berghahn Books.

Schleichert, Hubert. 2003. "Moritz Schlick's Idea of Non-Territorial States." In F. Stadler, ed., *The Vienna Circle and Logical Empiricism.* Dordrecht: Kluwer Academic.

Schneider, David M. 1968. *American Kinship: A Cultural Account.* Englewood Cliffs, NJ: Prentice-Hall.

Schneider, David M., and Kathleen Gough, eds. 1961. *Matrilineal Kinship.* Berkeley: University of California Press.

Schuessler, Jennifer. 2003. "The Novelist and the Animals: J. M. Coetzee's Unsettling Literature of Animal Rights." *Boston Globe,* October 12.

Schutz, Alfred. 1932 [1967]. *The Phenomenology of the Social World.* Evanston: Northwestern University Press.

Schutz, Alfred, and Talcott Parsons. 1978. *The Theory of Social Action: The Correspondence of Alfred Schutz and Talcott Parsons.* Edited by R. Grathoff. Bloomington: Indiana University Press.

Schweber, Libby. 2006. *Disciplining Statistics: Demography and Vital Statistics in France and England, 1830–1885.* Durham: Duke University Press.

Serres, Michel. 1980 [1982]. *The Parasite.* Translated by Lawrence Scher. Baltimore: Johns Hopkins University Press.

——. 1983 [1991]. *Rome: The Book of Foundations.* Translated by Felicia McCarren. Stanford: Stanford University Press.

——. 1990 [1995]. *The Natural Contract.* Translated by Elizabeth MacArthur and William Paulson. Ann Arbor: University of Michigan Press.

Sewell, William H. 1980. *Work and Revolution in France: The Language of Labor from the Old Regime to 1848.* New York: Cambridge University Press.

Sha, Xin Wei. 2005. "Whitehead's Poetical Mathematics." *Configurations* 13:77–94.

Shanin, Teodor, ed. 1971. *Peasants and Peasant Societies.* Baltimore: Penguin.

Shapin, Steven, and Simon Schafer. 1985. *Leviathan and the Air Pump: Hobbes, Boyle and the Experimental Life.* Princeton: Princeton University Press.

Sharma, J., A. Angelucci, and M. Sur. 2000. "Induction of Visual Orientation Modules in Auditory Cortex." *Nature* 404:841–47.

Sharma, Kalpana. 2000. *Rediscovering Dharavi: Stories from Asia's Largest Slum.* New Delhi: Penguin.

Shell, Susan Meld. 2003. "Kant's 'True Economy of Human Nature': Rousseau, Count Verri, and the Problem of Happiness." In B. Jacobs and P. Kain, eds., *Essays on Kant's Anthropology.* New York: Cambridge University Press.

Shellenberger, Michael, and Ted Nordhaus. 2004 "The Death of Environmentalism: Global Warming Politics in a Post-Environmental World." www.thebreakthrough.org.

Sheth, Dhirubhai L. n.d. "Micro-Movements in India: Towards a New Politics of Participatory Democracy." www.cbs.ubc.ca/participatory/docs/sheth.pdf.

Shiva, Vandava. 2005. *India Divided: Diversity and Democracy Under Attack.* New York: Seven Stories Press.

Shiva, Vandava, and Radha Holla Bhar. 2001. *An Ecological History of Food and Farming in India.* Delhi: RFSTE/Navdanya.

Shiva, Vandava, Radha Holla Bhar, and Afsar H. Jafri. 2002. *Corporate Hijack of Biodiversity: How WTO-TRIPS Rules Promote Corporate Hijack of People's Biodiversity and Knowledge.* Delhi: Navdanya.

Shulman, Seth. 2006. *Undermining Science: Suppression and Distortion in the Bush Administration.* Berkeley: University of California Press.

Siegel, James. 1997. *Fetish, Recognition, Revolution.* Princeton: Princeton University Press.

——. 1998. *A New Criminal Type in Jakarta.* Durham: Duke University Press.

——. 2006. *Naming the Witch.* Stanford: Stanford University Press.

Slattery, Dennis Patrick. 2000. *The Wounded Body.* Albany: State University of New York Press.

Slotkin, Richard. 1973. *Regeneration through Violence: The Mythology of the American Frontier, 1600–1860.* Middletown, Conn.: Wesleyan University Press.

Smith, Barbara Herrnstein. 2005. *Scandalous Knowledge: Science, Truth and the Human.* Edinburgh: Edinburgh University Press.

Smith, Caitlin. 2006. "Edmund Husserl and the Crisis of Europe." *Modern Age* 48(1): 28–36.

Smith, Craig S. 2005. "A Project to Remodel Grape Genes." *New York Times,* Sept. 26, A3.

Smith, Marquard, ed. 2005. *Stelarc, the Monograph.* Cambridge: MIT Press.

Smith, Marquard, and Joanne Morra, eds. 2006. *The Prosthetic Impulse: From a Posthuman to a Biocultural Future.* Cambridge: MIT Press.

Snyder, Laura. 2006. *Reforming Philosophy: A Victorian Debate on Science and Society.* Chicago: University of Chicago Press.

Sombart, Werner. 1911 [2001]. *The Jews and Modern Capitalism.* Ontario: Batoche Books.

de Sousa Santos, Bonaventura. 2006. *The Rise of the Global Left: The World Social Forum and Beyond.* London: Zed.

——, ed. 2007. *Another Knowledge Is Possible: Beyond Northern Epistemologies.* New York: Verso.

Spengler, Oswald. 1918–23 [1926]. *The Decline of the West.* New York: Alfred A. Knopf.

Sperling, Stefan. 2006. "Science and Conscience: Stem Cells, Bioethics and German Citizenship." Ph.D. diss., Princeton University.

Spiro, Melford. 1967. *Burmese Supernaturalism: A Study in the Explanation and Reduction of Suffering.* Englewood Cliffs, NJ: Prentice-Hall.

——. 1982. *Oedipus in the Trobriands.* Chicago: University of Chicago Press.

Stadler, Friedrich. 1991. "Aspects of the Social Background and Position of the Vienna Circle at the University of Vienna." In T. Uebel, ed., *Rediscovering the Forgotten Vienna Circle.* Dordrecht: Kluwer Academic.

Stadler, Peter. 2006. "Herodotus and the Cities of Mainland Greece." In C. Dewald and J. Marincola, eds., *The Cambridge Companion to Herodotus.* New York: Cambridge University Press.

Stafford, Barbara Maria. 2004. "Romantic Systematics and the Genealogy of Thought: The Formal Roots of a Cognitive History of Images." *Configurations* 12:315–48.

Stark, Werner. 2003. "Historical Notes and Interpretive Questions about Kant's Lectures on Anthropology." In B. Jacobs and P. Kain, eds., *Essays on Kant's Anthropology.* New York: Cambridge University Press.

Starrett, Susan G. 2006. *Wittgenstein Flies a Kite.* New York: PI Press.

Steiner, George. 1971. *In Bluebeard's Castle: Some Notes Towards the Redefinition of Culture.* New Haven: Yale University Press.

Stelarc and Ross Farnell. 1999. "In Dialogue with 'Posthuman' Bodies: Interview with Stelarc." In Mike Featherstone, ed., *Body Modification.* London: Sage.

Stelarc and Marquard Smith. 2005. "Animating Bodies, Mobilizing Technologies: Stelarc in Conversation." In M. Smith, ed., *Stelarc, the Monograph.* Cambridge: MIT Press.

Stengers, Isabelle. 1993 [2000]. *The Invention of Modern Science.* Translated by Daniel W. Smith. Minneapolis: University of Minnesota Press.

Stewart, Kathleen. 1996. *A Space on the Side of the Road: Cultural Poetics in an "Other" America.* Princeton: Princeton University Press.

Stiegler, Bernard. 1998. *Technics and Time.* Translated by Richard Beardsworth and George Collins. Stanford: Stanford University Press.

Stocking, George. 1968. *Race, Culture and Evolution: Essays in the History of Anthropology.* New York: Free Press.

Stone, Christopher D. 1972. "Should Trees Have Standing: Toward Legal Rights for Natural Objects." *Southern California Law Review* 45:450–501.

Stott, William. 1973. *Documentary Expression and Thirties America.* New York: Oxford University Press.

Strathern, Marilyn. 2004. *Commons + Borderlands: Working Papers on Interdisciplinarity, Accountability and the Flow of Knowledge.* Oxford: Sean Kingston.

Stringer, Tish Marie. 2006. "Move! Guerilla Media, Collaborative Modes and the Tactics of Radical Media Making." Ph.D. diss., Rice University.

Stuchtey, Benedikt, ed. 2005. *Science Across the European Empires, 1800– 1950.* New York: Oxford University Press.

Suchman, Lucy. 1987. *Plans and Situated Actions: The Problem of Human-Machine Communications.* New York: Cambridge University Press.

Sullivan, Nikki. 2001. *Tattooed Bodies: Subjectivity, Textuality, Ethics and Pleasure.* Westport, Conn.: Praeger.

Sunder Rajan, Kaushik. 2006. *Biocapital: The Constitution of Postgenomic Life.* Durham: Duke University Press.

——, ed. Forthcoming. *Lively Capital: Directions in the Anthropology of Science.* Durham: Duke University Press.

Sung, Wen-Chin. 2006. "Global Science: The Convergence of Biotechnology and Capitalism in China." Ph.D. diss., Harvard University.

Surya, Michel. 1992 [2002]. *Georges Bataille, An Intellectual Biography.* Translated by Krzysztof Fijalkowski and Michael Richardson. New York: Verso.

Tailbear, Kimberly. 2008. "Native-American-DNA.com: In Search of Native American Race and Tribe." In Barbara Koenig, Sandra Soo-Jin Lee, and Sarah Richardson, eds., *Revisiting Race in a Genomic Age.* New Brunswick: Rutgers University Press.

Takacs, David. 1996. *The Idea of Biodiversity: Philosophies of Paradise.* Baltimore: Johns Hopkins University Press.

Tambiah, Stanley J. 1986. *Sri Lanka: Ethnic Fratricide and the Dismantling of Democracy.* Chicago: University of Chicago Press.

——. 1992. *Buddhism Betrayed? Religion, Politics and Violence in Sri Lanka.* Chicago: University of Chicago Press.

———. 1996. *Leveling Crowds: Ethnonationalist Conflicts and Collective Violence in South Asia.* Berkeley: University of California Press.

Taussig, Karen-Sue. 2009. *Ordinary Genomes.* Durham: Duke University Press.

Taussig, Michael. 1980. *The Devil and Commodity Fetishism in South America.* Chapel Hill: University of North Carolina Press.

———. 1987. *Shamanism, Colonialism, and the Wild Man: A Study in Terror and Healing.* Chicago: University of Chicago Press.

———. 1992. *The Nervous System.* New York: Routledge.

———. 1993. *Mimesis and Alterity.* New York: Routledge.

———. 1997. *The Magic of the State.* New York: Routledge.

———. 2003. *Law in a Lawless Land.* New York: New Press.

Tawney, R. H. 1936. *Religion and the Rise of Capitalism: A Historical Study.* London: John Murray.

Tax, Sol. 1953. *Penny Capitalism: A Guatemalan Indian Economy.* Washington: Smithsonian Institution Press and Government Printing Office.

———, ed. 1953. *An Appraisal of Anthropology Today: International Symposium on Anthropology.* Chicago: University of Chicago Press.

Taylor, Charles, et al. 1992. *Multiculturalism.* Charles Taylor with respondents. Princeton: Princeton University Press.

Taylor, Peter J., Saul E. Halfon, and Paul N. Edwards, eds. 1997. *Changing Life: Genomes, Ecologies, Bodies, Commodities.* Minneapolis: University of Minnesota Press.

Terranova, Tiziana. 2007. "Futurepublic: On Information Warfare, Bioracism and Hegemony as Noopolitics." *Theory, Culture and Society* 24(3): 125–45.

Thompson, Charis. 2005. *Making Parents: The Ontological Choreography of Reproductive Technologies, Inside Technology.* Cambridge: MIT Press.

Thompson, E. P. 1968. *The Making of the English Working Class.* London: Victor Gollantz.

Toutounchian, Iraj. 2006. "Integrating Money into Capital Theory: A Legal Perspective." Paper presented at the Seventh Harvard Islamic Finance Conference, April 23.

Traweek, Sharon. 1988. *Beamtimes and Lifetimes: The World of High Energy Physicists.* Cambridge: Harvard University Press.

———. 1996. "Kokusaika (International Relations), Gaiatsu (Outside Pressure), and Bachigai (Being Out of Place)." In Laura Nader, ed., *Naked Science: Anthropological Inquiry into Boundaries, Power and Knowledge.* New York: Routledge.

Troeltsch, Ernst. 1912 [1931]. *The Social Teaching of the Christian Churches.* New York: Macmillan.

Tsing, Anna Lowenhaupt. 2005. *Friction: An Ethnography of Global Connection.* Princeton: Princeton University Press.

Tunstall, Kate E., ed. 2006. *Displacement, Asylum, Migration: The Oxford Amnesty Lectures, 2004.* London: Oxford University Press.

Turkle, Sherry. 1995. *Life on the Screen: Identity in the Age of the Internet.* New York: Simon and Schuster.

Turner, Victor. 1967. *The Forest of Symbols: Aspects of Ndembu Ritual.* Ithaca: Cornell University Press.

——. 1968. *Drums of Affliction: A Study of Religious Processes Among the Ndembu.* Oxford: Clarendon Press.

——. 1969. *The Ritual Process: Structure and Anti-Structure.* Chicago: Aldine.

——. 1974. *Dramas, Fields, and Metaphors: Symbolic Action in Human Societies.* Ithaca: Cornell University Press.

——. 1987. "Bodily Marks." In Mircea Eliade, ed., *Encyclopedia of Religion* 2:269–75. New York: Macmillan Free Press.

Tylor, Edward Burnett. 1871. *Primitive Culture: Researches in the Development of Mythology, Philosophy, Religion, Language, Art and Custom.* London: J. Murray.

——. 1889. "On a Method of Investigating the Development of Institutions Applied to the Laws of Marriage and Descent." *Journal of the Royal Anthropological Institute* 18.

Uebel, Thomas E., ed. 1991. *Rediscovering the Forgotten Vienna Circle: Austrian Studies on Otto Neurath and the Vienna Circle.* Dordrecht: Kluwer Academic.

——. 1992. *Overcoming Logical Positivism from Within: The Emergence of Neurath's Naturalism in the Vienna Circle's Protocol Sentence Debate.* Atlanta: Rodopi.

Ulmer, Gregory. 1985. *Applied Grammatology.* Baltimore: Johns Hopkins University Press.

——. 1989. *Teletheory: Grammatology in the Age of Video.* New York: Routledge.

——. 1994. *Heuretics: The Logic of Invention.* Baltimore: Johns Hopkins University Press.

Vale, V. 1989. *Modern Primitives: An Investigation of Contemporary Adornment and Ritual.* San Francisco: Research Publications.

Vargas, João H. Costa. 2006. "When a Favela Dared to Become a Gated Condominium: The Politics of Race and Urban Space in Rio de Janeiro." *Latin American Perspectives,* issue 149, 33(4): 49–81.

Vaughan, Daine. 1997. *The "Challenger" Launch Decision: Risky Technology, Culture, and Deviance at NASA.* Chicago: University of Chicago Press.

Venkataraman, G. 1992a. *Bose and His Statistics.* Hyderabad: Universities Press.

——. 1992b. *Chandrasekhar and His Limit.* Hyderabad: Universities Press.

——. 1994. *Bhabha and His Magnificent Obsessions.* Hyderabad: Universities Press.

Vickery, John B. 1973. *The Literary Impact of* The Golden Bough. Princeton: Princeton University Press.

Virno, Paolo. 2004. *A Grammar of the Multitude.* Cambridge, Mass.: Semiotext(e).

Visvanathan, Shiv. 1985. *Organizing for Science: The Making of an Industrial Research Laboratory.* Delhi: Oxford University Press.

——. 1986. "Bhopal: The Imagination of a Disaster." *Lokayan Bulletin* 5(1).

——. 1997. *A Carnival for Science: Essays on Science, Technology, and Development.* Delhi: Oxford University Press.

Visvanathan, Shiv, and Harsh Seth. 1989. "Bhopal, A Report from the Future." *Lokayan Bulletin* 7(3).

Vivanco, Luis A. 2006. *Green Encounters: Shaping and Contesting Environmentalism in Rural Costa Rica.* New York: Berghahn Books.

von Hilgers, Philipp. Forthcoming. "The Discourse Analysis Machine: The Visitation of the Blind Spot." In Henning Schmidgen, Julia Kursell, and Hans-Jörg Rheinberger, eds., *The Experimentalization of Life: Configurations between Science, Art, and Technology.* Chicago: University of Chicago Press.

Waldby, Catherine, and Robert Mitchell. 2006. *Tissue Economies: Blood, Organs, and Cell Lines in Late Capitalism.* Durham: Duke University Press.

Wallace, Anthony. 1969. *The Death and Rebirth of the Seneca.* New York: Random House.

Wang, Ban. 2004. *Illuminations from the Past: Trauma, Memory, and History in Modern China.* Stanford: Stanford University Press.

Wang, David Der-Wei. 2004. *The Monster That Is History: History, Violence, and Fictional Writing in Twentieth-Century China.* Berkeley: University of California Press.

Warner, Deborah Jean. 2000. "From Tallahassee to Timbuktu: Cold War Efforts to Measure Intercontinental Distances." *Historical Studies in the Physical and Biological Sciences* 30(2): 393–415.

——. 2000. "Political Geodesy: The First Department of Defense World Geodetic System." Manuscript. Washington: Smithsonian Institution, National Museum of American History.

Warner, William Lloyd. 1949–51. *The Yankee City Series.* 5 vols. New Haven: Yale University Press.

——. 1961. *The Family of God.* New Haven: Yale University Press.

Warwick, Andrew. 2003. *Masters of Theory: Cambridge and the Rise of Mathematical Physics.* Chicago: University of Chicago Press.

Watts, Sheldon. 1997. *Epidemics and History: Disease, Power and Imperialism.* New Haven: Yale University Press.

Weber, Max. 1904 [1930]. *The Protestant Ethic and the Spirit of Capitalism.* London: Allen and Unwin.

——. 1918 [1947]. "Science as a Vocation." In H. H. Gerth and C. Wright Mills, eds., *From Max Weber: Essays in Sociology.* London: K. Paul, Trench, Trubner.

——. 1920. *Gesammelte Aufsätze zur Religionssoziologie.* Tübingen: J.C.B. Mohr.

——. 1922 [1968]. *Economy and Society.* Edited by Guenther Roth and Claus Wittich. New York: Bedminster Press.

Weinberg, Steven. 2001. *Facing Up: Science and Its Cultural Adversaries.* Cambridge: Harvard University Press.

West, Cornell. 2005. "Exiles from a City and from a Nation." *Observer/UK,* Sept. 11.

White, Hayden. 1973. *Metahistory: The Historical Imagination in Nineteenth-Century Europe.* Baltimore: Johns Hopkins University Press.

Whitelaw, Mitchell. 2004. *Metacreation.* Cambridge: MIT Press.

Whiteside, Kerry H. 2002. *Divided Natures: French Contributions to Political Ecology.* Cambridge: MIT Press.

Whyte, W. F. 1943. *Street Corner Society.* Chicago: University of Chicago Press.

Wildavsky, Aaron. 1995. *But Is It True? A Citizen's Guide to Environmental Health and Safety Issues.* Cambridge: Harvard University Press.

Willis, Paul. 1977. *Learning to Labour.* Farnsborough: Saxon House.

Willoquet-Maricondi, Paula. 1999. "Fleshing the Text: Greenaway's *Pillow Book* and the Erasure of the Body." *Postmodern Culture* 9(2).

Wilson, Elizabeth. 2004. "The Brain in the Gut." In *Psychosomatic: Feminism and the Neurological Body.* Durham: Duke University Press.

Wilson, Holly. 2006. *Kant's Pragmatic Anthropology: Its Origin, Meaning and Critical Significance.* Albany: State University of New York Press.

Winch, Peter. 1958. *The Idea of a Social Science and Its Relation to Philosophy.* London: Routledge and Kegan Paul.

Winson, Frederick. 1958. *The Space Child's Mother Goose.* New York: Simon and Schuster.

Wittgenstein, Ludwig. 1969. *On Certainty.* Edited by G. E. M. Anscombe and G. H. von Wright. New York: Harper and Row.

Wolfe, Cary. 2003. "In the Shadow of Wittgenstein's Lion: Language, Ethics, and the Question of the Animal." In Cary Wolfe, ed., *Zootologies: The Question of the Animal.* Minneapolis: University of Minnesota Press.

Wolhforth, Charles. 2004. *The Whale and the Supercomputer: On the Northern Front of Climate Change.* New York: North Point Press.

Wood, Allen W. 2003. "Kant and the Problem of Human Nature." In B. Jacobs and P. Kain, eds., *Essays on Kant's Anthropology.* New York: Cambridge University Press.

Worsley, Peter. 1957. *The Trumpet Shall Sound: A Study of Cargo Cults in Melanesia.* London: MacGibbon and Kee.

Wylie, Sara. 2006. "Living the Landscape: Natural Gas Development and the Cultivation of Contested Disease." Paper presented at the annual meeting of the Society for the Social Study of Science, Vancouver.

Young, Allan. 1995. *The Harmony of Illusions: Inventing Post-Traumatic Stress Disorder.* Princeton: Princeton University Press.

Zaloom, Caitlin. 2004. "The Discipline of the Speculator." In A. Ong and S. Collier, eds., *Global Assemblages: Technology, Politics and Ethics as Anthropological Problems.* New York: Blackwell.

Zargooshi, Javaad. 2001. "Quality of Life of Iranian Kidney 'Donors.'" *Journal of Urology* 166:1790–99.

Ziai, Hossein. 1990. *Knowledge and Illumination: A Study of Suhrawardi's Hikmat al-Ishraq.* Atlanta: Scholars Press.

——. 1992. "Source and Nature of Authority: A Study of Suhrawardi's Illuminationist Political Doctrine." In C. Butterworth, ed., *The Political Aspects of Islamic Philosophy,* Cambridge: Harvard University Press.

——. 1996. "The Illuminationist Tradition." In S. H. Nasr and O. Leaman, eds., *History of Islamic Philosophy.* London: Routledge.

Ziai, Hossein, and Oliver Leaman. 1998. "Illuminationist Philosophy." www.muslimphilosophy.com.

Žižek, Slavoj. 1991. *Looking Awry: An Introduction to Jacques Lacan through Popular Culture.* Cambridge: MIT Press.

——. 2004. *Organs without Bodies: On Deleuze and Consequences.* New York: Routledge.

MICHAEL M. J. FISCHER
is Andrew W. Mellon Professor in the Humanities and professor of
anthropology, and science and technology studies at the Massachusetts
Institute of Technology. His previous books include *Emergent Forms of Life
and the Anthropological Voice* and *Mute Dreams, Blind Owls, and Dispersed
Knowledges: Persian Poesis in the Transnational Circuitry* (both published by
Duke University Press).

Library of Congress Cataloging-in-Publication Data
Fischer, Michael M. J., 1946–
Anthropological futures / Michael M. J. Fischer.
p. cm. — (Experimental futures : technological lives, scientific arts,
anthropological voices)
Includes bibliographical references and index.
ISBN 978-0-8223-4461-2 (cloth : alk. paper)
ISBN 978-0-8223-4476-6 (pbk. : alk. paper)
1. Anthropology. 2. Ethnology. 3. Interdisciplinary approach to knowledge.
I. Title. II. Series: Experimental futures.
GN27.F57 2009
301—dc22   2008055244